*the complete*

# A-Z
# BUSINESS
# STUDIES

*handbook*

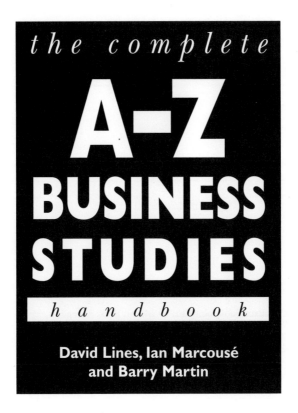

*the complete*

# A-Z
# BUSINESS
# STUDIES

*handbook*

**David Lines, Ian Marcousé
and Barry Martin**

Hodder & Stoughton

A MEMBER OF THE HODDER HEADLINE GROUP

Order queries: Please contact Bookpoint Ltd, 39 Milton Park, Abingdon,
Oxon OX14 4TD. Telephone: (44) 01235 400414. Fax: (44) 01235 400454.
Lines are open from 9 am - 6 pm Monday to Saturday, with a 24-hour
message answering service. Email address: orders@bookpoint.co.uk

*British Library Cataloguing in Publication Data*

Lines, David
  Complete A–Z Business Studies Handbook
  2Rev.ed
  658

ISBN 0 340 65467 8

First published 1996
Impression number    10  9  8
Year                         2004  2003  2002  2001  2000  1999

Typeset by GreenGate Publishing Services, Tonbridge, Kent.
Printed in Great Britain for Hodder & Stoughton Educational,
a division of Hodder Headline Plc, 338, Euston Road, London NW1 3BH
by Redwood Books, Trowbridge, Wiltshire.

# HOW TO USE THIS BOOK

The *A–Z Business Studies Handbook* is an alphabetical textbook designed for ease of use. Each entry begins with a one-sentence definition. This helps the user to add precision to the completion of reports or case studies.

Entries are developed in line with the relative importance of the concept covered. *Bundesbank* is covered in a few lines, whereas a central business issue such as *change* receives half a page. The latter would provide sufficient material to enrich an essay. Numerate topics are developed through the use of worked examples. All formulae are set out explicitly.

The study of business can be developed further by making use of the cross-referenced entries. For example the entry for *distribution channels* refers the reader to *breaking bulk*. Cross-referenced entries are identified by the use of italics. The authors have limited the use of cross-referencing to important, linked concepts. Therefore essay or project writing should benefit from following the logical pathway indicated by italicised entries.

Business Studies students have always had difficulties with the language of the subject. This stems from several factors:

- different firms have their own terminology, and their own ways of using words
- the media use or invent phrases (such as 'white knight'), some of which prove temporary, while others need assimilating into a modern business course
- textbooks recommended by the exam boards use different terms for essentially similar concepts (such as contribution pricing and marginal cost pricing)

The *A–Z Business Studies Handbook* is a business glossary providing a single solution to these problems. In addition, the entries have enough detail to make it a valuable reference/revision companion. This Second Edition provides full coverage of the new GCE A level and Advanced GNVQ syllabuses.

To aid the revision process, carefully selected lists are provided at the back of the book, such as the 'Top 40 terms in marketing'. Those facing examinations can use the lists to make the best use of the *Handbook* during their revision time. The revision recommendations are split into modules, for ease of use. Separate lists are provided for the two main A level syllabuses (AEB and Cambridge) and for the concepts required to tackle Business Advanced GNVQ unit tests.

A new feature of this, the second edition of the *Handbook*, is a section on examiners' terms. Starting on page PPP, this provides an explanation of the trigger words used on exam papers, such as 'analyse', 'discuss' and 'evaluate'.

We hope that the *A–Z Business Studies Handbook* proves an invaluable resource, fully relevant from the first to last day of a business course and then on into working life.

David Lines, Ian Marcousé, Barry Martin.

# ACKNOWLEDGEMENTS

The idea for the *A–Z Business Studies Handbook* came from discussions with students at John Ruskin College, Croydon. It was developed further at meetings of the Nuffield Economics and Business Project team and in discussion with David Lines.

The book took a year to research and write. The authors were fortunate to have the assistance of a number of people and organisations. Among the organisations were the Banking Insurance and Finance Union (BIFU), the City Business Library, the Advisory Conciliation and Arbitration Service (ACAS) and the Advertising Association.

The individuals fell into two groups. First, the family aides. Maureen Marcousé did much of the research into employment practices and laws. Fiona Martin proved a hawk-eyed proof reader. Jill Lines provided ideas and support throughout. The other people to be thanked are the team at Hodder and Stoughton, especially Tim Gregson-Williams.

Researching, writing and editing a book of this size requires teamwork and hard work. It also requires the occasional willingness to sacrifice technical accuracy in favour of clarity. A considerable amount of time went into checking the entries, but if any mistakes have slipped through, the authors apologise and accept full responsibility.

Ian Marcousé

**ABC:** see *activity-based costing*

**above the line** promotion is the advertising of a product or service through consumer media such as television, magazines, newspapers and radio. It contrasts with *below the line* activity such as sponsorship, trade promotions, and on-pack competitions.

**absenteeism** measures the rate of deliberate workforce absence as a proportion of the employee total. Ideally this statistic would exclude absence due to ill-health, though it may be impossible to distinguish between genuine absences and truancy.

$$\text{FORMULA:} \quad \frac{\text{number of staff absent}}{\text{staff total}} \times 100$$

Main causes of absenteeism include: *alienation*, poor staff welfare systems, stress, poor working conditions.

Remedies include: pay systems linked to attendance, *job enrichment*, better *human relations*, better working conditions.

**absorption costing** calculates the unit cost of an item after allocating a proportion of the estimated fixed *overheads*, i.e. each unit must absorb its fair share of the overheads.

Pros:
- ensures that prices are set after all costs have been considered
- requires thought about the most accurate method for allocating overheads

Cons:
- ignores the problem that *fixed costs per unit* can only be estimated accurately if demand/output can be predicted
- often undermined by imprecise methods of *overhead allocation*

**ACAS:** see *Advisory Conciliation and Arbitration Service*

**accelerator:** the theory that investment spending by firms is a function of the rate of change in consumer demand or output. Therefore if demand is rising, firms' requirements for more capital equipment will accelerate the economic growth that is already taking place.

**accountability** is the extent to which a named individual is held responsible for the success or failure of a policy or a piece of administration. When a company's management structure is clear, staff will know what authority has been given to them, and by whom. If that authority is exercised poorly, the employee should be held to account for his or her mistakes.

Pros:
- clear accountability is the basis for providing two of Professor *Herzberg*'s 'motivators': achievement and recognition for achievement
- in order to correct mistakes it is essential to know how they came about – usually a function of people's decision-making or communication failures

Cons:
- if a firm operates in an atmosphere of mistrust, accountability can be seen as a threat; managers may fear that overambitious sales targets have been set with a view to proving their incompetence

**accounting equation:** the principle that the book value of a company's *assets* must equal the finance that has purchased those assets.

FORMULA:   assets employed = capital employed

**accounting packages:** software programs used to maintain a company's accounts on computer. They can be used to record financial transactions, maintain balance and prepare statements and reports.

**accounting period**: the period of time, typically a year, over which an organisation records revenues and expenses, cash flows and changes in assets and liabilities. At the period end the final accounts are drawn up and can be compared with the previous period. The business should keep the same accounting period to ensure *consistency*.

**accounting principles:** a chosen set of accounting conventions that must be applied consistently if company accounts are to be useful to observers. These include: *matching* costs to related revenues; valuing assets with *prudence*; making the assumption that the firm is a *going concern*; and establishing accounting rules to ensure objectivity, i.e., minimising personal judgement in the drawing up of accounts.

**accounting ratios:** see *ratio analysis*

**accounting records**: the books or ledgers where regular entries are made from which the trial balances and final accounts are prepared. They include the sales ledger (customers' accounts), purchases ledger (suppliers' accounts), cashbook and general or nominal ledger. To prevent the general ledger being overcrowded, journals are created for listing transactions, before a total is transferred to the ledger. For example, daily sales might be recorded in the sales journal and the total posted to the ledger at the end of the day.

**Accounting Standards Board:** the body which lays down the accounting standards that firms should follow and checks on whether the standards are being met. If concerned about an issue, the Accounting Standards Board may review the Statement of Standard Accounting Practice (SSAP) that governs the problem, or may issue a new *Financial Reporting Standard (FRS)* to cover it.

**accounting system**: this consists of the system of double-entry, the accounting equation and the conventions or principles. Together they form a coherent system to provide consistent and reliable records.

**accounts:** a systematic way of recording the financial history of an organisation over a certain time period. The principal accounts kept are the *balance sheet, profit and loss account,* and *cashflow statement.*

**accreditation of prior learning (APL)** is the award to trainees of credits towards the completion of a course based upon what they already know. This requires courses to be broken up into small units and for careful recording of who has achieved what.

**accruals:** according to the *matching principle,* expenses (and *revenues*) are to be allocated in the accounts to the time period in which the cost (or benefit) to the organisation is felt. An invoice may not yet have been paid for a benefit already received, e.g. a gas bill. If so, the expense must still be shown in the accounts despite the fact that no cash has been paid. It would appear as an accrued expense under *current liabilities* in the *balance sheet*.

**accumulated depreciation:** in each accounting period, depreciation is deducted from the *book value* of a *fixed asset*. All the amounts deducted are added up or accumulated to calculate the *net book value* of the asset at the end of the latest period so that:

FORMULA: historic cost − accumulated depreciation = net book value

**accumulated profit** is the total retained profit a firm achieves over its lifetime. Also known as *reserves*, accumulated profit forms part of the *shareholders' funds*. A common mistake is to assume that accumulated profit represents an asset that can be used or liquidated. It is a source of long-term finance that has already been invested in *fixed assets* or *working capital*. If a firm needs cash today, it must look at its assets not its past profits.

**acid test ratio** measures a firm's ability to meet its short-term debts, i.e. to pay its bills. The firm's total *current liabilities* are compared with *current assets* excluding *stock*. This is because it can be hard to turn stock into cash, such as for a clothing company when fashion turns against it.

FORMULA: $\dfrac{\text{currents assets} - \text{stock}}{\text{current liabilities}}$

Accountants recommend that this figure should be about 1, i.e. that there should be about £1 of liquid assets for every £1 of short-term debt.

---

Worked example: extract from the Rochelle Clothing Ltd balance sheet

|  |  | £000 | £000 |
|---|---|---|---|
| Current assets | Stock | 160 | |
| | Debtors | 80 | |
| | Cash | 60 | 300 |
| Current liabilities | Creditors | 180 | |
| | Tax due | 45 | |
| | Overdraft | 55 | 280 |
| Net current assets | | | 20 |

Acid test ratio $= \dfrac{300 - 160}{280} = 0.5$

This means that the firm has only 50p of highly liquid assets for each £1 of short-term debt: very low liquidity.

---

**acquisition accounting** the term given to methods used by accountants to make *take-overs* and *mergers* seem beneficial financially. Most are based upon manipulation of earnings per share (a measure of the profits made by a firm). This would be pointless if it was not for the fact that firms which appear to have rapidly rising profits find it easier and cheaper to raise capital than other firms. The *Accounting Standards Board* is introducing new *Financial Reporting Standards* to try to prevent deceptive accounting practices, but past evidence indicates that whenever economic and financial booms occur, *creative accounting* booms as well.

**ACT:** see *advanced corporation tax*

**activity-based costing** allocates central *overheads* to a *cost centre* in line with the estimated benefits received. For example, if the personnel department spends 50 per cent of its time recruiting sales staff, then the sales department should cover 50 per cent of personnel's costs.

Pros: • overhead costs are covered so that a potential loss is avoided
• the method of allocation is more logical than many other approaches (such as allocating as a proportion of sales)

Cons: • collecting the data may be expensive and ineffective, such as getting staff to fill in time sheets to record how long they spent on different departments' work
• allocations may be more reliant on guesswork than accountants would like

**activity chart:** a diagram showing the time sequence necessary for the successful completion of a task.

**adding value**: the process by which firms add value to a product. This may take a very simple form: for example cleaning your car or motorbike before you sell it makes it seem worth more in the eyes of the purchaser. Therefore you have added value. Note that this has no effect on the actual performance of the car or motorbike, so the notion of 'value' is very subjective. Another example is the development of pre-wrapped sandwiches in supermarkets. The sandwiches themselves are not changed, but the way they are packaged and presented convinces customers they possess more 'value' and so they pay more for them.

**ad hoc research** is tailor-made to meet a *market research* need that cannot be satisfied by standardised surveys such as *retail audits*. It is one-off research, for example, to discover what proportion of 16-19-year-olds want to have a credit card.

**administration:** when a company in severe financial difficulties brings in an administrator whose task is to protect the best interests of the shareholders by keeping the business going. The administrator may need to sell off some *assets*, but is most unlikely to close down the whole firm. If the financial problems cannot be resolved a *receiver* might be called in. He/she would act in the best interests of *creditors*, possibly by liquidating all the firm's assets.

**administration systems:** The different structures which support business organisations such as finance, human resources, post room and so on. Since such systems do not contribute directly to profits, it is vital that they are efficient. The increasing use of IT in accounting packages has had a profound impact upon administration systems in recent years.

**advanced corporation tax (ACT):** the compulsory early payment by firms of a proportion of their expected profit tax liability. This advanced payment of *corporation tax* hits firms' *cash flow* but improves the government's cash and therefore spending position.

**advertising** is paid-for communication through media such as television, newspapers or radio. Most advertising can be categorised as either *informative* or *persuasive*, or a combination of the two.

**advertising agency:** a firm specialising in creating, planning and executing a client's advertising strategy. Agencies are usually divided into three main departments, all of which draw upon the work of market research:

| | |
|---|---|
| Planning: | decides which type of consumer to target the advertising at, and the strategy for doing so |
| Creative: | designs and writes the advertisements and commercials, including the *slogans* and catch-phrases |
| Media: | plans and buys the media time or space to reach the *target market* as cost-effectively as possible |

**advertising campaign:** the complete realisation of the client firm's strategy, i.e. all the advertisements appearing for a certain product within a specified time period.

**advertising elasticity** measures the extent to which changes in advertising spending affect *demand*. If a relatively small change in spending caused a major shift in demand, the product would be termed advertising elastic.

FORMULA: $$\frac{\text{percentage change in demand}}{\text{percentage change in advertising spending}}$$

---

Worked example: if a firm doubled its advertising spending and demand rose from 20 000 to 28 000 units as a result, its advertising elasticity is:

percentage change in demand = 8 000 ÷ 20 000 × 100   = + 40%
percentage change in advertising spending          = +100%

advertising elasticity = $\frac{+\ 40\%}{+\ 100\%}$ = 0.4

---

The concept of advertising elasticity has a major flaw: it ignores time. It assumes that extra money spent on advertising today will generate extra sales today or tomorrow. In fact, firms such as Nestlé know that additional spending on a product such as KitKat will have virtually no immediate pay-off. Their hope is that increased advertising presence will boost the long-term image of the brand, thereby helping sales in the years to come. Such benefits could never be measured in the way needed to calculate a firm's advertising elasticity.

**advertising ethics** are the moral issues raised by the persuasive power of *advertising*. Laws prevent advertisements from containing untruths, but do not force firms to state the whole truth. This allows companies to use advertising images that exaggerate or mislead. An ethical company should reject such an approach.

**Advertising Standards Authority (ASA)** is a self-regulatory organisation set up to ensure that advertisements are kept socially acceptable. It administers the *Code of Advertising Practice*. Critics suggest that because it is financed by advertisers, the ASA is not harsh enough on advertisements that appear to break the code.

**advertising strategy** is the plan for meeting advertising objectives. Frequently, these objectives consist of targets that are not directly linked with sales volume, such as improving consumers' awareness of a brand name. The strategy will set out the *target market*, the preferred media for reaching these potential customers, and the overall style of the advertising. The *advertising agency* puts the strategy into practice.

**Advisory Conciliation and Arbitration Service (ACAS)** was set up in 1975 as an independent source of expertise in preventing or settling industrial disputes. It is the organisation companies, unions or individuals turn to when seeking an expert, unbiased conciliator or mediator. Upwards of 70 000 individual conciliation cases are handled each year. ACAS has a reputation for unbiased advice that has been helped by its policy of not commenting publicly on the strength of the case of either side to a dispute. (See *conciliation* and *arbitration*.)

**after-sales service** is the appreciation that customer needs do not end when a sale has been made. Spare parts and maintenance may have to be provided, and friendly, supportive advice should always be available. Efficient after-sales service may be a vital factor in encouraging a high level of repeat purchase.

**aged creditors analysis** means listing your unpaid bills from suppliers in age order, with the most overdue account at the top of the list. By paying the oldest account first, you hope to maintain good relations with your creditors.

**aged debtors analysis** means listing the unpaid bills of your customers in age order, with the most overdue account at the top of the list. The rank order may then be categorised, as below:

Worked example:

| Age of debts | No. of accounts | Total outstanding |
|---|---|---|
| 120+ days | 32 | £14 500 |
| 90–119 days | 63 | £89 000 |
| 60–89 days | 110 | £54 000 |
| Under 60 days | 55 | £12 000 |
| TOTAL | 260 | £169 500 |

This analysis provides the data to enable a firm to focus its debt collection efforts on the really bad payers. In the above example, a computer could identify the 32 customers who were more than 120 days late in paying, and print out a strong reminder letter to each.

**ageism** is discrimination based on a person's age. This is legal in the UK, but may result in the neglect of older employees' experience.

**agenda:** the notification to those attending a meeting of the topics to be discussed and the order in which each will be tackled.

**agent:** an independent person or company appointed to handle sales and distribution within a specified area. An agent's income comes from the commission or *mark-up* they make on each sale.

Pros:   •  for a small firm the appointment of agents removes the need for the high set-up and overhead costs of a distribution network
      •  as agents work solely for a percentage of the *sales revenue* they may work harder than a salaried *salesforce*

Cons:   •  if the agent sells many different products, he or she may not give yours enough attention

**aggregate demand** is the total level of demand in the economy. It consists of: consumer spending on goods and services, the investment expenditure of firms, government spending, and net revenue from abroad (export earnings less spending on imports). See *circular flow of national income.*

**AGM:** see *annual general meeting*

**AIDA:** this stands for Awareness, Interest, Desire, Action. It is a standard marketing approach to promoting the sales of a product. The four stages of AIDA suggest:

- first ensure brand or product awareness – perhaps through an outrageous advertising campaign that grabs people's attention
- second, stimulate consumer interest - perhaps by making your product seem different or novel
- third, make people desire your product, perhaps through the images created by your advertising or by giving free samples in-store
- finally, provoke action, through, for example, sales promotions such as a money-back trial offer.

**aims** are the long-term intentions that provide a focus for setting *objectives.* They are usually expressed qualitatively, sometimes in the form of a *mission statement.* A typical corporate aim might be 'to produce the finest chocolate in Europe'. From this starting point a firm can build a series of quantifiable targets, such as to increase its consumer quality rating from fifth in Europe to third within three years.

**alienation** is the state of mind that results from a boring, unpleasant and meaningless job. It is most likely to occur in a situation of high *division of labour,* or when the workforce rejects the approach or objectives of senior management. Once established, alienation is very hard to dispel. Improved *human relations* or *job enrichment* could only work after the apathy and mistrust have been overcome.

**allocative efficiency** is the extent to which resources are allocated effectively between competing market wants or needs.

**allotment of shares:** in a new share issue, a subscriber for the shares may not get all the shares wanted because of *excess demand.* The application is scaled down and the subscriber receives an allotment or allocation accordingly.

**alpha stock:** the shares of first-class companies quoted on the stock market, so rated because of their successful record and low risk.

**Alternative Investment Market (AIM):** a market for buying and selling shares in firms which are too small or too young to be quoted on the full London Stock Exchange. AIM became the successor to the Unlisted Securities Market (USM) in 1995.

**amalgamation:** the merging of two or more divisions of a business, perhaps as part of a *rationalisation* process.

**amortisation:** the *depreciation* of *intangible assets* such as *goodwill.*

**Annual Abstract of Statistics** is published once a year by HMSO (Her Majesty's Stationery Office). It contains key economic and social statistics such as the rate of capital investment and the level of unemployment.

**annual general meeting (AGM):** a meeting held by *public limited companies* to which all shareholders are invited in order to:

- approve the year's accounts
- vote on resolutions and the election or re-election of board directors
- have the opportunity to put questions to the company chairman

**annual pay round:** the convention that pay and conditions of employment will be reviewed each year. Employers may negotiate new terms with employee representatives (*trade unions* or *staff associations*) or may impose a settlement on staff. The annual pay round usually results in pay increases in line with inflation, sometimes in return for employee agreement to change working practices in order to improve *productivity*.

**annualised hours agreement:** the acceptance by an employee of working hours that are measured per year instead of per week. As a result, the company is able to obtain higher working hours at seasonally busy periods of the year without needing to offer overtime payments. This is an example of *flexible working*.

**annualised percentage rate (APR)** measures the interest charges on a loan or credit as a percentage of the loan amount outstanding. This is an attempt to ensure that borrowers can compare the true cost of credit from different lenders. APR contrasts with the highly misleading flat rate method of interest calculation, which makes the interest charge appear much lower than it really is. Lenders are legally required to quote the APR on loans so that the necessary consistency is achieved.

**annual report and accounts:** at the end of each accounting year a company must produce a set of accounts to be sent to every shareholder and to *Companies House* (for public scrutiny). The annual report must include: a *balance sheet*, a *profit and loss account*, a *cashflow statement*, a *directors' report* and an *auditor's report*.

**anti-competitive activities:** where a firm in a dominant market position uses its powers to restrict or eliminate competition. Such actions undermine free competition within a marketplace and may therefore lead to poorer customer service or higher prices. For example, in 1995 British Airways apologised for actions taken by employees which could have threatened the survival of the rival Virgin Atlantic airline. In other cases, firms as prestigious as ICI and British Steel have been fined by the European Commission for price fixing.

Anti-competitive activities can take many forms:

- exclusive dealing, i.e. forcing suppliers to deal exclusively with the dominant firm
- refusing to supply distributors who handle competitors' products
- *full line forcing*, i.e. where the dominant firm requires distributors to stock all of its product line, thus preventing a rival from getting a toehold even in a niche
- tie-in sales, where the dominant firm requires the purchaser to buy a package which not only includes the good of primary interest but others as well, for example a consumer may be offered a guarantee only on the understanding that the product is serviced by the supplying firm
- aggregated discounts, i.e. where a distributor is given a discount for the total sales over a year or any other lengthy period. This encourages the distributor to stay with the dominant firm and discourages competitors

Such activities come under the Competition Act 1980, and are therefore subject to review by the *Office of Fair Trading.*

**apportioned costs** are *overheads* that have been allocated in an arbitrary way to cost or *profit centres.* An example would be allocation of *corporate advertising* expenditure as a proportion of the sales volume of each brand held by a firm.

**appraisal** is the process of assessing the effectiveness of a process or an employee. It is usually conducted by comparing goals with outcomes. An employee appraisal might be conducted through a questionnaire but is more commonly a one-to-one discussion between employee and manager. The conversation will focus upon the employee's performance, perhaps in relation to pre-set indicators such as timekeeping, customer sales levels, and contribution to teamwork. The appraisal interview may take place annually or more frequently; it will usually end with discussion of career prospects and training needs.

**apprenticeship** used to be the main way in which young people learned to become skilled workers. The apprentice would be allocated to a master craftsman who would explain and demonstrate the different facets of the trade. Over a four, five or even seven-year period, a series of written but mainly practical tests would have to be passed before the young worker could be declared a craftsman. As technology reduced the need for such skills in more and more jobs, the need for such a lengthy process was reduced. Unfortunately, Britain has not produced a modern vocational training system to replace apprenticeships.

**appropriation account:** the section of the *profit and loss account* that shows how the firm has used its after-tax profits (its *earnings*). Part may be paid to *ordinary shareholders* as dividends, part to *preference shareholders*, and the remainder will be retained within the company as investment capital. The part of the appropriation account that is retained adds to the balance sheet reserves.

**APR:** see *annualised percentage rate*

**aptitude test** is a test of an individual's ability to perform specific tasks, such as typing speed and accuracy. It often forms part of recruitment and selection procedures.

**arbitrage** is trading between two or more markets when profitable opportunities arise. For example, if the pound equals 2 000 lire on the Italian foreign exchange market and 2 050 in London, a profitable arbitrage deal can be made by buying pounds in Italy and selling them in London. In this way currency dealers' actions ensure that different market rates keep in line with each other.

**arbitration** is resolving a dispute by appointing an independent person or panel to judge the appropriate outcome. The arbitrator will listen to both sides to the dispute then make his or her decision. If both sides have agreed it in advance, this decision can be legally binding. Otherwise, either side could reject the arbitrator's decision. (See also *conciliation, Advisory Conciliation and Arbitration Service* and *pendulum arbitration.*)

**arithmetic average (mean):** the arithmetic mean or average of a distribution is a *measure of central tendency* which is calculated by dividing the total value by the number of occurrences.

$$\text{FORMULA:} \quad \frac{\text{sum of (variable} \times \text{frequency)}}{\text{sum of frequencies}}$$

The mean is a useful measure and can be subject to further calculations but it is distorted by extreme values and may not be a whole number or the same as one of the items in the distribution.

**ARR:** see *average rate of return*

**articles of association:** one of two documents required by law to establish a limited company. It sets out the internal rules under which the company will operate and its relationship with its shareholders. Examples include: the way meetings are conducted, the types of shares and the rights attached to each type, and the powers of the directors. Together with the *memorandum of association*, the articles are submitted to the *Registrar of Companies*. They can be viewed by anyone on payment of a fee.

**ASA:** see *Advertising Standards Authority*

**assembly line** is the final stage in the manufacturing process, where components and *sub-assemblies* are fitted together to make the finished product. The assembly line usually works on the basis of high *division of labour*, with the use of conveyor belts to move the parts from one stage to the next.

**asset:** anything providing a flow of benefits to an organisation over a certain time period. Those reported as assets on a *balance sheet* are the ones which can be given a monetary value, usually because they have been bought and a value thus obtained. Assets show how an organisation has deployed the funding available. Assets represent what is owned by an organisation or what is owed to it.

**asset-led marketing** bases the firm's marketing strategy on its strengths (instead of purely on what the customer wants). An example of this was the use of the Mars Bar as the starting point for Mars to move into the ice-cream market.

**assets employed:** the book value of all the firm's assets minus *current liabilities*. It is calculated by adding fixed (long-term) assets to (short-term) working capital.

**asset stripping** occurs when a *predator* takes over a target company because it feels that the market price of the target's assets is higher than its *stock market* value suggests. Thus the stock market is undervaluing the target company whose assets can be stripped out individually and sold in total for more than the price the predator pays. The sum of the parts is greater than the whole (the opposite of *synergy*).

**asset structure:** the way a firm balances its holdings of assets broadly between fixed (long-term) and current (short-term).

**asset turnover:** a measurement of a firm's ability to generate *sales turnover* from its asset base. Its importance is that unless the assets owned by a business can produce income, they must represent a drain on its resources and/or efficiency. Business people like to use the phrase 'making the assets sweat'; by this they mean working all the firm's assets hard enough to generate high sales. For example, a fast-food chain might decide to close down its 10 worst performing outlets because even though they are profitable, the firm's capital could be employed more effectively in branches with a higher asset turnover.

$$\text{FORMULA:} \quad \frac{\text{sales}}{\text{net assets}} = \text{asset turnover}$$

**assisted areas:** carefully defined parts of the UK in which government grants may be given to persuade firms to locate there. These grants are available for production and service businesses. They represent an element of the government's *regional policy*.

**auction** is a method of selling based on gathering buyers together to bid for the item being sold. Buyers compete openly, with the highest bid being the winner.

**audit:** an independent check on the financial accounts of an organisation. It is conducted by auditors who are professional accountants. In the wake of a series of unexpected company failures in the late 1980s and early 1990s, auditors came under repeated criticism for their failure to clarify accounting irregularities to the shareholders. It was pointed out that although the process should be independent, the fact that the client firm was selecting and paying the auditor might undermine that independence.

**auditor's report** is part of an organisation's annual accounts and will be read carefully by shareholders, *creditors*, employee organisations and others to check for indications of concern. If satisfied, auditors will report that the accounts reveal a *true and fair view* of the organisation's affairs for the period. If the auditors qualify their remarks, there may be cause for concern.

**authorised cheque signatories:** directors or staff with the authority to sign cheques on behalf of a company, club or any other organisation. Usually, two signatures are required on every cheque to reduce the chance of fraud.

**authorised share capital:** the value of *share capital* which a company may issue, i.e. sell, to raise funds. This is found in the *memorandum of association*. A company may choose not to issue all its authorised share capital, ensuring the ability to raise new funds from existing and new shareholders at any time in the future.

**authoritarian leadership style** assumes that information and decision-making are best kept at the top of the organisation. This may be because the senior managers lack trust in the competence or good faith of their staff, or it may reflect acute pressures on the firm that force the directors to make rapid, difficult decisions. (See also *leadership style*.)

**autocratic leadership style:** see *authoritarian leadership style*

**automatic stabiliser:** part of the economic system which helps to iron out fluctuations in the *trade cycle*. The most common example is social security expenditure and, in particular, unemployment benefit. As the economy goes into *recession* more people become unemployed, and so government expenditure rises to pay dole to those out of work. This maintains demand at a higher level than would otherwise be the case were the unemployed simply left with no money at all.

**automation** uses machinery to replace human labour. This may reduce total costs, but could result in a more inflexible production process. This makes a firm more vulnerable to changes in consumer taste or increases in competition. Modern, *lean production* techniques emphasise the need for flexible automation, using computer-controlled machines that can quickly be reprogrammed to perform different tasks.

**autonomous group working** is a term used to describe the delegation of set tasks to a team of workers. They are given the power to decide how best to complete the task; to decide if there should be a team leader and if so, who; and to decide who should do what. It is a process of decentralised teamworking.

**AVCO:** see *average cost of stock*

**average cost of stock (AVCO)** is a way of determining the closing stock valuation at the end of the financial year. It is calculated as the units left in stock multiplied by the average price paid for the stock over the accounting period just ended.

**average cost** is the total cost divided by the number of units produced. It is also known as unit cost.

FORMULA:   average costs = $\dfrac{\text{total cost}}{\text{units of output}}$

---

Worked example: a firm buys materials at 50p per unit and spends £1 000 on weekly overheads: the production rage is 4 000 per week.

So average costs are: $\dfrac{(\pounds0.5 \times 4\ 000) + \pounds1\ 000}{4\ 000} = 75p$

---

This figure must be treated with great caution as it is highly deceptive. It gives the impression of being a constant figure per unit. In fact it varies at different levels of output because if fewer units are produced, the fixed cost element per unit rises. This can be seen in the diagram below.

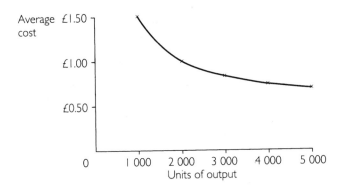

*Average costs falling as output rises*

**average fixed costs** fall in the short run as output increases because the fixed costs are spread more thinly over the larger number of units produced.

FORMULA:   average fixed costs = $\dfrac{\text{total fixed costs}}{\text{units of output}}$

**average rate of return (ARR):** a calculation of the average annual profit on an investment as a percentage of the sum invested.

FORMULA:   $\dfrac{\text{total profit over project life} \div \text{number of years}}{\text{capital outlay on project}} \times 100$

It provides the firm with a percentage figure that can be compared with the percentage rates of return on other uses of its capital. It can also be judged against the rate of interest to identify the rewards the firm is hoping to receive for the risks involved in its investment. The diagram shows a situation where a firm anticipates a 15 per cent ARR at a time when interest rates are 12 per cent. It must then make a judgement about whether a 3 per cent real return is sufficient given the risks involved. If the investment is by Marks and Spencer PLC in a new store opening, the risk may be low enough to justify going ahead. For the launch of a new computer software house, however, a 3 per cent reward for risk would be hopelessly inadequate.

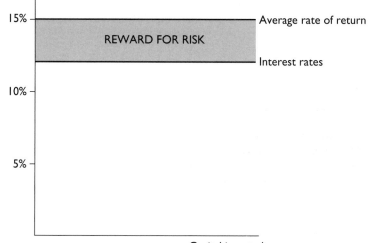

*Diagram to show how to interpret an average rate of return (ARR)*

Worked example: a 4-colour printing press will cost Colour Co. £120 000. It is expected to generate the following net cash flows over its four years of useful life:

| Year 1 | £38 000 |
| Year 2 | £60 000 |
| Year 3 | £60 000 |
| Year 4 | £34 000 |

Step 1  Calculate total cash contribution over lifetime:

£38 000 + £60 000 + £60 000 + £34 000 = £192 000

Step 2  Deduct the investment outlay to find lifetime profit:

£192 000 − £120 000  = £72 000

Step 3  Calculate average annual profit:

£72 000 ÷ 4  = £18 000

Step 4     Take the annual profit as a percentage of the sum invested:

$$\frac{£18\ 000}{£120\ 000} \times 100\ = 15\%$$

**backdata** is past research information that can be used to interpret new findings. For example if a survey finds that 47 per cent of beer drinkers say they would buy a new American malt liquor, how could one translate that into a sales forecast? Only by comparing the result with backdata on the research and actual performance of past product launches. If a new German lager had, a year ago, received a 45 per cent result and, since then, had actual sales worth £40m. a sales forecast of more than £40m. could be made for the malt liquor.

**back to the knitting:** a curious phrase meaning that a firm should return to the core activities it knows best. In other words it should reverse a *diversification* strategy.

**Backward (or upstream) vertical integration:** means buying out a supplier, e.g. a chocolate manufacturer buying a sugar producer.

Pros: to the company

- close links with suppliers aids new product development
- control over supply quality, quantity and delivery times

Pros: to the consumer

- more innovative products available
- more reliable supply of goods

Pros: to the workforce

- secures a market for supplier's products; improves job security
- working in a big firm provides more career opportunities

Cons: to the company

- assumed guarantee of demand may make supply division complacent
- increases firm's dependence on one industry (opposite to *diversification*)

Cons: to the consumer

- complacency may lead to cost increases and then to price rises
- firm's control over its supplier may reduce variety of goods available

Cons: to the workforce

- the bidder may integrate the supplier into its own factory, causing job losses
- being part of a larger firm may mean loss of team spirit

**bad debt:** an unpaid customer's bill for goods or services sold on *credit* which is now thought unlikely to be settled, perhaps because the customer is in *liquidation*. As a credit sale has been already included as *revenue* in the organisation's books, the bad debt needs to be charged to the *profit and loss account* as well as to the *book value* of debtors.

**badge engineering** means selling products that are mechanically identical, but which are distinguished by different brand names ('badges'). This used to be true of Rolls Royce and Bentley cars.

**balance of invisibles** is the term used to describe that part of the *balance of payments* account which registers exports and imports of invisible payments and receipts. Exports and imports are categorised as either visible or invisible. Visible trade is that which involves goods, such as cars and machinery, i.e. those which you can clearly see and touch. Invisibles include services such as banking, insurance and tourism, which you cannot see and touch. Traditionally, the UK has run a surplus on invisibles thanks mainly to its finance sector, which has paid for its deficit on the *balance of trade*.

**balance of payments:** the sum of the nation's income and expenditure on foreign trade. It consists of the current account and the capital account. It could be compared with an individual who has a current account and a savings account in a bank. Together they represent his or her wealth. If that person is overdrawn on their current account, the savings account will have to make it up. Overall, though, there will be a balance. Note that within the overall balance of payments there is the *balance of invisibles* and the *balance of trade*.

**balance of trade** is the term used to describe that part of the *balance of payments* account that registers exports and imports of visible goods. The UK has been importing more visible goods than exports since the last quarter of the nineteenth century, and this has been paid for by the surplus on *invisibles*.

**balance sheet:** a statement of an organisation's *assets* and *liabilities* at a precise point in time, usually the last day of the financial year. Liabilities must equal assets thanks to the accounting convention of *double-entry bookkeeping*. An alternative way of interpreting a balance sheet is that liabilities (capital employed) show where the capital came from and assets show how and where the capital is employed. So assets employed must equal capital employed, as shown in the diagram below.

| Balance sheet for A–Z Ltd 31 December 199- | | |
|---|---|---|
| | £000s | £000s |
| Fixed assets | | 450 |
| Stocks | 125 | |
| Debtors | 160 | |
| Cash | 45 | |
| Less trade creditors | (260) | |
| Net current assets | | 70 |
| ASSETS EMPLOYED | | 520 |
| Long-term liabilities | 135 | |
| Share capital | 25 | |
| Reserves | 360 | |
| CAPITAL EMPLOYED | | 520 |

**Baldridge Award:** the most prestigious quality award for companies based in the United States. The award criteria are based on ten core concepts:

- customer-driven quality
- leadership

- *continuous improvement*
- *employee participation* and development
- fast response
- design quality
- long-term outlook
- management by fact (based on measuring data such as absenteeism)
- partnership by development
- *corporate responsibility* and *citizenship*.

**ballots** are the process of voting for or against a course of action. Ballots authorising *industrial action* must meet the requirements of the *Trade Unions Act 1984* and the *Employment Act 1988*. These demand that ballots must be secret, must offer voters an alternative which stops short of strike action and must include a warning that strike action may lead to dismissal. Only if the industrial action receives more than 51 per cent support will the union be immune from being sued.

**banking covenants** are formal agreements between a firm borrowing money and its bank that set out the limits within which the company can operate. For example, a bank lending £200 000 to a firm may insist that no more than £100 000 be borrowed from any other source. If the firm breaks its covenant, the bank can insist that the loan be repaid. Failing re-payment, the firm could be placed into the hands of a *receiver*.

**Bank of England:** the UK's *central bank*. It is responsible for the issue of notes and coins in the economy, and also, more importantly, for implementing *monetary policy* including interest rate and exchange rate policies. As a state-owned organisation, it works closely with the government and the *Treasury*. There have been calls to make the Bank of England independent, mainly because of the perceived success of the *Bundesbank*, the German central bank, in guiding the West German economy. Another important role of the Bank of England is acting as a watch-dog for all banking activities. It was widely criticised after the collapse of BCCI and Barings.

**bank rate:** his is the interest rate set by the *Bank of England* in consultation with the *Chancellor of the Exchequer*. This rate then applies throughout the banking world, and in turn applies to loans taken out by individuals and firms. It is therefore an important weapon in *monetary policy*, which attempts to influence the level of economic activity.

**bankruptcy:** an individual or an *unincorporated* body may request (petition for) bankruptcy or be declared bankrupt when unable to settle its *liabilities* or if acting in such a way as to lead *creditors* to think that it is unable to settle, e.g. by refusing to communicate with them. Note that the term bankruptcy should not be applied to *limited liability* companies (see *insolvency* and *liquidation*).

**bar chart:** a diagram used to give a quick comparison between variables, e.g. monthly *sales revenue* of a company's three products. The values are plotted vertically and time horizontally. The heights of the bars represent the values. While good for impact, the bars lack precision and it may be difficult to ascertain actual values from the vertical axis. Also distortion can be created by selecting the width of bar inappropriately and by starting the vertical scale at above zero.

**bar coding** is the recording of data in a form that can be read instantly by a laser beam. When used on packaging it enables each sale to be recorded, thereby providing accurate stock records.

**barriers to communication** are physical or attitudinal reasons why messages fail to be received.

Physical reasons include:

- noisy environments making conversation impractical
- geographic distance, as when firms have their production in the North-East but their head office in London

Attitudinal reasons include:

- *intermediaries* deciding not to pass a message on (a complaint, for example)
- the unwillingness of an alienated worker to listen

**barriers to entry** are obstacles put in the way of new firms entering a market. The ability of existing firms to maintain such obstacles will depend on their marketing and financial power. See *anti-competitive activity*.

**barriers to trade** are obstacles put up by countries to stop imports entering their domestic market. They can be classified as either visible, such as tariffs or quotas, or invisible, for example when a country keeps changing the technical specifications of imports so that very few conform and are allowed entry. Barriers to trade are a form of *protectionism*.

**barter** is the swopping of goods or services to conduct a non-monetary transaction. It is likely to be needed when the deal is between different countries, one of which has a currency which cannot be converted freely.

**base weighted index:** a composite *index number* representing the average value of a number of items weighted according to their importance in the overall index. For consistency the weight or importance of each item must be constant over time.

**base year:** where *time series* data are put into *index number* form, the year chosen to have a value of 100 in the index series is called the base year.

**basic pay:** an agreed regular wage excluding any bonus, shiftwork, or profit-sharing supplements.

**batch production** is the manufacture of a limited number of identical products, usually to meet a specific order. Within each stage of the production process, work will be completed for the whole batch before the next stage is begun. This provides some *economies of scale* compared with *job production*, but not as many as through *flow production*.

**bear market:** a period of pessimism and falling share prices on the *stock market*. Individuals who anticipate this happening sell shares in the expectation that they will be able to buy them back in the future at a lower price. To a certain extent it results in a self-fulfilling prophesy, in that if everyone sells, more shares will come onto the market, and their price will indeed fall. A bear market is the opposite of a *bull market*.

**below the line** is a marketing term to indicate promotional activity other than main media advertising. It includes price and added value promotions, *point-of-sale* displays, and *sampling and selling*. Below-the-line activity is most commonly used for tactical or short-term reasons rather than for long-term image building.

**benchmarking** means setting competitive performance standards against which progress can be measured. These standards are based on the achievements of the most efficient producers within a market-place (if you can find out their figures). They ensure that production managers focus upon the competitive environment, instead of looking purely at this year's achievements compared with previous years'. Benchmarking is seen as a vital element in achieving *world class manufacturing*.

**Betriebsrat:** German for *works council*. In Germany it is a legal requirement that all large firms must have a works council (a consultation forum for workers and managers). The success of this policy has been a major influence on European Union pressure for all EU members to do the same.

**bias** is a factor that causes data or an argument to be weighted towards one side. Statistical bias occurs when a *sample* has – by chance or by mistake – an overweighting towards one subgroup (e.g. too many pensioners within a research sample). Personal bias occurs when a decision-maker consciously or subconsciously favours one side over another. *Scientific decision-making* methods such as *investment appraisal* or *decision trees* are supposed to avoid bias. In fact, the results they produce will depend upon the assumptions made, and they may reflect personal prejudice or bias.

**bilateral** talks or arrangements are those that occur between two parties. Therefore discussions on trade between the American and British governments could be termed bilateral trade negotiations.

**binding arbitration:** see *arbitration* and *pendulum arbitration*

**biotechnology** is the attempt to harness nature for commercial purposes such as the manufacture of medicines. Whereas pharmaceutical drugs, food colourings and flavourings have traditionally been based scientifically on chemistry, the intention is that advanced biology will become more important in future. Biotechnology is best known for genetic engineering, but it is the vast worldwide market for medicines that most attracts investors into this high-risk, high-tech area.

**blacking** is the refusal to deal with goods or personnel of a firm, usually because they have been involved in strikebreaking.

**blacklist:** a list of names of people or companies that a firm or country will not deal with.

**Blake's grid:** a diagram on which can be plotted the characteristics of a leader in order to identify his or her leadership style.

**blending** is a *linear programming* technique designed to show the factors limiting the achievement of an objective, and how best to operate within those constraints. The *constraints* are shown as straight lines on a graph, and at one vertex (i.e. where at least two lines intersect) the optimum value of the objective will be found. Blending will typically be used in short-run problems of resource allocation in controlled conditions, e.g. allocation of factory production time for various products in order to minimise cost. As with other linear programming techniques, complex problems can best be solved with the use of computing power, as the calculations become very lengthy.

**blind product test** is a consumer test of the qualities of two or more rival products. What makes it a 'blind' test is that the brand name and therefore image of the product is hidden from the consumer.

**block release** is off-the-job training based on blocks of time at college (such as three months). It is an alternative to the more common system of *day release*.

**blue chip:** a company that is so large, well established and soundly financed that it can be regarded as a secure investment or employer.

**blue collar union:** a *trade union* that represents manual workers.

**body language** is the conscious or unconscious use of the body to convey unspoken messages. A shrug of the shoulders may convey indifference, while an aggressive stance may undermine a manager's attempt to apologise to a subordinate.

**bonus issue:** a free issue of shares to shareholders on a proportional basis e.g. one for every five already held. For fuller information see *scrip issue*.

**bookkeeping:** recording a firm's transactions in a series of account books on the basis of *double-entry* accounting. From these books a *trial balance* can be arrived at, from which a full set of accounts can be drawn up.

**book value:** the *balance sheet* value of an asset. For *fixed assets* this is the *historic cost* minus *accumulated depreciation*. For stocks it is the lower of cost and *net realisable value*. In either case, the stated book value depends on assumptions made by the business, and is therefore only as reliable as the individuals concerned and the information they have available to them.

**Boston Matrix:** a method of analysing the current position of the products within a firm's portfolio, in terms of their *market share* and growth within their market-place. Devised in America by the Boston Consulting Group, this system of product portfolio analysis is far more sophisticated than the *product life cycle*. The Boston Matrix points out not only the importance of market share, but also that firms want products that can support each other's development. Product life cycle theory implies that declining brands have no future other than to die, whereas the Boston Matrix shows that an ageing brand can be a *cash cow* to be milked for the benefit of a rising star or to finance the changes needed to a problem child.

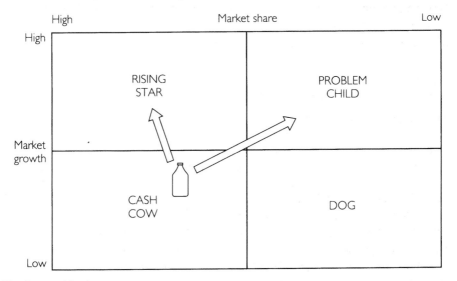

*The Boston Matrix*

**bottlenecks** are hold-ups in the assembly lines for a firm or for a whole economy. They are caused by an inability to increase supply to match an unexpected surge in demand. In past boom years, for example, there have been shortages of microchips, forcing producers of a huge range of products to slow down their rate of output. Within an individual firm, bottlenecks might be caused by poor management planning; trying to rush more output through the factory than is possible using the available labour, material or capital resources.

**bottom line:** jargon for the bottom line of a *profit and loss account,* or the estimated *net profit* on a specific activity or project. Care must be exercised to see which version of profit is meant.

**BRAD:** see *British Rate and Data*

**brainstorming:** a group activity in which members are encouraged to say the first answer that strikes them about how to solve a problem, no matter how weird. Having obtained as many ideas as possible, the group will consider each one in more detail. It is a way of encouraging more creative solutions than the normal carefully considered, safety-first ideas that managers may put forward.

**brand accounting:** see *creative accounting*

**branding:** establishing an identity for your product that distinguishes it from the competition. Marketing managers often talk about the personality of their brands as if referring to people. Successful branding adds value to an item and can ensure *brand loyalty.*

**brand leader:** the brand with the highest percentage share of a specific market or segment. This has become an increasingly valuable position as retailers have become more powerful over recent decades. Supermarkets such as Sainsbury's have such strong *own-label* products that they do not have to stock every national brand within a sector. Usually, they stock the brand leader, their own label, and just one other brand. Therefore the second biggest selling brand often has to compete fiercely with the numbers three and four for shelf space, and that means cutting prices to the bone. Only the brand leader is able to negotiate on equal terms with the retail giants.

**brand loyalty** exists when consumers repeat-purchase your product on a regular basis. Such customers are unlikely to be price sensitive, therefore your product's *price elasticity* will be low. This enables you to increase the price level without much effect upon demand. Brand loyalty can be active or passive:

- active loyalty stems from a conscious decision on the part of your customers that they prefer the taste, look, quality, or image to that of the competition
- passive loyalty stems from consumer inertia, from people's tendency to become used to a purchasing pattern from which they do not bother to change; for new products, this is the hardest marketing problem to overcome

**brand mapping:** see *mapping*

**brand standing:** a measure (in effect an audit) of where one firm's brand stands in consumer affections compared with rivals. This is monitored regularly by the use of *market research* into the images, attitudes and usage of those within the *target market.*

**breach of contract:** breaking a term laid down in a legal contract and therefore being liable to be taken to court or to be sued.

**break-even chart:** a line graph showing total revenue and costs at all possible levels of *output* or *demand*, i.e. at every point from an output of zero through to maximum capacity. This enables the reader to see at a glance the profit at any output level that interests them (by looking at the vertical difference between revenue and costs).

The chart comprises three lines: *fixed costs*, total costs and total revenue. They are plotted with pounds on the vertical axis and output on the horizontal axis.

Fixed costs:      form a horizontal straight line

Total costs:      line starts at fixed costs and rises as a diagonal straight line

Total revenue:   line starts at 0 and rises as a diagonal straight line

To construct the chart, first set out a grid with the following headings:

| Quantity | Revenue | Variable costs | Fixed costs | Total cost |
|---|---|---|---|---|

In the quantity column should be no more than three figures:

**1**  0 units

**2**  Maximum output (which might have to be assumed)

**3**  A convenient point between them (probably halfway).

---

Worked example: compile a table of data for a firm with fixed costs of £40 000, variable costs of £1, a selling price of £2, and a factory capable of producing 50 000 units:

| Quantity | Revenue | Variable costs | Fixed costs | Total cost |
|---|---|---|---|---|
| 0 | £0 | £0 | £40 000 | £40 000 |
| 25 000 | £50 000 | £25 000 | £40 000 | £65 000 |
| 50 000 | £100 000 | £50 000 | £40 000 | £90 000 |

From this information the graph can be drawn as follows, with pounds on the vertical axis and output on the horizontal.

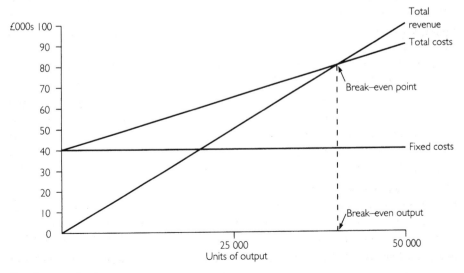

*Break-even chart*

**break-even point:** the intersection of total revenue and total cost on a *break-even chart*. It can be calculated without drawing the chart as shown below:

FORMULA:  break-even output = $\dfrac{\text{fixed costs}}{\text{contribution per unit*}}$

*selling price – variable cost

---

Worked example:

$$\frac{£40\ 000}{£2 - £1} = 40\ 000 \text{ units}$$

---

**breaking bulk:** see *wholesaling*

**British Rate and Data (BRAD):** a monthly publication that lists out all the advertising media available in the UK, from THE TIMES to THE GROCER. Each entry gives the address of each medium, together with the cost of buying advertising space. It is available at many local libraries and is ideal for discovering real advertising costs for projects or business plans.

**British Standard 5750** is the best known certification of quality management within the country. Its supporters believe that it ensures standards that can be relied on by purchasers. Critics consider it a bureaucratic nightmare: a triumph of paper over performance. What is not in doubt is that BS 5750 does not guarantee a quality standard. It is a system for ensuring that firms set quality targets and then monitor their actual performance in relation to those targets. By implication, then, a firm could hold a BS 5750 certificate for setting and achieving a relatively low quality target.

**British Standard 7750** is a certification of environmental management standards. It is a tool by which an organisation can recognise whether it is achieving acceptable environmental standards. In the longer term, it is hoped that it will become as important a market differentiator as BS 5750.

**British Standard 7850** measures a firm's progress towards achieving TQM (*total quality management*)

**British Standards Institute (BSI):** the body responsible for setting quality and performance standards over a wide range of product fields. Seeing the BSI *kitemark* logo on a product should give consumers confidence that it has been manufactured to a high quality and safety standard.

**brown goods:** a collective term for electrical household goods that were traditionally made with wood castings, such as televisions and hi-fis.

**BS 5750:** see *British Standard 5750*

**BS 7750:** see *British Standard 7750*

**BSI:** see *British Standards Institute*

**Budget (the)** sets out the government's income and expenditure plans for the forthcoming year. Government income is raised through *direct* and *indirect taxes* on firms and individuals, and spent on goods and services such as defence, education and social security benefits such as unemployment benefit. Note that the budget does not have to balance; if expenditure is greater than income it is known as a *budget deficit*, and if income is greater than expenditure it is known as a *budget surplus*.

**budget:** a forward financial plan usually involving a *cash-flow forecast*, forecast sales and forecast costs. The budget is a kind of route map that should have been set in the light of the company's objectives for the period. Divergences from a budget figure can be analysed by *variance analysis*. Budgets can be used as a discipline, a coordinator, a motivator, a monitoring and control device and a trigger for remedial action, as well as a test of forecasting ability.

**budgetary control:** progress throughout an accounting period can be checked by regularly comparing actual with budgeted figures for *revenues* and *expenses*. Variances can then be investigated. Regular monitoring may correct divergences to allow changes within the budget to cope with the unexpected. (See also *variance analysis*.)

Worked example: budgetary control through variance analysis

All figures in £000s

|  | January | | | February | | | March | | |
|---|---|---|---|---|---|---|---|---|---|
|  | Budg | Act | Var | Budg | Act | Var | Budg | Act | Var |
| Revenue | 85 | 80 | (5) | 95 | 86 | (9) | 110 | | |
| Materials | 36 | 34 | 2 | 42 | 39 | 3 | 46 | | |
| Fixed costs | 42 | 44 | (2) | 45 | 45 | – | 45 | | |
| Profit | 7 | 2 | (5) | 8 | 2 | (6) | 19 | | |

**budget deficit:** the result of government expenditure being greater than its income. The difference has to be made up by boosting the money supply, or by borrowing, which the government can do by selling *gilt-edged securities* or by attracting more savings into Premium Bonds or other *National Savings* products. Heavy government borrowing may, however, have a knock-on effect on other parts of the economy, if the government's demand for money crowds out private sector firms seeking loans. This may harm the 'real' economy. Certainly such action is likely to increase interest rates, making life hard for businesses and individuals with heavy borrowings.

A budget deficit may be caused by structural or cyclical factors:

- structural: a long-term tendency for spending to exceed revenue, perhaps because government spending is more popular politically than government taxation
- cyclical: in a recession, tax receipts inevitably fall because people are out of work, and firms are making less profit. In addition more people out of work means more spending on social security benefits such as unemployment benefit

Cyclical causes should be self-correcting when the economy recovers. Structural causes will not disappear unless tackled directly.

**budget surplus:** when government revenue exceeds its spending. See *budget* and *budget deficit*.

**buffer stock:** the desired minimum stock level held by a firm just in case something goes wrong. Possible causes include a supplier's failure to deliver, the discovery of substandard supplies or an unexpected increase in demand. The more efficient the firm and its suppliers, the lower the buffer needed. Those aspiring to a *just in time* production system set their sights on removing the buffer stock completely. This would release capital to be put to more profitable use elsewhere in the business.

**building society:** an organisation that provides interest-paying savings facilities, using the funds raised to provide households and small businesses with mortgages (long-term loans) to buy property. Since the Building Society Act 1986, the societies have been able to provide many other banking facilities, such as *overdrafts*. Traditionally, because there were no outside shareholders, building societies reinvested all profits back into the business. In recent years there has been a trend for societies to turn themselves into public limited companies, thereby making themselves indistinguishable from banks, both in law and in the profit motive.

**built-in obsolescence:** see *obsolescence*

**bulk buying** means purchasing in large enough quantities to secure a lower price per unit. This is an important *economy of scale* and is a reason why firms are attracted to *horizontal integration* (mergers). Traditionally, even small firms thought it sensible to buy in large quantities, gaining discounts but needing to hold stocks for a long time. This desire to buy in bulk has become unfashionable due to the focus on *just in time* production and *stock control.*

**bulk decreasing good** is one which loses size and/or weight during its manufacturing process e.g. steel and glass making. Because the reduction in bulk decreases transport costs, industries which do this tend to be located close to their supply of raw materials. (See *industrial location.*)

**bulk increasing good** is one which increases in size and/or weight during its manufacturing process, e.g. car body shells and soft drinks. Because adding weight and/or size increases transport costs, industries which do this tend to be located close to their market and the consumers. (See *industrial location.*)

**bull market:** a period when prices on the *stock market* are on a rising trend. Individuals who anticipate this happening buy shares in the expectation that they will be able to sell them in the future at a higher price. Sometimes this can get out of hand, so that the speculation on a high rising market begins to develop a momentum of its own, which has no relationship to the real value of the companies themselves. Such a market can only be sustained by its own momentum, and once a hint of doubt sets in it collapses very rapidly. Exactly this happened in the 1929 *Wall Street Crash* and again in October 1987. Both were followed by long, deep *recessions.* A bull market is the opposite of a *bear market.*

**Bundesbank:** the German *central bank.* Unlike the *Bank of England* it is independent of the government. The reunification of Germany in 1990 tested the Bundesbank's determination to keep to a strict anti-inflation policy because the costs of rebuilding the East German economy proved to be far greater than had been anticipated. This had an impact throughout Europe because of the considerable power and influence of the German mark on the *Exchange Rate Mechanism (ERM).* It has been suggested that the Bundesbank may well set the pattern for a *European Central Bank* should one ever come into existence.

**bureaucratic:** a process or management that is rooted in paper-based checks and counterchecks on decisions or actions. As a consequence, creativity is likely to be stifled and decision-making both slow and cautious.

**business confidence** is widely assumed to be a major factor in decisions regarding firms' manpower plans, investment plans and stock levels. It is measured regularly by many research groups, of which the best regarded is the *CBI*'s Quarterly Survey. Many believe that confidence can produce a self-fulfilling prophesy, with an optimistic outlook causing the investment spending and stockbuilding that makes the economy grow. This can lead governments to 'talk up' the economy in recessionary times.

**business cycle:** the regular pattern of upturns and downturns in demand and output within the economy that tend to repeat themselves every five years or so. The causes of this cyclical pattern to economic activity are not fully known, but are partly explained by:

- bunching of investment spending which, by definition, need not be repeated for some years
- government policies that aim for rapid growth just prior to election dates (leading to *inflation* and therefore the need to constrain the economy post-election)
- the impact of stockbuilding and, later, *destocking* on the whole economy

For managers, the key point to remember about the business cycle is that it has existed for over 150 years. Therefore, even when economic prospects look especially rosy, they should remember that a *recession* may follow the current boom. So the company should always ensure that its *liquidity* is high enough and borrowings low enough to survive an unexpectedly bad year or two.

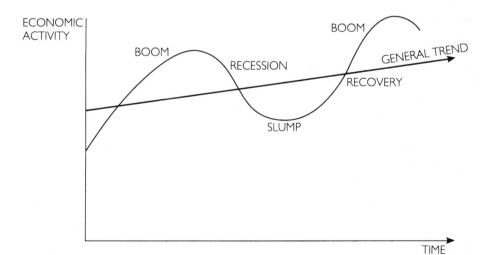

*The phases of the business cycle*

**business entity:** a term used to show that when a *limited liability* firm is founded, it becomes a separate legal being (entity) from the individual who founded the business. It is this separation of the person from the company that enables the shareholders to enjoy limited liability.

**business environment** is the combination of factors which lie outside an individual firm's control, but which have an effect on its performance. Such factors include economic circumstances, changing technology, government legislation and policy, the social environment, *pressure group* activity and the ethical climate.

**business ethics:** see *ethics* and *ethical code*

**Business Monitors** are government-produced statistics showing quarterly *output* within a series of manufacturing and construction sectors. For instance, if information was required on production trends for umbrellas, Business Monitors would provide this piece of *secondary data*. They are published by HMSO and are available through subscription or in business-orientated public libraries.

**business plan:** a report detailing the marketing strategy, production costings and financial implications of a business start-up. The plan is useful for helping the *entrepreneur* to think his or her idea through, though it is mainly drawn up to persuade investors or lenders to inject capital into the business. The main sections of a business plan are:

- a *marketing plan* showing the market gap, product positioning and competition within the chosen market-place
- an account of the entrepreneur's business experience and financial commitments
- a *cash-flow forecast*
- a projected *profit and loss account* and *balance sheet* for the end of the first year
- details of the finance needed from the investor, and the forecast rate of return on the investor's capital
- a brief account of the long-term forecasts and plans of the business

**business objectives:** targets set by the board of directors that affect decision making throughout the organisation. Examples might include:

- to break even
- to make a 20 per cent return on the capital invested in the business
- to become known as the technological leader within a marketplace (for example, Sony in the audio and video markets).

A business plan will be devised to attempt to achieve the objectives set.

**business process re-engineering** see *re-engineering*.

# C

**CAD:** see *computer aided design*

**Cadbury Committee:** set up to report on the financial aspects of *corporate governance*, it recommended a voluntary *code of practice* relying heavily on non-executive directors. Among its other proposals were:

- separation of the roles of *chairman* and *chief executive*
- firms should set up audit committees with a strong independent element

**called-up share capital** is the face value of all the shares that have been paid for by shareholders. A *share* has a *nominal value* written on the face of the share certificate, say £1. A share may be issued fully paid at par and so the buyer pays £1 in full for the share. Alternatively this share may be issued partly paid, say for 40p, so the called-up capital is 40p and the uncalled 60p. Future owners of this share will have to meet this 60p call at some time, or sell the share. Called-up share capital will be the same as actual *share capital* except when some shares are still partly paid.

**CAM:** see *computer aided manufacture*

**cannibalisation** is the effect of a new product launch on sales of a firm's existing brands. If Mars launched a mint Mars Bar they would worry that its sales would eat away at sales of the standard Mars Bar. This would need to be taken into account when estimating the profitability of the new product.

**CAP:** see *Code of Advertising Practice* or *Common Agricultural Policy*

**capacity** is the maximum amount the organisation can produce in a given period in the short run, i.e. without extra *fixed assets* and/or fixed *overheads*. Capacity is often difficult to estimate as more output can often be produced by a more intensive use of *plant* e.g. motivated workforce, better materials, better maintenance or *shift working*.

**capacity utilisation** is the extent to which the maximum capacity of the firm is being used, i.e. actual output as a percentage of maximum potential output.

$$\text{FORMULA:} \quad \frac{\text{actual output per period}}{\text{full capacity output per period}} \times 100$$

A firm's capacity utilisation is of considerable financial importance, because of the impact of fixed *overheads* per unit on profit margins. If a 40 000 unit factory has fixed overheads of £400 000 a year, full capacity working carries *fixed costs per unit* of £10. Should demand halve to 20 000 units, fixed costs per unit double to £20. So high capacity utilisation keeps fixed costs per unit down, by spreading the overheads over many units of output. Low utilisation can push a firm into severe loss making, forcing it to consider a strategy of *rationalisation*.

**capital:** to an economist, capital is one of the *factors of production*, the others being land, labour and entrepreneurship. To the business person it means funds invested in the company, either from the shareholders (*share capital*) or from lenders (*loan capital*). Both, however, recognise that capital is stored-up wealth, which when combined with the other factors of production, can be used to make goods and services more efficiently.

**capital allowances** are the amounts of the purchase cost of *fixed assets* which can be charged to profit in each year and thus reduce the tax liability. These allowances are not the same as *depreciation* which is assessed according to the company's own policy; capital allowances are assessed according to the rules of the tax authorities.

**capital budget:** a forecast or estimate of the resources available for use by an organisation for capital expenditure on projects or assets. This is separate from the revenue budget which is a forecast or estimate of revenues and expenses of the operations of the organisation. The building of a new factory would appear in a capital budget, while expenditure on heating it would be in the revenue budget. Both capital and revenue budgets should be related to the cash flow forecast or cash budget which will forecast the cash movements overall.

**capital employed** is the total of all the long-term finance of the business, consisting of loans, *share capital* and *reserves*. It provides the funds for obtaining the company's assets, therefore capital employed equals assets employed.

**capital expenditure** is spending on new *fixed assets* such as machinery or new buildings. This affects the *balance sheet*, as a cash purchase would cause cash to fall while the fixed asset total rises. Capital spending does not, however, have any direct effect on the *profit and loss account*. This is because the cost of capital expenditure is only charged to the profit and loss account through *depreciation*, i.e. the cost is spread over the useful lifetime of the asset.

**capital gain:** a gain arising from the increase in value of an *asset*, which becomes apparent when the asset is sold for more than its *historic cost* or is subject to professional revaluation, e.g. property. A capital gain is accounted for in the balance sheet through an increase in *shareholders' funds*.

**capital gearing** measures the proportion of *capital employed* that is financed by long-term liabilities such as *debentures*. Capital gearing is, as a percentage:

FORMULA: $\dfrac{\text{long-term liabilities}}{\text{capital employed}} \times 100$

A highly geared organisation is heavily reliant on borrowing and is therefore vulnerable as it must meet interest payments to lenders, whatever its earnings. A gearing level above 50 per cent is regarded as uncomfortably high.

**capital goods:** another term for a *fixed asset* such as *plant* or machinery.

**capital intensive** means that the way a good or service is produced depends more heavily on capital than the other *factors of production*. Examples of production systems which are very capital intensive include steel production and oil refining. A capital intensive production process will require very high spending on plant and machinery, causing fixed costs to represent a high proportion of total costs. This will give it high *operational gearing*.

**capital market:** the banks and other lenders that provide funds for long-term business investment. The capital market can be compared with the money market which provides shorter term loans, although in practice the line between the two is increasingly blurred.

**capitalisation** of interest charges or other costs represents one of the most extraordinary accounting practices, turning costs into assets. Expenditure can either be treated as a running cost, affecting the *profit and loss account* or as a capital cost, affecting the *balance sheet*. The distinction between capital and revenue expenditure is usually clear-cut, but there are some costs that can be capitalised in a way that can be thought of as *window-dressing*. For example, are interest charges on borrowed money a running cost or an asset? The former, surely. Yet many property companies draw up their accounts on the basis that interest payments form an inevitable part of the cost of building a property, and therefore form part of the value of a semi-completed site. Thus the interest payments are capitalised, adding to balance sheet assets.

**capitalism** is the social and economic system which relies on the market mechanism to distribute *factors of production* in the most efficient way.

**capital : labour ratio** measures the proportion of those two factor inputs in the production of a good. A good with a high capital : labour ratio is said to be *capital intensive*, and *labour intensive* when the reverse is true. Some economists have argued that a purely quantitative measure such as this is unhelpful. The quality of the capital and the labour (e.g. how well the workforce is trained) is more important.

**capital rationing** is a situation in which tight financial constraints force a firm to choose between projects that are all attractive. Were there no capital shortage, all the projects would be adopted.

**capital structure** refers to the way an organisation has arranged its funding between *ordinary shares, preference shares* and *debentures*. Its importance is that shares pay *dividends* which may be waived in bad trading years, whereas debentures pay interest which cannot be passed.

**captive market** is a group of potential customers who are virtually unable to obtain alternative supplies because one company has a *monopoly* position. Isolated villagers would represent a captive market for a small village shop and are likely to be charged high prices as a consequence.

**cartel:** the name given to a group of producers who make an agreement to limit output in order to keep prices high. In order to do this they must control a large proportion of the output, and they must agree on levels of production. Probably the best known cartel is the *Organisation of Petroleum Exporting Countries (OPEC)*. The problems with cartels are:

- that if they do force a high price it will encourage other producers to enter the market
- the members of the cartel may cheat by secretly producing more than laid down in the cartel agreement in order to gain revenue

In most countries cartels are illegal because of their potential to exploit customers.

**cascading** is the process of passing important information or training down the hierarchy. Each director holds a meeting with senior managers; each senior manager then passes on the knowledge to the managers below; each of them . . . and so on until the whole staff have been fully briefed. It is a more time consuming but much more effective communication method than a huge meeting or lecture.

**cash** is the most liquid of *assets*. All other assets are measured against it in order to define *liquidity*. The speed with which assets can be turned into cash depends on how saleable they are. The disadvantage with holding cash is its *opportunity cost*, in other words the loss of potential interest or profit. Strictly speaking, notes and coins are the only forms of cash, but other forms are so near cash as to be virtually indistinguishable. These might include cheques and credit cards.

**cash and carry** is a wholesale operation which offers rapid, local service to *retailers*, but without providing credit or delivery.

**cash balance:** a firm's net cash position at a point in time, as shown by the bank statement.

FORMULA:   cash at start + cash inflows − cash outflows = cash balance

**cash book:** the book where all receipts and payments by cash or cheque are recorded. The cash book should tally with the firm's cash and bank accounts.

**cash cow:** a brand that has a high share of a declining market. Firms use their cash cows to generate the cash to invest in newer products with greater growth prospects. The cash generation (or 'milking') is achieved by pushing prices up as high as possible while minimising expenditure on *research and development, market research* or *advertising*. See *Boston Matrix*.

**cash flow** is the sum of cash inflows to the organisation minus the sum of cash outflows, over a specific period. Inflows can arise from cash sales, *debtors* paying up, interest received or disposal of assets. Outflows can be caused by cash purchases, settling *creditors*, or asset purchases. As not all these items pass through the *profit and loss account*, cash flow and *profit* are different concepts. Profit may be affected by non-cash items such as credit given and taken, *depreciation* and *stock valuation*.

**cash flow forecast:** a detailed estimate of a firm's future cash inflows and outflows per month. From this can be derived the monthly *cash flow* and, by adding together each month's figures, the cumulative cash position. As the worked example below demonstrates, a firm may face a period of negative cash flow that is purely temporary. As long as it has been forecast, *overdraft* arrangements can be made with the bank to ensure that temporary finance is available.

Worked example: cash-flow forecast

(All figures in £000s)

|                 | Jan  | Feb  | Mar  | Apr  |
|-----------------|------|------|------|------|
| Cash at start   | 45   | 30   | (20) | (5)  |
| Cash inflows    | 115  | 130  | 150  | 170  |
| Cash outflows   | 130  | 180  | 135  | 145  |
| Net cash flow   | (15) | (50) | 15   | 25   |
| Cumulative cash | 30   | (20) | (5)  | 20   |

**cash flow statement:** an account that shows the sources and uses of cash within a firm over its financial year. Whereas a cash flow forecast is based upon estimates of the future, a cash flow statement records what has happened in the past, i.e. it shows historic cash flow. Following the Companies Act 1985, it succeeded the Sources and Application of Funds as one of the three financial documents that must be published each year by every public limited company.

**cash on delivery (COD):** if a seller wishes to speed up cash inflow, or where the purchaser's creditworthiness is uncertain, cash is demanded before goods are released on delivery.

**category killer**: a retailer offering such an attractive proposition to such a large share of the market as to threaten the survival of all competitors. The term came into use in Britain when Toys 'R' Us swept into a powerful market position with its wide range of stock, free parking and heavy television advertising.

**caveat emptor** means 'let the buyer beware'. In other words, however much consumer protection legislation there is, buyers always have a responsibility to take reasonable care over their purchases.

**CBI:** see *Confederation of British Industry*

**CD Rom** stands for 'compact disk read only memory'. It is a method of information storage and recall via a computer. Like a music CD, it can be played and information accessed, but no new material can be added to it. Data such as newspapers and encyclopaediae are increasingly being put on CD Rom.

**cell production** splits a continuous-flow production line into self-contained units. Each cell will produce a significant part of the finished article, enabling the cell workforce to feel committed to their *complete unit of work*. It is part of what the management consultant *Schonberger* calls 'building a chain of customers', which he believes to be a vital part of *just in time (JIT)* production.

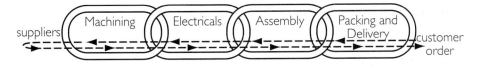

*Cell production*

**central bank:** all countries have a central bank whose main function is to issue notes and coins, and to regulate the banking system. Britain's central bank is the *Bank of England*, in Germany it is the *Bundesbank* and in the United States it is the *Federal Reserve Bank.*

**centralised organisation:** one in which decision-making powers are kept at the top of the hierarchy rather than delegated. The same term applies to geographic centralisation, in which local branches (or shops) work within a pattern tightly laid down by head office.

**centralisation** is drawing decision-making powers from the local or lower-level parts of the organisation, and concentrating them within the head office or centre. Its opposite is *decentralisation.*

Pros:  • centralisation allows consistent policies to be applied throughout the firm
       • it ensures that quick decisions can be made without consultation

Cons:  • centralisation reduces the input of the day-to-day experts (the shop-floor staff) into the firm's decision-making
       • it risks demoralising branch managers who feel powerless or mistrusted

**Central Office of Information (COI):** the government department that deals with all the *advertising* and *public relations* campaigns for the government. Examples of the COI's work would include drink-drive campaigns and recruitment advertising for the armed forces.

**Central Statistical Office (CSO)** is the government's data collection and processing agency, whose statisticians provide a wealth of information on the economy, society and business. The CSO is responsible for the production of key *secondary data* sources such as the *Annual Abstract of Statistics* and *Economic Trends*. All CSO material is published by HMSO (Her Majesty's Stationery Office).

**centring:** a technique used in the *moving averages* method of forecasting to ensure that the moving average trend data coincides directly with a time period. In a four quarter moving average, for example, two successive four quarter averages are added together, and the result divided by two. This establishes a centred average which shows the trend figure for the third quarter. Centring is needed whenever the moving average is based on an even number of pieces of data.

Worked example: centred averages

| YEAR 1 | Sales average | Four quarter average | Centred average |
| --- | --- | --- | --- |
| Quarter 1 | 900 | | |
| Quarter 2 | 1 200 | | |
| | | 1 150 | |
| Quarter 3 | 1 300 | | 1 175 |
| | | 1 200 | |
| Quarter 4 | 1 200 | | |
| YEAR 2 | | | |
| Quarter 1 | 1 100 | | |

**CEO:** see *chief executive officer*

**Certification of Incorporation:** issued by the *Registrar of Companies*, this gives a company its legal personality and enables it to trade.

**ceteris paribus** is a Latin phrase meaning 'other things being equal'. This is a vital assumption in a lot of economic analysis, for it enables one to assume that no variables are influencing a situation other than those under consideration. An example would be that when measuring a product's sales following a price increase, one can only draw conclusions about the product's *price elasticity* if one assumes other things are equal, i.e. ceteris paribus.

**chain of command** is a vertical line of authority within an organisation enabling orders to be passed down through the *layers of hierarchy*.

**chairman (or chairperson):** the elected chair of the meetings of an organisation. A company chairman will not only run the meetings of the board of directors, but may also take responsibility for the long-term aims and objectives of the business, leaving the managing director to determine and execute the strategy and to run the business day to day.

**Chambers of Commerce** are groups of business people in a town or city who gather together as a *pressure group* to look after the interests of local firms. They provide information and help for small companies as well as promoting trade fairs and exhibitions. They may work with *Training and Enterprise Councils (TECs)* to improve levels of training in their areas.

**Chancellor of the Exchequer:** the person responsible for running the nation's economy. He (there has not yet been a woman Chancellor) sets out the government's tax and spending plans once a year and can make certain other changes, such as alterations to interest rates, throughout the year.

**change** is a constant feature of business activity. The key issues are whether it has been foreseen by the company – and therefore planned for – and whether it is within the company's control. Extensive change may come from sales growth: requiring new management structures, new *layers of hierarchy*, new divisions or *profit centres*. Such organisational change may be difficult, but one could say, fairly, that failure would be due to bad management. Yet there may be failure. Growth may lead the company to become stiflingly *bureaucratic*, causing bright, young people to leave. Or extensive delegation to profit centres may backfire, as managers struggle to live up to their new responsibilities.

More problematic is unforeseen change. A small business that has a product which suddenly becomes very popular has many serious threats. An overstretched management may let costs get out of control: overtime payments, company cars, expenses and so on. *Quality control* may slacken in the rush to meet orders, leading to high returns (and therefore refunds) and a poorer reputation. Capital spending on new, bigger capacity will drain cash from the company. Worse, it may prove wasted if demand falls away as rapidly as it came. This example combines two problems: unforeseen change and change that is outside the company's control. Yet the firm could have brought the change within its control by ensuring steady, moderately geared, liquid growth, rather than frenetic, risky expansion.

External change is usually the hardest to control or even influence. Changing tastes or fashions, new laws or taxes, increased competition, or changes in the economy: all are major external constraints. The firm will try to affect these areas (by advertising or through *pressure group* activity), but may not succeed. In which case it must ensure that it is prepared to respond quickly and appropriately to whatever change occurs. *Contingency plans* are formulated to succeed in this aim. These will cover the marketing tactics and production planning needed in the short term. Long-term health will often depend on the product range and degree of *diversification* in the business. A sharp tax increase on whisky will not damage a company with extensive beer, wine and soft drinks interests.

**change management:** the process of planning, preparing, implementing and evaluating changes in business strategies or working methods. The key underlying factor in change management is trust. For only if staff have faith in the motives and competence of the managers concerned will they help to implement the desired change. Successful management of change requires:

- people whose motivation and trust makes them willing to accept and even harness it

- brand names with the consumer loyalty to ensure continuing, high sales revenues
- knowledge and confidence in several different markets
- the financial resources to be able to invest in new products or methods

**Chapter 7:** the section of the US Federal Bankruptcy Act 1978 that provides for the *liquidation* of a company which cannot reasonably be expected to return to a viable operating condition. Typically, a company in financial trouble will first turn to *Chapter 11* of this Act. If the company cannot be turned round it may end up in Chapter 7: liquidation.

**Chapter 11:** a section of US Federal Bankruptcy Act 1978 that allows a firm in financial difficulties to protect itself from its creditors for a period of time. Filing for Chapter 11 fends off the threat of *liquidation* while managers attempt to return the firm to financial health.

**charismatic leader:** one who motivates employees to strive to meet an objective through the force of his or her personality.

**chartered accountant:** one who has achieved a publicly recognised qualification from a professional association and can therefore charge higher fees to reflect higher qualifications.

**chief executive officer (CEO):** the director in charge of all operations within a business. In Britain, the term 'managing director' has usually described this function, but the American version CEO seems to be gaining popularity. The CEO is answerable to the chairman of the board of directors, although some companies combine these functions. This results in an individual having a degree of power that concerns those with an interest in *corporate governance*.

**chinese walls:** the wall of silence that is supposed to exist in *merchant banks* between those advising firms on *take-over bids* and the bank employees who are stock market dealers. If the dealers hear of a bid in advance, they could make huge profits by buying shares that are about to rise in value, but will lay themselves open to accusations of *insider dealing*.

**chinese whispers:** the way in which a message passed orally along a chain of people becomes distorted.

**CIM:** see *computer integrated manufacture*

**circular flow of national income:** a *macroeconomic* concept referring to the interconnectedness of the economy. Firms need workers who are paid from the sales of goods which are bought by *consumers*.

**circulating capital:** the funds flowing through a business enabling it to carry out its usual operations. Also known as *working capital* and defined as *current assets* minus *current liabilities*.

**Citizens' Charters** were introduced in 1992 to provide rights for individuals when dealing with state-run organisations, especially where such organisations appeared distant and non-accountable. The scope of the Charters is wide, ranging from the reasons for motorway cones being in place to waiting times in doctors' surgeries. In practice, the targets set may be too loose to be genuinely effective, and critics perceive the Charters more as a *public relations* exercise than a real attempt to raise standards.

**citizenship**: the extent to which a business acts as a good citizen, such as in clearing up its own mess and pollution, behaving well towards others and acting in the best interests of the whole community.

**The City** refers to the City of London and its financial services sector. The latter includes the banking system, the Stock Exchange, the money markets, the insurance industry and commodity exchanges.

**City Business Library:** located in Basinghall Street, London EC1, this is an exceptionally well-stocked and well-staffed public reference library for business. Its collection of *Mintel, EIU, Business Monitors*, trade magazines, *Extel cards* and innumerable other reports is invaluable for project work.

**civil law:** legislation which covers offences that are not automatically prosecuted by the police. The civil law gives the individual the right to pursue a grievance by taking another person or corporation to court.

**classical management theory** was formulated by observing how large organisations worked, and concluded that the main management functions were: forecasting, planning, organising, commanding, coordinating and controlling. The main theorist, Henri *Fayol*, believed that a clear hierarchy and the specialisation of tasks were the keys to effective management.

**classified advertising:** lines of advertising text used to inform people about second-hand items for sale or about job vacancies. Unlike *display advertising*, classified advertisements have no pictures or even headlines. Accordingly it is the cheapest form of *informative advertising*.

**class intervals** are the dividing lines chosen in order to group data into categories for purposes of analysis, e.g. there might be 12 days when sales volume was greater than 25 and no greater than 30. The class interval is five units. (See *frequency distribution*.)

**clearing bank** is the name given to the main high-street banks. They are so called because they developed by 'clearing' cheques, i.e. by paying cash for cheques drawn against them. (See also *commercial banks*.)

**clerical union:** an organisation designed to represent the interests of white collar workers at their places of work. (See *trade union*.)

**client groups:** a term used in the financial services industry to denote specific types of customer, such as young couples with children.

**client-server computing** means processing data on networks of computers, some providing computing or data services to the network, the rest serving as work stations.

**clocking-in** is a method of recording the exact arrival and leaving time of each employee. Abolishing this system has become a key element in the pursuit of *single-status* conditions in factories that once expected blue-collar workers to clock in while white-collar staff did not need to.

**closed question:** a question to which a limited number of pre-set answers are offered, e.g. Do you buy a newspaper nowadays? Yes ❑ No ❑

Pros: • ticking boxes is much quicker and easier for the respondent, so closed questions ensure a higher response rate

- a limited number of answers makes them easy to process and analyse

Cons:
- provides no scope for comment or qualitative input
- impossible to anticipate all the possible answers

**closed shop:** a workplace where employees must belong to a *trade union*. It can only occur by agreement between the employer and the union. The enforcement of 100 per cent union membership was made illegal in the *Employment Act 1988*.

**cluster sample:** respondents drawn from a relatively small area selected to represent a particular aspect of a product's *target market*. For example, the cluster may be a seaside town chosen by a producer of sun lotion.

**CNC machine:** see *computer numerical control machine*

**COD:** see *cash on delivery*

**Code of Advertising Practice (CAP):** the document that sets out the boundaries of what is acceptable within an advertisement, as laid down by the *Advertising Standards Authority*. For example, the Code states that advertisements for alcoholic drinks should not feature people who are or who look under 25. If a member of the public complains about an advertisement to the Advertising Standards Authority, the test will be whether the advertisement breaks the Code.

**code of practice:** a form of *self-regulation* devised and run by an employers' organisation that lays down appropriate standards for firms operating within the industry. It is a way of improving the industry's public image and of avoiding government legislation and regulation. Although codes of practice are most obvious within industries with poor reputations such as time-share holidays, many conventional sectors also have them. Critics believe that rogue companies will always surface within a system of self-regulation. Advocates of codes of practice believe that industry experts can supervise their own industry more effectively and more economically than the State.

**co-determination** is the German system for *industrial democracy* within large firms. All companies with 2 000 or more staff must have an equal number of employer and employee representatives on a supervisory board of directors. This is to promote the idea that all those working for the company have a common interest in its success.

**COI:** see *Central Office of Information*

**coincident indicator:** a monthly economic statistic that can be taken as an indication of the health of the economy currently. A good example would be the demand for motor cars.

**collateral** is the security offered to back up a request for a loan. Usually the only acceptable form of collateral to a bank is property, since that tends to appreciate in value, whereas other business assets depreciate. For small business start-ups, the owners' personal property is often the only asset substantial enough to provide the security demanded by the banks.

**collective bargaining** is when one or more *trade unions* negotiate with management on behalf of a whole category of employees within an organisation or plant. Such negotiations usually cover pay, fringe benefits, working conditions and working practices. A benefit to the firm of collective bargaining is that a single negotiation can settle pay issues and potential disputes for a year. Less appealing to the employer is that the single negotiation gives the trade unions more power through solidarity.

**collusion** occurs when firms act in concert with each other, perhaps over *market sharing agreements* or price fixing. The word has strong implications of working together for reasons that are not in the public interest, though there is no reason why firms should not share marketing data or *research and development* effort.

**command economy:** an economic system controlled by the decisions of those at the centre of government. This contrasts with the Western model of free or social markets in which economic decisions are made by producers in response to demand from customers. The command economy rejects the notion of the *invisible hand* in favour of a system that hopes to distribute resources more fairly, but seems to be more *bureaucratic* and less able to supply goods of the right quality and quantity to meet consumer demand. The collapse of the command economies of the USSR and the Eastern bloc countries and the low living standards which prevailed before their collapse indicates the inefficiency which results from such a system.

**commercial banks** are those banks whose activities are directed at making a profit by borrowing from customers at an interest rate lower than that at which they lend. This makes them different from a *central bank*. Because customers who deposit their money with banks only ever need a small portion of that money in cash, commercial banks can lend the rest to other customers, who in turn only need a small proportion as cash, and so the remainder can again be lent to yet further customers … and so on.

**commercial mortgages** are loans made by banks or building societies for the specific purpose of purchasing commercial property such as shop premises. The property serves as security on the loan.

**commodity:** any good – as opposed to a service - which can be bought and sold. The term is usually applied to markets in which there is almost no product differentiation. These include commodities traded in commodity markets such as unprocessed tea, sugar, rubber, wool and so on. Businesses may also talk about a consumer market as 'having become a commodity market'. This would mean that customers have come to choose products or brands solely on the basis of price.

**Common Agricultural Policy (CAP)** is the scheme by which agricultural production within the *European Union* is organised. It was set up by the Treaty of Rome as a way of helping small-scale and relatively inefficient European farmers to survive. It sets prices which are often above world prices so that if high levels of production threaten to drive farm prices down, the CAP buys up the extra at a pre-set intervention price. In theory, if there is large intervention one year and stocks rise, they can be used up in future years. In practice, however, such things as 'wine lakes' and 'butter mountains' have developed because there is no reason for farmers to limit their production as it can all be bought at the intervention price. The CAP is very expensive to operate, and works against the UK which generally has an efficient large-scale agricultural sector. The UK's payments into the CAP largely explain why, despite being one of the poorer members of the EU, the UK is the second largest net contributor to the budget.

Pros: • it stabilises farm incomes
  • it enables marginal producers to stay in business e.g. sheep farmers on Welsh hills
  • it has helped to make Europe self-sufficient in food production

Cons:
- it is expensive to operate
- it is open to corruption
- it raises food prices above world levels. This hurts consumers, and it hurts poor consumers more than rich ones

**communication** is the interaction between people, focusing primarily on the transfer of information. A communicator chooses an appropriate *transmission mechanism* in order to communicate with the intended receiver of the message. Communication can only be said to have succeeded once a response (*feedback*) has been achieved.

There is a tendency to believe that businesses need *more* internal communication, as if that would be beneficial in itself. This may not be the case, because people can feel swamped by too much communication – especially if it is passive, such as memos to all members of staff. *Herzberg* and others have emphasised the importance of direct communication in the psychology of motivation.

**communication channels** are routes through which communication occurs. Examples include *team briefing* sessions, *works councils,* plus the *chain of command* within an organisation. Communication channels can be "open" or "closed". The latter means that access to the information is restricted to a named few. The former "open" means that any staff member is welcome to see, read or hear the discussions and conclusions.

**communication net** (or network) is a diagram representing the actual communication structure within an organisation. The most common types are the wheel and the circle. As the diagram below indicates, the circle gives strong, team-based communication whereas the wheel gives control to the person at the hub.

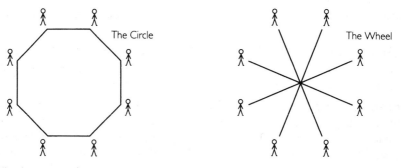

*Communication networks*

**Companies Act 1985:** the main piece of legislation governing modern company law in England, Scotland and Wales. It sets out the legal procedures for forming a company, running a company and winding it up:

- to form a company, the founders must present two documents to the *Registrar of Companies*: the *memorandum of association* and the *articles of association*
- to run a company, directors must ensure that accounting information is presented to shareholders in a form that complies with the Companies Act 1985, and that the accounts must be available for public scrutiny at *Companies House*
- winding up a company can be done via compulsory or voluntary *liquidation*

**Companies Act 1989:** a conscious attempt to bring UK company law into line with EU law. Among its provisions is to allow a firm to start up with a *memorandum of association* that places little restriction on a firm's trading freedom.

**Companies House** is where the *Registrar of Companies* holds the financial and ownership details on all the limited companies in the country. As laid down in the *Companies Act 1985*, all these records have to be available to the public. Students working on a project requiring the latest accounts for a company will find that the Cardiff and London bases for Companies House can provide the information required (for a fee of around £6).

**company formation**: the process of founding an incorporated (and therefore a limited liability) business. This requires submitting to the *Registrar of Companies*:

- a *Memorandum of Association*
- *Articles of Association*
- a fee

Then shares can be issued and trading commence.

**company objectives:** see *corporate objectives*

**company secretary:** appointed directly by the board of directors, the company secretary is the chief administrative officer of a business, usually responsible for the company's legal affairs.

**Company Securities (Insider Dealing) Act 1985** made *insider dealing* a criminal offense carrying up to two years' imprisonment. Fierce a deterrent though that seems, there have been so few successful prosecutions of insider dealing that the value of this law could be questioned.

**company union** is a Japanese approach whereby all workers within a firm are automatically represented by a trade union structure that is employed by the firm itself. Critics regard the lack of independence as a fundamental flaw.

**comparative advantage:** the idea that countries can benefit from specialising in the production of goods at which they are relatively more efficient. In this way consumers within each country gain the maximum benefit from international trade. At first, this may seem strange, because a country like the United States would seem to have an advantage at producing all goods when compared with a less developed country such as Somalia. However, it is easy to see that while the US may be one hundred times more efficient than Somalia in the production of maize, it is probably one thousand times more efficient at the production of cars. It therefore benefits everyone if the US produces cars, and Somalia maize, and then they trade.

**competence-based qualifications** are those based on identified achievements such as writing a letter or operating a word-processing package.

**Competition Act 1980:** an Act which allowed anti-competitive practices such as the refusal to supply to be investigated by the *Monopolies and Mergers Commission*. It was designed to extend *competition policy* to cover existing – especially public sector – monopolies. Under the Act, a complaint about a nationalised industry would go to the *Office of Fair Trading (OFT)* which could decide whether the matter deserved a full Monopolies and Mergers Commission investigation.

**competition policy:** since *monopolies* are considered to be against the interests of consumers and the public in general, governments legislate to restrict them. In the UK, the *Monopolies and Mergers Commission* has the job of policing monopolies under the guidance of the *Office of Fair Trading (OFT)*. Any merger which creates a market share of 25 per cent or more is likely to be referred by the OFT to the Monopolies and Mergers Commission, who will investigate whether the merger is thought to be in the public interest. Increasingly the power of the EU has come into play in this area under Article 86 of the Treaty of Rome.

**competitive pricing** means setting a price for a product or service based on the prices charged by competitors. This can be subdivided into two types:

1 In a market with low *product differentiation*, where all producers are price takers, no one has the market power to set a price higher than the competition.
2 In a market dominated by a *price leader*, a less important brand would have to price at a discount in order to sell a significant sales volume.

**competitive tendering** is the practice of encouraging *private-sector* firms to compete to undertake tasks that were formerly done by council employees. This encourages those applying to find new, more efficient methods of carrying out the task, but often results in lower wages and/or poorer conditions of service for the employees.

**complaints procedure:** the process whereby a customer complaint is resolved to his or her satisfaction and the problem communicated to management to prevent its repetition. Some organisations have a special department for dealing with complaints. This is likely to be efficient, but may insulate other staff from hearing the causes of customer dissatisfaction. The ideal method is to ensure that all staff are trained to deal with – and resolve – complaints immediately. This is likely to achieve the desired effect: a contented customer who will return in future.

**complementary goods** are products that complement each other, such as bread and butter, cars and tyres, fish and chips. Because usage and demand are connected in this way, if the price of one product rises, demand for its complement is likely to fall. The amount by which these movements take place is determined by their *price elasticity*.

**complete unit of work** means organising the production process so that the task of each worker or team represents a significant part of the whole. This move away from high *division of labour* is regarded by Professor *Herzberg* as a key factor in providing *job enrichment*.

**components** are manufactured parts used within production or assembly. They might be bought in from suppliers or produced within the factory.

**compound interest:** the way that the value of a lump sum can build up sharply if the interest is reinvested. For example, although intuition would suggest that savings earning 10 per cent a year would double in value every 10 years, the impact of compounding is:

|  | Apparent growth (10% uncompounded) | Actual growth (at 10% compound) |
| --- | --- | --- |
| After 5 years | + 50% | + 61% |
| After 10 years | + 100% | + 159% |
| After 20 years | + 200% | + 575% |

Compound interest means that the capital sum will grow at an increasing rate as interest is earned on the interest. For example, with an interest rate of 10 per cent:

Year 1 £100 + £10.00 = £110.00
Year 2 £110 + £11.00 = £121.00
Year 3 £121 + £12.10 = £133.10

**computer aided design (CAD)** enables designers and draughtsmen to store, retrieve and modify their work using multi-dimensional images.

**computer aided manufacture (CAM)** involves the computer in a variety of manufacturing tasks beyond the use of robots on the *production line.* These include *stock control* and ordering goods.

**computer integrated manufacture (CIM)** is the use of computers to coordinate every aspect of production, from product design through *stock control* to production scheduling and control.

**computer numerical control (CNC) machines** are those that respond to numerical instructions programmed into their memory in advance of the production process taking place. This enables them to produce a wide range of different tasks in an automated response to their computerised instructions.

**concentration ratio** is the extent to which a market is dominated by a small number of large firms (at one extreme) or a large number of small firms (at the other). It can be measured in a number of ways e.g. by *capital employed,* turnover or number of employees.

**conciliation** is the attempt to get both sides in a dispute to reconcile their differences. An independent conciliator might be found from ACAS, the *Advisory, Conciliation and Arbitration Service.* He or she would listen to the views of both sides, look for possible common ground, then encourage both sides to meet to discuss a compromise.

**conditions of employment** are the details of pay, working hours and holiday time that are set out in an *employment contract.*

**confectioner, tobacconist, newsagent (CTN)** is the trade term for ordinary newsagents or sweetshops.

**Confederation of British Industry (CBI):** the premier employers' association, listing most of the country's leading firms in its membership. The CBI's main functions are:

- to be a lobbying service for industry within the government and elsewhere, promoting the legislation and economic policies favoured by the *private sector*
- to promote the image of industry as a worthwhile career, especially among students
- to provide its membership with well-researched, nationally applicable research such as the CBI's Quarterly Survey of Economic Trends

**confidence level:** a measurement of the degree of certainty to be attached to a conclusion drawn from a *sample* finding. For example, if a pre-election opinion poll puts the Conservatives 3 per cent ahead of Labour, how confident can one be of a Tory

41

victory? Clearly, not 100 per cent certain since the research finding is not based on the whole population. Market researchers only feel happy to draw conclusions from findings that have a 95 per cent chance of being right (i.e. 19 times out of 20). The term given to that is a 95 per cent confidence level.

**conglomerate:** a firm which is comprised of a series of disconnected businesses. This provides the strength derived from *diversification* but has the potential weakness of a lack of focus. The modern approach to the management of a conglomerate is to delegate power very extensively to the different businesses within the group. This is to enable each business to act as its own core with its own strategy and focus.

**conglomerate mergers** occur between firms which have no clear connection with each other's business, either horizontally or vertically (see *horizontal* or *vertical integration*). The advantage to the firm of such a move is that it spreads risk, and may increase overall profit potential.

**conscience spending** occurs when consumers spend because they feel, for a variety of reasons, that they 'ought' to buy the good or service. Charities often exploit this situation in their advertising and, especially at Christmas, by offering cards or small gift items for sale.

**consensus** is the area of agreement between people. It may be tacit rather than explicit. In other words it may not have been discussed and agreed formally. It is a key principle of Japanese management that a strategy should not be implemented until a consensus has been arrived at.

**consensus-based decision making** means waiting until all relevant staff agree before putting a decision into effect. Critics of this Japanese tradition suggest this slows decision making and prevents tough decisions being taken. On the other hand, careful thought by all the staff affected should result in the right actions being taken, and the psychological effect of such a democratic procedure may benefit morale enormously.

**constant prices** are used when it is important to measure a variable in a way that avoids including the effect of inflation. For example, real income is measured in constant prices. This will involve the selection of a *base year*, so that the variable is expressed in, for example, 1990 prices.

**consistency** states that the accounting methods used to prepare firms' published financial data must be kept consistent so that proper conclusions can be drawn from the figures. This is an important accounting concept as it ensures that trends are a result of real changes in performance, not merely the consequence of an accounting change. For example the stated profit of a firm could be boosted by an accounting change that lengthens the assumed useful life of an asset, thereby reducing the annual *depreciation* charge. This would go against the principle of consistency.

**consolidated accounts** are the sum of the accounting data from all the divisions of a business, after allowance has been made for transactions within the group. They show the aggregate figures for all the sections of a group of companies consisting of a *holding company* and its *subsidiaries*. So the consolidated accounts show the *profit and loss account* and the *balance sheet* for the whole group.

**constraint:** a limitation on a firm's ability to meet its objectives. *Internal constraints* are those within the firm's control; *external constraints* are beyond it. Often, however, internal and external constraints interact, muddying the dividing line between them. For instance, a rise in interest rates (external) is primarily a problem for firms with high borrowings (internal).

**constructive dismissal** occurs when an employee resigns from a job because the employer has acted unlawfully, or broken the contract of employment. A black worker who has suffered racist abuse from a manager could take the company to an *industrial tribunal* on grounds of constructive dismissal.

**consultation:** asking for the views of those who will be affected by a decision. These views should then be taken into account by the executive responsible for taking the decision. It is important to distinguish between consultation and *delegation*. The latter means passing decision-making powers down the hierarchy, whereas consultation keeps power at the top.

**consumable:** any product that is not *durable*, i.e. can only be used or consumed once. Typical examples include food, detergent and petrol.

In addition, all services would be classified as consumables. From the business point of view, their significance is that:

- consumables do not share the *market saturation* problems of durables, therefore demand is more constant
- due to the possibility of regular purchasing it is easier to build strong *brand loyalty* towards consumables
- consumables are less subject to falling demand during *recessions* (whereas durables suffer as customers postpone replacement purchases)

**consumer:** a person who purchases or consumes a product. Manufacturers of children's products are aware that their consumers are often not the purchasers. This is why advertising for products such as breakfast cereals are often a strange combination of health information (for parents) wrapped up in jazzy, fun cartoon images (for children).

**consumer credit** is the means by which people buying goods can delay payment and so spread the cost. Purchasing in this way usually requires a deposit and carries a rate of interest. One of the most common types of consumer credit is *hire purchase* (HP).

**Consumer Credit Act 1974** lays down the regulations covering the purchase of goods on *credit*. Its intention is to prevent consumers signing unfair contracts and also to ensure that purchasers know exactly what interest rate they are to be charged for the credit they receive. For the purposes of the Act, the term 'credit' includes any form of cash loan, including bank overdrafts and credit cards. Specific measures include:

- regulating the terms (especially the small print) allowable within a credit contract
- the rule that all advertising or display materials quoting *credit terms* must also state the *annualised percentage rate (APR)* of interest

**consumer durables** are goods which are owned by households but which are not immediately consumed by them. Examples include washing machines, dishwashers, cars and televisions. In effect, they are the *capital goods* of households.

**consumer panel:** a group of consumers within a firm's *target market* used on a regular basis for *market research* exercises. A typical use of a panel is for product testing, using the known tastes of the panellists to decide on the qualities of new product ideas, or of changes to the composition of existing products.

Pros: • keeping the same sample saves the recruitment cost of finding new respondents every time
 • avoids the problem of unmatched samples

Cons: • panels will become expert in the product field being tested and therefore become unrepresentative of the general public
 • any bias within the sample chosen may not become evident because there may be no other comparative samples

**consumer profile:** a quantified picture of a company's customers, showing the proportions of young to old, men to women, middle class to working class and so on. (See *demographic profile*.)

**consumer protection** legislation is that group of laws passed to control the worst excesses of past business practices towards their customers. Included within this legal grouping are:

• *Sale of Goods Act 1893* and *1979*
• *Trades Descriptions Act 1968*
• *Unsolicited Goods and Services Act 1971*
• *Consumer Credit Act 1974*
• *Competition Act 1980*
• *Weights and Measures Act 1985*
• *Food Safety Act 1990*

**consumer resistance** is the term given for the factors that prevent potential customers from buying a particular product. The reasons for resistance may be active or passive. If people dislike the idea of whisky mixed with cream, they will actively resist trying or buying an Irish cream liqueur. An example of passive resistance would be a consumer who does not try a new brand of detergent because of loyalty to the Persil brand. Consumer resistance to a new product must be found out long before the product launch. Remedies may be to offer free samples in retail outlets, or to sell keenly priced trial packs.

**consumerism** is an approach that places the interests of the consumer at the heart of discussions about business decisions or activities. This could be contrasted with trade unionism, which places the interests of workers first. The best known consumerist organisation is the Consumers' Association, publishers of WHICH? magazine.

**Consumers' Association (CA)** is an independent organisation that lobbies on behalf of its consumerist membership and produces the monthly magazine WHICH?.

**consumer sovereignty** is sometimes referred to by the saying 'the consumer is king', which means that the consumer, by his or her purchasing habits determines what is produced in the market-place. In practice, the existence of market friction such as imperfect information, as well as market imperfections like *monopolies* mean that the consumer is far from sovereign.

**consumers' risk** is the statistical risk of being sold an item which lies outside the standards advertised. In *quality control*, producers apply statistical tests to the processes of production, filling and packing, but to save time and money they do not check every item sold. The producer must ensure that the consumers' risk is low enough to minimise the probability of loss of reputation.

**contingency planning** means preparing for unwanted or unlikely possibilities. Since Perrier Water's setback when it was found to contain traces of benzine, firms include disaster planning as one contingency. Plans might also be prepared in case of:

- a severe *recession*
- *bankruptcy* of a major customer
- a sudden surge of demand

Contingency plans can be prepared on computer models that provide the opportunity to ask and answer *what if? questions*.

**contingent liabilities** are possible future *liabilities* that depend on uncertain factors and therefore do not have to be included on a *balance sheet*. They should be itemised in the notes to published accounts (and a value placed upon them), though there have been cases of substantial liabilities arising that had never been mentioned in the accounts. A contingent liability differs from a *provision* only in that the latter can be estimated with more certainty and therefore should be valued on the balance sheet.

**continuous improvement**: see *kaizen*.

**continuous research** consists of *surveys* that are carried out on a regular basis, such as every month. Firms might do this to monitor brand awareness and *brand standing*.

Pros: • warns of any slippage in *brand loyalty* or image
- helps measure the success of advertising campaigns

Cons: • regular research will be expensive over the year, therefore may not be economic for a small firm
- accuracy relies on asking the same questions each month, which is less flexible than *ad hoc research*

**contracting out** means placing with independent suppliers a task that used to be done in-house, i.e. within the organisation. *Private-sector* firms, councils or nationalised industries might contract out services such as cleaning, refuse disposal, or even the production of components. Contracting out is a reversal of *vertical integration*.

Pros: • might lead to lower costs as the contractor's wage rates do not have to be as high as those within the organisation
- putting the service out to *tender* invites new management thought on how to improve efficiency

Cons: • the subcontractor's employees may be less motivated towards providing the quality the organisation wants
- from the employees' viewpoint, working for a subcontractor may mean more intensive work for less pay

**contract of employment**: see *employment contract*

**contribution** is total *revenue* minus total *variable costs*. Therefore contribution minus *fixed costs* equals *profit*. It is a measure of the amount each product or department contributes towards covering the fixed overheads of the business. Once the latter have been covered, all further contribution is straight profit. The contribution of a product line or of even a department is its revenue minus the costs which would disappear or could be avoided if it were discontinued. Contribution gives a clearer picture by removing general *overheads* or fixed costs which are difficult to allocate.

Revenue £150 000

minus
£60 000
Variable
costs
equals

Contribution £90 000

Contribution
of
£90 000

minus
Fixed costs of
£56 000
equals

Profit of
£34 000

*Contribution*

---

Worked example: calculating profit by use of contribution

    Question: if a firm sells 20 000 units at £7.50, has £3 of variable costs and £56 000 of fixed costs, what is its profit?

| Answer: | Total contribution | – | Fixed costs | = | Profit |
|---|---|---|---|---|---|
| | (£4.50 × 20 000) | – | £56 000 | = | |
| | £90 000 | – | £56 000 | = | £34 000 |

---

**contribution costing:** the valuation of a product's cost solely on the basis of *variable cost*, i.e. excluding *fixed costs* or *overheads* which are difficult to allocate (especially in multi-product companies).

**contribution per unit** is the amount each unit sold contributes towards covering the fixed *overheads* of the business. Once the *fixed costs* are covered, all extra contribution is profit.

Contribution per unit is one of the most useful concepts in business studies. Among its applications are:

- for calculating profit: (contribution per unit demand) – fixed costs
- for calculating break-even output: fixed costs ÷ contribution per unit
- for calculating appropriate minimum prices when considering a strategy of *price discrimination*

**contribution pricing:** the setting of prices based on the principle that as long as an item is sold for more than the *variable cost*, it is making a contribution towards the *overheads* of the business. This notion may lead a firm towards one of two approaches to pricing: *price discrimination* and *loss leaders*. For exam purposes, the main consequence of contribution pricing is its effect on the acceptance of additional customer orders at cut prices. A standard exam question runs as follows:

---

Worked example: contribution pricing

The BG Co has sales of 2 000 units at £5. Its fixed costs are £3 000, variable costs are £3 and average costs are £4.50. BG's sales director has just phoned through with an extra order for 500 units at £4 each. Should it be accepted?

Answer: the immediate thought is that if average costs are £4.50, it must be unprofitable to accept an order at £4. That is wrong, however, because if fixed costs have already been covered and variable costs are £3, any price above £3 is profitable. The order will in fact generate an extra 500 × £1 = £500 profit (assuming BG Co has the capacity to produce the extra units).

---

**contribution statement:** a table of data setting out the contribution made by different departments or products to covering the company's fixed *overheads*.

|  | Brand X | Brand Y | Brand Z | Company total |
|---|---|---|---|---|
| Revenue | 100 | 200 | 300 | 600 |
| Variable costs | 50 | 75 | 150 | 275 |
| Contribution | 50 | 125 | 150 | 325 |
| Fixed costs |  |  |  | 300 |
| Profit |  |  |  | 25 |

In the above example, all three brands make a positive contribution. However, if the total *fixed costs* were allocated equally to each of the three (£100 each), Brand X would show a loss of £50. This might encourage a manager to halt production of X. Yet without the £50 contribution made by Brand X, the fixed costs would not be covered so the firm would make a loss. So although a contribution statement is a useful way of presenting data, it must be treated with care.

**contributory negligence** occurs when an employee injured in a workplace accident is partly at fault and therefore has contributed to the occurrence. In such a case, if the employer is taken to court over the accident, any compensation payment will be reduced in line with the negligence. In other words if the accident is considered half the employee's fault, the award will be halved.

**control:** one of the two key factors involved in successful *delegation*; the other being trust.

**controlling interest** in a company is achieved when an individual or organisation owns one more than 50 per cent of the voting shares. A great deal of influence, if not effective control, can be exercised at lower levels of ownership. Once an individual or an organisation such as a *pension fund* or *unit trust* gains a substantial block of shares, they may gain representation on the board of *directors*.

**Control of Substances Hazardous to Health (COSHH):** government regulations that lay down procedures for controlling unsafe substances. They are based on the provisions of the *Health and Safety at Work Act 1974*:

- the 1989 regulations require employers to prevent or control exposure to substances that are dangerous on contact, inhalation or ingestion
- the 1990 regulations require employers to apply appropriate measures for storing and handling dangerous substances, and coping with emergencies concerning them.

The COSHH regulations require all employers to carry out assessment, control, monitoring, health surveillance and training in relation to substances hazardous to health. Within individual workplaces, it will often be the safety representatives who work to ensure that employers pay proper regard to their COSHH obligations.

**convenor** is the elected head *shop steward* within a large factory. The convenor chairs meetings among the shop stewards and is likely to be the chief negotiator with the local management.

**convergence** is the idea of bringing the *European Union's* economies and currencies into line with each other. This is an essential prerequisite to *European Monetary Union (EMU)* and a single currency. Unless all the countries have similar levels of economic activity, rates of *inflation* and interest rates, joining the currencies together could cause major economic upheavals.

**convertible currency:** one which can be exchanged for another currency without limit. At its simplest level, this means if you go abroad you can take as much *sterling* out of the country as you like, or exchange it before you go. At another level it means that companies can move large sums out of and into currencies as they wish.

**convertible shares:** loan stock or *loan capital* paying interest at a fixed rate but which on a predetermined future date may be converted into *ordinary shares* at a price set today.

**cooperative** is an organisation run by a group of people, each of whom has a financial interest in its success and a say in how it is managed. That group might be the producers (as with agricultural cooperatives handling the packing and storage of several farmers' crops), the workers, or the customers (as with retail cooperatives).

**coordination** means ensuring that the work of many different people interlinks within a single plan. It is a major management function which can become hard to achieve when a great deal of decision-making power is delegated. The difficulty of coordinating the workings of a large organisation is a key *diseconomy of scale.*

**copyright** is the legal protection against copying for authors, composers and artists. Unlike *patents*, there is no requirement to register an author's copyright. The law on copyright is governed by the Copyright, Designs and Patents Act 1988.

**core activities** are the operating divisions that the firm sees as central to its corporate strategy. Other, more diversified functions may be seen as peripheral to the firm's purpose, and therefore sold off or closed down.

**core workers** are those people – managers, technicians and skilled workers – who are essential to a company. They give the organisation its distinctiveness. Because they are essential the organisation seeks to bind them to itself with secure, full-time employment at high salary levels and with good conditions and *fringe benefits*. Such people have become a shrinking proportion of the total labour force over recent years. Commentators such as *Professor Handy* believe this trend will continue, as firms come to prefer the flexibility of *peripheral* and *freelance workers*.

**corporate advertising:** an *advertising campaign* to boost the image of the company rather than to sell a particular brand.

Pros:
- can increase sales of a whole range of products if, like Heinz, the company name is also the brand name
- can make the company more attractive to potential shareholders, suppliers and employees

Cons:
- can be regarded as a luxury, especially in times of recession
- has often been used to correct image problems caused by the company's own unethical behaviour (e.g. banks overcharging or oil companies polluting)

**corporate governance** is an American term raising questions about who controls the boardrooms of public companies and whose interests do they and should they serve? In theory, the shareholders have voting powers over company directors, but in practice these are rarely exercised. Practical power resides with institutional investors such as pension funds, but they rarely step in unless they see the company dividends or share price threatened. In Britain, issues of corporate governance became prominent after a series of City and company scandals revealed a moral vacuum at the top of many businesses. The *Cadbury Committee* was set up to address the issues raised.

**corporate hospitality** means treating clients to an enjoyable, usually luxurious, time away from work. Common examples include days out at Wimbledon, Henley and Twickenham. Critics see such activity as bordering on bribery; advocates see it as useful social contact.

**corporate identity:** the design package that aims to create the company image desired by a firm. This may consist of a *logo*, a company uniform, the colour and style of the firm's stationery or even company cars and vans.

**corporate image:** the view of a company held by its customers, employees, and the public at large. For a bank, the ideal image might be: large, reputable, long-established yet innovative, approachable. *Market research* would aim to find the image characteristics desired by the customers, which would in turn influence decisions on *corporate advertising* and *corporate identity*.

**corporate objectives** are the *goals* of the whole enterprise. These should be based upon the firm's mission/aims. The corporate objectives govern the targets for each division or department of the business. They provide a mechanism for ensuring that authority can be delegated without loss of co-ordination. Among the most common corporate objectives are:

- to ensure long term, stable growth in real terms
- to spread risk and achieve growth through *diversification*
- to concentrate upon the firm's core skills
- to maximise *market standing*
- to add value through continuous technological *innovation*
- to achieve *profit maximisation* in the short to medium term

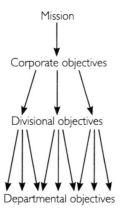

*Corporate objectives*

**corporation tax** is the tax which companies have to pay as a percentage of their profits. Although tax rates can be changed each year in the *Budget*, the level has usually ranged between 30 and 35 per cent. Smaller firms pay a lower tax proportion, of around 25 per cent.

---

Worked example: Company A pays 34 per cent tax on profits while the smaller Company B pays 25 per cent

|  | Company A £000 | Company B £000 |
|---|---|---|
| Revenue | 9 500 | 1 200 |
| Total costs | 7 300 | 840 |
| Pre-tax profit | 2 200 | 360 |
| Corporation tax | 748 | 90 |
| Profit after tax | 1 452 | 270 |

---

**correlation** is a measurement of how close a causal link there is between two or more sets of numerical data. Highly correlated data would form a predictable pattern, such as that for every £100 extra spent on advertising, sales rise £500. If the correlation is total, the data will form a straight line, as shown on the next page.

A danger with statistical correlations is making assumptions about cause and effect. Perfume advertising is at its heaviest in the weeks prior to Christmas. Sales follow the same pattern. Yet it would be foolish to suppose that this proves the effectiveness of the advertising. Perfume companies advertise at Christmas because that is when the public is most receptive to their advertising. The sales and advertising data are correlated, but that does not in itself prove which factor is the cause and which is the effect.

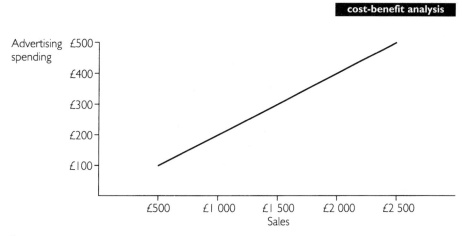

*Correlation between advertising and sales*

**corporate responsibility** is the idea that organisations have to consider environmental and ethical factors in their decision making as much as those concerned with profit. The Cadbury Report (1992) spurred many companies into action, so that, for instance ICI now issues a separate environmental report; and many companies undertake *environmental audits* of their activities to examine the impact they are having. In 1988 BP issued its 'Policy on Business Conduct and Code of Business Ethics' which required employees not only to abide by statutory requirements but also to the BP code of conduct.

**COSHH:** see *Control of Substances Hazardous to Health*

**cost accountant:** one who is employed to decide how costs are to be allocated to different product lines. This is information on which key decisions may be based, such as the pricing or even the discontinuation of a product.

**cost accounting:** the aspect of *management accounting* that is concerned with the allocation of costs to different product lines. The techniques of cost accounting include *standard costing* and *variance analysis*. The cost accountant provides the detailed information to enable marketing and production managers to make pricing, promotional and new product decisions.

**cost-based pricing:** setting a price on the basis of production costs rather than market conditions. This can only be sensible for a firm with little or no direct competition. The two main cost-based pricing methods are *mark-up* and *cost-plus*.

**cost-benefit analysis** means weighing up the financial and social costs of an action or decision against the financial and social benefits. This requires a quantification of the *external costs* (such as pollution) and of the social benefits (such as jobs). This can be very difficult to achieve, which may undermine the analysis. For example, whereas it is known that taking a person off the dole queue saves the Treasury more than £9 000 per year, it may be impossible to calculate the cost of noise or air pollution.

Cost-benefit analysis is usually applied to *public-sector* projects where the benefits and costs cannot all be assessed on a commercial basis and where it is difficult to price or value them because of the absence of a market. *Private-sector* firms make their business decisions on the basis of their internal revenues and costs, i.e. those that affect their internal company accounts. A cost-benefit analysis of the Channel Tunnel would consider the damage to the countryside, the advantages of a more efficient market as well as the excavation cost and expected fare revenues.

FORMULA:    social benefit − social costs = cost-benefit analysis

Within which

social benefit = internal (company) revenues + external benefits
social costs = internal costs + external costs

**cost centre:** a department or section of an organisation to which specific costs can be allocated. If a large company splits itself up into cost centres, various benefits can result:

- team spirit is easier to generate among 20 people than among 2 000
- each individual knows that personal effort to cut costs can have an impact within a small budget, but not within a 2 000 strong workforce
- by identifying the costs generated by each department, the firm is better able to make decisions (especially if *benchmark* data is available from national sources or from elsewhere within the company)

(See also *profit centres* and *overhead allocation*.)

**cost of goods sold (COGS):** see *cost of sales*

**costing** is the process of determining the cost of producing or supplying a product or service to the customer. It may be based upon historic information, or *standard costing* may be used to monitor the present and forecast the future.

**cost of living:** the money spent by the average household on necessities and luxuries over a period of time. This is difficult to determine precisely because each individual spends a different proportion of his or her income on different things. For example, a couple with two young children will probably spend a high proportion of their income on food and housing. In contrast, a middle-aged couple may spend a high proportion on holidays. If the mortgage rate goes up, the young couple will face a much larger rise in their cost of living than the middle-aged one. The government attempts to measure the cost of living using a 'basket of goods' which research has identified as the average household's expenditure. The best known measure of the cost of living is the *retail price index (RPI)*.

**cost of sales** is the accountant's calculation of the *direct costs* that can be attributed to the *sales revenue* generated over a trading period. The cost of sales can then be deducted from revenue to show the *gross profit*. This is the first stage in constructing the trading account of a firm's *profit and loss account*.

The calculation of cost of sales is quite tricky because of the accounting principle known as *matching*. This makes it necessary to exclude from the purchases total any costs of building up stocks for sale in the next financial year. In order to achieve this, cost of sales is calculated as on the next page.

FORMULA:    opening stock + purchases − closing stock = cost of sales

Worked examples: a firm's trading account

|                        | £     | £   |
|------------------------|-------|-----|
| Sales revenue          |       | 100 |
| Opening stock          | 20    |     |
| Add purchases          | 50    |     |
|                        | 70    |     |
| less closing stock     | (15)  |     |
| Cost of sales          | 55    | 55  |
| Trading or gross profit |      | 45  |

**cost-plus pricing** means adding a set profit percentage to the estimated total costs per unit.

Worked example: a firm with fixed costs of £40 000 per month and variable costs of £1 per unit wants to price its product on the basis of 25 per cent cost plus. Monthly sales are estimated at 100 000.

Total costs per unit    = fixed costs per unit   + variable costs per unit
                        = £40 000 ÷ 100 000   + £1
                        = £0.40                + £1

Total costs p.u. + 25%  = £1.40 × $\frac{125}{100}$ = £1.75

So the price is £1.75

Pros:  • cost-plus ensures that any cost increases will be passed onto the customer in the form of higher prices, thereby protecting the firm's profit margins
       • it may be the only way of pricing a job for which the amount of work cannot be predicted, such as *research and development* into a supersonic military aircraft.

Cons:  • cost-plus can only be applied in a situation where no effective competition exists; this is because it means setting prices with no reference to the market situation. So although it is the ideal pricing method, few companies are in a position to use it
       • by ignoring market conditions, the firm may be missing out on the further profit opportunities offered by *price discrimination*

**cost-push inflation** occurs when rising production costs force firms to increase their prices to protect their profit margins. In particular, *trade unions* are accused of making wage demands greater than productivity increases, causing employers to raise the prices of their goods, hence causing *inflation*. The usual response to this is that trade unions are only protecting their members' living standards, and if prices rise in the rest of the economy, it is unfair to expect workers to suffer a reduction in their standard of living. The causes of inflation are complex, and probably result from the interaction of cost-push with *demand-pull inflation*.

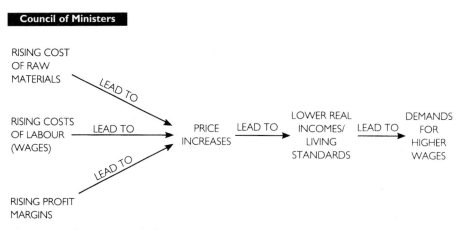

*The causes of cost-push inflation*

**Council of Ministers:** the *European Union's* main decision-making body. Its membership comprises one government Minister from each of the 15 member states. The Minister chosen will depend upon the issue under discussion. If the meeting is focusing upon the European economy, the *Chancellor of the Exchequer* is likely to be the UK's representative.

**counter-cyclical policy** is when a government takes steps to iron out fluctuations in economic activity (see *business cycle*). When the economy is booming, the government will try to stop it 'overheating' by reducing its own spending on goods and services. In times of *recession* it will follow the opposite course. To a certain extent this is automatic; in a recession there is more unemployment, so government spending has to rise to pay for more unemployment benefit. The automatic elements are known as *'automatic stabilisers'*.

The tricky part is deciding when to apply policy measures which are not automatic. Getting the timing wrong will make the situation worse. If the *Chancellor* believed the economy was coming out of recession he might reduce government spending on, say, roads. If, however, the recovery did not happen as expected, the reduction of incomes in the road building industry would make the recession worse.

**counter trading** (or contratrading) is the use of *barter* as a way of financing an international trade deal. This may be necessary for an exporter who has a good sales prospect in a country that has no *foreign exchange* with which to pay. So instead of accepting payment in an unreliable (perhaps inflationary) foreign currency, the exporter will arrange to be paid in a tradable *commodity* such as oil.

**county court:** the court to which one might take a legal dispute that is too large for the *small claims court*. The district judge can handle civil claims of up to £5000.

**craft union:** an organisation set up to represent the interests of highly skilled workers, most of whom would have served *apprenticeships*. (See *trade union*.)

**creative accounting** is the name given to legal but questionable accounting practices that massage the figures (and therefore ratios) on published company accounts. The two focal points for creative accounting are the stated profit for the trading period and the balance sheet ratios relating to financial health. During the 1990s, the *Accounting Standards Board* has been trying to minimise the scope for presenting legal but misleading accounts.

Among the main creative accounting techniques are:

- brand accounting, meaning to obtain a valuation for brand names a company owns, and then place them on its *balance sheet*; this boosts *shareholders' funds* and therefore cuts the firm's apparent *gearing* level
- *capitalisation* of interest, by which the interest costs of financing a property development are recorded as an addition to the value of the property asset, instead of as a business cost; so instead of the interest cost being a deduction from the *profit and loss account*, it is recorded as an addition to the firm's balance sheet
- *acquisition accounting*
- *off-balance-sheet financing*
- *window-dressing*

**creative tension:** the stimulation to thought and motivation that can come from exchanging views with others on a problem that has no clear-cut solution.

**creativity** is the spark that can provide an innovative solution or decision. It may be a quality that certain individuals possess naturally, but it will only become evident within an organisation that nurtures it. Some *top-down managements* lay down company policies for dealing with virtually every eventuality. This removes the flexibility of operation that is the essential background for creative solutions to problems. A firm wishing to foster creativity might:

- encourage *group discussions* among the workforce based on *brainstorming*
- accept that all ideas are worth considering
- encourage open, *direct communication*
- accept that mistakes are to be learnt from, not condemned

**credit** exists as soon as someone has acquired goods or services without paying for them at once or by paying for them with someone else's money. A credit sale means that the organisation acquires the *current asset* of *debtors* rather than cash. A sale is recorded in either case.

**credit controller:** an employee in an accounts department who monitors the *debtors* of the organisation to ensure that agreed limits are not exceeded and that the cash inflows are received promptly.

**credit clearance** is the process of obtaining a banker's agreement that a customer is creditworthy. When members of the public pay with cheques or credit cards, their banks are often phoned to make sure that they can afford items. When dealing with other companies, more detailed checks are made because a firm might be able to hide behind the shelter of *limited liability*.

**credit factoring:** see *factoring*

**credit insurance** involves paying a fee (premium) in return for the guarantee that if a customer fails to pay for a credit purchase, the insurer will pay. It is therefore a guarantee against *bad debts*. A common way of obtaining credit insurance is as part of a *factoring* service. Export credit sales can be insured through the *Export Credit Guarantee Department (ECGD)*.

**credit note:** a document informing a business customer that its account has been credited, probably due to an unintentional overcharge or because the customer has returned items that were faulty.

**creditor days:** a measurement of the average number of days a company takes to pay its suppliers.

FORMULA: $\dfrac{\text{trade creditors}}{\text{average daily sales (at cost)}}$

---

Worked example: calculating creditor days

Question: the JBM Company's cost of sales last year was £1 460 000 and trade creditors amounted to £200 000. Calculate their creditor days.

Answer:

Step 1    Calculate average daily sales: $\dfrac{£1\ 460\ 000}{365\ \text{days}} = £4\ 000$

Step 2    Apply formula: $\dfrac{\text{trade creditors}}{\text{average daily sales}} = \dfrac{£200\ 000}{£4\ 000} = 50$

The average credit period from suppliers was 50 days.

---

This information is useful because:

- firms considering supplying the company can build the payment delay into their *cash-flow forecast*
- existing suppliers can check whether they are being treated fairly (if, for example, a supplier was being paid 30 days later than the average, it could justifiably complain)
- bankers and suppliers can check on the financial health of the business; a slide towards later and later payment might indicate cash-flow problems

**creditors** are those to whom the organisation owes money, perhaps through having purchased goods or services on *credit* so that payment is still outstanding. Creditors appear under *current liabilities* in the *balance sheet*.

**creditors meeting:** a meeting arranged to confirm the appointment of a *receiver* to a company that has just gone into *liquidation*. The creditors would also have the opportunity to ask the proposed receiver questions about the likelihood of any payments of the cash they are owed.

**credit rating:** a judgement made by bankers about the financial health of a business and therefore how safe it would be to provide them with goods on *credit*. The credit rating will be based upon the strength of the firm's *balance sheet* and on its recent financial history. The best known credit rating service is the American company Moody's. Any firm with Moody's top rating (triple AAA) is in a position to borrow at the best possible terms.

**credit terms:** the time allowed by a supplier before the customer must pay for the good or service received. This is usually 30, 60 or 90 days from the time the invoice has been presented, though customers may try to take longer to pay than this. Business credit is usually interest free.

**criminal law** applies to those committing a criminal offense such as fraud. Such offenders should be pursued by the police and prosecuted. This contrasts with the *civil law* which only results in lawbreakers being sued if an individual or organisation takes them to court.

**crisis management:** the response of an organisation to a severe, probably unexpected threat to its well-being or even survival. Many firms devise *contingency plans* to cope with predictable crises (such as a fire at a key supplier's factory), but the actual crisis will rarely go according to plan. Therefore a named, top executive is likely to be put in charge. It is quite possible that this person will manage the crisis in a far more authoritarian manner than usual, due to the need for quick decision-making.

**criterion level:** the thresholds set by senior management as a way of appraising the acceptability of an investment proposal. The following table gives an example:

| Appraisal method | Criterion level | Minimum or maximum |
| --- | --- | --- |
| Pay-back period | 2 years | Maximum |
| Average rate of return | 16% | Minimum |
| Net present value | 10% of outlay | Minimum |
| Internal rate of return | 20% | Minimum |

**critical activity:** an activity which is on the *critical path*. If it is delayed, the minimum duration of the whole project is lengthened.

**critical path:** the network activities that must be completed in the shortest possible time in order that the project duration can be minimised. The critical path can be found by identifying the activities that have no *float time*. By identifying the *critical activities*, managers can ensure that they are supervised most closely, taking care also to ensure that the resources required are available at the right time.

**critical path analysis** is the term used to describe the process of breaking down a project into its component activities, placing them in the right sequence, then

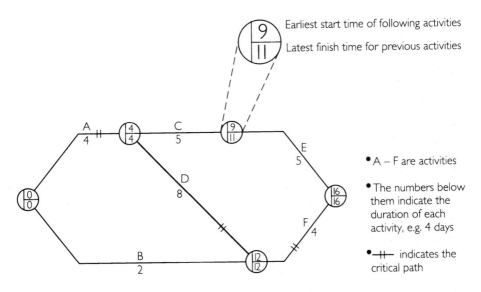

*Critical path analysis network*

deciding when to schedule them. Many projects, such as in building or marketing, can be divided into separate activities, which can be put into a logical sequence in a network diagram. The duration of each activity can then be estimated. Some activities will be critical: if they are delayed, the project will take longer than its minimum time. The shortest possible duration in which the project can be completed is determined by the activities on the *critical path*. A non-critical activity may be delayed up to its total float before the project is threatened. *Critical activities* have no *float time* at all.

**cross-price elasticity** measures the responsiveness of demand for one good to a change in the price of another. So, if the price of apples falls, the demand for pears is likely to fall as consumers switch to purchasing apples. It is measured by applying the following formula:

$$\text{FORMULA: } \frac{\text{percentage change in quantity demanded of good X}}{\text{percentage change in price of good Y}}$$

The closer the competition between goods X and Y, the higher will be their cross-price elasticity.

**CSO:** see *Central Statistical Office*

**CTN:** see *confectioner, tobacconist, newsagent*

**culture:** the culture of an organisation is the (perhaps unwritten) code that affects the attitudes, decision-making and management style of its staff. Examples of different business cultures include:

- goal-orientated, bonus-seeking, youthful culture based upon success at any price
- hierarchical culture based on respect for seniority, tight official communication channels and the avoidance of mistakes
- lively, growth-orientated culture based upon commitment to the product and the company

The culture will affect *resistance to change* within the business and therefore the ability of a new boss to impose his or her style or decisions upon subordinates.

**cumulative data** is generated by adding up consecutive numbers within a series. For instance a firm with sales of 100 units per month in the period January–March has cumulative sales of:

January 100
February 200
March 300

It follows that if April's cumulative figure is 380, monthly sales have fallen to 80 units. Alternative terms for cumulative data include accumulated data and year to date.

**cumulative preference shares** pay their shareholders an annual return that is a fixed percentage of their investment capital and is guaranteed to be paid in full before ordinary shareholders receive any *dividends* at all. *Preference shares*, unlike *ordinary shares*, pay dividends at a fixed percentage rate of the *nominal value*. Nevertheless, in a bad year it is possible that the firm will not be able to pay its preference shareholders at all. With cumulative preference shares, past unpaid dividends must be paid in later years before ordinary shareholders are paid anything. Therefore the cumulative preference share is the most secure form of shareholding.

**currency swaps** are ways in which firms avoid the problems of international currencies which fluctuate in value. A swap takes place when a currency is simultaneously bought and sold. This may be done by purchasing a currency on the spot market, and at the same time selling it on the forward market. This is a way of *hedging*.

**current asset:** anything owned by the organisation which is likely to be turned into *cash* before the next balance sheet date, usually within one year. Typical current assets are *stock*, *debtors* and *cash*. The balance of current assets over *current liabilities* is called *working capital* and, in essence, finances the organisation's day-to-day running.

**current cost accounting (CCA)** is the attempt to allow for *inflation* in company accounts by basing asset values and profit figures on the replacement cost of assets instead of their *historic cost*. In inflationary times this would make *balance sheet* asset valuations higher, but profit figures lower. Disputes among accountants over the validity of this exercise have hindered the widespread acceptance of current cost accounting methods.

**current liability:** anything owed by the organisation which is likely to be paid in cash before the next *balance sheet* date, usually within one year. Typical current liabilities are *creditors, overdrafts, dividends,* and unpaid tax.

**current ratio:** see *liquidity ratio*

**curriculum vitae (CV):** the 'story of life', i.e. the itemisation of a job applicant's qualifications, experience and interests. It should provide sufficient detail to enable a recruiter to build a picture of the applicant's suitability, to provide references that can be taken up, and to give starting points for discussion at interview.

**customer loyalty** implies such positive purchaser attitudes as to ensure a high rate of repeat purchase. This could be achieved through the quality of the product or service, the level of sales and/or after-sales care, or from the power and attraction of the product image.

**customer satisfaction** measures how well an organisation has lived up to the expectations of its customers. Kwik Save customers might judge their shopping experience primarily on the basis of low prices. Harrods customers will be more concerned about impressive service in impressive surroundings. Monitoring satisfaction requires a survey of the factors customers are looking for, then regular (perhaps monthly) research to track trends in customer satisfaction.

**customer service:** this covers all the activities that affect the customer's experience of dealing with an organisation. This will include the impressions created by the manner, appearance and training of staff, plus the reality of how well the customer's needs or wants can be satisfied. Businesses offering a high level of customer service will add value to their products, enabling them to charge a higher price, while ensuring customer loyalty. Also see *after-sales service*.

**CV:** see *curriculum vitae*

**cycle time** is how long it takes for a job function to repeat itself. In other words if a car assembly worker has to fit 30 windscreen wipers an hour, his or her job cycle time is two minutes. The higher the *division of labour* the higher the repetition and the lower the cycle time.

**cyclical unemployment** is the consequence of an economic downturn within the *trade cycle*. Such unemployment can be expected to last for approximately as long as the *recession* itself, typically 12–24 months. A government that wishes to prevent or relieve cyclical unemployment could:

- take *counter-cyclical* economic measures
- encourage wage flexibility so that company wage bills fall automatically during recessions, without requiring redundancies (see *profit-related pay*)

**cyclical variation:** in *time series analysis,* this is the variation which can be attributed to the economic or *trade cycle.* For example the increase in demand for *consumer durables* after a period of *recession* may be cyclical rather than indicate a change in the underlying trend.

REVISION: There are two sets of revision lists and a glossary of examiners' terms at the back of this book to help you prepare for exams or unit tests. See pages 307–312 for unit tests in GNVQ Business Advanced and pages 313–325 for examinations in A level Business Studies. See pages 326–329 for explanations of examiners' terms such as 'analyse' and 'discuss'.

# D

**damages:** money awarded by a court to a plaintiff in compensation for something suffered or lost. The money will have to be paid by the defendant. This may occur if a firm has been sloppy about product safety and a customer injury results.

**data:** facts of any kind, whether in number or verbal form. Although this is the correct explanation, business people are inclined to use the term to mean numerate information only.

**database**: a collection of information, usually stored on a computer. Examples of databases used in business include lists of customers and suppliers. Such information can be quickly and easily accessed, added to and interrogated, so that, for instance, it might be possible to ask the database for the names of all customers living in the North-East of England.

**Data Protection Act** came into force in 1984 to protect individuals who have information on them held on computers. Organisations which hold such information have to register with the Data Protection Registrar, and have to agree to levels of accuracy and security. The Act gives people the right to see their personal file, for example one held by a bank on a customer's creditworthiness.

**dawn raid:** an unannounced, rapid raid intended to succeed through surprise. The term is used for *stock market* share raids, when a firm making a *take-over* buys up as many shares as possible before the bid announcement is made. This enables it to buy some shares cheaply, and to establish a base shareholding upon which to build. A dawn raid can also be used to describe the unexpected arrival of tax or *Office of Fair Trading* officials to inspect a company's books.

**day release** is *off-the-job training* for employees who are given paid time off work each week to complete a college-based course that will lead to extra qualifications.

**DCF:** see *discounted cash flow*

**dead stock** means stock that is no longer being used or purchased. It is therefore lying around using up space that could be utilised more profitably in some other way. On recognising that stock is dead a firm should write its value down to zero in its accounts. Typically firms will try to sell it off at a substantial discount, or accept that it should simply be thrown away.

**debenture:** a fixed interest, long-term security with underlying *collateral*, usually land. So a £100 000 10 per cent debenture dated 31st December 2010 would pay £10 000 a year before tax to the registered holders until 2010. If the company defaults, the collateral can be sold to repay the lender, much like a building society *mortgage*. Debentures are an alternative to shares as a means of raising long-term *capital*. They do not dilute control but create the risks associated with raising the *gearing* level.

**debit:** a debit item in the system of *double-entry bookkeeping* means an increase in an *asset* or an expense, or a reduction in a *liability* or a revenue account.

**debit card:** a payment card similar to a credit card, except that each month's bill must be settled up in full at the end of the month. The best known debit card is American Express.

**debrief:** a meeting to hear what a researcher or interviewer has discovered and to discuss what conclusions can be drawn.

**debt factoring:** see *factoring*

**debtor days**: the average length of time customers take to pay for goods bought on credit. The higher the debtor days figure, the longer the credit period taken by customers. This forces the supplier to tie up more of its capital in *debtors*, leaving less for other parts of the firm such as *fixed assets* (e.g. up-to-date machinery) and *stock*.

$$\text{FORMULA:} \quad \frac{\text{debtors}}{\text{sales} \div 365} = \text{debtor days}$$

There is no rule of thumb for evaluating the debtor days figure, though research shows that medium-sized manufacturers have to wait 80 days for payment, while shopkeepers tend to have a much lower figure (since most customers pay by cash, cheque or credit card).

**debtors** are the people who owe you money. On a *balance sheet*, they represent the total value of sales to customers for which money has not yet been received. The way an organisation manages its debtors is often a key to its *liquidity*. Successful credit control ensures that credit is not extended to potentially *bad debtors* and that late-payers are chased.

**debtors turnover** is an accounting ratio which measures the speed with which debtors pay up.

$$\text{FORMULA:} \quad \frac{\text{annual sales}}{\text{debtors}}$$

$$\text{Example:} \quad \frac{\text{sales}}{\text{debtors}} \quad \frac{£1\,200\,000}{£200\,000} = 6 \text{ times}$$

A value of 6 implies that debtors pay up on average every two months. Caution is needed as sales may not be even through the year and some debtors may take much longer to pay and indeed some may be *bad debts*. The figure given could be end-of-year debtors or might be an average for the year. An alternative ratio to debtors turnover is *debtor days*.

**debt rescheduling** may occur when a firm with heavy borrowings finds that it cannot meet the repayments. The lenders could apply to the courts for the firm to be put into *liquidation*, or they may choose instead to reschedule the debts. This would mean extending the term of the loans and thereby postponing the repayment dates. It might also include an *interest holiday*, i.e. a period when the borrower does not have to pay interest on the loans. Lenders might offer these facilities because they expect to get a higher proportion of their capital back than if the firm was liquidated.

**decentralisation** means devolving power from the head office to the local branches or divisions. This includes passing authority for decision-making 'down the line', thereby accepting less uniformity in how things are done. Traditionally, firms such as Sainsbury's and Marks and Spencer have been highly centralised.

Pros: • decentralisation can *empower* local managers, encouraging them to be more innovative and motivated
  • it reduces the volume of day-to-day communication between head office and the branches, therefore giving senior managers the time to consider long-term strategy

Cons: • reduction in uniformity may unsettle customers who expect every Sainsbury's to look the same, or every McDonald's hamburger to contain just one slice of gherkin
  • head office is in a position to measure the success of every aspect of the product and sales mix, therefore its instructions may prove more profitable than local managers' intuition

**decentralised organisation:** one in which decision making powers and financial resources are passed down the hierarchy to empower junior and local managers. Whereas in a *centralised organisation* a local store manager has to apply the rules set out by head office, decentralisation enables junior staff to make decisions in line with local circumstances and opportunities.

**decile:** the total accounted for by one tenth of a population. For example, if all the households in Britain were ranked in order of wealth, the lowest decile would be the 10 per cent of the population with the least wealth. To measure the distribution of wealth within society, the proportion of national wealth owned by the lowest decile could be compared with the highest decile.

**decision-making model:** see *scientific decision-making*

**decision tree:** a diagram that sets out the options available when making a decision plus the outcomes that might result by chance. A decision tree shows the decisions and the chance events together with an estimate of the probability of their occurrence. It sets out the actual values or pay-offs to be expected at the end of each branch. These

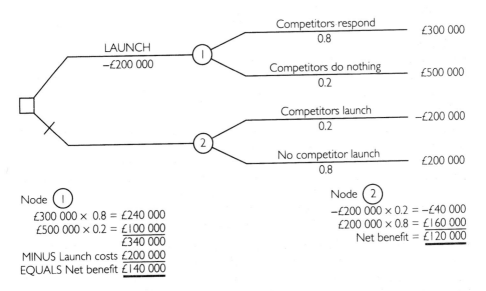

*Decision tree showing whether or not to launch a new product*

can then be adjusted by the probabilities to reach *expected values* which represent the average pay-off if the decision was taken many times.

Pros:
- sets out problems clearly and encourages a logical and quantitative approach
- the tree diagram can act as a focal point for discussion within a management meeting
- shows not only the (average) expected values for each decision, but also sets out the probability of any specific result occurring (e.g. a 20 per cent chance of making a £1 million loss)

Cons:
- hard to get meaningful data, especially for estimated probabilities of success or failure
- exceptionally easy for a manager with a case to prove, to bias the result in his or her favour

**declining balance method:** a *depreciation* method that makes a high charge to a *fixed asset* in its first year of life but reducing amounts thereafter. Each year's depreciation is calculated at a set percentage of the previous year's book value. If, for example, the charge was set at 40 per cent, a £20 000 company car would be depreciated as follows:

|  | Annual depreciation | Cumulative depreciation | Book value (on balance sheet) |
|---|---|---|---|
| Purchase date | – | – | £20 000 |
| After 1 year | £8 000 | £8 000 | £12 000 |
| After 2 years | £4 800 | £12 800 | £7 200 |
| After 3 years | £2 800 | £15 680 | £4 320 |

This method ensures that the balance sheet values of assets are recorded at more realistic levels than when using *straight line depreciation.* This is because assets such as cars do lose their value in the way set out above; heavily in the first year, less so in subsequent years.

**deed of partnership:** when forming a *partnership*, the partners may choose to draw up a partnership deed which is a legal agreement setting out the rights and responsibilities of the partners and the division of profits and losses. This is particularly important as partners do not enjoy *limited liability* unless they are limited partners. If no agreement exists, the provisions of the Partnership Act 1890 apply.

**deficit:** when income falls short of expenditure. The opposite is a surplus. The terms are used generally instead of profit and loss for *non-profit-making organisations* such as charities, or in economics when describing balances such as the government's finances or the country's *balance of payments.*

**deflation** is downward pressure upon the level of economic activity, usually in an attempt to reduce *inflation.* In other words it is a period of falling demand and prices. It is usually accompanied by reduced output and rising unemployment. Deflationary policies are those which are designed to reduce demand by the use of *fiscal* or *monetary policies.*

**deindustrialisation** means the long-term decline in Britain's relative position as a world manufacturer. Writers using the term are usually looking for thoroughgoing changes in society and government policy in order to halt the trend. The main causes of deindustrialisation are said to be:

- *short-termism*
- *stop-go* economic policies
- the social class divide (*them and us*)
- poor education and vocational training

**delayering** is the removal of one or more *layers of hierarchy* from the management structure of an organisation.

Pros:
- leads to a wider *span of control*
- gives greater responsibilities and workload for each staff member
- reduces the number of *intermediaries* between the bottom and the top
- reduces overhead costs

Cons
- staff may become overstretched (causing stress)
- may just be a euphemism for making people redundant

**delegation** means passing authority down the hierarchy (see *decentralisation* and *empowerment*). It can only work successfully on the basis of mutual trust. The boss must trust the subordinate to complete the tasks efficiently, while the subordinate must be sure that the boss is not just passing on dull or impossible tasks. The other key element in delegation is control. Can the boss bear to relinquish control over a task? If not, the delegation is phoney.

**delivery note:** a document presented for signature to a purchaser of goods, materials or components when delivery is made. A copy is then sent to the supplier's accounts department to trigger a request for payment.

**Delphi technique:** a form of subjective long-range forecasting which relies on the use of expert panels achieving consensus. It might be used to attempt to predict the sales of video cameras in eastern Europe in the year 2010 rather than the sales in the UK next December. The latter would be handled better by a quantitative method.

**demand** is the desire to own a good or a service. Demand which can be translated into purchases is known as *effective demand*. When everyone's effective demand in a country is added together it is known as *aggregate demand*.

**demand curve:** a graphical presentation of the likely level of demand for a product at a range of different prices, i.e. the relationship between price and demand. As one might expect, the curve indicates that as price rises, demand falls (as customers switch to cheaper alternatives).

**demand-pull inflation** is the process by which prices rise because there is excess demand in the economy. It is the same as when people go to an auction. If there are insufficient goods available to satisfy them, the prices of the goods which are there will be bid up. (See *cost-push inflation*.)

**demarcation** is the dividing line between one job function and another. For example, it used to be common for maintenance workers in factories to be split into mechanics and electricians. Nowadays, firms favour *multi-skilling*, which does away with demarcation lines and therefore prevents *demarcation disputes*.

**demarcation disputes** are *industrial disputes* about an attempt to change existing *demarcation* lines. They occur because of the possible threat to employment if two jobs are combined into one.

**demerger** occurs when a firm is split into two or more parts, either by selling off parts, or by floating them separately on the *Stock Exchange*. Demergers occur because:

- firms involved in *take-overs* often find that their new purchases offer fewer *economies of scale* than expected, so they prefer to focus on their original business
- take-overs are often financed by heavy borrowings, so in times of economic downturn firms may try to sell off non-core business to cut their debts or interest payments

**Deming W E** (b. 1900): an American engineer whose post-1945 work on product quality at the Hawthorne lighting plant led him to be invited to help the Japanese rebuild their industries after the Second World War. His emphasis on achieving quality through *statistical process control* was well learned and appreciated by the Japanese. They regard him as one of the founders of *total quality management* and have named their premier quality award after him.

**democratic leadership** means running a business or a department on the basis of decisions agreed among the majority. This might be done formally through a voting system, but it is much more likely to be an informal arrangement in which the leader delegates a great deal, discusses issues, acts upon advice, and explains the reasons for decisions. The main difference between democratic and *paternalistic leadership* lies in the degree of *delegation* and in the willingness to go along with the decisions of the majority.

**demographic profile:** a statistical breakdown of the people who buy a particular product or brand, e.g. what percentage of consumers are aged 16–25? What percentage are male? The main categories analysed within a demographic profile are the customers' age, gender, social class, income level, and region. Main uses of profile information are:

- for setting quotas for research surveys
- for segmenting a market
- for deciding in which media to advertise (VOGUE or THE SUN?)

**denationalisation** means returning to the *private sector* a business that was previously operated by the *public sector*. (See *privatisation*.)

**Department of Trade and Industry (DTI)** is responsible for carrying out the government's policies on the industrial base of the nation. It is involved with a wide range of activities including *regional policy, competition policy* and overseas trade.

**depot** is a storage area or warehouse, usually to hold stocks for local distribution.

**depreciation** is the process of allocating the *historic cost* of a *fixed asset*, less any forecast *residual value*, to its estimated useful life. The annual depreciation expense, which does not involve a movement of cash, is a notional charge to the *profit and loss account*. Each year the profit is reduced by the annual depreciation and the *net book value* of the asset is correspondingly reduced. The net book value of the asset is therefore equal to historic cost minus accumulated depreciation to date. The estimated

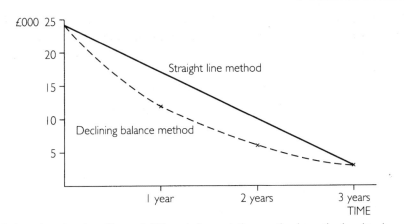

Depreciation, showing the effects of different depreciation methods on the book value of a fixed asset

life of the asset and its residual value are forecasts, and if the asset is ultimately sold for more than its net book value, a surplus on disposal arises. The two methods of depreciation used most commonly are *straight line* and the *declining balance method.*

**depression:** a prolonged period of negative growth, or growth that is well below the long-term average. Whereas a *recession* occurs regularly as the bottom phase of a country's *trade cycle*, a full-scale depression is much rarer. Where recession ends and depression begins is a matter for debate, and it may be that it is only time which turns a recession into a depression. In other words a recession becomes a depression if it continues for a long time. Few would argue that the depression of the 1930s was one such period. Whether the late 1980s/early 1990s period should be termed recession or depression remains in doubt.

**depth interview:** a one-to-one interview in which the interviewer has no pre-set questionnaire, but tries to obtain information and ideas through informal discussion. It is a form of *qualitative research* in which a psychologist will be trying to discover the reasons behind people's attitudes or purchasing decisions.

**deregulation** is the removal of government rules, regulations and laws from the workings of business. This might include scrapping *wages councils*, or ending *monopoly* rights to supply services such as letter delivery or bus services.

Pros:
  • less regulation means fewer regulators need be employed by the government or local councils (cutting public spending and therefore cutting tax levels)
  • less regulation should encourage more competition

Cons:
  • many rules affecting business were to stop exploitation; is this acceptable nowadays?
  • competition does not necessarily provide what society wants, it may only provide what is profitable (such as buses in the daytime but not at night)

**derivatives trading**: paying for the right to buy or sell a commodity in the future, at a price fixed today. Derivatives trading can take place in foreign currencies, agricultural produce, metals or in any other tradeable item. Two of the most common forms of derivatives trading are *hedging* and options. Firms can use hedging to reduce the risk of profits being hit by a sharp change in the price of a commodity. Options, however, are a highly geared, risky form of speculation. In 1995, the famous British merchant bank, Barings, was bankrupted by the derivatives trading of one of the bank's dealers, Nick Leeson.

**design mix:** how the firm combines three key design elements in order to fit the market gap that has been identified. The three are:

- aesthetic appeal (appeal to the senses)
- function (how well the product works and lasts)
- economic manufacture

**deskilling** occurs when a new machine or process changes a job that was once a source of craft pride into a repetitive or mundane task such as feeding or minding a machine.

**desk research** means finding out information from already published sources, perhaps from trade magazines, from government statistics or from on-line computer *databases*. It is also known as secondary research.

**desktop publishing (DTP)** is computer software which organises material including text, pictures, shading and different font sizes on to a page or pages. The result can be seen on a VDU and then be downloaded to a printer. As word-processing packages have become more sophisticated the distinction between them and desktop publishing software has reduced.

**destocking** is the deliberate attempt to reduce a firm's stockholding by cutting orders of materials or by cutting production levels. This is usually undertaken by organisations at the beginning of a *recession*, when orders begin to fall. Businesses can cut stocks of raw materials quickly by reordering less from suppliers. This represents a cut in the suppliers' levels of *demand* which reinforces the recession. Stocks are usually financed by *overdraft* borrowing from banks on which interest is paid, so there is a strong incentive to destock when interest rates rise.

**destroyer pricing:** another term for *predatory pricing*

**destruction pricing:** another term for *predatory pricing*.

**devaluation** is the deliberate decision by a government to reduce the value of its currency in relation to foreign currencies. This boosts the international competitiveness of the country's products. In the case of the UK's devaluation in Autumn 1992, £1 bought approximately 15 per cent fewer German Marks, French Francs and American dollars than before. This made it more expensive for British consumers to buy foreign goods, therefore making home-produced goods more attractive. Devaluation also boosts the competitiveness of exports, thereby improving the *balance of payments*.

---

Worked example: effects of a devaluation on exporters
> Before devaluation: exchange rate £1 = 3 Deutschmarks (DM)

> Good A is made in the UK and sells for £1. If it is exported to Germany at the current exchange rate it will be priced at 3DM.

Then devaluation causes the rate to change to £1 = 2DM

Good A still sells for £1 in the UK, but the exporter can now make a pricing decision based upon two attractive alternatives:

1. Hold the Deutschmark price constant, i.e. at 3DM, in which case the exporter will now receive 3DM / 2DM = £1.50. This will mean no change in export volume, but a 50 per cent rise in export revenue per unit.

2. Cut the Deutschmark price in line with the lower exchange rate, i.e. from 3DM to 2DM. This holds the UK revenue per unit at £1, but should boost demand dramatically, as the German consumer sees the price cut 33 per cent from 3DM to 2DM.

Pros:
- makes a country's exports more competitive
- make imports more expensive and less price competitive
- should therefore boost the country's *balance of payments*

Cons:
- may represent an 'easy option' for firms, so that they don't have to control their costs
- imposes *cost-push* inflationary pressures on an economy due to rising import prices

**developing country:** a country with a developing manufacturing base, but which has a national income that is not yet big enough to provide sufficient saving to sustain the investment required for more growth. Many developing countries have been dependent on *primary sector* products for their growth in the past, but as prices for such products are notoriously unreliable, growth has often been intermittent.

**development area:** a geographical region designated by government to receive special help due to its depressed economic circumstances. The British government may offer selective regional assistance to encourage a business to locate within a development area. Increasingly the *European Union* has played a major role in offering grants to such areas to encourage regeneration.

**devolving power** means delegating it to a person or organisation at a lower level within a hierarchy. (See *delegation*.)

**dictatorial leadership:** the use of power by giving out orders, rather than consulting or delegating. It implies what *McGregor* termed a *Theory X* attitude on the part of the leader, i.e. the assumption that employees have little ability or desire to contribute fruitfully to the decision-making process. The dictatorial leader is also likely to threaten or penalise those who fail to succeed in the tasks they have been set. (See *authoritarian, paternalistic* and *democratic leadership*.)

**differential piece-rate** means paying workers a higher rate per unit of production once a target figure has been achieved. This was a key element in F W *Taylor*'s recommendations to his clients. Its purpose was to gear up the incentive effect of piece-rate, encouraging unproductive workers to look for other jobs, while efficient workers could enjoy high rates of pay.

---

Worked example: producing pairs of jeans on differential piece-rate

- Between 0 and 100 pairs per week ............................80p per pair
- Above 100 pairs .........................................................£1.60p per pair

Worker No 1 produces 90 pairs and therefore earns £72 (90 × 80p)
Worker No 2 produces 160 pairs and therefore earns £176 (100 × 80p + 60 × £1.60)

---

**differentials** are the proportionate differences in pay between one grade of worker and another. They are likely to reflect different levels of skill or responsibility. When differentials are narrowed, workers on the higher rate of pay may feel that their skills and status are being downgraded.

**dilution of control** occurs when an existing shareholder is unwilling to increase his or her investment in a company that is looking for extra *share capital*. For example, if a shareholder's 1 000 shares represent 10 per cent of a firm's 10 000 issued shares, the stake will be diluted to a 5 per cent holding if the firm doubles its share issue to 20 000. This issue becomes much more important if the shareholder is the family owner of the business, and the family's holding is just above 50 per cent. Then a *rights issue* might cause the family to lose control of its business.

**dilution of earnings** occurs when a firm's decision to increase its *share capital* leads to a fall in *earnings per share*. This will occur if profits (earnings) rise by a lower proportion than the increase in share capital. There are two main circumstances in which earnings dilution may arise:

- when a *rights issue* takes place
- when a firm buys up another company; if the latter proves to be less profitable than the original firm, earnings dilution is likely

**diminishing balance method**: see *declining balance method*

**direct communication** means communication that is not through *intermediaries*. It is an alternative to the conventional system of communicating through official, formal channels. Professor *Herzberg* considered this a vital element in *job enrichment*, as it supported the requirement for direct *feedback*.

**direct controls:** a general term to describe the government's power to influence business and the economy through direct intervention, such as legislation or administrative action. For example, direct controls may be imposed by the *Bank of England* on the *commercial banks* in order to limit their lending. The Bank also specifies the type and amount of lending rather than using more indirect methods such as *monetary policy*. Such controls are more likely to be imposed by an *interventionist* government, or at a time of grave economic crisis.

**direct cost:** any cost which can be allocated precisely to a *cost centre* and which varies in direct proportion to activity or output. Common examples of direct costs are materials and *piece-rate* labour.

**directive leadership** involves letting subordinates know exactly what is expected of them and giving specific directions on how they must go about their tasks. Subordinates are expected to follow the organisation's rules and regulations to the letter. A leader might adopt this approach because of a lack of confidence in the abilities and self-discipline of the subordinates. This has similarities to McGregor's *theory X.*

**direct labour:** the staff directly involved in the production process, who therefore represent a *direct cost.*

**direct mail** is advertising or promotional material that is posted to specific address-es selected from a mailing list. For example, a car manufacturer might use a mailing list of those who have passed their driving test within the last six months. A common term for direct mail is 'junk mail'. Advertisers know that a high proportion will end up in the waste bin, but experience teaches them that perhaps 2 per cent of those mailed will respond. The question is whether that 2 per cent will generate enough business to justify the cost of the exercise.

**direct marketing** is marketing activity that is aimed directly at the customer, such as *direct mail,* door-to-door selling, or door-to-door leaflets.

**director:** a senior manager proposed by the *chief executive* and elected by share-holders to represent them on the main decision-making committee, the board of directors. Directors may either be executive or non-executive. Executive directors are employees of the company, usually with the responsibility for running a large division or department. *Non-executive directors* are not company employees; they are experi-enced senior managers from other firms, appointed to give independent advice. It has always been hoped that non-executive directors would be sharp critics of the internal management, taking special care to look after the interests of the company's shareholders. Experience has not always borne this out, however, as too many have been friends or business associates of the chief executive.

**directors' report:** a statutory element in a *public limited company*'s annual report which informs shareholders of: future developments, the firm's health and safety pol-icy, any political or charitable donations, directors' shareholdings and *share options,* plus any changes in board personnel.

**direct response** (marketing) is activity designed to get the customer to contact the advertiser directly, such as by filling in a form for a holiday brochure or telephoning to buy a CD advertised on television. The great advantage of this form of advertising is that the company can measure the cost-effectiveness of each medium used, and therefore build up a picture of the best ways to spend its advertising budget.

Worked example: measuring direct responses to a campaign advertising for members to join a Book Club

| Publication | Type of space | Cost per advert | Number of new members | Cost per new member |
|---|---|---|---|---|
| TV Times | Colour page | £28 000 | 1 240 | £22.58* |
| Sunday | Colour page | £32 000 | 1 575 | £20.32 |
| Observer | Colour page | £14 000 | 564 | £25.71 |

* Cost per member = cost / members, e.g. £28 000 / 1 240 = £22.58

In this example SUNDAY is the most cost-effective advertising medium, as it has the lowest cost per member.

**direct sales:** selling directly to the end-user, without going through an outlet such as a shop. This might be achieved through door-to-door selling, telephone selling, direct response TV or press advertising.

**direct taxation** is paid from an individual's income or wealth (for instance *income tax*), as opposed to *indirect taxes* which are paid on goods and services purchased (for instance *VAT*).

**dirty float** is the term used to describe a *floating exchange rate* which operates only within certain bands. In other words the *central bank* will intervene to prevent the exchange rate exceeding those limits.

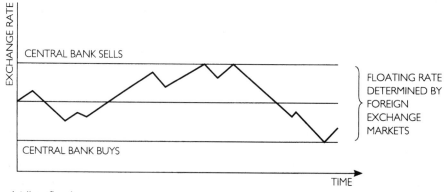

A 'dirty float'

**disaster planning** became a common form of *contingency planning* during the 1980s and early 1990s, after a series of sudden shocks hit major firms, such as the Zeebrugge ferry disaster and the Perrier Water contamination scandal. It involves visualising possible types of disaster that might hit the firm, then deciding:

- which team of senior managers would be best suited to tackling the crisis
- where they would meet
- what resources they would require (telecommunications etc.)

**disciplinary procedure** is the formal process by which employees can be taken to task for failure to meet their employment contract. If the employee does not change his or her attitude or behaviour, it will lead to verbal then written threats of dismissal. The disciplinary stages are:

1 verbal warning
2 written warning
3 final written warning
4 *dismissal* (if a further offence is committed within 12 months of a final written warning)

**disclosure of information** is the process of releasing factual data to enable outsiders to make a judgement or decision. For many years British *trade unions* have complained that they cannot trust the stance of managers in industrial negotiations because of their failure to disclose key facts. Company secrecy over industrial accident rates, pollution emissions and recycling levels also makes it hard for environmental campaigners to pressurise firms into accepting their *social responsibilities*. This is why many *pressure groups* feel that the law should force firms to disclose more information in their *annual report and accounts*.

**discounted cash flow (DCF):** an *investment appraisal* technique based on *cash flow forecasts* and the *opportunity cost* of money. A project requires a capital outlay which should generate positive cash inflows over future years. These estimated future cash inflows are each multiplied by a *discount factor* between zero and one, since money at some future date is worth less to the firm than the same sum in hand today. The longer the wait for a future sum, the lower its *present value*. When discounted, these future cash flows can be totalled; from this the capital outlay can be deducted to give the *net present value (NPV)* for the project. If this is positive the project is economically viable. (See *net present value* for a worked example.)

**discount factor:** the adjustment which must be applied to an estimated future *cash flow* to convert it to *present value*. The calculation of discount factors is a lengthy, complex process that is not required in examinations. Candidates are provided with the relevant figures. When undertaking business projects, however, it can be valuable to show an understanding of how the figures are derived.

Discount factors are the inverse of *compound interest*. Suppose the organisation expects to receive £10 000 in three years' time and the current interest rate is 10 per cent. The present value is the sum of money which would compound up to £10 000 if left in the bank to earn 10 per cent per year. The calculation and use of discount factors requires three steps:

   **1** Calculate the effect of compound interest over three years:

     After 1 year each £1 becomes £1.10
     After 2 years each £1 becomes £1.21 (£1.10+10%)
     After 3 years each £1 becomes £1.33 (£1.21+10%)

   **2** Take the inverse of the Year 3 figure:

$$\frac{1}{£1.33} = £0.75$$

   **3** Apply the known value of each pound in three years' time to Year 3's forecast cash flow, i.e. discount the future pounds to allow for the loss of interest over the next three years:

     £10 000 × 0.75 = £7 500

**discretionary income:** the income left to a household after deduction of income tax, national insurance and contracted outgoings such as mortgage payments.

**discriminatory pricing:** see *price discrimination*

**diseconomies of scale:** factors causing higher costs per unit when the scale of output is greater, i.e. causes of inefficiency in large organisations. The main factors are:

   1 Communication costs: in small firms, internal communication is mainly oral, which is cheap and highly effective since *feedback* is inbuilt. Large firms have many *layers of hierarchy* so messages may be distorted as they pass through *intermediaries*. Consequently much communication is done

through memos, reports or written requests. These require the time and therefore pay of typists, filing clerks and messengers. Worse still, written messages are less effective and less motivating than conversation, so they involve more costs through inefficiency.

2 Coordination costs: in small firms, decisions are usually made by the proprietor, perhaps after consulting staff. One person taking the decisions ensures *coordination* of the firm's strategy and actions. Large firms require *delegation*, as one person cannot make hundreds of major decisions competently. Yet *empowering* managers to make their own decisions can result in different departments heading in different directions. So regular meetings are required to ensure coordination. This is why research shows that managers spend over half their time communicating. That time represents a considerable extra *overhead* cost for the firm to bear.

**dismissal:** being dismissed ('sacked') from a job due to incompetence or breaches of discipline. Note that this is different from *redundancy*.

**display advertising:** a term for advertisements that use different type styles, photographs and captions to convey information as well as images to the target audience. This is in contrast to *classified advertising*.

**disposable income** is that part of your income that is available to spend as you wish. In other words your gross income of £200 per week has tax, *National Insurance*, pensions etc. deducted from it so that you may only have £150 to spend as you wish. That is your disposable income.

**disputes procedure:** the formal process by which a dispute between management and *trade union* will be progressed. For example, it may be laid down by written agreement that a pay dispute will be put to an *ACAS*-appointed *arbitrator* before any *industrial action* is taken.

**distance learning** is the teaching of academic subjects by post (or *electronic mail*). Managers may develop their skills by specialist courses in accountancy or personnel management, or may pursue general courses such as an MBA (*Master of Business Administration*). Distance learning avoids the need to give up work while studying, and cuts out the travelling time involved in part-time academic study.

**distinctive competence** is a competitive advantage that distinguishes one firm from another. It is the skill or asset upon which future strength can be built. For example the French company Bic have developed exceptional know-how in the manufacture of disposable plastic products; that is their distinctive competence. (See *asset-led marketing*.)

**distribution:** the entire process of getting products to where customers can buy them. This sounds easy, but actually requires considerable persuasion. Shop shelf space is limited, so if a retailer is to stock your product they must destock another. Furthermore, having obtained shop distribution, manufacturers have to battle constantly to keep it. (See *distribution targets*.)

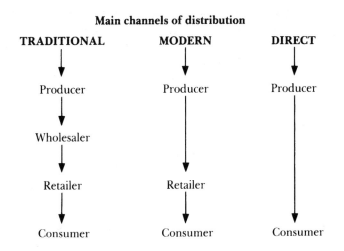

**Main channels of distribution**

| TRADITIONAL | MODERN | DIRECT |
| --- | --- | --- |
| ↓ | ↓ | ↓ |
| Producer | Producer | Producer |
| ↓ | | |
| Wholesaler | | |
| ↓ | ↓ | |
| Retailer | Retailer | |
| ↓ | ↓ | ↓ |
| Consumer | Consumer | Consumer |

**distribution channels**: the stages of ownership that take place as a product moves from the manufacturer to the consumer (see *wholesaling*).

**distribution of added value:** the notion that added value can be shared between those who contribute to it in different ways. For instance, added value could be shared so that wages and salaries had a larger proportion than profits. A trade union might well argue that the contribution of the workforce to added value through increased productivity justified such a redistribution. Managers might disagree.

**distribution of income** is the spread of income earned by different groups of people within an economy. The intention of taxation and social security benefits is usually to redistribute income from the richer towards the poorer members of society. Since 1980, the move in Britain towards more *indirect taxation,* taken with the reduction of income tax and social security benefits, widened the gap between the rich and the poor.

**distribution resource planning** is a sophisticated computer software package that can record and plan how products can be delivered to customers on time at the lowest possible cost (given the constraints the company works within).

**distribution targets** are set to motivate the *salesforce* to obtain distribution in as high a percentage of target outlets as seems feasible. This might be achieved by:
- offering high *profit margins* to retailers
- heavy advertising in trade magazines
- giving sales staff big incentives to work and sell hard

**diversification** is the spreading of business risks by reducing dependence on one product or market. It is an important business objective, be it for a small ice-cream producer wanting security from cool summers, or for *multinational* firms wanting to move into new growth markets. The opposite of diversification is *focus.*

Pros:
- improves prospects for long-term company survival
- can enable a firm in a saturated market to regain a growth path
- provides new outlets for a firm's skills and resources

Cons: • many diversifications have disappointed due to *diseconomies of scale* or failure to understand fully the new market-place (the customer, competition, etc.)

• the firm's core business may be weakened as resources are redirected towards new opportunities; the American writer Peter Lynch has called this phenomenon: 'diworsification'

**divestment** means selling off parts of the business that no longer fit the long-term strategy. This might be because they are no longer profitable, or because the firm wants to focus its management on the *core activities.*

**dividend cover** is the number of times the dividend declared could have been paid out of the *net profit* available after tax and interest. A figure of around three is usually felt to be desirable. Much below it and the firm is paying out such high dividends as to leave too little for reinvestment. Above it and the shareholders could reasonably question whether the firm's dividend pay-outs are too mean.

**dividend per share (DPS)** is the total dividend declared by the *directors* divided by the number of shares issued.

FORMULA: $\dfrac{\text{total dividends}}{\text{shares issued}} = \text{dividends per share}$

**dividend policy:** the proportion of profits after tax a company's directors decide to pay out to shareholders in the form of annual dividends. The higher the payout, the less there is to reinvest to make the business bigger or more efficient. Higher retained profits should enable the firm to pay higher dividends in future. So the more profit that is retained today, the greater prospects of benefits tomorrow. Shareholders would have to agree to such a policy. They can vote on it at the AGM; if they disagreed with the policy they could sell their shares.

**dividends** are a share in the profits of a company distributed to its shareholders according to the rights which the shares give them. Dividends must be paid (after interest charges) on *preference shares* before *ordinary shares.* Preference share dividends are fixed but ordinary share dividends are declared annually by the directors and voted on at the *annual general meeting.*

**dividend yield** is the annual *dividend per share* expressed as a percentage of the market price of the share. The dividend is a matter of record but the market price may fluctuate constantly. If the share is being upgraded by the *stock market*, its price will rise and therefore the yield will fall. Dividend yield is an important consideration for share buyers who need an annual income from their savings to boost their regular earnings (for example, pensioners). Investors can compare a share's dividend yield directly with building society rates, to help decide where to place their savings.

FORMULA: $\dfrac{\text{dividend per share}}{\text{market share price}} \times 100 = \text{dividend yield}$

**division:** a major operational part of a business. It is likely to have its own *chief executive* or *chairman* and may have a separate location from the head office. It will function as a business within a business.

**division of labour** means breaking a job down into small, repetitive fragments, each of which can be done at speed by workers with little formal training. This enables firms to hire labour cheaply and plentifully, but may lead to serious problems of low *motivation* and even alienation of the workforce. Professor *Herzberg* maintained that unless workers have a *complete unit of work* they cannot be motivated. Nevertheless, the degree of specialisation implied by division of labour can enable an individual to become expert at his or her job and can increase *productivity*.

**divorce of ownership and control** is a phrase conveying concern that although the shareholders own public companies, managements run them. This might lead to conflicting loyalties with managements pursuing objectives that help their own careers or job satisfaction, rather than looking after shareholders' best interests. Many past *diversification* moves and *take-over bids* seem to have offered little real benefit to shareholders.

**dog:** a term given by the Boston Consulting Group to describe a product with low *market share* within a market with low growth. The Group recommend that dogs be considered for discontinuation, in order to concentrate time and resources on more profitable brands. Dogs form one part of the *Boston Matrix*.

**dollar ($):** the currency of the United States of America. Because of the importance of the US economy in terms of world trade, many goods are traded internationally in dollars. For example, oil produced in the North Sea by the UK will be sold to another country at a price given in dollars. From 1945 the dollar was virtually the world's common currency, but as the economic, political and social influence of the US has declined with the growth of Japan and Europe, especially Germany, so also has the power and influence of the dollar.

**double-entry bookkeeping** is a system of accounting whereby one event is recorded in two accounts, as a *debit* in one and as a *credit* in another. This recognises that all financial transactions have a dual nature. For example, if you go to buy a chocolate bar, not one but two things occur. You hand over 30p (cash minus 30p) and receive a piece of (very temporary) stock (stocks plus 30p). The use of double-entry ensures that *assets* always equal *liabilities* and therefore *balance sheets* always balance (unless a mistake has been made).

**doubtful debts** are sums owed to a firm by companies that are thought unlikely to be able to pay. When the firm becomes sure that the sums will never be received, they become *bad debts* and cause a *write off* on the firm's accounts.

**Dow Jones Index** is the name for the New York's Stock Exchange daily market index. Dating back to 1928, the index takes the average price of thirty major stocks which together account for 25 per cent of its *market capitalisation*.

**down-market:** a product or advertisement aimed at working-class or low-income households; the opposite of *up-market*.

**downside** is the possible or actual consequence of a decision turning out badly. If the downside is relatively small compared with the potential benefits of a decision, the *risk:reward ratio* is said to be favourable.

**downsizing**: this term has two separate uses:

    1  moving computer applications from *mainframe computers* to less expensive but no less powerful personal computers

2 reducing the size of a business to meet a new, lower demand level; the term downsizing is often used as a euphemism for a round of *redundancies*. Due to the negative connotations of the term <u>down</u>sizing, some firms now use a further euphemism - <u>right</u>sizing

**downtime** is when machinery is needed but not being used. This may be because of a breakdown, lack of spare parts, or when resetting the machine for a different product specification to be manufactured. Downtime might be measured in minutes or as a proportion of the day's working hours. It represents a waste of resources and adds to *fixed costs per unit* by restricting the volume of *output* from a given *production line*.

**downward communication** is the passage of information down the *chain of command*, from senior to junior staff.

**DPS:** see *dividend per share*

**drawings** represent the salary taken out of an *unlimited liability* firm by its proprietors. What is left on the *profit and loss account* after drawings is the firm's retained earnings.

**Drucker, Peter:** a highly influential management writer and consultant who popularised the concept of management by objectives. His ideas were firmly rooted in the case histories of major corporations such as IBM and General Motors, making his writings far more business-specific than motivation theorists such as *Maslow*.

**DTI:** see *Department of Trade and Industry*

**dummy line:** an activity in *critical path analysis* which does not really exist except to show a logical dependence. Accordingly it has a zero duration. It is shown as a dashed rather than a solid line.

**dumping** describes the selling of a good in another country at less than its cost price. A country may dump for a number of reasons:

- to earn foreign exchange: this was a common practice amongst countries formerly under communist control. Items such as cameras were sold at less than their cost price in order to earn western currency
- to get rid of excess production: in the early 1990s the USA fined European steel manufacturers for such dumping
- to destroy the foreign industry in order to create a monopoly so that prices can be adjusted back to high levels in the future.

**duopoly** is where there are only two producers in the market. This may result in what appears to be a highly competitive market, usually based on *non-price competition*, such as *advertising*. However, there may also be a certain amount of *collusion*, either explicit or implicit, in order to guarantee high profits for both firms, and to keep out other potential competitors. Because there are only two producers, the actions of one are clear to the other, and so each business decision will be based on how it is expected that the competitor will react to the decision, as well as how consumers will respond.

**durable:** see *consumer durable*

**earliest start time (EST)** of an activity in *critical path analysis* is the earliest it can start given that all preceding activities have been completed as speedily as possible. The ESTs on all activities within a network are calculated from left to right, by adding the duration of the preceding activity to its own EST.

**earnings:** when applied to a company, means *profit* after tax.

**earnings per share (EPS):** a ratio showing the after-tax *profit* available for distribution to shareholders. The company directors recommend and the shareholders vote on how much of that profit will be paid as dividends and how much will be *ploughed back* into the company.

FORMULA: $\dfrac{\text{profit after tax}}{\text{number of shares}}$

---

Worked example: if DG Ltd makes a profit after tax of £40 000, what is the EPS if the issued share capital is £200 000 of £0.25 share?

DG has $\dfrac{£200\ 000}{£0.25}$ = 800 000 shares issued

EPS = $\dfrac{£40\ 000}{800\ 000}$ = £0.05 i.e. 5p per share

---

**EC:** see *European Community*

**ECGD:** see *Export Credit Guarantee Department*

**economic expectations** refer to people's anticipation of the way the economy is likely to develop in the future. Such expectations can have a profound effect. For instance, firms will not invest in new *plant* and machinery if they believe they will not get an adequate return, even if the rate of interest is low. Consumers will not spend money in the shops, whatever the level of prices, if they believe that the economy is in *recession* and that their jobs are at risk.

**economic growth** describes the way real incomes per head increase over time. A nation's growth is measured in terms of *gross national product*, or *national income*. The reasons for growth are complex, although it can be explained in terms of increasingly efficient uses of the *factors of production* to provide more and more goods and services. It is important to note that increases in national income do not necessarily yield increases in welfare, because some aspects of growth bring disadvantages such as increased noise, pollution or congestion.

**economic indicators** are the monthly statistics that provide information on the country's economic performance. *Leading indicators* give a prediction of future events, *coincident indicators* show the state of the economy today, and *lagging indicators* show the health of the economy in the recent past. All are subject to considerable error, so it is unwise to draw any conclusions from one month's data.

**economic man** is an assumption that human behaviour is based upon rational economic motives such as the desire for financial gain and fear of financial pain. It underpinned the writings of Adam *Smith* in the eighteenth century and F W *Taylor* in the early twentieth century. It is also at the heart of what *McGregor* called a *theory X* attitude on the part of managers.

**economic order quantity** is the attempt to calculate the optimum stock order level, given the delivery costs compared with the cost of holding stock. The higher the delivery cost in relation to the *stockholding cost*, the larger the order level should be (to minimise the number of deliveries). The economic order quantity fails to consider the *buffer stock* level, or the *opportunity costs* to the firm of being out of stock. It therefore cannot be thought of as a comprehensive model of stock control.

**Economic Trends:** a monthly publication by HMSO that lists and charts the latest government statistics on the economy. It is a usual source of *secondary data* for project or assignment work.

**economies of scale** are the factors that cause average costs to be lower in large-scale operations than in small-scale ones. In other words, doubling the *output* results in a less than double increase in costs; the cost of producing each unit falls because factor inputs can be used more efficiently. Economies of scale fall into a number of categories, divided into internal and external economies. The following are internal:

- specialisation, i.e. with a large workforce it is possible to divide up the work process and then recruit people whose skills exactly match the job requirements; staff can then be trained and become highly effective at carrying out their limited task
- technical economies, such as the use of automated equipment where it is more cost-effective than labour; this is only feasible when the *fixed costs* of the machine can be spread thinly over many units of output
- purchasing economies are the benefits of bulk buying, i.e. obtaining supplies of materials and components at lower unit costs, thereby cutting variable costs
- financial economies stem from the lower cost of *capital* charged to large firms by the providers of finance. Banks charge lower rates of interest and equity investors are more willing to accept low *dividend yields* from bigger firms. This is because large firms are usually more diversified and less vulnerable to *liquidation* than small firms

External economies are the advantages of scale that benefit the whole industry, and not just individual firms. So if an industry is concentrated in one geographical area it is likely that a pool of labour will be attracted and trained, perhaps by a local college, which will have specialised skills useful to the whole industry and from which each firm will benefit. Similarly, a large grouping of firms will attract a network of suppliers, whose own scale of operation should yield economies such as lower component costs.

**Economist Intelligence Unit (EIU):** a sister company to the ECONOMIST magazine that provides carefully researched *secondary data* on particular countries or markets. Its monthly publication RETAIL BUSINESS is a valuable source of sales and distribution information about UK consumer markets and products.

**ECU:** see *European Currency Unit*

**EDI:** see *electronic data interchange*

**EEC:** see *European Community*

**effective demand** is the desire to buy backed by the ability to pay. Text books often suggest that the price of a *commodity* is determined by *supply* and *demand*. In such cases the author really means effective demand.

**efficiency** means using resources effectively. It can be calculated in many different ways; the most common measurements are:

- labour efficiency: *productivity* (output per worker)
- production efficiency: *wastage* (percentage of scrap within the process)
- financial efficiency: *asset turnover* (the amount of sales generated from the firm's assets)

**EFTA:** see *European Free Trade Association*

**EFTPOS:** see *electronic funds transfer at point of sale*

**EGM:** see *extraordinary general meeting*

**eighty/twenty rule:** also called 'Pareto analysis', this is a maxim which states that 80 per cent of benefits, or disbenefits, tend to come from 20 per cent of items. Thus, 80 per cent of total profit tends to come from 20 per cent of items stocked or made and 80 per cent of breakdowns come from 20 per cent of the machines. The value of Pareto analysis is that it indicates clearly to managers that their efforts are best spent on the key 20 per cent rather than spread too thinly.

**EIU:** see *Economist Intelligence Unit*

**elasticity of demand** is the measurement of how customer demand is affected by a change in price, advertising spending or incomes. It is measured by percentage or proportionate changes. For example, price elasticity is measured by the formula:

$$\text{FORMULA:} \quad \frac{\text{percentage change in demand}}{\text{percentage change in price}}$$

For fuller details, see *price elasticity, advertising elasticity* and *income elasticity*.

**elasticity of supply** is the responsiveness of supply to changes in price. It is measured by percentage or proportionate changes, and goods are classified depending on whether the value of the elasticity is less than one (inelastic), one (unitary), or more than one (elastic). Unlike *price elasticity*, elasticity of supply is always positive because a movement of price one way will always result in a movement of supply in the same way (see the table on the next page).

**electronic communications technology**: all the forms of information technology that involve communication. At the time of writing these include: *e-mail, fax,* enhanced telephones (such as voice-mail), *electronic data interchange* (EDI), computer *networks*, tele and *video conferencing* and interactive television (often through touch screens). The speed of technological change means that many of these may be obsolete within a few years, making it risky for firms to invest heavily in them.

| Definition and example | Value | Called | Verbal explanation |
|---|---|---|---|
| % change in quantity supplied / % change in price<br><br>e.g. +10% / +20% | <1 | inelastic | A percentage rise (fall) in price results in a less than proportionate rise (fall) in quantity supplied |
| % change in quantity supplied / % change in price<br><br>e.g. +10% / +10% | 1 | unitary | A percentage rise (fall) in price results in an equally proportionate rise (fall) in quantity demanded |
| % change in quantity supplied / % change in price<br><br>e.g. +20% / +10% | >1 | elastic | A percentage rise (fall) in price results in a more than proportionate rise (fall) in quantity demanded |

*Elasticity of supply*

**electronic data interchange (EDI)** is on-line communication between computers, usually personal computers communicating with mainframes. It is used by retail branches to transmit details of their day's trading to a central computer which orders replacement supplies from the distribution depot. In turn, the depot's EDI link with suppliers brings fresh supplies from the manufacturers.

**electronic funds transfer at point of sale (EFTPOS):** a payment system whereby the retailer is credited from the customer's bank account by means of a plastic card, when the purchase is made. In the UK this is often known as a 'Switch' card.

**electronic mail (e-mail)** involves sending messages from one computer to another, either internally or to those outside an organisation. This rapid communication is especially useful for posting detailed data such as daily sales broken down by product line.

Pros:
- unlike paper communication, sending and storing e-mail generates very low marginal costs
- the ease and speed of response to an e-mail message makes feedback more effective
- avoids the telephone problem of finding people at their desks

Cons:
- it can be impersonal and therefore potentially alienating
- can be intercepted and so cannot be used for confidential material (Microsoft chief Bill Gates has said that 'I'm not the only one who reads e-mail sent to askbill@microsoft.com')
- as with any other form of communication, its effectiveness can be undermined by overload, for example from junk e-mail.

**e-mail:** see *electronic mail*

**embargo:** an order forbidding trade with a particular country, perhaps imposed by the United Nations against a country that has broken international laws or conventions.

**empire building** is when a manager makes decisions with the objective of increasing his or her own department or sphere of influence.

**employee appraisal:** see *performance appraisal*

**employee share ownership (ESOP):** a programme for providing a public limited company's employees with a share stake in the business. If each individual's share-holding is large enough, this might encourage greater sympathy with the firm's profit motive and therefore eliminate a feeling of them-and-us. Unfortunately, both staff and directors are inclined to turn their shares into cash at the earliest opportunity, undermining the exercise.

**Employment Gazette**: a magazine published by the Government Statistical Service that provides articles and numerical data about the employment trends within Britain, sometimes in comparison with other leading economies. It is a valuable source of *secondary data* for project work.

**employers' association:** an organisation representing the views and interests of the companies within a sector or industry. It is financed by members' subscriptions and is expected to provide value for money by:

- its success as a *pressure group*, for example in influencing the taxes the government imposes or cuts on products
- its research success, either by compiling sales figures from all the firms within an industry, or by initiating studies that can help the members cope with foreign competition. Part of the motivation towards this research may be *public relations*
- providing a negotiating team that can agree minimum pay and conditions throughout the industry with employees' trade union representatives

**Employment Act 1980:** the first of five Employment Acts passed by Mrs Thatcher's Conservative governments. Its main features were:

- repeal of the existing procedures for trade union recognition, thereby enabling firms to refuse to negotiate with unions
- *picketing* restricted to 'own place of work'
- lawful *secondary action* limited to direct supplier or customer
- first move against the *closed shop*, making closed shops allowable only if 80 per cent of the workforce vote in favour
- reductions in employment and compensation rights for employees of small firms

**Employment Act 1982** provided further tightening of the 1980 rules. The main measures were:

- further restrictions on lawful *industrial action* by redefining a 'lawful dispute'
- removal of trade union immunity from authorising unlawful industrial action (making unions liable for damages of up to £250 000)
- dismissal of strikers made easier
- *closed shop* union membership agreements made harder to enforce

**Employment Act 1988** tightened up the controls on union operations by:

- insisting that all voting members of national union committees must be elected by postal *ballot* of the entire membership
- protecting union members from being disciplined by unions for ignoring strike calls or *picketing*, even after a ballot in favour of industrial action

- laying down the specific wording to be used on voting papers in *industrial action* ballots

**Employment Act 1989** was designed by the Secretary of State for Employment to 'remove outdated, unnecessary barriers to women's employment and relieve young people and their employers of a mass of bureaucratic restraints'. Opponents argued that the 'barriers' were far from outdated. The Act's main provisions were:

- removing all restrictions on the hours of work of young people, including the prohibition of night work
- removal of discriminatory legislation against women, such as the former ban on women working underground in mines
- dissolving the Training Commission and the Industrial Training Boards

**Employment Act 1990:** last of a series of Acts passed by Conservative governments during the 1980s designed to 'free up the labour market', i.e. to reduce the influence of government and especially *trade unions.* Its main provisions were:

- to make it unlawful for an employer to refuse to employ a non-union worker; that meant the end of the *closed shop*
- to make unlawful any remaining forms of *secondary action*
- to make trade unions liable for virtually any *industrial action* taken by their members
- to allow employers to dismiss any individual for taking part in an *unofficial strike* without the individual having the right to complain of *unfair dismissal* to an *industrial tribunal*

**employment agency:** a *private sector* business that acts as a job centre, charging employers a fee if they decide to recruit one of the candidates sent along by the agency for interview.

**employment contract:** a legal document that sets out the terms and conditions governing an individual's job. It details the employee's responsibilities, working hours, rate of pay and holiday entitlement. By signing it, an employee agrees to abide by its terms. If, therefore, the employee joins in with strike action he or she can be dismissed for having broken the contract.

**Employment Training (ET):** a government-funded training scheme provided for the long-term unemployed. Individuals are supposed to have their needs identified and provided for by training agents. Critics suggest that the lack of suitable places means that 'clients' are often given training that provides little prospect of regaining employment.

**empowerment** is providing the means by which subordinates can exercise power over their working lives. Whereas *delegation* might provide the power for a subordinate to carry out a specific task, empowerment is more all-embracing. It implies a degree of self-regulation; the freedom to decide what to do and how to do it.

**EMS:** see *European Monetary System*

**EMU:** see *European Monetary Union*

**enablers:** factors or resources that make it possible for a firm to meet or beat its targets/objectives. They may be internal, such as good personnel, or external, e.g. a strong economy. Enablers are the opposite of *contraints.*

**end-game strategies** are plans for dealing with the decline phase of the *product life cycle*. Theory suggests that the only response to decline is to cut marketing spending and cut prices. However, the huge profitability of the UK cigarette market suggests that more positive end-game strategies are possible.

**endowment mortgages** are a way of financing a house purchase that involves the payment of loan interest plus payments into an endowment insurance fund. Although this type of mortgage might prove good value if held for the entire 20 or 25 year term, it is extremely poor value if cashed in before then. As only 20 per cent of borrowers hold their endowment policy for the full term, it follows that 80 per cent lose out. In many cases home-owners suffer considerable financial loss as a consequence of acquiring their home through an endowment policy. The traditional repayment mortgage is very much better value, but as endowment policies provide substantial commissions to the salesmen or firms that sell them, the endowment remains far more common than it should be.

**enforcement agencies** are the government bodies or self-regulatory agencies that have the power to investigate and punish breaches of legally enforceable or voluntarily agreed codes of business behaviour.

**enterprise** is the organisation of *factors of production* in such a way as to generate profits. The term also means showing initiative and entrepreneurship.

**enterprise allowance:** a regular payment from the government to those starting up a business, to help supplement their personal income during the first year of trading.

**enterprise culture:** a social climate which applauds the profit motive in general and starting a small business in particular. The term was widely used in the 1980s and formed a key element in *Thatcherism*.

**Enterprise Investment Scheme:** a government initiative offering tax incentives to encourage direct equity investment in companies which are not quoted on the stock exchange. Individuals can obtain 20 per cent tax relief on share purchases made this way and firms can raise up to £1 million per year through the scheme. Announced in the 1993 Budget, it replaced the Business Expansion Scheme. It is designed to help close the 'equity gap', in other words the shortage of share capital available to expanding small to medium sized companies.

**enterprise union:** a company union founded and run in conjunction with the employer. This is a common form of union in Japan, though British workforces are inclined to doubt its independence.

**enterprise zone:** a town or small area hit by severe unemployment that is given government *grants* or tax advantages to encourage greater business investment. When first set up in 1981, the zones were expected to act as a magnet, attracting inward investment that would spread prosperity throughout the surrounding area. Despite generous incentives such as 10 years free of local rates and 100 per cent tax allowances, enterprise zones proved a disappointment. Much of the 'extra' investment was diverted from sites just outside the zones, providing little additional employment. In 1989, when there were 27 zones established, the government announced that no more would be created.

**entrepreneur:** an individual with a flair for business opportunities and risk taking. The term is often used to describe a person with the entrepreneurial spirit to set up a new business.

**environmental audit:** an independent check on the pollution emission levels, wastage levels and recycling practices of a firm. If measured annually and published, such an audit could encourage companies to invest in improved environmental practices. During the 1990s Body Shop, ICI and IBM have all conducted and published environmental audits annually. Unless forced to do so by legislation, however, it is hard to see why poorly performing companies should carry out this exercise.

**environmental policy:** a written statement of a firm's approach to dealing with the environmental disturbance or hazards it may face or create. A paper-towel manufacturer, for example, might adopt a policy that covers:

- planting a new tree for every one its suppliers cut down
- including an average of at least 30 per cent recycled paper in its products
- getting at least 20 per cent below the minimum pollution emission standards ruling within the *European Union*

**EPS:** see *earnings per share*

**equal opportunities:** a situation where employees and potential recruits have equal chances of being employed or promoted, whatever their sex, race, colour, religion or disability. The pursuit of this goal has been frustrated by personal and organisational discrimination. For example, in Northern Ireland it can be difficult for Catholics to gain employment in predominantly Protestant organisations. In the whole of Britain, job applications by blacks are much less likely to succeed than those of whites.

A political consensus in the 1970s enabled the *Equal Opportunities Commission* and the Commission for Racial Equality to be set up. The former seeks to promote sex equality, the latter to overcome discrimination on grounds of race.

Many large firms employ an equal opportunities officer whose job is to monitor procedures, attitudes and outcomes regarding discrimination within the business. The officer will check that:

- *job descriptions*, advertisements and application forms have no inherent bias
- the shortlisting of candidates is carried out on objective criteria (such as educational achievement)
- the interviews are conducted fairly
- the statistics of those appointed (or promoted) suggest that minority groups have been given equal opportunities
- the proportion of disabled employees meets the government target of 3 per cent (this only applies to firms with over 20 employees)

Although these systems could work effectively to provide equal opportunities, the evidence shows that many firms give this issue a low priority. Success will require either tougher laws or a change in social attitudes. (See *Sex Discrimination Act, Race Relations Act, Equal Pay Act*.)

**Equal Opportunities Commission:** an organisation set up by the *Sex Discrimination Act 1975* to promote the ideas and practices required to eliminate sex discrimination in education, advertising and employment.

**Equal Pay Act 1970:** a statute requiring employers to provide equal pay and conditions to those doing the same jobs, or work of equivalent difficulty. This had some effect in narrowing the pay gap between men and women, though it took the European Union's Equal Pay Directive 1975, to establish fully that equal pay should be given for work of equal value. This regulation enabled shop workers to claim successfully that cash-till operation is as valuable and demanding a job as working in the (male-dominated) warehouse. Despite some successes, however, women's pay remains significantly below that of men.

**equilibrium** is the notion of a market where *demand* and *supply* are equal to each other. In a product market this will produce an equilibrium price; in the labour market, an equilibrium wage; and in the market for *capital*, an equilibrium rate of interest. The problem with these ideas is that they are static, whereas in practice, market prices tend to be in a constant state of change, with equilibrium, if it is ever reached, little more than a fleeting accident.

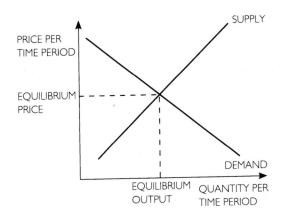

*Equilibrium in the market for goods*

**equity capital** is the name given to shares; equity being the word for equal. Therefore equity capital means *share capital*. In the UK, equity shareholders have one vote per share and each share has an equal right to distributed profits. Some books, however, treat equity as if it means all *shareholders' funds*, i.e. share capital plus *reserves*.

**ergonomics** is the study of the movement of energy involved within the work process. Like *method study*, a researcher would measure the effort that goes into producing a particular item in a particular way. As a consequence the company could decide what equipment would be most helpful, plus practical issues such as seating, lighting and factory layout.

**ERM:** see *Exchange Rate Mechanism*

**EST:** see *earliest start time*

**ET:** see *Employment Training*

**ethical code:** a document setting out the way a company believes its employees should respond to situations that challenge their integrity or social responsibility. The focus of the code will depend on the business concerned. Banks may concentrate on honesty, and chemical firms on pollution control. It has proved difficult to produce meaningful, comprehensive codes; Natwest Bank, for example, took two years to produce its ten-page document. The typical code might include sections on:

- personal integrity – in dealings with suppliers and in handling the firm's resources
- corporate integrity, such as forbidding *collusion* with competitors and forbidding *predatory pricing*
- environmental responsibility – highlighting a duty to minimise pollution emissions and maximise recycling
- social responsibility – to provide products of genuine value that are promoted with honesty and dignity

Critics of ethical codes believe them to be *public relations* exercises rather than genuine attempts to change behaviour. What is not in doubt is that the proof of their effectiveness can only be measured by how firms actually behave, not by what they write or say.

**ethical investment:** stock market investment based on a restricted list of firms that are seen as ethically sound, for example:

- they do not make products such as cigarettes or arms
- they act responsibly towards the environment
- they are good employers.

If many share buyers applied ethical principles, responsible firms would receive a reward in the form of a rising share price.

**ethics** are the moral principles that should underpin decision-making. A decision made on ethics might reject the most profitable solution in favour of one of greater benefit to society as well as the firm. Typical ethical dilemmas in business include:

- should an advertising agency accept a cigarette manufacturer as a client?
- should a firm in a take-over battle hire a private detective to investigate the private lives of the rival executives?
- should a producer of chemicals sell to an overseas buyer it suspects will be using the goods to produce chemical weapons?

If public opinion and media pressure force firms to take the publicity impact of their decisions into account, this may change the decisions made. This would not mean, however, that the firm was becoming more ethically minded. An ethical decision means doing what is morally right, it is not a matter of scientific calculation of costs and benefits.

**European Central Bank:** an institution to be set up as part of *European Monetary Union (EMU)* that will control the supply of the European common currency in the same way as the *Bank of England* looks after the interests of sterling.

**European Commission** is the civil service of the *European Union*, but with one important difference from the UK's civil service in that the Commission actually proposes legislation. The Commission is headed by the President and 16 other Commissioners (two each from the five big States and one from each of the smaller ones). Proposals for any new EU regulations and directives pass from the Commission to the *European Parliament* for debate and possible modification before going to the *Council of Ministers* for approval or rejection.

**European Community:** the name for the European Union before November 1 1993.

**European Court of Justice** is the judicial arm of the European Union's legal system. The court makes judgements on European law and Treaties when they are in dispute. The Court has the power to fine firms, but it can only apply moral pressure on governments. This has often resulted in the slow implementation of European law by some member states.

**European Currency Unit (ECU):** a stable means of exchange between the foreign currencies of Europe derived from a weighted average of the value of those currencies. The ECU may form the basis of the future European common currency if economic and monetary union becomes a reality.

**European Economic Area (EEA**) is the agreement signed in the autumn of 1991 between the members of the *European Union* and the *European Free Trade Association.* The EEA allows greater access for goods from EFTA into the EU, while encouraging the EFTA countries to bring their legislation into closer alignment with EU laws. For some countries within EFTA, particularly Austria and Sweden, the EEA was seen as a halfway house to full membership of the EU.

**European Free Trade Association (EFTA)** is the rival organisation to the *European Union.* It was set up in 1959 and included the UK, Norway, Sweden, Denmark, Austria, Portugal and Switzerland. It was enlarged with the inclusion of Iceland and Finland, but the UK and Denmark left in 1973, and Portugal in 1986 when these three countries joined the *European Union.* In 1991, EFTA and the EU reached agreement on the free movement of goods, services, capital and people, and it is the intention of both organisations to move towards total integration under the name of the *European Economic Area.*

**European Monetary System (EMS):** the bringing together or harmonisation of the financial arrangements of the member states of the *European Union.* It is the first phase of a movement which, it is hoped, will eventually lead to *European Monetary Union (EMU).* The heart of the EMS is the *Exchange Rate Mechanism (ERM)* and the *European Currency Unit.* By using funding agreements operated by the European *central banks* it was hoped that the EU currencies could stay within fairly close bands of each other.

**European Monetary Union (EMU)** will result in all member states using a common currency, such as the *ECU.* The breakdown of the *Exchange Rate Mechanism* in 1992 put the move to EMU in some doubt, and it seems likely that some countries, notably Germany, Austria, France, Holland and the Benelux countries (Belgium, the Netherlands and Luxembourg) will move to monetary union before the others. The target date for European Monetary Union is 1999.

Pros:
- more efficient i.e. there are no exchange costs, no need for forward or spot markets and foreign exchanges
- easier for producers and consumers to compare products, which should stimulate efficiency gains
- it should ease transfers of people into a wider job market, as well as easing travel generally

Cons:
- a feeling of a loss of national identity, through the loss of a national currency
- in order to work, the nations involved will have to bring their economies

into closer alignment, particularly rates of *inflation*. This is difficult, especially where countries have to deflate in order to bring this about

**European Parliament:** the elected chamber of the *European Union*. The members sit each month alternately in Strasbourg, France, or in Brussels, Belgium. They debate and amend proposals put forward by the *European Commission* (the European civil service) before they are passed to the *Council of Ministers* for approval or rejection. The Parliament is quite restricted in its powers. As the only directly elected European institution, the Parliament feels it ought to be given more powers, and indeed it is slowly having greater influence. Members of the European Parliament were first directly elected in 1979.

**European Union (EU):** The EU was formed in November 1993, following the *Maastricht* Treaty. It replaced the European Community, which in turn had replaced the European Economic Community. It currently consists of the following members: France, Germany, the Netherlands, Belgium, Luxembourg, Italy (the first six members), the UK, Denmark, Ireland (joined 1973), Greece (1981), Portugal and Spain (1986), Sweden, Finland and Austria (1995). The EU was established under the Treaty of Rome in 1957 with the objective of removing all trade barriers between member states. The background to this was the desire to form a political and economic union which would prevent the possibility of another war in Europe. The success of the EU, particularly in its early days is seen by the speed with which it dwarfed the *European Free Trade Association (EFTA)* which was set up in 1959 as a rival to the EU.

In the autumn of 1991, agreement was reached with the EFTA countries to form closer links within what is called the *European Economic Area (EEA)*. This builds on the Single European Act which came into force in 1987, and the abolition of all trade and other restrictions which was effective under the Act from January 1 1993 to form the *Single European Market*. The Maastricht Treaty, which came into force November 1 1993, laid the foundations for even greater unity. It was seen as a move towards a federal Europe (although the UK had the word 'federal' removed from the Treaty, and secured opt-out clauses on *European Monetary Union* and the *social chapter*). This fear of closer political as well as economic ties persuaded the populations of both Norway and Switzerland to vote against joining the EU when referendums were held in 1994.

For some countries, however, the attraction of membership remains very strong. Turkey has consistently made overtures, but has been turned down because of its record on human rights. Other southern countries such as Malta and Cyprus are possible members but most of the established EU members are more concerned with consolidating capitalism and sound democracies in the former USSR sphere of influence in Eastern European. It is possible that the Czech Republic will gain entry by the turn of the century, but Slovenia, Romania, Bulgaria, Hungary and Poland may have to wait some time. Some of these countries, especially Poland, have large agricultural sectors which could add to the problems of the *Common Agricultural Policy*.

The institutions of the EU are shown in the diagram on the next page.

Pros: • it offers a huge market of over 360 million people. Its size offers the possibilities of *economies of scale*. The combined strength of the EU creates a potentially powerful trade bloc
- • by creating competition it reduces costs and increases efficiency as well as encouraging innovation
- • investment is encouraged, especially inward investment from non-EU countries like Japan who are seeking to produce within the EU's boundaries
- • it offers the possibility of income and wealth redistribution within Europe and offers greater career choices for EU citizens

Cons: • the budget has not always been wisely spent. In particular the Common Agricultural Policy has distorted spending in favour of agriculture, has led to over-production in certain areas and fostered corruption
- • the bureaucracy of some elements of European law making has made some people think that law making should be delegated to member States. This is the idea of *subsidiarity*
- • countries outside the EU bloc, especially those in the Third World see the Union as another conspiracy by the rich western economies to keep them poor (by trade advantages for EU members over non-members)
- • individual members still tend to put national interests before those of the wider community. Although laws have often been passed, they have not always been applied with equal force

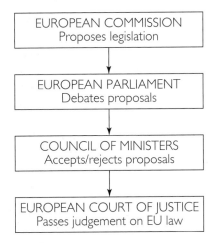

**exceptional item:** an entry in the *profit and loss account* which arises from ordinary trading, but is so large or unusual as to risk distorting the company's trading account. Therefore it is listed separately as an exceptional item. An example would be unusually large *bad debt* charges.

**excess capacity** means having more storage or production potential than is likely to be used in the foreseeable future. Therefore the *capacity utilisation* will be low and the *fixed costs per unit* of output will be relatively high. Firms faced with excess capacity might rationalise by closing down one production site or renting out spare space to another firm.

**excess demand** describes the situation where *demand* exceeds *supply*, as in the following diagram:

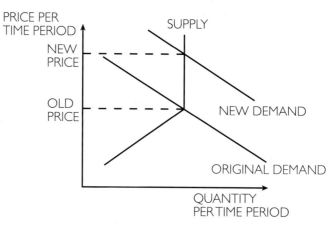

PRICE PER TIME PERIOD

NEW PRICE

OLD PRICE

SUPPLY

NEW DEMAND

ORIGINAL DEMAND

QUANTITY PER TIME PERIOD

*Excess demand*

The result of excess demand is the same as if there were two or more people bidding for a single item at an auction: its price would rise. Excess demand is therefore seen as one of the two main causes of *inflation*, the other being *cost push*. Excess demand may occur at the recovery stage of the *trade cycle* before firms have restocked following a *recession*, and also at the peak of the cycle as all the slack in the economy has been taken up so that increasing production is very difficult.

**exchange controls** are limits set by law on the dealings in gold and foreign currency which a country's citizens can make. In effect, it prevents a country's *exchange rate* from settling at a market-determined price, because it is a way of fixing the market. Exchange controls were abandoned by the UK in 1979, and by all the member states of the *EU* in 1993.

Pros: • can counter a *balance of payments* deficit by limiting the value of imports to the value of export earnings
• allows the internal price level to be established by the workings of the internal economy rather than external factors such as the exchange rate

Cons: • discourages international trade
• may encourage other countries to follow suit

**exchange rate:** the price of one country's currency expressed in terms of another. In the press, the pound sterling is often compared to its value against the German mark, the US dollar, or a 'basket of currencies' (an average of a number of major currencies). Anyone going on holiday abroad will know that there is a rate for all other currencies against the pound. The exchange rate between different countries is kept in line through *arbitrage* operations.

**Exchange Rate Mechanism (ERM):** the way currencies are brought into line under the *European Monetary System (EMS)*. Countries belonging to the ERM agree to keep their *exchange rates* within a range of values known as currency bands. On entering the ERM, a government decides on an appropriate rate and agrees to keep it within either 2.5 per cent or 6 per cent of the value. The 2.5 per cent range is known as the narrow band and the 6 per cent range as the wide band.

**exchange rate policy** is, in the UK, the government's policy on the international value of the pound sterling. There are two extremes of exchange rate policy:

- a fixed rate where the *central bank* intervenes by buying when market pressures are forcing the value down (and *vice versa*)
- a freely floating exchange rate where the central bank does not intervene at all

Prior to 'Black Wednesday' in September 1992, the UK's exchange rate policy was to keep sterling within the *European Monetary System*, which meant keeping it within quite narrow bands against the other European currencies. Since 1992 the UK's policy has been to operate floating exchange rates.

**excise duty** is a tax levied by HM Customs and Excise on goods produced for home consumption, as opposed to customs duties which are levied on imports. Excise duties are paid on a wide range of goods, the best known being alcohol and petrol. In the case of some products this can lead to distortions. In the case of beer, for example, the duty is raised on its alcoholic content. This might encourage a brewer to weaken the beer and so reduce the excise duty paid whilst keeping the retail price the same, thereby increasing profits.

**executive summary:** a précis of a report's main findings and conclusions to enable busy managers to gain a quick understanding and to decide which parts are worth reading in full. The executive summary is therefore placed at the front of a report, even though it will have been written last. It should be remembered that although communication is often seen as a good thing, senior executives are often faced with communication overload – making it hard for them to find the time to think about long term strategy. Executive summaries are a way of reducing the time taken on written communication.

**ex-factory price** means the price charged by a manufacturer to direct purchasers. These will either be wholesalers or large retailers. The latter add on their mark-up to determine the *retail selling price*.

| | | |
|---|---|---|
| Ex-factory price | £4.50 | |
| Wholesale price | £6.00 | Wholesaler mark-up 33% |
| Retail price | £9.00 (+ VAT) | Retail mark-up 50% |

So although the consumer pays £9+VAT the producer receives just £4.50 per unit.

**exit interview:** a procedure for finding out why staff are leaving the organisation; it might be an informal discussion or filling out a structured questionnaire. A personnel officer would analyse the findings on a regular basis to find out whether people are leaving due to stress, pay, personality clashes, or lack of challenge. Exit interviews can reveal a great deal about the causes of satisfaction or frustration among the workforce, as those leaving can be more open than those staying. It is a practice that most progressive firms do automatically, as the findings can help the managers devise improved personnel strategies.

**expansion pricing:** price reductions that are part cause and part an effect of economies of scale. For products with high fixed costs such as microchips, a virtuous circle can occur whereby:

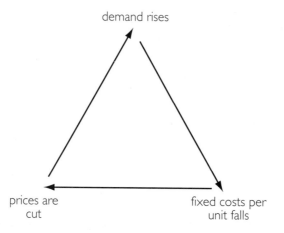

demand rises

prices are cut

fixed costs per unit falls

**expectancy theory:** the view that *motivation* depends on employees' *expectations* as to the outcome of their efforts. If people know what they want from an outcome and believe they can achieve it, they will be highly motivated towards it. This theory is mainly associated with *Vroom* and contrasts with *Maslow* and *Herzberg*'s emphasis on people's needs.

**expectations** are what people believe will happen in the future. Economists and business leaders place great importance on expectations because they assume that they influence people's behaviour. If, for example, people believe that house prices will rise sharply, they may rush to buy before the price rise occurs. The extra *demand* will pull prices up, making it a self-fulfilling prophesy.

**expected value** is the average value of the possible outcomes resulting from a decision, weighted by the probabilities of achieving them. Used in *decision tree* analysis, it is the monetary value that would be expected on average from a decision if it was repeated many times.

**expense:** a payment for something of immediate benefit to the business. It causes a debit on the accounts and is charged to the current *profit and loss account.* Maintenance costs and wages are expenses; these are also known as *revenue expenditure.*

**expert systems:** highly developed computer software often used in diagnosing or analysing business problems or methods. Expert systems provide instant detailed and expert information from a database which can be asked questions and can also ask its own questions and offer possible solutions. The latter function encourages commentators to call this 'artificial intelligence'.

**exploitation** means taking advantage of a situation or resource for one's own gain. The term implies that the gain will be at the expense of others. Exploitation could be used to describe the employment of labour at very low wages, or the profitable extraction of a scarce mineral from a Third World country.

**exponential smoothing** is a method of *time series analysis* in which the data from more recent periods is given heavier weighting than that from earlier years. This is hoped to make forecasts more accurate.

**export:** the sale of a product or service overseas

**Export Credit Guarantee Department (ECGD)** is a government department offering a service of guaranteeing that if foreign importers of UK-produced goods fail to pay, then it will step in and pay instead. It is a way of insuring UK exporters against *bad debts* overseas. By offering such a service, exports are encouraged. As with any insurance policy, fees are charged, and critics of the British government have pointed out that ECGD charges much higher premiums to British exporters than the governments of France, Germany and Japan do to their own companies. In this way, the competitiveness of British exports is hindered. In 1991, the ECGD's short-term export credit insurance business was privatised.

**export marketing:** devising a strategy for developing and sustaining profitable sales overseas. Although largely the same as UK marketing, selling overseas has certain points of difference:

- gaining *distribution* is likely to be harder and far more expensive, so most firms use local *agents* who already know and have access to the local distribution channels
- the exporter must decide whether to keep the product the same in all markets (benefiting from *economies of scale*), or to tailor make it for differing local tastes; the latter should generate higher sales, but the former will keep unit costs down and therefore might be more profitable
- brand names may have different meanings in different languages and should therefore be researched (the German soft drink Pschitt was tested in the UK but failed)

**Extel cards** provide up-to-the-minute information on the published accounts of *public limited companies*. Looking up the data you want on an Extel card is a quicker and cheaper process than a company search at *Companies' House*.

**extension strategy:** a medium- to long-term plan for lengthening the life cycle of a product or brand. It is likely to be implemented during the maturity or early decline stages within the life cycle. Extension strategies can be divided into two categories, defensive and offensive.

Defensive: a plan designed to postpone the obsolescence of a product by a year or two, perhaps to keep sales going until a replacement can be launched. Examples include car manufacturers' 'special editions', which usually offer different paintwork, slightly different equipment and a bouncy name.

Offensive: a plan to revitalise or reposition a product to give it a wholly new, long-term market. Horlicks becoming Instant Horlicks achieved this, as it shifted a bedtime drink to an anytime drink. Even more noteworthy was Johnson and Johnson's repositioning of its Baby Powder and Baby Oil to appeal to women instead of just the babycare market.

Types of extension strategy include:

- redesigning or reformulating the product ('New improved!')

- adding an extra feature ('Now with ...!')
- repositioning its price and image (usually downmarket)
- changing the packaging and advertising imagery to appeal to a new or additional market sector.

Note that sales promotions or extra advertising spending alone would not be regarded as extension strategies. They are ways of boosting sales that could work equally well at any stage of the life cycle.

**external constraint:** a factor outside the control of the enterprise that restricts it from meeting its objectives. Main types of external constraint include:

- changing consumer tastes
- competitors' actions
- economic circumstances (especially the level of interest rates, the value of the pound, consumer and business confidence, and the level of *aggregate demand*)
- legal constraints
- social attitudes and *pressure group* activity

**external costs** are negative consequences of an activity that are paid for by people or organisations other than the originator of those costs. For example, the sulphur emissions from power stations cause acid rain that damages forests; the cost of this is borne by the owners of the forests, not the electricity companies. As external costs do not affect the *profit and loss account* of the firm causing the costs, it has no direct incentive to minimise the pollution. This is why government intervention is required to force the polluter to pay (or stop). (See *cost-benefit analysis*.)

**external economies of scale:** see *economies of scale*

**external environment:** the circumstances within which firms operate that are outside their control. (See *external constraints*.)

**external financing** means obtaining capital resources from outside the firm's resources or accounts. This can only be done in one of three ways: debt, *share capital*, or *grants*.

Debt can be obtained for day-to-day (short-term) transactions or for longer-term capital needs. Among the ways of borrowing for the short term are: bank *overdraft*, *trade credit* and credit *factoring*. For the longer term are bank loans, commercial mortgages and *debentures*.

Share capital can be obtained via a *rights issue*, the issue of *preference shares*, or by a *flotation* of the company's shares on the *Stock Exchange*.

Grants could come from the *European Union*, the government's *regional policy* or from a local enterprise board. It should be remembered, however, that grants provide only a tiny fraction of the capital needs of business.

**external growth** comes from outside the firm, such as by acquiring or merging with another firm. This is the easiest way to grow rapidly, but results in a huge number of managerial problems based on the difficulty of integrating a new business, management and *culture*. *Internal growth* is a far safer way of expanding, though it may be too slow to allow the firm to capitalise on exciting short-term prospects.

**externalities** are those costs or benefits which occur as a result of the main opera-tion of the business but which are not part of the firm's *profit and loss account.* Examples include *pollution* and congestion, costs that are the result of production but which are borne by the community, not the business. There are moves for some *external costs* to be passed back to organisations, such as by legislation that forces firms to pay for any smoke emissions from their factories. Where it is possible to 'make the polluters pay', firms have an incentive to minimise their costs by minimising the pollution.

External benefits can arise through the effect on local service and supply industries of new firms opening up in an area, or from the spill-over effect of new technology, such as in defence or related industries. An example of an external benefit from the development of space exploration was Teflon which was used to produce non-stick saucepans.

An attempt to account fully for external as well as internal costs and benefits is made through *cost-benefit analysis.*

**extraordinary general meeting (EGM):** a shareholders' meeting called in addi-tion to the normal *AGM.* This might be to gain approval for a *rights issue* or for a vote of confidence in the chairman.

**extraordinary items** derive from events or transactions that fall outside the ordi-nary activities of the company and which are therefore not expected to recur frequently or regularly. The most common example is the cost of closing a business division or factory. Extraordinary items used to be excluded from the main section of the *profit and loss account* because of their potentially distorting, one-off nature. Now, under the modern *Financial Reporting Standards* extraordinary items are included.

**extrapolation:** in forecasting the near future it can be assumed the recent past will be a good guide. This is known as extrapolating from the past to the future. When *trend* values have been established, they can be plotted on a graph and extrapolation by eye or by mathematical means can be undertaken.

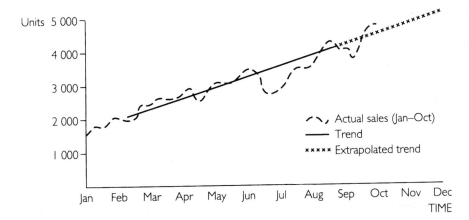

*Extrapolation of a sales trend*

**extrinsic motivation** is a drive to succeed that comes from outside the job itself. It might be stimulated by the promise of financial reward or promotion. Professor *Herzberg* characterises such a process as 'movement' rather than *motivation*, which he believes to be less desirable.

**extrinsic rewards** are the financial or status rewards that may stem from a job but are not a fundamental part of it.

REVISION: There are two sets of revision lists and a glossary of examiners' terms at the back of this book to help you prepare for exams or unit tests. See pages 307–312 for unit tests in GNVQ Business Advanced and pages 313–325 for examinations in A level Business Studies. See pages 326–329 for explanations of examiners' terms such as 'analyse' and 'discuss'.

**F**

**face-to-face interview:** an interview conducted in person, so that the interviewer and the respondent are face to face. This contrasts with a telephone survey or a *self-completion questionnaire.*

Pros:
- the interviewer can assess the *body language* of the respondent when the questions are being answered
- face-to-face interviews gain higher *response rates* than self-completion questionnaires; this reduces the chance of a biased sample

Cons:
- respondents are less likely to make critical comments face to face
- face-to-face interviewing is time consuming and expensive

**factor:** an organisation that provides a *factoring* service. Most are subsidiaries of banks.

**factoring** is a banking service which provides up to 80 per cent of the value of invoiced sales as a cash advance, and then organises the collection of the debt. Many organisations which sell mainly on *credit* carry high values of *debtors* in their *current assets.* This ties up cash that could be used more effectively elsewhere in the business. An alternative is to sell these debts to a specialist debt collector called a factor. The procedure is as follows (assuming a £40 000 sale to a customer on two month's credit):

1 Today, a £40 000 order is delivered to the customer, and the bill (invoice) is presented. A copy of the bill is sent to the factor who sends a £32 000 (80 per cent) cheque immediately
2 In two months' time the factor contacts the customer, requesting payment. When the customer pays, the factor deducts a fee (usually amounting to around 5 per cent, or £2 000 in this case) and then sends the balance to their client.

Worked example: cumulative cash inflows with and without factoring

|  | Today | In one month | In two months |
|---|---|---|---|
| Without factoring | £0 | £0 | £40 000 |
| With factoring | £32 000 | £32 000 | £38 000 |

Although many small firms feel that the loss of 5 per cent of revenue is too high a price to pay, factoring provides important cost savings that could totally offset the factor's fees. These include:

- lower administration costs in the process of collecting and chasing up customer bills
- the cash provided by the factor reduces *overdraft* requirements (and therefore interest charges)
- the factor takes on the risk of *bad debts*, reducing uncertainty for the client

Further advantages include: bringing cash inflows forward, providing the finance for further production; and making cash inflows more predictable, to increase the accuracy of *cash-flow forecasts*. Among the disadvantages are: the *factor*'s fee would take too high a proportion of a low profit margin business (a 4 per cent fee would take half the profits of a firm operating on margins of 8 per cent); the factoring company reserves the right to refuse to let you deal with a customer thought uncreditworthy; the credit checking procedures might upset your customers.

**factors of production** include land, labour, capital and enterprise. Enterprise is not considered to be a special factor of production by some economists because they regard an *entrepreneur* as someone who, whilst having special skills, is nonetheless just a part of labour. Others argue that without entrepreneurship the other factors would not be combined in order to produce profit, and hence increase living standards. The factors are rewarded as follows:

- land receives rent
- labour receives wages
- capital receives interest
- entrepreneurship receives profit.

**factory farming** is the use of *production-line* techniques to ensure maximum *output* from farm livestock with the minimum of inputs. This usually means that the animals live in isolation in very confined spaces, and are fattened up with the aid of hormones. It is a good example of where *profit maximisation* could be thought to conflict with *ethics*.

**factory inspectors** are employed by the *Health and Safety Executive* to check that firms are complying with relevant UK and EU legislation, such as the *Health and Safety at Work Act 1974*.

**Fair Trading Act 1973** set up the *Office of Fair Trading (OFT)*, the government agency responsible for providing ministers with advice on legislation and action with regard to *monopolies*, *mergers* and *restrictive practices*.

**fast moving consumer goods (FMCG)** are branded products in markets when high sales volumes occur due to regular purchasing. FMCG markets include breakfast cereals, chocolate, hair care and detergents.

**fax (facsimile machine):** a way of transmitting photocopies via telephone lines, thereby enabling detailed, legally valid written information to be communicated instantly.

**Fayol, Henri** (1841–1925) was a French management pioneer who focused on the problems of organisational structure within large firms at the turn of the century. Whereas his American contemporary, F W *Taylor*, concentrated on the efficiency of shop-floor labour, Fayol looked at senior management. He was largely responsible for introducing the concepts of *chain of command*, the *organisational chart*, and *span of control*.

**feasible region:** the area on a *blending* graph bordered by *constraint* straight lines which contains the complete set of possible or feasible solutions to the problem described. The *optimum* always lies at the intersection of two of the constraints.

**Federal Reserve Bank** (known as the 'Fed') is the *central bank* of the United States. The American banking system includes a large number of quite small banks. As a result, American banks are more difficult to regulate than in the UK.

**feedback** is response to a piece of communication. Without it the communicator cannot know whether the communication has been received effectively. This could not only cause operational problems (such as stocks not being reordered), but may also undermine *motivation*. This is because communicators have a psychological need for response to their efforts. For instance, if homework goes unmarked students will soon lose the impetus to produce more, and any that is done will be of poor quality.

**field trials:** testing a new or improved product on consumers within your target market. For example, 400 households might be asked to use a new detergent for a month, then be interviewed on its qualities compared with their regular brands. If the brand name of the product is kept hidden from the households, this is known as a *blind product test.*

**fieldwork** is the process of carrying out field research. An example would be a *market research* survey, which could be conducted through face to face interviews in the street, or via a postal or telephone survey.

**FIFO:** see *first in, first out*

**financial accounting** s largely concerned with reporting and the production of the financial accounts according to the requirements of the *Companies Acts* so that users of accounts have an accurate view of the firm's financial position.

**Financial Reporting Exposure Draft (FRED):** a draft version of a proposed new accounting standard issued by the *Accounting Standards Board* for consultation.

**Financial Reporting Standards (FRS):** an accounting standard issued under the authority of the *Accounting Standards Board.* The first standard was issued in 1991 and aimed to improve the reporting on *cash flow* in published company accounts.

**Financial Services Act 1986** set up a system of self-regulation in the City which was intended to ensure that only those considered 'fit and proper' would be able to operate within the financial markets. It was supposed to ensure that the fees and charges made by the financial services businesses would become more explicit. In fact, major providers of financial services such as the life insurance industry managed to keep their charges hidden.

**financial year:** the national financial year runs from 6 April to 5 April and so income tax changes apply accordingly. Each individual person or company may make up its accounts annually to any date. The essence of a financial year is simply to create a consistent reporting period.

**financing requirements:** the capital a firm needs to carry out its plans for the coming trading periods. If this cannot be achieved through *internal financing*, it will be found from external sources such as share issues, loans or grants. The length of time the financing requirements are needed is important. At some future point the plans should become self-financing.

**first in, first out (FIFO)** is the standard practice in all systems of *stock rotation*. In other words the oldest item purchased should be the first to be used or sold. This practical matter should not be confused with the following entry, which shows how accountants use the term.

**first in, first out (FIFO):** a method of stock identification in which it is assumed that stock is used and sold in the order in which it came into the business, i.e. first (stock) in, first (stock) out.

At the end of an accounting period, *stocktaking* and valuation are carried out. If all stock is purchased at the same buying-in price it makes little difference whether FIFO or *LIFO (last in, first out)* is chosen. When stock buying-in prices change, however, it affects the valuation. For example, in a situation of rising prices, FIFO will give a higher value for closing stock than LIFO. Because of the way *profit* is calculated, a pound extra on closing stock value raises profit by £1. So the method of identifying closing stock is important as it affects firms' reported profits.

The fact that the FIFO method is used does not mean necessarily that stock was actually used in that order; it is only an assumption about the order in which stock was used.

Advantages of FIFO over LIFO:

- ensures that the *balance sheet* stock valuation is more accurate, as the valuation is based upon the cost of purchasing the stocks bought recently
- for the calculation of the tax due on business profits, the Inland Revenue only allows FIFO to be used; therefore few British firms use LIFO

**fiscal policy** is government policy towards its raising of revenue and its level of (public) spending. The task of setting fiscal policy is undertaken by the *Chancellor of the Exchequer*. It is arrived at in the following order:

1  establish government economic objectives
2  decide on the correct balance between government revenue and government spending (known as the fiscal or budgetary balance)
3  make the individual decisions that are compatible with **1** and **2** and maximise political advantage. They may include increasing the tax on petrol or cutting government spending on the National Health Service.

In the *circular flow of national income*, taxes represent a withdrawal that is balanced by government expenditure on such items as pensions, unemployment benefit and so on. If the government takes in more than it spends, consumer spending power is reduced and *demand* falls, thus slowing down the economy. If it spends more than it takes in then it increases demand and therefore increases economic activity. Because of the impact on demand, fiscal policy is often called 'demand management', as opposed to *monetary policy* which attempts to control the economy through the money supply and interest rates. From a government's point of view, fiscal policy has the following advantages and disadvantages:

Pros:
- government spending injected into the economy has a *multiplier* effect as it moves through the economy. For instance, if an unemployed person gets a job helping to build a new road, some of his or her wages will be spent on things which previously could not be afforded, such as new clothes. This creates demand in the clothing industry, so more people are employed to make clothes, which creates more income and so on. If the clothes are made abroad, however, it is the overseas economy and workforce that benefits
- revenue can be raised either through direct taxation e.g. *income* and *corporation tax* or through indirect taxation e.g. *VAT*. Governments can alter the

mix of the two for policy reasons, such as reducing direct taxation, which some believe has an important impact upon people's incentives to work

Cons: • the timing of government intervention is crucial, yet extremely difficult to judge
 • many large-scale projects take a long time to have any effect on the economy. For instance, if a new motorway is to be built, it may take years of planning before the first contractor moves on to the site, by which time the economy may have recovered
 • some economists believe that government spending has a 'crowding out' effect, meaning that any boost to the economy from the *public sector* is at the cost of the *private sector*

**fishbone chart:** a diagram used in Japanese *quality circles* that acts as the visual focal point for discussion of a problem. These causes are grouped into categories known as the four Ms: men, methods, machines and materials. Having focused on the causes, the team leader will then look for ideas from the group about how the problem can be solved.

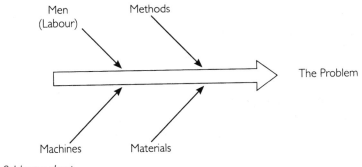

The fishbone chart

**fitness for purpose:** a judgement on how well a product or service is matched to customers' requirements. The expression is often used in relation to product characteristics such as reliability, styling and performance. Many academics regard fitness for purpose as being the key test of product quality.

**fixed assets:** items of a monetary value which have a long-term function and can be used repeatedly. These determine the scale of the firm's operations. Examples are land, buildings, equipment and machinery. Fixed assets are not only useful in the running of the firm, but can also provide *collateral* for securing additional *loan capital*.

**fixed costs** are the expenses that do not alter in relation to changes in demand or output (in the short term). They have to be paid whether the business trades or not. Examples are rent, *depreciation* and interest charges.

**fixed costs per unit,** also known as *average fixed costs*, are total *fixed costs* divided by the units of output produced. While total fixed costs cannot be changed by definition in the short run, fixed costs per unit continually fall as output or activity is increased up to the *capacity* level.

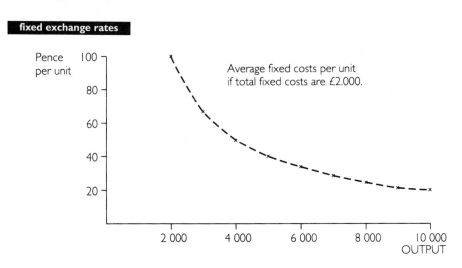

Pence per unit

Average fixed costs per unit
if total fixed costs are £2.000.

*Fixed costs per unit*

**fixed exchange rates** are currency rates which are not permitted to respond to changes in the demand for currencies. In practice, there is always some movement, but the rate is controlled by *central bank* intervention. If the pound came under selling pressure, the market reaction would be a fall in the exchange rate. Under a fixed system the central bank, in this case the *Bank of England* would step in to buy pounds with reserves of gold or foreign currency. In other words it would make up for the shortfall in demand.

**fixed overheads:** see *overheads*

**fixed rate loan:** a loan on which the interest rate payable is determined at the outset and does not vary with the market rate of interest.

Pros: • enables interest costs to be budgeted accurately
     • the firm is protected from the potentially serious impact on *overheads* of sharp rises in interest rates

Cons: • fixed rate loans are inflexible, as they are taken out for specific time periods (such as five years)
     • timing must be right; it is easy to become tied to a high fixed interest payment just before market rates fall

**fixtures and fittings** are the internal fabric of a building: its decor, equipment and fittings. For service businesses, expenditure on fixtures and fittings can be considerable. Therefore they can form a major component of a firm's *fixed assets* and of its *depreciation* provisions.

**flat organisation (or hierarchy):** a management structure based on a wide *span of control*, therefore requiring relatively few *layers of hierarchy*. This results in:

• good *vertical communication* as there are few management layers between the bottom and top of the company
• the need to delegate a high proportion of the tasks and decisions
• higher motivation potential, given the greater responsibility delegated to junior managers and staff

**flexed budget:** a form of *variance analysis* in which the budgeted figures are adjusted in line with changes in sales volume before being compared with the actual outcomes. This avoids the problem of conventional variance analysis, which fails to identify whether variance is due to external factors or the firm's inefficiency. In the worked example below, sales volume proves to be 20 per cent above the forecast level. The conventional budget shows a buoyant revenue variance which prevents the steeply rising costs from damaging profit too greatly. The flexed budget adjusts the forecast figures by the 20 per cent increase in volume. It therefore can show far more clearly the way in which the firm has allowed cost increases to rob them of a potentially lucrative month.

Worked example: flexed budget

| | Conventional Budget | | | Flexed Budget | | | |
|---|---|---|---|---|---|---|---|
| | Budg | Act | Var | Budg | Flex-budg | Act | Var |
| Revenue | 250 | 300 | + 50 | 250 | 300 | 300 | — |
| Labour | 100 | 130 | – 30 | 100 | 120 | 130 | – 10 |
| Materials | 50 | 70 | – 20 | 50 | 60 | 70 | – 10 |
| Overheads | 70 | 75 | – 5 | 70 | 70 | 75 | – 5 |
| Profit | 30 | 25 | – 5 | 30 | 50 | 25 | – 25 |

**flexibility** in business usually means the ability and willingness to change methods of working. This relies on a workforce that is multi-skilled and is not too resistant to *change*. A flexible worker would be capable of doing many different jobs, perhaps when filling in for an absentee.

**flexible specialisation:** a manufacturing theory stating that because modern markets are broken down into small niches, yet customer tastes are always changing, the successful firm must be able to produce specialised products flexibly. This requires machinery that can quickly be reprogrammed, instead of conveyor-belt driven plants designed to mass-produce a single item. Flexible specialisation implies a move back to batch production and places a premium upon a multi-skilled, adaptable workforce.

**flexible working:** the acceptance by staff and management that rigid *demarcation* lines lead to inefficiency, and therefore that *labour flexibility* is preferable for long-term success. The same term is also used to describe a staffing pattern that is not dependent upon full-time, permanent jobs. In this context flexible working means a willingness to work on a temporary or part-time basis.

**flexitime:** an *employment contract* that allows staff to complete their agreed hours of work at times that suit the employee. This can give a greater sense of control to workers who have repetitive jobs, and helps parents with small children.

**floating exchange rate** applies to a currency which responds to supply and demand on the foreign exchange markets without *central bank* intervention.

Pros: 
- requires no gold or foreign currency reserves
- responds to the automatic discipline of the market
- accepts that 'you can't buck the market' (to use Mrs Thatcher's phrase)

Cons: • firms cannot predict future rates, adding to the uncertainties involved in business decision-making, which might restrict trade
 • leaves the international competitiveness of a country's goods to a market that is often affected by speculative money flows; these may have little to do with the underlying state of the economy and its *balance of payments*

**float time** is the amount of spare time available to complete an activity within a project. It is an important element in *critical path* (network) *analysis*. There are two ways of calculating float time:

 1 total float, which measures the spare time available so that there is no delay to the project as a whole, e.g. if an activity lasting two days can start on day three and the following activity must start on day nine, there are four days of total float available.

FORMULA:    LFT    −    duration    −    EST
        (this activity)                 (this activity)
           9    −    2    −    3    = 4

 2 free float, which measures the spare time available so that there is no delay to the following activity; this is a tighter requirement, so the result will never be higher than for total float.

FORMULA:    EST    −    duration    −    EST    = free float
        (next activity)                 (this activity)

**flotation:** the term given to the launch of a company on to the *stock market* by the offer of its shares to the public.

**flow chart**: a diagram setting out the activities needed to complete a project and their timescales. A flow chart can identify:

 • how one activity may depend on the outcome of another
 • the activities crucial to the successful completion of the project
 • how long the whole project should take to complete ...
 • ... and therefore when final payment can be expected.

**flow production** is the manufacture of an item in a continually moving process. Each stage is linked with the next by a conveyor belt or in liquid form, so that the production time is minimised and production efficiency is maximised. The diagram

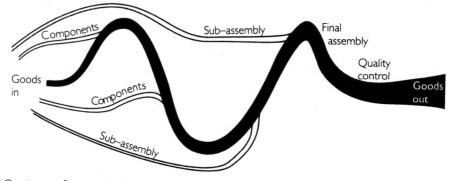

*Continuous flow production*

on page 106 shows a continuous system in which sub-components are being fed into the main production line just as streams flow into a river. In order to operate effectively, a flow system needs high capacity utilisation, as the highly mechanised line is likely to be expensive to purchase, install and maintain. Therefore high demand levels are needed to spread the *fixed costs* over many units of output.

**FMCG**, see *fast moving consumer goods*

**focus** upon the core of the business represents the opposite corporate strategy to *diversification*. Focus might be achieved by selling off fringe activities or by the decision to stop developing new products outside the core market.

**focus groups:** an American term for *group discussions*, i.e. small-scale, in-depth research into the reasons behind consumers' habits and attitudes.

**Food Act 1984:** *consumer protection* legislation that has been incorporated into and strengthened within the *Food Safety Act 1990*.

**Food Safety Act 1990** is a wide-ranging law which strengthens and updates *consumer protection* in the food sector. This brought food sources, and by implication farmers and growers, specifically under food safety legislation for the first time. It made it an offense to sell food which is not of the 'nature or substance or quality' demanded by the purchaser. Other key features include:

- premises selling food must register with the local authority
- those handling food must receive appropriate training
- enforcement officers can issue an improvement notice or, in extreme cases, an emergency prohibition notice
- the harmonisation of UK laws and standards with those of Europe

**footloose** companies are those with no firm commitment to any specific location. The term is most often used in relation to *multinational* organisations.

**Footsie (FT–SE 100):** a widely quoted index denoting shifts in the average share price level among 100 of the largest public companies in the UK. The market prices are plotted regularly through each working day and their *weighted average* is the basis of the index. A rise in the index indicates greater confidence in the financial community about UK economic prospects generally so the Footsie is considered an important *leading indicator*. The term stands for the Financial Times–Stock Exchange 100, though it is usually referred to as Footsie.

**Fordism:** the application of Henry Ford's faith in *mass production* run by autocratic management. This implies high *division of labour* and little workplace democracy, but with the consolation of high wages.

**forecasting:** estimating future outcomes such as next year's sales figures. Although forecasts can only be guesses of the future, the aim is to base the guesswork on the best possible information. There are three main sources for this:

- projecting an established trend forward (*extrapolation*)
- *market research* into consumers' buying intentions
- consulting experts with proven ability at anticipating trends (the *Delphi technique*)

**foreign exchange market (FOREX)** is the market where dealers buy and sell currencies either 'spot' i.e. for immediate exchange, or 'forward' i.e. at a rate agreed today for some future time, such as in three months' time. Currencies are bought and sold depending on the demands of international trade but also for reasons of speculation. The major world trading markets are in London, New York and Tokyo.

**foreign exchange profits/losses** are those which result from buying and selling a currency in the expectation that its value will rise or fall in the future. For instance, in September 1992, foreign exchange dealers decided that the pound was overvalued within the *Exchange Rate Mechanism*. They therefore sold pounds and bought other currencies, particularly the German mark. When the pound was devalued, the dealers were able to take huge profits by exchanging their marks back into pounds.

**foreman:** a supervisor of *manual workers*. The foreman is likely to be in charge of discipline, timekeeping, productivity levels and product quality. The role of foreman should not be confused with that of the *shop steward*.

**formal communication** takes place within the official channels, i.e. the lines of communication approved by senior management. An example would be a marketing manager talking to the marketing director: his or her immediate boss. Within that channel any form of communication is regarded as formal. Beware of muddling formal communication with written and informal with oral. (Also see *informal* and *direct communication*.)

**Fortress Europe** describes the possibility that a Europe with a single market might build an import protection wall around itself, keeping out American and Japanese imports.

**forward buying** means contracting to buy a certain quantity of goods or foreign currency at a price agreed today, for delivery at a specific future date. This can act as insurance against unforeseen problems that may damage the profitability of an export order, such as a sudden jump in oil prices due to war breaking out in the Middle East.

**Forward (or downstream) integration:** means buying out a customer, e.g. the chocolate firm buying up a chain of newsagents.

Pros: to the firm

- control of competitive forces within one's sales outlets, as when a brewery owns pubs and off-licences
- controlling the display and sale of products

Pros: to the consumer

- it could be said that less competition means less pressure to cut product cost or quality
- may benefit from more expert sales staff

Pros: to the workforce

- control of competition should mean greater job security (in the long run)
- opportunity for better training on the products

Cons: to the firm

- control over outlets (customers) may cause complacency and inefficiency
- consumers may not like outlets dominated by one firm's products: hitting sales

Cons: to the consumer

- control over competition in retail outlets may lead to high prices and poor consumer choice
- those in country areas or small towns may have no other outlets to go to

Cons: to the workforce

- staff in retail outlets may find that their owner dictates all buying and display decisions
- any customer dissatisfaction is likely to lead to lower job satisfaction

**FOX:** see *Futures and Options Exchange*

**franchise:** a business based upon the name, *logos* and trading method of an existing, successful business. To obtain a franchise requires the payment of an initial fee and the signing of a contract that places tight restrictions upon the *franchisee*, including:

- limitation on the area of operation
- design of premises to be exactly as laid down by the *franchisor*
- all supplies to be purchased from the franchisor
- an annual payment to the franchisor based upon a percentage of the franchisee's turnover

Despite these costs and constraints, business start-ups based upon franchising have a far lower failure rate than independent firms. This is due to the following advantages of franchising:

- the niche, trading strategy and methods have been tried and tested elsewhere, reducing many of the risks associated with business start-ups
- the name and *logos* may have wide customer recognition and loyalty, ensuring high demand from day one
- part of the annual payment goes into an advertising fund that finances much larger advertising campaigns than could be afforded by an independent; television advertising has played a major part in the success of franchise businesses such as McDonald's and Pizza Hut

Despite these considerable advantages, potential franchisees should never forget that running any business is very demanding and involves significant risk. Franchising has attracted some would-be *entrepreneurs* who lack the experience or the personality to lead a company.

**franchisee:** a person or company who has bought the local rights to use the name, *logos* and training method of another company (the *franchisor*).

**franchisor:** the holder of the *franchise* who will sell the local rights to suitable *franchisees*. From the franchisor's point of view, this can be a far better way to expand the company than via the traditional route of opening up more managed branches or outlets.

Pros:
- prevents the cash drain or heavy borrowings required to develop a business quickly enough to take advantage of a market opportunity; with franchising, growth is paid for by the franchisees
- franchisees have the direct financial incentive to be far more motivated than salaried managers

- a firm with many franchise outlets needs less middle management than one with managed outlets, thereby reducing the overhead costs and improving *vertical communications*

**FRED:** see *Financial Reporting Exposure Draft*

**free enterprise:** circumstances in which firms are allowed to start up and operate free from government involvement or regulation. The term tends to be used with reference to small or medium-sized firms and implies a fiercely competitive market. This might prove inaccurate as unregulated markets can become dominated by *monopolies* or *cartels*.

**free float:** see *float time*

**freehold:** the right to own a piece of land and/or property for evermore. Freeholds can become substantial, long-term *assets* with a strong impact on the *balance sheet*. They can provide the security (*collateral*) that banks want before lending money, or be the basis of raising cash via a *sale-and-leaseback* contract.

**freelance:** a self-employed person who expects to earn a living by providing a service to different clients at irregular intervals. As they are not employed on a permanent basis, freelancers need to work especially hard at keeping their clients satisfied.

**free trade** exists when trade between countries is not restricted in any way by *tariffs*, *quotas*, or other barriers. It is based on the theory of *comparative advantage*, which argues that every country will be better off if it specialises in producing goods at which it is comparatively more efficient. The *World Trade Organisation (WTO)* accepts the notion that more trade benefits everyone, and through successive 'rounds' has sought to reduce trade barriers around the world.

**frequency distribution:** where events occur many times, the values they have on each occasion can be recorded to see the frequency with which each value occurs. Examples might be daily sales of a chocolate bar, or the precise length of a bolt to be used in car production. Distributions can be presented as *histograms* or as line graphs.

**frictional unemployment** occurs in the time delay between losing one job and finding another. By its nature it is temporary, as opposed to *structural unemployment* which is more fundamental and therefore longer term. If a government wished to reduce frictional unemployment it could improve the quality of service in Job Centres, so that the newly unemployed are able to find work more quickly.

**Friedman, Milton** (b. 1912) is an American economist whose views on *monetarism* had a great influence on Conservative governments during the 1980s. His work at Chicago University helped give rise to the 'Chicago School' of economists. Their view of governments' responsibility for poor economic growth due to *interventionist policies* and overtaxing made them recommend a *laissez-faire* approach.

**friendly societies:** non-profit making savings organisations similar to building societies. To encourage their continued use, successive governments have allowed every household to save a limited amount tax free with a friendly society.

**fringe benefits:** any benefit received by employees in addition to their wages or salary. Common fringe benefits are a company pension scheme, a company car, discounts when buying the firm's products and the provision of sports facilities. All add to the cost of employing labour, but are expected to pay for themselves by their contribution to staff loyalty and therefore the reduction of *labour turnover.*

**FRS:** see *Financial Reporting Standards*

**full costing** is an attempt to allocate all costs incurred in an organisation to *cost centres.* The intention is to ensure that all costs are covered and the possibility of losses by underpricing is avoided. *Direct costs* can be relatively easily allocated to an activity or a product. Some direct *overheads* may be easy to allocate but most are indirect overheads and cannot be allocated easily. An example of full costing would be allocating 35 per cent of the overhead cost of rent to the machine shop if the machine shop has 35 per cent of the factory space. A widely used alternative method is *contribution costing.*

**full cost pricing:** another term for *cost-plus pricing*

**full employment** is the level of employment which provides jobs for all those who wish to work apart from those *frictionally unemployed.* It implies that the capital stock of the country is fully utilised. What level of unemployment in the UK now represents full employment is a matter of some debate. Structural change, which includes an increasing rate of technological advance, appears to be creating higher and higher levels of unemployment at each trough in the *trade cycle.*

**full line forcing** is a *restrictive* (trade) *practice* whereby a retailer wanting to buy one brand or product from a supplier is told that unless they stock the full product range they can have nothing. As in-store space is limited, if the retailer accepts this manufacturer's full range it may not be worthwhile to stock any rival products. This is a way in which producers can attempt to achieve monopoly distribution in retail outlets (especially smaller ones). The manufacturers of ice-cream and of batteries have been accused of full line forcing in the past. Retailers wanting to fight against it could make a complaint to the *Office of Fair Trading,* but they would be worried that a powerful manufacturing firm might stop supplying them with the key brands demanded by customers.

**function:** an individual's job role, defined broadly within headings such as marketing, production, personnel or finance. Therefore a business structured by function is organised into departments such as the above. This contrasts with businesses structured by product or by *matrix.*

**functional organisation** is based on a hierarchy in which each department operates separately under the leadership of those at the top of the pyramid. *Coordination* stems from the top, but may be hard to achieve at the lower management layers due to the separation of job functions into the different departments. This form of structure can be contrasted with the more flexible *matrix* organisation.

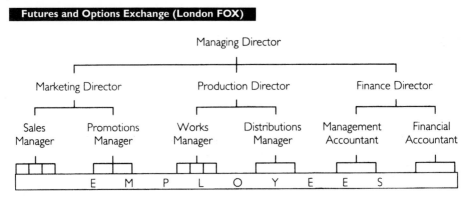

*A functional organisation*

**Futures and Options Exchange (London FOX):** the trading floor in the City of London where dealing takes place in future purchases or options-to-purchase in a wide range of *commodities*.

**futures trading** is when *commodities* or financial assets are bought or sold at some time in the future at an agreed price. In London such trading in financial assets occurs on the floor of LIFFE (*London International Financial Futures Exchange*). Commodities such as wheat, oil, wool, and many other products can also be bought or sold 'forward'. This can be purely speculative, but it can also be vital for a business to protect itself against possible exchange rate or commodity price fluctuations (see *hedging*).

# G

**G7:** see *Group of Seven*

**Galbraith J K** (b. 1908): a Canadian-born economist who popularised the works of J M *Keynes* and contributed to an understanding of the workings of large corporations and of the motives of firms and politicians. His writings were sceptical of *free enterprise*, as in his criticisms of the idea that the free market satisfies people's needs. In his book THE AFFLUENT SOCIETY (4th ed. Deutsch, 1985) he spoke out strongly against the persuasive power of advertising:

> As a society becomes increasingly affluent, wants are increasingly created by the process by which they are satisfied.

Galbraith's account of THE GREAT CRASH 1929 (3rd ed. Penguin, 1988) is one of the most readable insights into that dramatic event.

**Gantt chart:** a horizontal *bar chart* in which the activities needed to complete a project are shown in the right order and at the right time. This is a way of planning to ensure that the project can be completed on time and with maximum efficiency. On the vertical axis are the activities and on the horizontal scale is time. The Gantt chart is a useful visual supplement to a *critical path* network.

**gap** (in the market): an identifiable market opportunity that has not yet been exploited. The term might be used in relation to:

- market segments, such as an age group that has not been catered for
- products, such as a flavour of fruit juice that has not yet been marketed
- distribution, such as a new, *impulse purchase* product that is not yet being distributed to garages, cinemas and other non-standard outlets

**GATT:** see *General Agreement on Tariffs and Trade*

**GDP:** see *gross domestic product*

**gearing** measures the proportion of *capital employed* that is provided by long-term lenders. The gearing ratio is:

$$\text{FORMULA:} \quad \frac{\text{long-term liabilities}}{\text{capital employed}} \times 100$$

If loans represent more than 50 per cent of capital employed, the company is said to be highly geared. Such a company has to pay interest on its borrowing before it can pay dividends to shareholders or reinvest profits in new equipment. Therefore the higher the gearing, the higher the risk. The gearing ratio measures financial risk by use of *balance sheet* figures: the *interest cover* ratio measures this risk by means of *profit and loss account* figures.

**gee whiz graph:** a graph drawn to a scale that exaggerates a trend (to produce the effect: 'gee whiz!'). This is achieved by starting one of the axes (usually the vertical one) at above zero. It is useful to remember that examiners prefer axes to start at zero, in order to prevent the deception implied by the gee whiz graph.

**General Agreement on Tariffs and Trade (GATT)** was established after the Second World War to encourage the growth of international trade by removing or reducing *tariff* and non-tariff barriers. In 1995 GATT was succeeded by the *World Trade Organisation (WTO)*.

**general or nominal ledger:** the books where a small business could keep all its financial records and accounts. As the business grows, this needs to be divided up into:

- a sales ledger (record of debtors)
- a purchases ledger (record of creditors)
- a cash book for recording the receiving and paying of cash and cheques

Sometimes journals are set up to record details which are then transferred to the general ledger periodically. For example, sales are recorded in the sales journal and totals transferred to the general ledger weekly.

**general union:** an organisation founded to represent the collective interests of employees from within any industry and with no specified skills. General unions tend to attract unskilled or semi-skilled workers.

**generic brands** are those that are so totally associated with the product that customers treat the brand name as if it was a product category. Examples include Hoover (vacuum cleaner) and Bacardi (white rum). This could be said to be the ultimate marketing achievement.

**gilt-edged security** is a type of *government security*. It is used by governments to borrow the sums needed to cover their *budget deficits*. Originally such stock certificates were literally edged with gold leaf, hence the name. This is no longer true, but it is the case that a gilt is a totally safe form of investment because no government would refuse to pay up when the gilt matures.

**glass ceiling:** the invisible barrier of discrimination that prevents women or non-whites from getting promoted to the top of organisations. In many businesses and professions, women form the majority of the workforce, yet hold a tiny minority of the senior posts. *Equal opportunities* legislation was supposed to break through the ceiling, but discriminatory attitudes have proved very hard to overcome.

**global brands** are branded products that have been marketed successfully worldwide. Examples include Coca-Cola, McDonald's and Bacardi. Although there may be a degree of tailoring to local tastes (such as more salads at McDonald's located in hotter countries) the key to global brands is standardisation. In other words, a Big Mac should taste the same in Tokyo as in Manchester. As so many global brands are American in origin, some critics worry that different national traditions are being swept aside in a shift towards the American way of life.

**globalisation** of the international economy suggests that because there is an increasing world market in goods and services (especially currency flows), it is becoming difficult for any government to pursue policies outside the worldwide consensus. In such a world, the *transnational* company is king.

**GNP:** see *gross national product*

**goals** are targets that act as a focus for decision-making and effort, and as a yardstick against which success or failure can be measured. The word goals is used interchangeably with *objectives*.

**going concern:** the accounting assumption that unless there is evidence to the contrary, the organisation will continue its usual operations into the foreseeable future. Therefore *assets* can be valued at cost (minus *depreciation*) as their actual market value is considered irrelevant. This assumption can be thought to conflict with the notion of *prudence*, especially in the case of new, small companies.

**going rate:** the prevailing percentage wage rise being received by employees during a *pay round*. Its level is likely to be determined by the rate of price inflation and the degree of demand for labour. If the going rate is 6 per cent, workers will see that level of pay rise as the least they can expect.

**goodwill** arises when a business is sold for more than the *balance sheet* values of its assets. A purchaser is prepared to pay more than this for the business as a *going concern* because it may have an established name and reputation as well as a favourable location. Goodwill is then shown in the purchaser's balance sheet as an *intangible asset*. Goodwill is a technical accounting term which should not be confused with the everyday use of the word.

**go-slow:** a form of *industrial action* in which employees keep working, but at the minimum pace allowable under their terms of employment. This will lose them any bonuses, but will ensure that they receive their basic pay. If conducted at a time of year of high demand, a go-slow could be successful in applying considerable pressure upon an employer.

**government economic objectives** are the goals laid down by the political party in government. It was long thought that all governments pursued a mix of objectives including: steady *economic growth*, low *inflation*, low unemployment and a modest *balance of payments* surplus. There have been periods, however, when the pursuit of low inflation has been the primary economic objective. This has come into conflict with other aspects of policy, such as low unemployment.

**government securities** are sold by governments as a form of borrowing from households or firms. It is a way of making up for a shortfall in money raised through taxation, i.e. a *budget deficit*. The most common forms are *Treasury bills* and *gilt-edged securities*.

**government spending:** see *public spending*

**grant** a government or charitable subsidy of a business investment or activity.

**grapevine:** the network of informal communication contained within every organisation. It will spread rumours that may undermine the public statements of senior management, but only if those statements are incorrect or incomplete. In firms with an *authoritarian leadership style*, the grapevine may be condemned for spreading gossip, whereas a *democratic leader* might see it as a useful supplement to other lines of communication.

**Great Depression:** the term used to describe the period following the Wall Street Crash of 1929. In the years afterwards, unemployment hit 20 per cent in Britain and 33 per cent in America and Germany. The most important lessons that can be learnt from it are:

- the impact of the economy on political life (in Germany, mass unemployment brought Adolf Hitler to power)

- the dangers of allowing the banking system to collapse
- that positive government action to bring about recovery can be successful

**greenfield site:** a site for a new factory that has no history of the manufacture of the product in question. Despite the implication of the countryside, the same term would be used for an urban site. Among the firms that have succeeded on greenfield sites are Nissan UK and Toyota UK; a well-known failure was De Lorean motors in Northern Ireland.

Pros: 
- the site can be chosen on modern not historic criteria
- traditional restrictive labour practices will not hinder productivity

Cons: 
- no pool of local labour with the right skills or temperament
- local infrastructure not geared towards the product

**greenhouse effect:** the theory that global warming is taking place as a consequence of a build up of carbon dioxide preventing heat from the sun leaving the earth's atmosphere. Carbon dioxide is thought to be increasing due to deforestation, industrial pollution and excessive use of petrol-driven cars. Worldwide concern about the greenhouse effect put many industrial companies under pressure to reduce air pollution emissions from *pressure groups* such as Friends of the Earth.

**green pound:** an artificial exchange rate used for calculating payments to farmers out of the *Common Agricultural Policy*. If the green pound is devalued, food prices in British shops are likely to rise.

**grey market:** an unofficial market where buyers and sellers can trade legally (as opposed to the black market where trade is illegal). A grey market can develop when public interest in a new share issue is so high that people want to buy shares before the day official dealings start. More importantly, it is the grey market in goods that limits the effectiveness of price discrimination. When Fisher-Price was selling its 'Activity Centres' at a markedly higher price in Britain than in Germany, Tesco stores started buying grey market supplies from Germany and undercutting the prices charged by their competitors. Fisher-Price was furious and tried to stop this unofficial distribution channel, but had no legal power to do so.

**grievance procedure:** the method by which an employee can raise a serious complaint about his or her treatment at work. This is usually set out in the staff handbook. A common intention is that the grievance should be settled as near to the point of origin as possible.

**gross domestic product (GDP)** is the sum total of the value of a country's output over the course of a year. It differs from *gross national product* because it does not include net income from abroad.

**gross margin** is the percentage of *sales revenue* which is *gross profit*.

FORMULA: $\dfrac{\text{gross profit}}{\text{sales revenue}} \times 100$

**gross misconduct:** a breach of an *employment contract* that is so fundamental as to warrant instant *dismissal*, without entitlement to holiday pay. Offenses considered to be gross misconduct will be set out in the contract of employment and will include: theft, deliberate disregard of safety rules, vandalism, gross insubordination, and breaches of company security.

**gross national product (GNP)** is calculated by adding the value of all the production of a country plus the net income from abroad. Net income from abroad is the income earned on overseas investments less the income earned by foreigners investing in the domestic economy. In most countries, the growth in real GNP per head of population is the main measure of economic growth.

**gross profit** is *sales revenue* minus *cost of sales* in the accounting period under review. Gross profit has not yet had *overheads*, interest and *depreciation* deducted from it and must not, therefore, be confused with *trading profit*. For a more detailed account, see *cost of sales*.

**group bonus scheme:** a performance incentive scheme based on the total *output* (or sales) of a group of workers. There are many different ways of organising such a bonus, but usually it will be based on the amount by which a target level has been exceeded. Compared with bonuses based on an individual's performance, group schemes have advantages and disadvantages:

Pros:
- encourages teamwork and thereby may improve morale
- more suitable when an individual's performance is dependent on others within the group

Cons:
- less direct an incentive, which may reduce its effectiveness
- pressure to achieve what the group expects may result in poor production quality

**group discussion:** a form of *qualitative research* in which a psychologist stimulates discussion among six to eight consumers chosen to represent the *target market*. The aim is partly to probe for the motives behind people's purchasing decisions (consumer psychology) and partly to use the group as a sounding board for new ideas. Usually a qualitative research programme will consist of between four and eight groups. (See *group dynamics*.)

**group dynamics** are the types of behaviour shown in small group situations such as *group discussions*. Among the common behaviour patterns are:

- the group becoming subordinate to the views of a dominant individual
- group members sparking excitement or anger off one another in a manner unlike the everyday routine of individuals' lives

Psychologists are trained to interpret and deal with such behaviour, but managers can sometimes find themselves overwhelmed as a meeting gets out of hand.

**group norms** are the types of behaviour thought acceptable within a workplace. Elton *Mayo*'s researches uncovered that group norms could exert so powerful a hold on workers that neither incentives nor exhortation could overcome them. For example, if bricklayers had come to see 300 bricks as a fair day's work, a new employee capable of 500 bricks might be very unpopular.

**Group of Seven (G7)** is the collective name given to the seven richest nations in the world: Japan, the USA, Germany, France, Canada, Italy and the UK. Because of their economic power they carry considerable political muscle, and consequently their meetings are reported widely.

**groupware** is software that runs across a computer network, coordinating the work of individuals within a team. Regardless of distance, each member's files are constantly and simultaneously updated. Groupware reproduces electronically the effect of putting everyone together in a room. Such a system would be especially useful on a construction project, where every decision by (for example) an architect would affect many others within a project team.

**guesstimate:** an estimate based largely on guesswork or intuition. Although firms want to make decisions on the basis of sound data (such as *market research* findings), there may be occasions when there is no time to collect it. For example, if Galaxy announced a two month promotion offering 20 per cent extra free, Cadbury's would have to decide immediately what effect this might have upon their chocolate sales, and decide whether to match Galaxy's offer. A sales guesstimate would be needed. *Scientific decisions* take time.

**hands-on management:** when senior executives get actively involved in the day-to-day problems of and decisions within the business. This might weaken the motivating power of *delegation*, but only if the senior manager insists on taking decisions that should be taken further down the hierarchy. Given Elton *Mayo*'s work on the *Hawthorne effect*, it is likely that active management involvement should aid motivation, though *Herzberg* would warn against over-supervision. If hands-on management is based on mistrust of the subordinates, and is effectively a form of snooping, the result could only be conflict.

**Handy, Professor Charles**: the author of many business books, notably *Understanding Organisations* and I*nside Organizations* (1990, BBC Books). Formerly an executive with BP Oil, Charles Handy has become a leading theorist about the future of organisations. He forecast in the 1980s the rise in contracted out and flexible work and the decline in the numbers employed securely as core workers.

**harmonisation** (of conditions of service) represents the move to *single status*, in which manual and white-collar workers have the same terms within their *employment contracts*. This does not mean that all are paid the same amount, but ensures that all are treated the same. In the recent past it was common for factory workers to be separated from management by different eating facilities, hours of work, types of payment, and with only managers getting company pensions.

**Hawthorne effect:** the beneficial impact on staff workrate and morale of an active, personal interest being shown by management. The term derives from *Mayo*'s researches into workplace behaviour at a factory at Hawthorne, USA between 1927 and 1932.

Mayo was a follower of F W *Taylor*'s methods and was attempting to measure the impact on productivity of improving the lighting conditions within the factory. He followed Taylor's scientific principles by testing the changes against a control, a section of the factory with unchanged lighting. Although productivity rose where the lighting was improved, Mayo was surprised to find a similar benefit where no physical changes had taken place.

This led him to conduct a series of further experiments which cast serious doubts on Taylor's assumptions about the absolute importance of money in motivation. The phrase 'the Hawthorne effect' remains in use worldwide as an example of the importance of *human relations* in business.

**headhunter:** a recruitment consultant who hunts actively for the right person for a job, instead of waiting for responses to an advertisement. The main benefit of this approach is that the headhunter may contact someone who is ideal for the job, but is not currently looking for work (and would therefore not notice an advertisement). Headhunting is expensive as it is labour intensive, but it is a common way of recruiting senior managers and professionals.

**Health and Safety at Work Act 1974** imposes on employers the duty 'to ensure, so far as is reasonably practicable, the health, safety and welfare at work' of all staff.

'Reasonably practicable' means that it is accepted that the risks of hazard can be weighed against the cost of prevention. The main provisions of the Act are:

- firms must provide all necessary safety equipment and clothing free of charge
- employers must provide a safe working environment
- all firms with five or more employees must have a written safety policy on display
- union-appointed safety representatives have the right to investigate and inspect the workplace and the causes of any accidents

The Act also set up the Health and Safety Commission to decide upon safety policy and the *Health and Safety Executive* to oversee the work of the *factory inspectors*. A major criticism of the Act and especially of government cutbacks since 1974, is that there are too few inspectors to have a meaningful deterrent effect.

**Health and Safety Executive:** a government-financed organisation set up to over-see the implementation of the 1974 *Health and Safety at Work Act*. It employs *factory inspectors* to investigate possible breaches of the Act and to give advice on improving safety practices.

**heavy industry:** a rather loose term denoting the producers of large, heavy prod-ucts usually from large-scale factories. Examples include the production of steel, lorries, cars and bulk chemicals.

**heavy user:** a regular customer who uses large quantities of a product or brand. For example, whereas the average consumer of Bounty bars may buy no more than one a month, the heavy user may buy three a week. It is widely accepted in marketing that, for most products, around 20 per cent of customers consume 80 per cent of sales (this is known as the 80/20 rule). Therefore a great deal of *market research* effort goes into identifying who the heavy users are, what they like about the product, and how best to reach them through advertising.

**hedging** (foreign currency) is a way of covering exchange rate fluctuations so that losses and risks are minimised.

---

Worked example: hedging operations

At a time when £1 = $2, an importer agrees to buy a product from the USA for $20 000. It will be delivered and paid for in six months' time. If the pound falls during that time to £1 : $1, the firm would now have to pay £20 000 for it instead of £10 000. So to cover itself, the importer should have bought dollars on the 'forward' mar-ket at £1 : $2. If the exchange rate did not move in that time the hedging fee would be lost. In the circumstances, though, the halving of the pound's value would cause no problems because the hedging would ensure that the dollars will be sup-plied at £1 = $2. This would save £10 000, minus the hedging fee.

---

In practice, foreign exchange movements are nowhere near as extreme, but the spot and *futures* markets are important in helping traders to conduct international busi-ness without having to guess what the exchange rate will be in six months' time.

**Herzberg, F** (b. 1923): an American psychologist whose researches in the 1950s led him to develop the *two-factor theory* of job satisfaction. Although many have criticised him for drawing conclusions about workers as a whole from a sample drawn solely from accountants and engineers, Herzberg's theory has proved very robust. Many firms have put his methods into practice, often with considerable success. Part of the reason for the interest shown by business leaders was because Herzberg offered a practical approach to improving motivation through *job enrichment*. This, he stressed, should not be confused with *job rotation*.

Herzberg's stress on redesigning workplaces and work systems to provide more ful-filling jobs was a major move away from the ideas of Ford and *Taylor*. Despite this, Herzberg could be criticised for making too little of the role of groups and teams at work. His focus on the job made him lose sight of the motivational power of team spirit.

**hierarchy of needs:** Abraham *Maslow*'s theory that all humans have the same type of need which can be classified into a single hierarchy. They span from the lower order, physical needs through social needs towards the higher order, psychological needs. Maslow believed that each need has to be fulfilled totally before the next becomes important. By the time all needs have been catered for, the individual will be motivated by self-actualisation, in other words psychological growth and develop-ment. Yet if the threat of *redundancy* occurs, the individual's focus will return to the basic needs, such as security.

Maslow's five categories of need:

1  Physical, the requirement to eat and sleep (and therefore earn an income).
2  Safety, the need for security.
3  Social, the desire for friendship, love and a sense of belonging.

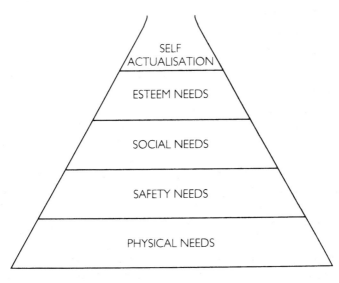

*Maslow's hierarchy of needs*

4 Esteem, to have respect from others and, more importantly, self-respect.

5 Self-actualisation, to fulfil one's potential through actions and achievements. Note that Maslow did not believe that this could be satisfied fully; in other words, people will always strive to develop further and achieve more. Hence the funnel at the top of the pyramid diagram above.

**hierarchy of objectives:** a diagram to show the logical order in which a firm should determine its *objectives*. First the *aims* must be agreed, then the medium to long-term objectives, and finally the *strategies* for achieving the objectives. Although these elements can be determined in advance at board level, changing daily circumstances may force short-term, tactical objectives to be set that might not be fully in harmony with the overall aims. (See *corporate objectives*.)

**Higher National Diploma (HND):** a practically based higher education qualification that is usually tackled by those who do not have high enough grades for a degree course. Despite this, some employers consider an HND in Business Studies a better preparation for business life than a degree, due to its focus on project work, problem-solving and work experience.

**higher order needs:** see *hierarchy of needs*

**Highland Park plant:** the huge factory in Detroit (USA) at which Ford achieved the breakthrough to moving, conveyor-belt assembly of cars in 1913. This heralded the start of the *mass production* era and therefore the beginning of the end for many craft manufacturing skills. Just prior to the switch to the mass production system, it had taken 750 minutes to assemble each car. By the spring of 1914 it took only 93 minutes, an 88 per cent reduction.

**hire purchase:** a system of obtaining *credit* for the purchase of an *asset* whereby the purchaser puts down a proportion of the price as a deposit and pays the balance in equal installments over an agreed repayment period. The purchaser becomes owner when the last instalment is paid. The hire purchaser pays a fixed monthly sum that is likely to amount to a far higher total than for outright purchase. In the short term, however, the firm may be pleased to obtain a vital asset without a large outflow of cash.

**histogram:** a diagrammatic way of representing a *frequency distribution* in which the area of the block is proportional to the value of the variable measured. A histogram differs from a *bar chart* because the width of the bars can vary as well as the height.

**historic cost** is the original purchase price paid for an *asset*. The principle of valuing assets at their historic cost lies at the heart of standard accounting. *Balance sheets* value *fixed assets*, for example, at historic cost (minus *depreciation*).

**holding company** is one which holds a majority of the shares of other companies and thus controls them without direct involvement in their running. The degree of influence can vary depending on the management style of the holding company (see *Hansonisation*). It can operate as little more than an industrial bank, with the head office staff simply deciding on the most profitable uses of the company's funds.

**homeworking:** earning an income from work undertaken at home. Traditionally, homeworkers have completed labour-intensive, very low paid jobs such as hand-sewing or packing. Modern technology offers the possibility that more professional employees could work from home, armed with communication links such as *electronic mail, fax* and telephone.

**homogeneous products** are absolutely identical. Since most businesses spend a great deal of time and money trying to persuade consumers that their products are different from others, this might seem a strange idea. However, its use is in theoretical economics, which establishes a model of a perfectly competitive market. In this model products are assumed to be homogeneous in order to predict behaviour.

**horizontal communications** represent the passage of information between people on the same hierarchical level within an organisation, e.g. between section heads.

**horizontal integration** occurs where a firm takes over or merges with another firm at the same stage of production. The production process starts with raw materials being processed, then moves through manufacture and assembly to be sold to wholesalers and then retailers. Horizontal integration can occur at any of these stages. The merger of two breweries would be an example of horizontal integration, and would have the following advantages and disadvantages:

Pros: • increases market power over the next or the previous link in the process
 • enables greater *economies of scale* to occur

Cons: • may restrict customer choice
 • unequal market influence may increase costs overall by the exercise of monopoly power, and may thus attract the attention of the *Monopolies and Mergers Commission*

**horizontal promotion:** the Japanese idea that as those at the top of an organisation need to have a thorough grounding in every aspect of the business, to be invited to transfer to a different department represents an effective promotion. Improved status, salary and career prospects go hand in hand with a new challenge, even though the individual has not moved up to a higher rung on the hierarchical ladder.

Horizontal promotion is a key element in overcoming the main weakness of a flat hierarchy (one with a wide *span of control* and few *layers of hierarchy*). Namely that few layers of hierarchy mean few opportunities for vertical promotion. This could be seen as a demotivator for ambitious employees. Therefore seeing a sideways move as promotion is important psychologically.

**host country:** one which receives foreign investment from a *multinational company*. This provides advantages and disadvantages to the host:

Pros: • provides income and employment
 • helps the *balance of payments* initially by providing a demand for the host country's currency, and then by providing exports of finished goods
 • may provide new training and skills to the workforce
 • may encourage the growth of other domestic industries, and industrialisation in general

Cons: • agriculture may be changed from being based on long-term self-sufficiency to reliance on cash crops; these crops may receive high prices in the short term, but end up ruining the soil
 • once income and wage levels have been raised, the multinational may move on to the next source of cheap labour and/or raw materials

- the multinational may not adhere to the highest standards of safety and responsibility that it would be required to follow in other, more developed countries

**hostile take-over bid:** this is where a *predator* company wishes to acquire a target company and its actions are unwelcome. The predator offers a price for the shares of the target and, as soon as it has acquired a majority, it has management control. It can vote in its own directors at a general meeting. According to the take-over rules, the predator has a time-limit to persuade shareholders to accept the offer and during this period the two companies may publish their campaigns. By contrast, some companies agree terms and carry out an agreed *merger*.

**hot money** is used to describe speculative flows on foreign exchange markets. Whilst foreign exchange is necessary for trade to occur, it is also possible to hold cash in order to gamble on changes in rates. For instance, in September 1992 the pound left the *ERM* and was devalued by around 15 per cent against other European currencies. The immediate cause was largely because of flows of hot money. The speculative selling of pounds forced more and more pounds on to the market, thus increasing supply and forcing its value down. Although the *Bank of England* stepped in to buy as many pounds as it could (increasing demand), it simply could not match the hot money flows. In the end the speculators 'won' in the way described below:

---

Worked example: hot money speculation

> Current exchange rate: £1 : 10DM. A person holds £1 which she sells for 10 Marks in the hope and expectation that the exchange rate will fall. This does in fact occur, and the exchange rate changes to £1 : 8DM. So, with her 10 Marks she can now buy her original £1 back for 8 Marks, and with the remaining 2 Marks she can make 25p profit.

---

**human capital** is the degree of skill and training embodied in labour as a *factor of production*. As in financial capital, its value can be increased by investment, in this case in education. The education might be paid for by the state or privately, but it explains in part why a graduate might reasonably expect to earn more than someone with no qualifications. Although that is not always the case for individuals – pop stars with no qualifications earn more than almost every graduate – it is generally true of countries.

**human relations** is the aspect of management that Elton *Mayo*'s work highlighted. The *Human Relations School* promoted the benefits to morale and productivity of a *paternalistic* style of management in which the worker was to be seen more as a member of the family than as a mere *factor of production*. Among the policy outcomes were:

- a move to more social facilities surrounding work (sports teams, social clubs etc.)
- the appointment of personnel or welfare officers whose function was to look after the well-being of the labour force
- a move to greater communication and *consultation* between the management and the factory floor

**Human Relations School:** those managers and writers who supported *Mayo*'s views on the importance of *human relations* in the workplace. (See *Hawthorne effect.*)

**human resource management (HRM):** the responsibility of using and developing the organisation's personnel in the most productive way. This appears to be little more than restating the role of the personnel department, but HRM has some distinctive features:

- its spur has been the success of the Japanese at managing people, even though their firms rarely have personnel departments; so HRM represents a rethink by personnel professionals
- it places greater emphasis on development through training and career planning
- it has the potential to persuade <u>all</u> managers that the development of their human resources (subordinates) is <u>their</u> job, not the personnel department's

**human resourcing:** the elements involved in providing and managing staff with the right skills and attitudes to achieve the organisation's goals. See *human resource management.*

**hunch:** the intuition that can lead a decision-maker to go against the obvious or statistically proven route. This may prove a stroke of genius or a source of great embarrassment. In support of hunches is the statement by John Sculley, Chief Executive of Apple Computers:

> No great marketing decisions have ever been made on quantitive data. (D Rowan, THE INTUITIVE MANAGER, Little, Brown & Company, 1989)

**hygiene factors:** elements of working life that have the potential to cause dissatisfaction, such as salary, working conditions, status and over-supervision. (See *Herzberg.*)

**hyperinflation** is used to describe a situation where the value of money decreases so fast that it loses some, or all of its functions. Consequently, people resort to *barter* or to the use of some other commodity which has intrinsic value or to the use of a foreign currency. The exact level of inflation which turns into hyperinflation is not precise since it will be determined by psychological factors. The best known example of hyperinflation occurred in Germany in the 1920s, but in more recent times many South American countries have suffered from it, and Russia in 1992/3 began to experience its horrors. Hyperinflation tends to lead to the breakdown of societies because it leads to a major redistribution of income in favour of those with debts, and against those on fixed incomes (such as pensioners or savers).

**hypothesis:** a theory about how to explain or solve a problem. A manager would want to test a hypothesis by a numerate technique such as *quantitative research.*

**ICC:** see *Inter-Company Comparison*

**idle time** is the amount of time a work station is not operational. A work station can be a machine waiting to be used in a production process or a booking clerk in a railway station. The concept is most often met in *queuing theory* or in *simulation* exercises.

Causes:
- machinery breakdowns, perhaps due to old age or poor maintenance
- the time taken to reset machines when a different batch is to be produced

Effects:
- a high rate of idle time reduces labour productivity and therefore adds to wage costs per unit
- if the workforce is being paid *piece-rate* or a productivity bonus, idle time hits wage packets and therefore lowers morale

**IIP:** see *Investors in People*

**import:** the purchase of a product or service from overseas.

**import controls** are *tariffs* or *quotas* designed to limit the number of overseas goods entering the domestic market. In extreme cases, some goods are prevented from entering at all, which is called an *embargo*. Other forms of import controls are collectively called *non-tariff barriers*, which discriminate against imported goods in a more subtle way. One example of such a non-tariff barrier would be requiring excessive paperwork for imports, resulting in delays at the frontier.

**import penetration:** a measurement of the share of the home market taken by importers. Twenty-five per cent penetration means, therefore, that imports account for a quarter of sales within a market.

**import tariff:** a tax levied on an imported item at the point of entry to the country.

**improvement notice:** an order issued by a *factory inspector* that compels a firm to remove a hazard or improve a safety system within 21 days.

**impulse purchase:** an unplanned decision to buy a product or brand. Certain types of product are especially prone to impulse purchase, such as confectionery and snacks. This makes it worthwhile for retailers to display the items prominently (such as by the checkout) as impulse purchase products generate extra takings. If a manufacturer knows that its products are mainly bought on impulse it is likely to:
- increase spending on packaging design and display materials at the point of sale
- offer high retail profit margins in order to maximise distribution and give the shops a strong incentive to display the product in an eye-catching position

**incentives:** financial or equivalent rewards (such as free holidays) to stimulate action from staff or customers.

**income and expenditure account:** the equivalent of a *profit and loss account* that records the year's trading for a non-profit-making organisation such as a charity or club.

**income elasticity** measures the way in which demand changes when consumers' real incomes change.

FORMULA: $\dfrac{\text{percentage change in demand}}{\text{percentage change in real incomes}}$ = income elasticity

There are two main elements in a product's income elasticity:

1 Is the income elasticity a positive or negative figure? Most goods have positive income elasticity, meaning that people buy more of them when they are better off. The term '*normal goods*' is given to these.

Products with negative income elasticity include sausages, bread and supermarket own label goods. When consumers feel better off they switch from these cheaper foods to more luxurious ones. For example, if the demand for sausages fell by 2 per cent in a year when real incomes rose 5 per cent, the income elasticity of sausages would be –2% /+5% = –0.4. Products such as this, with negative income elasticity, are known as '*inferior goods*'.

2 What is the degree of elasticity? As with price elasticity, a value of more than one indicates an elastic demand, while less than one means inelastic demand. Luxury items will tend to be highly income elastic: in other words quite a small drop in the living standards of consumers can lead to a substantial fall in demand for expensive sports cars, perfumes or whiskies. Necessities such as toothpaste and detergents are income inelastic.

---

Worked example: Market research reveals that following an increase in disposable income of 10 per cent, the demand for aftershave rises by 22 per cent. What is the income elasticity of demand for aftershave?

Formula:

Income elasticity of demand $= \dfrac{\text{percentage change in demand}}{\text{percentage change in income}}$

so in this example: $\dfrac{22\%}{10\%} = +2.2$

---

**incomes policy** is a way of controlling inflation by restricting increases in wages and salaries. This can be attempted in a number of ways, including:

1 Setting legal limits: the problem with this approach is that they can be avoided by giving employees 'perks' such as cars or expense accounts.
2 Restricting pay where the government has direct control, namely in the public sector; this often results in distortions within the labour market because pay differentials are altered, and stores up potential unrest when the pay freeze comes off.
3 By exhortation: unfortunately this rarely works either because incomes policies are often attempting to cut real wages, so they may be resisted quite fiercely by staff.

**income tax** is paid as a proportion of an individual's gross pay after certain allowances have been deducted. It is levied in a series of steps designed to ensure that no one can become worse off by moving into a higher tax band. As the *Chancellor of* *the Exchequer* changes the tax rates every year it is impossible to provide up-to-date information, so the following example assumes income tax bands set as follows:

| Income between | Tax rate % |
|---|---|
| £0 and £4 500 | 0 |
| £4 501 and £7 000 | 20 |
| £7 001 and £25 000 | 25 |
| £25 001 and above | 40 |

Worked example: income tax

**1** Toby earns £12 000 per year

| Income between | Tax % | Tax due |
|---|---|---|
| £0 and £4 500 | 0 | £0 |
| £4 501 and £7 000 | 20 | £500 |
| £7 001 and £25 000 | 25 | £1250 |
| Total | | £1750 |
| As a percentage of earnings | | 14.6% |

**2** Jill earns £30 000 per year

| Income between | Tax % | Tax due |
|---|---|---|
| £0 and £4 500 | 0 | £0 |
| £4 501 and £7 000 | 20 | £500 |
| £7 001 and £25 000 | 25 | £4500 |
| £25 001 and above | 40 | £2000 |
| Total | | £7000 |
| As a percentage of earnings | | 23.3% |

Although all taxes are undesirable from the viewpoint of those who must pay them, income tax has particular strengths and weaknesses compared with other ways of raising government revenue. Many people approve of its progressive nature; that is, it takes an increasing share of income from higher income earners (thereby reducing the burden on the less well off). Many of the better off feel that this is unfair however. In the above example, Jill is earning two and a half times more than Toby, yet paying four times the tax bill. A further argument against income tax is that it acts as a disincentive to work hard or seek promotion (because the government takes 25 or 40 per cent of every extra pound earned). Research has never been able to prove this theory, however.

**incompatible equipment:** hardware or software which cannot work effectively with equipment already owned by the organisation. This will reduce efficiency, especially of communications. It may also force the replacement of all the older equipment, at great expense.

**incorporation:** the process of becoming a corporate body, that is establishing a business as a separate legal entity. Before incorporation the owners of the business are liable personally for all of its debts. Becoming incorporated requires these steps:

- preparing a *memorandum of association*
- preparing *articles of association*
- sending these to the *Registrar of Companies* and applying for a certificate of incorporation

**Independent Broadcasting Authority (IBA):** the government-funded body that regulated independent television and radio until being split, in 1993, into the Radio Authority and the Independent Television Commission. It was responsible for the quality and social acceptability of the programmes. The scripts for television commercials needed approval from the IBA before they could be screened. Now the ITC checks that the content does not break the letter or the spirit of the *Code of Advertising Practice*.

**indexing:** see *index-linked*

**index-linked** means linking a value specifically to the changes in the *retail prices index* (RPI) (the standard measure of *inflation* in the UK). Thus pensions or some forms of savings may be indexed or index-linked so that their real value is preserved. The index linking of wages to the cost of living was tried in many European countries in the 1970s and 1980s. It was seen as a way of preventing trade unions from adding to *cost-push inflation* by negotiating pay rises above the current rate of inflation. In practice what happened was that if inflation rose by 1 per cent in a month, wages would follow automatically. This would leave real incomes unchanged, but would push industry's costs up so that they had to charge more for their goods. The price increases triggered another wage rise and so on. The result was that far from decreasing the rate of inflation, index-linking tended to perpetuate it.

**index numbers** are a convenient way of showing change in a set of data over time, called *time-series analysis*. Let us say a company had 28 000 employees in 1993, 33 600 in 1994 and 39 200 in 1995. If we make 1993 the base year and let the value for 1993 be equal to 100, then the other values are set relative to this. Therefore, in 1994 the index would be 120 (33 600/28 000 × 100) and in 1995 it would be 140. The index series tells us quickly that in 1994 employment rose by 20 per cent compared with 1993 and in 1995 by 40 per cent compared with 1993. As the table shows, the benefit of indexing is that it makes trends understandable at a glance.

|      | Staff<br>total | Staff<br>index (1993 = 100) |
|------|-------|------|
| 1993 | 28 000 | 100 |
| 1994 | 33 600 | 120 |
| 1995 | 39 200 | 140 |

**indirect cost:** a cost not directly attributable to a product line or a *cost centre*. It is probably, but not necessarily, a *fixed cost*. An example might be general maintenance charges in a factory. Under *full* or *absorption costing*, indirect costs are allocated in full to cost centres.

**indirect labour:** those employees such as office and cleaning staff who are not involved directly in the process of production or customer service.

**indirect sales** are sales through intermediaries, such as wholesalers, agents, distributors and retailers. In other words the producer has no direct communication with the consumer. *Direct sales* include door-to-door selling, telesales and direct response TV, radio or press campaigns.

**indirect taxation** is tax paid on goods and services, as opposed to *direct taxation* which is paid on income and profits. Examples of indirect taxation include *VAT* and *excise duty*. Indirect taxes are usually regressive, that is to say they take a higher proportion of a poor person's income than a rich person's. Since 1979, the UK has shifted the burden of taxation away from direct taxation to indirect, on the grounds that direct taxes are a disincentive to working harder or longer.

**individual bargaining** occurs when a firm negotiates with each employee in turn over salary levels and terms of employment. This takes place either when there is no *trade union* to undertake *collective bargaining*, or when individuals believe they can do better than the generally negotiated terms.

**indivisibility** is the machine utilisation problem that some equipment may be built to a large scale and not be divisible into smaller units. If all a firm needs is 600 units a week, but the smallest machine produces 1 500, it will have to accept operating permanently at only 40 per cent of capacity. This will push up *fixed costs per unit* and put a small producer at a considerable cost disadvantage.

**induction** is an introductory training programme designed to familiarise new recruits with the layout, health and safety, and security systems within the firm. The new employees might also be introduced to key personnel.

**industrial action:** measures taken by the workforce that will halt or slow output, in order to put pressure on management during an *industrial dispute*. Types of industrial action include: strike, *work-to-rule*, *overtime ban*, and *go-slow*.

**industrial advertising:** promoting products to industrial customers such as the owners of heavy lorry fleets, or the buyers of components such as gearboxes. As the target markets tend to be small, *direct mail* is often used, though so too are advertisements in trade or industrial magazines such as THE ENGINEER.

**industrial democracy** means the attempt to provide a workforce with channels through which the decision-making powers of the organisation can be influenced. *Trade unions* tend to be sceptical of the motives behind management initiatives in this area, suspecting that either the intention is to undermine the role of the union, or that the channels provided will only give a facade of democracy. Nevertheless, when used in the right spirit, the following forms of industrial democracy can be very successful:

- *worker director*, i.e. a board director elected to the board from and by the factory floor
- *works council*, a regular meeting point between management and unions
- *workers' cooperative*, i.e. the firm's workers owning a majority of the shares, thereby giving them a great interest in its success or failure

**industrial dispute:** a disagreement between management and the *trade union* representatives of the workforce that is serious enough for *industrial action* to be considered. The dispute might be resolved by successful *conciliation* or *arbitration*. Otherwise the union will consider balloting its members on whether to take industrial action.

**industrial espionage** means using the semi-legal or even illegal techniques of spies to gain information about a competitor or customer. Although this sounds far-fetched, there have been several past cases where major firms have used private detectives in this way. What this demonstrates is the enormous importance placed on information. Just as in a war, finding out the enemy's battle plans is invaluable, so in a *take-over* battle, businesses have gone to extraordinary lengths to find out their rival's next move.

**industrial inertia** is used to describe the situation when a firm or an industry stays in its original location after the reasons for it being there in the first place have disappeared. Reasons for industrial inertia include:

- the costs of upheaval may be too great to justify a move
- there may be external *economies of scale* which justify it staying where it is, such as local colleges which specialise in training the precise skills needed in the industry
- there may be marketing advantages which derive from a traditional location, such as Sheffield steel or Scotch whisky

(See also *industrial location*.)

**industrial location** is the decision taken on the geographical placing of firms and industries. The location of *heavy industry* was often based on the notion of '*bulk increasing*' or '*bulk decreasing*' *goods*. This meant that if the industrial process gained weight it would be located as near to the consumer as possible, whereas if it lost weight in the process it would be placed as near to the raw material source as possible. The soft drinks industry gains weight by adding water and so, for instance, Coca-Cola was originally sold to retailers in the form of a syrup to which soda was added at the point of sale. Even when Coke was sold in bottles, the syrup was sent to local bottling plants so that the relatively heavy product did not need to be transported very far. On the other hand, the steel industry is a considerable weight loser, and so it is located as close to its main raw materials – coal, iron ore and limestone – as possible. Today the bulk increasing/bulk reducing theory applies less because transport costs are a smaller proportion of total costs than they were. Communication links are better and the growth of the service sector has inevitably spread locations towards the consumer.

In recent years, it has been argued that profit-maximising behaviour is not always followed by some managers who locate in an area which is pleasant enough to suit their employees or themselves. Often, firms start up in a location close to the proprietor's home. This site may be clung to for many years after it has ceased to be economic to stay there (see *industrial inertia*). Also governments have affected some location decisions by offering *grants* and other incentives (see *regional policy*). This has affected the decisions of *multinationals* who are able to locate in whichever country minimises their costs.

**industrial marketing**: offering the right product at the right price at the right place and at the right time to sell profitably to business customers. In other words selling goods and services that are not aimed directly at consumers. Industrial marketing is used for:

- selling finished goods such as airplanes, lorries or office furniture
- selling raw materials or components such as steel or plastic computer casings
- selling services to businesses, such as waste disposal or legal and auditing services

In any of the above, industrial marketing is likely to imply a finely targeted approach – homing in on the few people in companies who will be involved in buying a product or service from outside. So whereas consumer marketing tends to aim at mass markets, industrial marketing is more focused.

**industrial policy** can be defined narrowly as the attempt by governments to coordinate production by prioritising particular sectors, or by investing directly in business enterprise. This was attempted by the Labour governments of the 1960s and 1970s, but with little success. A broader interpretation of industrial policy would include making fiscal, monetary and foreign currency decisions on the basis of business needs. This might include higher government spending on transport and communication *infrastructure*, and keeping the pound at a competitive level on the foreign exchange markets.

**industrial relations:** the atmosphere prevailing between a management and its workforce representatives, the *trade unions*. Anything that damages the relationship between the two sides might destroy the element of trust that is the key to good industrial relations.

**Industrial Society:** an organisation set up to promote good labour practices and good *industrial relations* in Britain. Its main role has been to educate managers and unions by spreading case histories about successes in *motivation*, cooperation or quality management.

**industrial tribunal:** an informal courtroom where legal disputes over *unfair dismissal* or discrimination can be settled. Each tribunal comprises three members, a legally trained chairperson plus one employer and one employee representative. The worker with the complaint against the employer can present his or her own case at little or no cost, but may be put at a disadvantage if the employer has hired a top lawyer. Industrial tribunals were established in 1964 and remain the place where most workplace legal disputes are settled.

**industrial union:** an organisation founded to look after the collective interests of all types of employee within a specific industry, e.g. the National Union of Mineworkers (NUM). Whereas most unions represent workers with a particular type of skill from many different industries (e.g. electricians), an industrial union would have clerical, skilled and unskilled members, all working in the same industry.

**inelastic demand** is where for a given percentage change in price there is a proportionately lower change in demand. It is the situation of a product that has low price sensitivity because consumers need it or think they need it. Examples of goods with inelastic demand are necessities like fuel and heavily branded items such as Levi's. If the price of Levi's rises by 10 per cent then demand might only fall by 5 per cent. In this case, the numerical value of its price elasticity would be: $5\% \div 10\% = 0.5$.

Any good having inelastic demand would have a lower number at the top (the numerator) than at the bottom (the denominator), and therefore the final value will always be less than one, but greater than zero. As with all elasticity of demand measures, it is conventional to ignore the minus sign, which should of course be a part of the equation since as one factor goes up (+), the other must go down (−), and vice versa.

**infant industries** are those just starting which are seen as needing protection from overseas competition. The argument is based on the notion that the industry will only be competitive once it has achieved *economies of scale* and therefore it needs protection until that has been achieved. This is particularly relevant to developing countries whose heavy industry is often particularly vulnerable, but also vital to increase incomes.

**inferior good:** a product for which demand rises when real incomes fall. This happens because the item is bought as a cheap substitute for a product thought more desirable. Examples include supermarket *own-label* brands, to which people turn when trying to economise. Inferior goods come into their own during *recessions*, when falling standards of living force consumers to switch to more economical products. A manufacturer that produces a range of products, half of which are inferior goods, would be in an excellent position to cope with the economic *trade cycle.*

**inflation** is a sustained rise in the average prices of goods within an economy. It is also useful to understand it as a fall in the purchasing power of money, since it is usual for wages to move ahead at least as fast as the price level. It can be divided into two types: *cost-push* and *demand-pull,* to distinguish between prices being pushed up by rising costs or being pulled up because demand has outstripped supply. In practice, the two very quickly become indistinguishable. As prices rise for whatever reason, people negotiate wage increases to maintain their standard of living, anticipating future levels of inflation and thereby helping those levels to come about. (See *inflationary expectations* and *inflationary spiral.*) Monetarists argue that inflation is brought about by an unnecessary increase in the money supply in excess of the production of goods and services available in the economy. If inflation reaches very high levels it is known as *hyperinflation.*

Inflation can have positive and negative effects on firms:

Pros:
- for firms with heavy borrowings, inflation reduces the real value of the sum outstanding, making it easier to repay the loan at the end of its life. For example, if a firm borrowed £4m. 10 years ago, and inflation since then had doubled the price level, the loan would be much easier to repay from the firm's doubled level of income
- small firms can benefit from consumers' increased price sensitivity, since theirs are usually the more *price elastic* products

Cons:
- the producers of major brands suffer as the regularity of price increases in the shops makes consumers focus far more on the price of what they buy. *Brand-loyal* customers start to look at prices instead of just picking their favourite from the shelf. This increased price sensitivity leads to brand switching towards the more competitively priced items, thereby reducing the *value added* by brand names. The owners of the brands must either cut their price premiums, or greatly increase their advertising expenditure in order to restore their value added
- just as consumers focus more upon prices, so workers become far more concerned about their wage levels, for unless they can obtain a pay rise at least as high as the level of inflation, their *real income* will fall. Therefore *industrial relations* can worsen sharply in inflationary times, with workers pushing their union representatives to be far more forceful about pay increases

**inflation accounting** is the attempt to eliminate the distorting effects of price rises from the underlying financial position of a firm. The most common method is *cur-*

*rent cost accounting,* which values assets and profits on the basis of current replacement cost instead of *historic cost.* The complexities of this procedure have prevented it from being adopted widely by the accounting profession. The most useful way of accounting for inflation on *profit and loss accounts* is the *LIFO* method of stock identification.

**inflationary expectations** are the views of the general public as to what will happen to the rate of *inflation* in the future. Usually, people anticipate that a period of rising inflation will continue into the future. For example, if the rate of inflation has risen from 4 per cent a year ago to 7 per cent today, people are likely to expect inflation to be 10 per cent by the same time next year. Therefore they might negotiate a pay rise of 10 per cent now in anticipation of that future level. By so doing, they add to costs and help to bring about that new level, so that their prophesy becomes self-fulfilling. (See *inflationary spiral.*)

**inflationary spiral:** the way in which price rises in one sector of the economy cause price increases in another, so that they spiral ever upwards. If the government allows too much *credit,* so that the *demand* for goods and services exceeds *supply,* prices rise and people will react by negotiating pay increases. One person's pay increase becomes another's price increase and so the spiral continues. Governments attempt to break the spiral by depressing demand within the economy or by imposing wage controls, such as the *public sector* pay increase limit of 1.5 per cent in 1993–4.

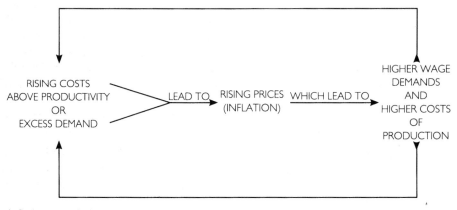

*Inflationary spiral*

**informal communication** means passing information outside the official channels. In a firm run on *authoritarian* lines this might be regarded as a serious breach of company discipline, especially if the message contained embarrassing information (such as details of a dangerous leak at a chemical plant). In a democratically run organisation, however, the management should not be attempting to keep secrets from the workforce, so informal communication should be accepted, even encouraged. After all, *direct communication* is often the quickest and most effective method, so why rely on the *layers of hierarchy* within the official channels?

There is, however, a danger of confusing informal with *oral communication*. This would be wrong because you can communicate written messages to the 'wrong' person just as easily as oral ones.

**informal group:** a group of employees who influence each other's behaviour and attitudes, either for or against the company's best interests. It was a key discovery of Elton *Mayo* that such groups were common, especially in organisations with weak *human relations*. He found that such groups often had unofficial leaders who wielded more effective power than the department head, especially in the setting of *group norms* regarding the work-rate considered acceptable.

**informal leader:** the unofficial head of an *informal group*.

**information overload:** the danger that a senior manager – wanting to be kept fully informed by all his or her subordinates – becomes swamped by the volume of information. As a result the manager may miss key points or fail to respond to urgent requests. Information overload can so reduce effectiveness as to put the employee under great *stress* through his or her inability to cope. The solution is usually to encourage the manager to delegate more wholeheartedly, trusting subordinates to get on with their tasks. This reduces the need for upward communication.

**information superhighway:** the promise of a hugely advanced form of telephone line that would enable consumers to call up video on demand or to use interactive shopping, banking or other services.

**information technology (IT)** includes the use of three electronic technologies: computing, telecommunications and microelectronics, and the way they gather, store, process and distribute information. The use of IT within an organisation tends to reflect the prevailing management style. Supermarket chains tend to concentrate on its potential for collecting vast quantities of data at shop-floor level and then transmitting it for head office analysis. So those at the top of the management hierarchy are pulling information up and then passing decisions back down to local branches. A leadership with a more democratic approach would use computer networks to allow information to flow more freely throughout the staff. This would provide an empowered workforce with the information needed for sound decision-making.

**informative advertising:** paid-for communication that provides messages based on facts rather than images. An extreme example is 'Car Boot Sale, Saturday 2.00, Town Hall'. Less clear-cut are the newspaper advertisements for electrical goods shops that scream persuasively about their sale bargains, but also provide information about prices and product specifications. The key issue about informative advertising is that it is unarguably in the public interest to be provided with useful facts. Information about the prices and product ranges offered by different shops helps competition by encouraging people to shop around. When advertising is under attack from critics of its persuasive powers, the defence is often to point to the benefits of the information it provides.

**infrastructure** is the name given to the road, rail and air links, sewage and telephone systems and other basic utilities which provide a network that benefits business and the community. One of the main advantages which industrialised countries have over less-developed ones is the existence of an efficient infrastructure. Building up such a system is very expensive, requiring a great deal of *capital* to be set aside, capital which poorer countries find difficult to afford. Successive British governments have been criticised for allowing our transport infrastructure to fall behind that of our main European competitors.

**injections** are items adding to the *circular flow of national income* and consist of government expenditure, exports and investment spending. They are 'matched' by *withdrawals* from the circular flow: taxes, imports and savings.

**innovation** means bringing a new idea into being within the market-place (product innovation) or workplace (process innovation).

Product innovation is of major competitive significance because consumers tend to fall into patterns of purchasing behaviour that change little over time. Therefore the *market shares* of the rival products may be quite static. Product innovation can change that, to the considerable advantage of the innovator. The sources of the innovation may be based on new technology, new design or a wholly new *invention*.

Process innovation is also of great significance as it can lead to major cost advantages over competitors. When the British firm Pilkington PLC invented a new way of making glass more cheaply and to a far higher quality standard (the float glass process), it provided not only a direct competitive advantage, but also earned considerable sums in licensing fees from overseas manufacturers.

**inputs** are the elements which go into producing a good or service such as the workforce, raw materials, components and capital.

**in-service training:** courses run to broaden, update or enhance the job knowledge of those at work.

**insider dealing or trading**: profiting personally from the use of information gained from the privilege of working within an organisation. For example, if a manager knew that his or her firm was about to make a *take-over bid* of £1.40 for a firm whose shares are currently £1, a guaranteed overnight profit of 40 per cent is there for the taking. Some say this is a victimless crime, because no one loses money directly. In fact, the manager has taken advantage of the shareholder who unwittingly sold at too low a price (£1). Insider dealing is illegal, but it has proved very hard to convict those caught doing it.

**insolvency** occurs when a firm's external *liabilities* are greater than its *assets*. In practice, this is likely to be revealed through the inability to meet financial obligations, e.g. the inability to raise the necessary cash through ordinary operations, asset sales or borrowing so as to make payments as they fall due. A business which continues to trade when insolvent is operating illegally.

**Insolvency Act 1986:** the legislation that sets out the possible ways of dealing with an insolvent company. The options include:

- a voluntary agreement between the company and its creditors to *recapitalise* the business
- putting the company into *administration* to try to reorganise the company in the best interests of shareholders and creditors
- *winding up* the company if there appears no way of saving it; this might be conducted by the administrator or by the appointment of a *receiver*

**Institute of Directors (IOD):** an employers' *pressure group* that has a stronger representation among small and service businesses than its main rival, the *Confederation of British Industry*. The IOD lobbies the government to try to obtain the economic and legal conditions that most benefit its members.

**Institute of Management (IM):** the professional association of managers that acts as a *pressure group* and as a disseminator of good practice. In 1992 the organisation changed its name from the British Institute of Management.

**institutional investors** are those who manage the portfolios of the *pension funds*, insurance companies and *unit trust* groups which, between them, own a majority of the shares listed on the *Stock Exchange*. The influence of these financial institutions has given rise to a heated and important debate. Critics say that because the portfolio managers' performance is measured every year, they focus too much upon the short-term share price performance of the firms they have invested in. This, in turn, makes them put too much pressure on companies to produce high short-term profits and *dividend* pay-outs. Few doubt that *short-termism* is a major competitive weakness of British industry; institutional investors may be one of its causes.

**intangible assets:** *assets* are intangible when they do not have a physical existence, i.e. cannot be 'touched'. Whereas *plant* and equipment are tangible, *goodwill* (the value of brand names) is intangible. This is the most common example as it frequently arises when business assets are sold. Other intangibles include *patents*, *trademarks* and *copyrights*.

**integration** refers to the bringing together of two or more companies, either by *take-over* or *merger*. (See *vertical integration*, *horizontal integration* and *conglomerate mergers*.)

**intellectual property** derives from the invention or ownership of *patents*, *trade marks*, *logos* or any other *copyright* material. If it can be given a monetary value it can be listed on a firm's *balance sheet* as an *intangible asset*.

**inter-company comparison (ICC):** a service offering (for a fee) a detailed analysis of the average accounting ratios for all the firms within a business sector. A biscuit manufacturer could therefore compare its own *stock turnover* or *gross margins* with the average level of its rivals. This is the most useful approach to *inter-firm comparison*.

**interest cover** measures the number of times a firm could pay its annual interest payments out of *operating* or *net profit*. This provides an assessment of financial risk as interest has to be paid whereas *dividends* may be passed. It is often used with the *gearing* ratio to assess a firm's long-term financial health.

$$\text{FORMULA: } \frac{\text{operating profit}}{\text{interest payments}} = \text{interest cover}$$

If interest cover is around one, it means that the whole of a firm's profit is eaten up by interest payments, leaving none for shareholders' dividends or for reinvestment into the business. A figure below one would be even worse, showing that the size of a firm's interest burden had pushed the firm into a loss-making position. Analysts often suggest that interest cover of around four is appropriate, meaning that profit is four times the level of the interest due on the firm's loans.

**interest holiday:** when banks allow a firm to postpone paying the interest charges on its bank loans. This may happen at the time of business start-up, when the new firm's *cash flow* will be poor or negative. Or, especially in times of *recession*, banks may grant an interest holiday to a firm that is in temporary difficulties. The danger of an interest holiday is that although the borrower does not need to find the money today, the interest payments are being added to the debt total, making it harder to repay when the 'holiday' is over.

**interest rates** represent the cost of borrowing money or, to put it the other way, the return for lending funds or for parting with *liquidity*. Interest rates also measure *opportunity cost* in that individuals give up the interest on their money by spending it on consumer goods rather than saving and receiving interest. Firms considering an investment project do so on the basis of whether the return from the project will exceed the interest paid if they borrow or foregone on own funds (opportunity cost). Interest rates can also be a key weapon of economic policy. If the government pushes interest rates up, consumer and business spending is likely to fall. High interest rates can also be used to support the exchange rate by attracting flows of short-term currency into the country.

**inter-firm comparison** is evaluation of a firm's financial performance by comparing it with one or more firms in the same industry and of a similar size. It is a commonly used method for interpreting financial ratios. For example, it is hard to know how to judge in isolation the knowledge that a firm has a *debtor days* figure of 68. If told that its closest rival's figure is 50, however, it would be clear that there are questions that need to be answered.

Useful though inter-firm comparison can be, however, it has significant limitations:

- different firms are likely to have different accounting methods (one may depreciate assets over three years, another over five years), indeed, some may be *window-dressing* their accounts; in either case the value of the comparison would be undermined
- there is no legal requirement that firms break down their accounts into their separate operating units; a shareholder wanting to compare Cadbury's ratios with those of Mars might not be aware that the Mars accounts comprise not only confectionery but also Pedigree Petfoods (Chum, Whiskas, etc.); this would render the comparison meaningless

**interim accounts** are those produced (and sometimes published) halfway through the financial year.

**intermediaries:** people within the official *communication channels*, through which messages must be passed in order to reach the intended receiver. As the diagram opposite shows, if employee A wants to communicate with manager J, the message has to go via intermediaries C, F and H. This will slow the message down and may lead to it becoming distorted. Even worse, C, F or H may either forget to send it on, or decide it is not worth passing on. Therefore the greater the number of intermediaries, the less effective the communication system. This is a fundamental problem for large firms and can represent a major *diseconomy of scale*.

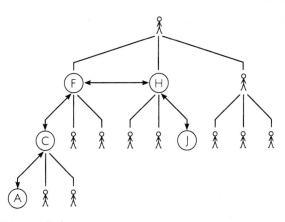

*Communication intermediaries*

**intermediate goods** are purchased by producers and include such products as materials and components (for short-term usage) or machinery and equipment for the long term.

**internal audit:** measuring the effectiveness of a firm's organisation and functions, to help identify internal weaknesses. This may be carried out by the firm's own managers or by external consultants. The results would rarely be published. Just such a procedure might have helped the merchant bank Barings to avoid the reckless trading that bankrupted the firm in 1995.

**internal constraint:** a factor within the company's control that is restricting it from achieving its objectives. The main internal constraints are:

- finance: has the firm the *cash flow*, the borrowing capacity or the profitability to finance its plans?
- marketing: does the firm have the marketing assets required, be it a brand name with a suitable image, or the distribution strength needed for success?
- people: have the staff the skills and experience to achieve what is required? If not, can retraining make up the ground?
- production: does the firm have the spare capacity to produce the volumes required?

(See also *external constraint.*)

**internal costs** are those expenditures that affect a firm's own accounts, such as wages and materials. This ignores the costs that the firm's actions may generate, but that may be incurred by other people or organisations.

**internal customers:** people within the organisation who are supplied with goods or services, for example a shop assistant being delivered stocks from the storeroom. Internal customers should be treated in as efficient and businesslike a way as external ones, for all the workings of a business are part of a chain that leads to the marketplace. Delays or sloppiness at any point can break the links in the chain. This issue becomes of crucial importance within a *just in time* production system, as there are no buffer stocks to mask inefficiency.

**internal financing:** the generation of cash from within the company's resources/accounts. This can be obtained from:

- *retained profits* (plus *depreciation*)
- *working capital* (by cutting stocks or *debtors*)
- the sale of *fixed assets* or under-performing divisions (for example, Grand Metropolitan financed the purchase of Burger King by selling off its hotels division)

**internal growth** arises from within a company, through increasing sales of existing products and/or the launch of new ones. This is likely to be a slower, steadier process than the alternative of buying up other firms (*external growth*). Even internal growth can be risky, however, if it is financed by debt. The ideal is expansion based upon reinvested profit.

**internal markets** can be created in large organisations such as the National Health Service in order to foster a spirit of competition and thereby encourage greater efficiency. The process requires that instead of just handing work over to the department that has always undertaken it, the job be given to whichever department can offer the lowest 'price'. In this way, less efficient departments will lose work and may therefore be forced to lose staff.

**internal rate of return (IRR)** is the discount rate which, when applied to a set of cash flows, makes their *net present value* equal to zero. The IRR can then be compared with the current market rate of interest, which represents the cost of capital. If the IRR is higher, the project is attractive. Alternatively, the company may set its own minimum discount rate as a criterion to test whether projects are viable and compare the IRR with that. The diagram below shows a project with an internal rate of return of 14 per cent. This beats the prevailing rate of interest (9 per cent) but does not meet the firm's own requirement of a 16 per cent minimum. Therefore the project would not be proceeded with (unless other, qualitative factors take precedence).

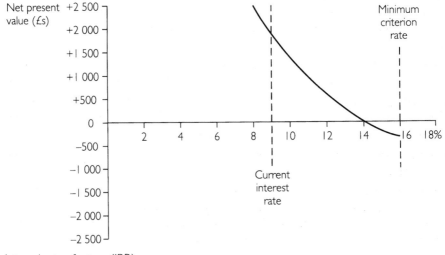

*Internal rate of return (IRR)*

**internal stakeholders:** groups within an organisation whose contribution to its performance can be seen as giving them a stake in its success or failure. Directors, managers and operatives come into this category, as might shareholders or customers in some circumstances. For example, the 'customers' of a football club would see themselves as part of the organisation; the directors of the club might choose to consult these supporters, thereby treating them as internal stakeholders.

**international competitiveness** measures the ability of firms to sell abroad and to compete with imports. It is determined by a number of factors, including price, quality, delivery and *after-sales service*. Such competitiveness will often be affected by the level of the foreign exchange rate, though successful exporting countries can succeed despite high and rising exchange rates. This shows that the price of goods is often not the main determinant of competitiveness. Germany and Japan, for instance, have thrived through well-designed, high-quality products such as BMWs and Sony televisions for which consumers are willing to pay a price premium.

**International Monetary Fund (IMF):** the banker to the world's *central banks*. In other words, if a country requires to borrow money (inevitably it would be foreign currency), it can apply for a loan from the IMF. It is then likely that the IMF would send a team of inspectors to the country who would advise on the conditions to be tied to the loan. Usually these conditions include cuts in *government spending* and cuts in the *money supply*.

**International Standards Organisation (ISO) 9000/9002** is a worldwide quality certification procedure of exact equivalence to *BS 5750*.

**international trade** consists of exports and imports between countries. Through the principle of *comparative advantage*, international trade should cause an improvement in people's living standards.

**Internet:** the worldwide linking of small computers and local area networks (LAN)s.

It is a non-commercial, unregulated network devoted mostly to communication and research with over 20 million users worldwide. For businesses, the internet offers the attractive prospect of providing the opportunity to make information available to customers worldwide. For example, a user can look up many things, from Singapore Airlines flight times and prices, to looking in the jewellery section of the Argos catalogue.

**interpersonal skills** are those used when communicating with and relating to other people. They include counselling, negotiating, consulting and making presentations.

**inter-union disputes** are disagreements between two or more of the *trade unions* representing the workforce at a particular company. This might lead to internal bitterness or even *industrial action*, with the managers no more than onlookers.

**intervention** (in foreign currency markets) is when a *central bank* steps in to buy or sell a currency in order to stabilise its exchange rate.

**interventionist:** an individual who believes that government intervention can help to make markets more efficient, and protect individuals from socially irresponsible business behaviour. Such a person is also likely to promote an active economic policy by government, as opposed to a *laissez-faire* approach.

**interventionist policies** are those pursued by governments that believe it is their duty to exert a strong influence over the running of a country's economy. Such intervention might include 'rescue packages' to help out large firms which have got into financial trouble, *prices and incomes policies*, and laws to provide stronger protection to consumers or workers. Many interventionist policies were derived from *Keynesian* beliefs that the state could help to iron out the extremes of the *trade cycle*. They were much in evidence in the UK from the early 1940s until 1979, when Mrs Thatcher's Conservative Government came to power. The new Prime Minister believed that government should stand back from the detailed working of the economy because markets are the most efficient way to allocate resources. Government's role, she argued, is simply to provide an efficient background against which markets can work. The theory on which this is based is called *supply side* economics, and is derived from the writings of Milton *Friedman*.

Among the most-favoured policies of interventionists are:

**Economic policy**

- *counter-cyclical* action
- prices and incomes control
- active support for new or manufacturing firms
- *regional policy*
- fixed exchange rates
- faith in using *fiscal policy*

**Policy towards business**

- tougher laws and higher fines for polluting and dangerous workplaces
- *wages councils* and industrial training boards
- controls on *dividend* payouts and boardroom pay levels.

**interviewee techniques** are the ways individuals should prepare for, carry out and follow up a job or appraisal interview. The techniques include:

- preparation: background research into the company
  phone to find out the interview procedure (a maths test? A panel interview?)
- execution: listen carefully to questions and instructions
  positive body language
- follow up: ask for a debrief on why you failed (or succeeded) at the interview stage

**interviewer techniques** are the ways executives should prepare for, carry out and follow up a job or appraisal interview. The techniques include:

- preparation: collecting written evidence in advance, such as an application form, a CV and references
- agreeing area of questioning with other panel members
- execution: making the interviewee feel at ease; asking and following up on questions; avoiding bias; closing the interview
- follow up: giving prompt feedback to applicants

**interviewing** is the process of obtaining information through questioning conducted face to face or over the telephone. There are two main business circumstances in which interviewing is used: as part of a job selection process and as part of a *market research* study. In either case, the interview can use *closed questions* to obtain specific (and quantifiable) information, or *open questions* that allow attitudes and ideas to emerge.

**intra-firm comparison** evaluates performance within the firm, often by using financial ratios. There are two methods of conducting this comparison: over time and between departments.

Comparisons over time give managers, shareholders and creditors an impression of the firm's progress. If a firm's *acid test ratio* this year is 0.6, it would be very reassuring to hear that last year it was 0.5 and the previous year 0.4. For internal users of the accounts, comparisons over time give important messages about trends in the firm's performance in relation to its objectives. External users, however, may be handicapped if the firm has changed its accounting practices or indulged in *window-dressing*.

Comparisons between departments are an essential piece of management analysis. Only if the firm knows that department A is obtaining a 30 per cent return on capital, while B generates only 12 per cent, can it decide how best to allocate its *capital expenditure* for coming years.

**intranet:** links between computers within a company to provide the same facilities to browse information and send e-mails that exist worldwide on the *Internet*. The advantage of an internal Internet (intranet) is that information confidential to the company can be published internally without outsiders having access. Glaxo, for example, uses an intranet to keep its research scientists up to date with discoveries made throughout the business.

**intrapreneurs:** employees working within a large organisation who are given the freedom and the resources to behave like *entrepreneurs*, i.e. taking risks and responding quickly to market changes.

**intrinsic motivation** means a drive to succeed that is from within the person. It occurs when individuals are doing a task they find satisfying, challenging or significant in the achievement of a meaningful goal. These are the drives that Professor *Herzberg* called the motivators, and can be contrasted with causes of *extrinsic motivation* such as pay and fringe benefits.

**intrinsic rewards** are the psychological satisfactions that accompany *intrinsic motivation*.

**invention:** the creation of a new product or process. If it represents a scientific or technical first, an invention can be *patented* to ensure that any user of the idea must pay royalties to the inventor. Britain has an impressive record at invention (including penicillin and the hovercraft), but a far poorer record at achieving the crucial next stage: *innovation*, i.e. bringing new ideas to the market-place.

**inventory:** another term for *stock*

**investment** means doing without consumption today in order to use *capital* to generate future returns. To an economist, investment means the purchase of capital equipment such as *plant* and machinery. On the *stock market*, investment means buying shares. In accounting terminology, investment might be in *fixed assets* or *working capital*.

**3i (Investors In Industry)** is an investment trust providing *venture capital* to small to medium-sized firms. It provides a mix of *equity* and *loan capital* to businesses which do not have access to the stock market. Typically these are independent companies with a turnover of between £1 million and £100 million. Most of 3i's clients operate in growth sectors or are in the process of completing *management buy-outs*.

**investment appraisal:** the set of techniques for determining whether a capital investment project should be undertaken or not, or for ranking investment projects in order of desirability. The techniques include methods using *discounted cash flows* such as *net present value* and *internal rate of return*, as well as *average rate of return* and *payback*. The advantage of using appraisal methods is that they avoid reliance on *hunch* or intuition alone. Nevertheless, it should be remembered that all four quantitative techniques are based on a forecast of the *cash flows* from an investment, which is not only subject to many variables but also to *bias* on the part of the forecaster.

**investment trust:** a company formed to invest in the shares of a wide range of other companies. Investment trusts are a long-established way for the small investor to invest in the *stock market* at relatively low risk.

**Investors in People (IIP)** is a government standard for employee consultation and training that establishes a procedure for 'relating training to your business plan'. Devised by the *Department of Employment*, it is administered by the *Training and Enterprise Councils (TECs)*. In order to achieve the standard, assessors from the TECs will ask:

- have goals been set for the business?
- have these been explained to the workers?
- have workers the right skills to meet those targets?

**invisible export:** the sale of a service to an overseas customer. As well as services such as banking, airline travel and insurance, visits by foreign tourists are counted as invisible exports, since they bring income in from overseas.

**invisible hand:** Adam *Smith*'s famous term for how the free market successfully and efficiently brings together willing sellers and willing buyers (through the *price mechanism*). If the product loses popularity, the lack of *demand* will force the price down until the buyers return, so the market-place will invisibly secure a balance between *supply* and demand. Adam Smith believed that people acting entirely out of self-interest unwittingly serve the community as a whole through the operation of this 'invisible hand'. Consequently he saw no need for government intervention in the workings of business.

**invisible import:** the purchase of a service from an overseas supplier.

**invisible trade** consists of imports and exports of services. They include financial services such as banking and insurance, as well as tourism and shipping. Invisibles account for approximately a quarter of world trade. Traditionally, the UK has enjoyed a surplus of invisibles, which has helped to pay for the long-standing deficit on *visible trade*.

**invoice:** another word for a bill. Where goods are sold for cash, an invoice may be given as proof of purchase and title. In the case of a credit sale the invoice should state the terms, e.g. payment within 30 days.

**inward investment** is the *capital* attracted to a region or a country from beyond its boundaries. An example of such investment is a Japanese car manufacturer opening an assembly plant in the UK.

**IRR:** see *internal rate of return*

**ISO 9000:** see *International Standards Organisation*

**issued share capital:** the amount of a firm's *authorised share capital* that has actually been issued (sold) to investors. The *memorandum of association* states the authorised share capital of a company, but not all the shares need be issued at once. Thus, under *shareholders funds* in the *balance sheet*, both the authorised and issued share capital may be listed. Shareholders can see whether further shares can be issued which would raise further funds but also dilute the ownership.

**IT:** see *information technology*

**ITV areas:** the division of the country into 13 marketing regions, each representing a different Independent Television franchise. Granada, for example, covers the North-West, so an advertiser with a strong market position in Lancashire might choose to advertise solely to the Granada TV region. This would cost about one tenth of the total for a national campaign, making TV advertising affordable for a company with a regional but not national presence.

---

### Doing a Business Research Assignment?

**The A–Z Business Studies Coursework Handbook** provides a full, clear account of how to set up, research and write up a business project. See page 330 for details.

---

# J

**Japanese way:** a term summarising the Japanese approach to management. Although there is a danger in over-simplifying (because Toyota and Nissan are as different from each other as Ford is from Rover), the Japanese way comprises three main elements:

- a strategic focus on the long term, in which the goal of a strong market position is more important than short-term profit
- a highly educated, highly trained workforce that is given a key role in improving production methods and quality; the *kaizen* (continuous improvement) group and the *quality circle* are ways of achieving this
- *lean production*, eliminating wastage of materials and time; hence *just in time (JIT)* production and *stock control* and the reduction in product development time that enables Toyota to get a new product idea to the market-place in half the time taken in the West

**Japanisation:** the process by which Western firms are attempting to follow the *Japanese way.*

**jargon:** the terms used among specialist employees that form a language which may mean little to outsiders. This may, indeed, be the motive behind its use.

**JIT:** see *just in time*

**job analysis:** an investigation into the demands of a job to identify the tasks and skills required for high performance (to draw up a *job description*). These can then be related to the abilities demanded from the employee in order to draw up a *job specification.*

**job description:** a detailed statement of the nature of the job, identifying the precise tasks and responsibilities involved. It is likely to form part of the individual's *employment contract.*

**job design:** deciding how the tasks required within a production process should be subdivided or grouped into specific job functions. The key decisions are between:

- high *division of labour* and a *complete unit of work*
- close supervision and self-checking

The role of job design is crucial in *job enrichment* and in *motivation* generally.

**job enlargement:** increasing the number of tasks and possibly responsibilities involved in a job. Examples of job enlargement are *job rotation* and *job enrichment.*

**job enrichment:** the attempt to motivate by giving employees the opportunity to use their abilities. This definition is closely based upon Professor *Herzberg*'s work, as job enrichment was the main policy recommendation that stemmed from his theories. Herzberg suggested that an enriched job should ideally contain:

- a range of tasks and challenges at different ability levels, some of which should be beyond the employee's experience to date

- a *complete unit of work*, in other words a meaningful task rather than a repetitive fragment
- direct *feedback*, by which the employee could know immediately how well he or she was performing

**job evaluation:** comparing the demands of different jobs in order to establish a systematic structure of gradings and pay scales. This will involve identifying the skills, experience and responsibility involved in each job. Given the psychological significance of *status* in the workplace, a job evaluation exercise may cause great disquiet. Those that receive lower gradings than expected may become demotivated.

**job flexibility:** see *flexible working*

**job grading:** another term for *job evaluation*

**job production** means producing a one-off item that has been tailor made to suit a specific customer. Although most of this type of production is undertaken by small firms (because there are no *economies of scale*), shipbuilding may operate on the same job basis. Also very common among smaller firms is a combination between batch and job methods. A baker might bake a dozen celebration fruit cakes. Some are then tailor made into wedding cakes while others are decorated for birthday cakes.

**job roles**: the official responsibilities held by individuals within the workplace, ranging from *director* and *manager* through to *supervisor, operator* and *assistant.* Each of these roles is different, but in general those further up the career ladder:

- have more responsibility for strategic decision making
- should have greater involvement in human resource issues such as recruitment, training, motivation, target setting and discipline
- need a wider range of skills, knowledge and experience.

**job rotation:** widening the activities of a worker by switching him or her around a number of work tasks. For example, a shop worker might spend two hours on the checkout, two filling shelves and another two in the warehouse. This is intended to relieve the tedium of the work, but has the useful side-effect of ensuring that if one person is absent, others can cover the job without difficulty.

**job satisfaction:** the degree to which an employee feels positively towards his or her present job function. Many writers have pointed out that the term is not only hard to define but also to measure. Indeed several believe it to be virtually irrelevant to managers, as it has not been possible to prove that higher job satisfaction results in higher job performance. Despite these reservations, the huge research effort and the management time spent considering the problems and opportunities involved suggests that job satisfaction is of great importance. Most clearly, job dissatisfaction can lead to *absenteeism*, high *labour turnover* and poor *industrial relations*. (See *Herzberg* and *job enrichment*.)

**job security:** the extent to which a job is, or seems to be, guaranteed for the foreseeable future. Although lack of job security would prevent a worker's *lower order needs* from being satisfied, it is possible that the implied threat would stimulate greater effort.

**job sharing:** when employees agree to divide the working week on a job in two, so that they each do half of the one job. This can be very useful for parents with young children, and may provide the employer with the bonus of having two, fresher minds on the one task.

**job specification:** a statement or listing of the characteristics required to do a job successfully. So whereas the *job description* describes the job, the job specification specifies the person. Drawing up a 'job spec' is one of the first stages in the recruitment process. It provides a yardstick against which the job applicants can be measured. Typical elements in a job specification include: educational qualifications, experience, impact on others, and special aptitudes (such as speed of thought).

**joint consultation:** regular meetings between management and *trade unions* to discuss important issues other than *collective bargaining*. A joint consultation committee is a communication forum in which the management's long-term strategy might be outlined, with requests for comments from the shop-floor.

**joint-stock company:** the traditional term for describing a limited company, i.e. a separate legal entity financed and owned by individual shareholders. Joint-stock companies may be *private limited companies* (Ltd) or *public limited companies* (PLC).

**joint venture:** when two or more firms set up a business division that will be operated jointly. This method avoids the need for a complete *merger*, with all the managerial problems that can entail. The potential problem with a joint venture is that the common interests that brought the firms together may shift, leaving the possibility of a messy divorce.

**Jonah complex:** *Maslow*'s view of the apprehensions employees may feel when faced with promotion, such as fear of being unable to cope.

**junk bond:** a fixed interest loan offering higher annual *dividends* than most bonds, but with far less security. The issuing of junk bonds was a major factor in the huge credit boom in America in the 1980s. It resulted in American firms becoming very highly geared, thereby turning the early 1990s recession into the longest for 60 years.

**just in case:** operating a production and distribution system with *buffer stocks*, just in case demand rises unexpectedly or there is a supply shortfall. Typically, this would require:

- a raw material buffer in case of a delivery failure or an unforecast increase in production
- buffers at every stage in the production process, to ensure continuous production even if one section was halted by a strike, equipment failure or high absence levels; this would add greatly to the level of work-in-progress (WIP)
- a stockpile of finished goods, enabling customer demand to be met immediately without affecting the production schedule directly.

This traditional system has tended to be replaced by *just in time* (*JIT*) production and stock control.

**just in time (JIT)** a manufacturing system which is designed to minimise the costs of holding *stocks* of raw materials, components, work-in-progress and finished goods by very carefully planned scheduling and flow of resources through the production process. It requires a very efficient ordering system and delivery reliability. It is usually implemented in conjunction with a shift from *mass* to *cell* production.

JIT also has enormous implications for managing the workforce. High stock levels act as a cushion against workforce indiscipline, be it absenteeism or strike action. Without them it is essential that managers encourage cooperation instead of confrontation. Factory workers need to be treated as valued members of a complete team - trusted, trained and consulted.

As a result, JIT can lead firms to rethink their approach to factory work. The traditional approach of splitting work into repetitive fragments results in an uncooperative workforce. So firms organise the workforce into teams, working together on large units of work instead of working in isolation on the same boring task.

From its origins in Japan, the JIT approach has spread widely throughout the West. In Britain, Rolls Royce has divided its car plant into 16 zones, each acting as a business within a business, responsible for purchasing, cost, quality and delivery. Rolls Royce's new approach has halved the break-even level from 2 800 cars per year to 1 400.

REVISION: There are two sets of revision lists and a glossary of examiners' terms at the back of this book to help you prepare for exams or unit tests. See pages 307–312 for unit tests in GNVQ Business Advanced and pages 313–325 for examinations in A level Business Studies. See pages 326–329 for explanations of examiners' terms such as 'analyse' and 'discuss'.

**k:** a common abbreviation of thousands (of pounds).

**kaizen:** a Japanese term meaning continuous improvement. The importance of this element in the *Japanese way* has often been overlooked. When General Motors realised how far their efficiency had slipped behind the Japanese car firms, they invested $billions in brand-new, highly automated production lines. Yet in the period it took to design, install and test the plant, the Japanese firms had moved the productivity goalposts by their continuous improvement policy. Furthermore, the Japanese improvements cost relatively little, as they were just shop-floor ideas on how to complete tasks more efficiently. Most were generated by kaizen groups that met regularly to discuss problems and solutions.

The diagram below shows the kaizen effect on productivity growth as compared with the traditional Western approach of large, technology-based leaps forward. Note that whereas the Western version would probably entail large-scale *redundancies*, steady productivity improvements are more likely to be accommodated by rising demand or by *natural wastage*.

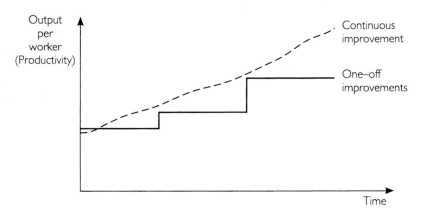

*Kaizen: continuous improvement*

**kanban:** the Japanese system of order cards that pull component supplies through a factory. This is the practical basis of the *just in time* production system. It often operates on the simple basis of two component bins. When one is empty, it is wheeled to the component production section with its kanban order card. That triggers production of the component that must be completed just in time before the other bin runs out of supplies. This approach minimises the amount of semi-completed stock within the factory, focusing minds on the need to avoid production hiccups that could quickly bring the factory to a halt.

**keiretsu:** a Japanese term for a group of companies that have interlocking minority shareholdings in each other. This encourages them to consult closely on long-term planning. Well-known keiretsu include Mitsui and Mitsubishi.

**Keynes J M** (1883–1946): unarguably the most important British economist of the twentieth century. His most important works included THE ECONOMIC CONSEQUENCES OF THE PEACE (first published 1919; latest edition Macmillan 1989), and THE GENERAL THEORY OF EMPLOYMENT, INTEREST AND MONEY (first published 1936; latest edition Macmillan 1973). Keynes was a major influence on Britain's successful handling of its wartime economy 1939–1945, and his ideas were adopted worldwide in the long period of economic growth between 1945 and 1970. (See *Keynesian*.)

**Keynesian:** a person whose economic ideas can be traced to those of J M *Keynes*. At the risk of over-simplification, these include:

- scepticism that the economy tends to stabilise at full employment; Keynes believed that government action might be needed to push an economy out of *recession* (such as extra spending on road-building)
- conviction about the desirability of *counter-cyclical policies* by government
- the belief that allowing people to suffer (through unemployment, for example) while waiting for the free market to bring the economy into balance is morally and socially unacceptable

**kitemark:** the symbol that shows that a consumer product has met the standards laid down by the *British Standards Institute (BSI)*.

**Kondratieff cycle:** the theory that in addition to the five year *trade cycle*, there exists a 50 year cycle of economic upturn and downturn. This theory was put forward by the Russian economist Kondratieff in the early twentieth century. It was dismissed by many economists until the *Great Depressions* of the 1880s and 1930s were duly followed (50 years later) by the frequent and severe *recessions* of the period from 1975–1992. The most widely accepted explanation for the Kondratieff cycle is that the introduction of a new technology causes disruption, but once established it forms the basis for many new products and jobs. In the 1930s the car was displacing rail, while in the 1980s the microchip was replacing mechanical technology.

**labour flexibility:** the ease with which a firm can change the jobs carried out by its staff. This is an important element in a firm's ability to cope with change within its market-place. The main factors determining labour flexibility are:

- workforce attitudes, including any resistance to change
- traditional labour practices, which may be restrictive and entrenched, such as rigid job *demarcation*
- the general skills of the labour force (have workers been encouraged to take general training courses or do they only know their specialist function?)
- the strength and attitude of the local *trade union*

**labour intensive:** a work process in which labour represents a high proportion of total costs. Such a situation is most likely to exist in the service sector, in a small firm, or in a firm operating on a *job* or *batch production* system. This contrasts with firms that are *capital intensive.*

**labour market** is the supply of labour (i.e. all those offering themselves for work) and the demand for labour (i.e. employers in both the *private* and *public sectors*), which together determine wage rates. Talking of a single market for this *factor of production* is quite misleading because it is made up of a vast number of smaller markets which have quite different characteristics: road repairers, brain surgeons and pop stars for instance.

**labour mobility** is the extent to which labour moves around in search of jobs, called geographical mobility, or the extent to which labour moves between jobs, which is known as occupational mobility. It is an indicator of a dynamic economy if such mobility is high. Geographical mobility depends on such things as available housing, costs of moving, communications and the importance of family ties, whilst occupational mobility depends on training facilities and a willingness to learn.

**Labour Relations Agency:** the equivalent of *ACAS* in Northern Ireland.

**labour stability:** a ratio measuring the proportion of the people employed at the start of the year who are still at the firm at the end of the period. It is, in effect, looking at the rate of *labour turnover.*

**labour turnover:** a measurement of the rate at which employees are leaving an organisation.

$$\text{FORMULA}: \frac{\text{number of leavers per year}}{\text{average number of staff}} \times 100$$

High labour turnover may be caused by:

- pay levels falling below comparable rates locally
- low morale, perhaps due to ineffective or *authoritarian leadership*
- an economic upturn creating many other job opportunities

The main effects of high labour turnover are:

- heavy overheads due to the costs of recruiting and training replacement staff frequently
- productivity reductions as new staff acclimatise
- the difficulties of building teamwork with an ever-changing team

**lagging indicator** is a term used to describe a signal which lags behind the true state of economic activity. Unemployment figures often lag behind in this way because, as the economy moves out of *recession*, firms experience an increase in their order books and respond by increasing output, initially by working overtime rather than by taking on more staff. Only when firms are convinced that the recovery is well under way will they employ more people. Therefore, unemployment tends to fall some time after the economy has begun to grow.

**laissez-faire** is a political and economic philosophy which believes that governments should avoid interfering in the running of business or any other part of the economy. A laissez-faire economist places faith in the ability of the free market to maximise business efficiency and consumer satisfaction. *Interventionists* note that the theory of laissez-faire was devised in the eighteenth century when small firms did compete freely. Today, many markets are dominated by a few large firms, so the theory of laissez-faire is less persuasive.

**laissez-faire leadership** occurs where the leader has minimal input, leaving the running of the business to the staff. *Delegation* would lack focus and coordination, making it hard for employees to feel a sense of common purpose. This style can stem from a leader's inability to provide the framework necessary for a successful democratic approach. Or it may be a conscious and brave policy decision to give staff the maximum scope for showing their capabilities. Some people will love the freedom provided, and produce highly creative work. Others will hate their unstructured job with its low input from the leader. (Also see *democratic, authoritarian* and *paternalistic leadership*.)

**lame duck:** a firm or industry which cannot compete and which is therefore likely to go into *liquidation* unless the government helps. Since 1979, all the main political parties have moved towards the view that the market should decide which companies should survive, not the government.

Advantages of government support for lame ducks are:

- financial support for firms may prevent the long-term financial and social costs associated with unemployment
- if large firms fail they will drag others down with them, firms which may themselves be perfectly efficient and profitable
- industries go through periods of structural change as demand alters, and this does not necessarily mean that they are inefficient

Disadvantages of supporting lame ducks are:

- the resources put behind struggling firms could, perhaps, be used more effectively in growth industries (or to cut taxes)
- if firms believe that failure will be cushioned by government they may lack the incentive to fight to become efficient and profitable
- past experience suggests that civil servants are poor at distinguishing between lame ducks and dead ones

**landfill waste tax:** a tax imposed per ton of waste dumped in landfill sites. Starting in October 1996, this tax is intended to make the polluter pay. This should provide an incentive for companies to minimise the waste they dump and maximise their efforts at recycling.

**last in, first out (LIFO)** is a method of stock identification designed to eliminate *inflation* from the calculation of a firm's profit. It achieves this by making the accounting assumption that the stock being used is the last stock purchased. Therefore what is left is assumed to be the oldest (pre-price inflation) stock.

By valuing the closing stock at the earliest price, the impact of rising prices upon a firm's costs is not allowed to boost its profit position artificially. Therefore, in times of inflation, LIFO gives a lower, more realistic profit statement. Unfortunately the fact that the closing stock is valued at the earliest price means that stock is under-valued on the *balance sheet*. So LIFO improves the accuracy of the *profit and loss account* at the cost of making the balance sheet less accurate. (See also *first in first out (FIFO)*.)

**latent needs** are those which exist but which consumers may be unaware of. A far-sighted entrepreneur may be able to identify such needs and produce a good or service which satisfies them. An example of such a product is the Sony Walkman. In research, consumers were unable to see how they would use a portable sound system. Sony was able to look further ahead and anticipate what became a worldwide sales success.

**lateral communication:** another term for *horizontal communication*

**lateral thinking:** the ability when faced with an apparently unsolvable problem to think creatively and either find a radical solution or realise the situation can be side-stepped altogether. This kind of creative thinking can pay especially handsome dividends in product development and in marketing, where originality can lead to exciting *innovations*.

**latest finish time (LFT)** is the date by which an activity on a *network* must be completed in order that following activities can be started in time to finish the project as quickly as possible. In order to calculate the LFT, you must first:

- draw up the network diagram
- calculate the *earliest start times* from left to right
- then work back from the earliest project completion time to see the latest time each activity can be allowed to finish

**latest start time (LST)** is the latest any activity can be allowed to start so that its completion will not delay the whole project.

**launch:** the programme of *stockpiling, distribution, advertising* and publicity required to thrust a new product before its *target market*. The launch may be national or regional depending upon the firm's confidence in the product, its available production capacity, and any known regional taste differences. Once sufficient stocks of the product are ready, the launch is likely to consist of three phases:

1 *Trade advertising* plus aggressive *salesforce* activity to get wholesalers and retailers to stock the product.
2 A large-scale *merchandising* campaign to achieve high visibility at the *point of sale*, e.g. display stands near the shop checkouts.

**3** A consumer advertising campaign, perhaps of TV commercials plus posters.

**layers of hierarchy** means the number of ranks within the organisational structure, i.e. the number of different supervisory and management layers between the shop-floor and the chief executive.

**LBO:** see *leveraged buy-out*

**leadership style:** the manner and approach of the head of an organisation or department towards the staff. The leader's manner affects the personal relationships involved. Will the leader inspire loyalty, affection, respect, trust? The style includes the use of *delegation* and *consultation*, plus the degree to which he or she gets involved personally in the daily problems of the business. Both aspects will be handled differently by each and every leader, but there are four categories of leadership style that are used widely for purposes of analysis: *democratic, paternalistic, authoritarian* (or dictatorial) and *laissez-faire.*

**leading indicator** is a term used to describe a signal which predates or predicts the true state of economic activity, such as the level of orders for machine tools. The *stock market* often leads in this way. For example, growing confidence that signs of a recovery are under way is often translated into rising share prices, as investors predict improving profits in the next year to eighteen months. The opposite also holds, with sharp falls in share prices indicating a falling off of activity in advance of the reality. Such leading indicators can be predictors of what is likely to happen to the 'real economy'.

**lead time:** the length of time a firm needs between receiving an order and delivering the finished product or service. Efforts by management at reducing lead times could result in considerable benefits in terms of customer satisfaction and faster turnover. Nevertheless, many customers would rather have a 100 per cent reliable delivery date than an apparently faster, but actually less reliable service.

**leakages:** see *withdrawals.*

**lean production:** a term used to describe the range of waste-saving measures inspired by Japanese manufacturing firms. These include *just in time*, shorter product development times and *flexible specialisation.* To the authors of THE MACHINE THAT CHANGED THE WORLD (Womack, Jones and Roos; Macmillan, 1990), lean production has replaced *mass production* as the world's most efficient system. This has caused huge problems of transition to major mass producers such as America's General Motors. (See also the *Japanese way.*)

**learning curve:** the process of gaining experience and knowledge that depends on learning from your mistakes. New employees and firms new to a market both go through the same learning process. The successful ones will be those that move up the learning curve as rapidly as possible, probably through a combination of good research and a willingness to experiment.

**learning organisation:** an enterprise that makes *continuous improvement* a central theme of its management approach. Therefore it is always willing to listen to new ideas and make the necessary changes – however radical.

For this to be successful there needs to be an open style of management, excellent internal communications and a sense of common purpose amongst managers and staff alike.

**lease:** a way of acquiring property for a restricted period of time; after the lease runs out, ownership returns to the freeholder. As it has value for the years of its life, a lease is recorded as a *fixed asset* on a firm's *balance sheet.*

**leasing:** a method of acquiring non-property *assets* without the need for the initial cash outlays implied by purchasing. This can also be done by renting or hiring equipment, though leasing is cheaper per month because the firm must contract to lease the assets for a period of two or more years. Compared with purchasing, leasing has various advantages and disadvantages:

Pros: • avoids the damage to *cash flow* caused by purchasing
• releases *capital* for other, perhaps more profitable uses
• depending on the terms of the lease, it may be possible to update your equipment at little or no extra cost
• most leasing contracts enable the firm to buy the asset cheaply at the end of the contracted term

Cons: • in order to provide the leasing company with a profit, it is inevitable that in the long run most leasing arrangements will prove more expensive than outright purchase
• when a firm leases a machine it does not own it; therefore it does not appear as an asset on the *balance sheet*; so if a firm leased all its equipment, its accounts may look worryingly short of assets

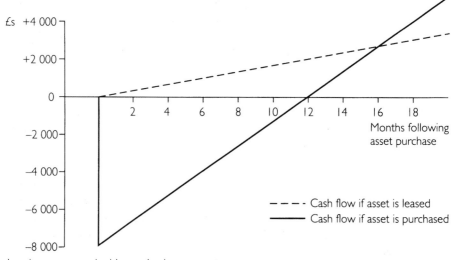

*Leasing compared with purchasing an asset*

**ledger:** the accounting book where daily transactions are recorded (on a *double-entry* basis). Ensuring that the ledgers are accurate is the job of a bookkeeper.

**legislation:** laws passed by Acts of Parliament.

**level playing field:** a phrase that sums up the need within a *market economy* for all firms to be competing on the same terms. If one national government is subsidising its steel producers, for example, they will have an unfair advantage over those from a country like Britain, which offers no State-aid to steel. The *single European market* is an attempt to provide a level playing field in relation to laws and regulations governing traded goods within the *European Union*. If product and factory regulations could be made the same throughout the EU, the trading field would have been levelled out.

**leverage:** the American term for *gearing* (i.e. the level of borrowing).

**leveraged buy-out (LBO):** the American term for buying out the shareholders of a firm using borrowed funds. Usually, such a buy-out is done by the managers of the business, hence the British term *management buy-out (MBO)*. Calling it a leveraged buy-out has the virtue of pointing to the main worry about this type of operation; the high *gearing* that results from a *take-over* that is based upon borrowed money rather than share capital.

**LFT:** see *latest finish time*

**liability:** a debt that may have to be paid within 12 months (current liability), after 12 months (long-term liability), or at no specified time (*shareholders' funds*). For an understanding of *balance sheets*, it is useful to remember that liabilities are sources of finance. They are the means by which the *assets* have been acquired. For example, an *overdraft* (current liability) is a source of short term-finance for the firm.

**liberalisation** is a term used to describe the freeing up of international trade from barriers such as *tariffs* and *quotas*. The *General Agreement on Tariffs and Trade (GATT)* was established to negotiate reduced barriers under a succession of so-called 'rounds'.

**licensing:** when the holder of a *patent* or *copyright* allows other firms to use their creation in return for a *royalty*. The royalty might be an agreed percentage of the value of the sales made by the licensee, or a fee per unit sold. The holders of the Batman name and *logo* might, for example, charge licensees £1 per Batman T-shirt and 10p per Batman pencil.

**LIFFE:** see *London International Financial Futures Exchange*

**LIFO:** see *last in, first out*

**light industry:** manufacturers of all items other than the large-scale output of *heavy industry*. Typical examples include food manufacture and printing.

**light user:** a customer who buys irregularly or in small quantities. (See *heavy user*.)

**Likert R** (1903–1981) pioneered the technique of human resource accounting which attempted to monitor the value to the firm of employee *motivation* just as conventional accounting monitors financial resources. For example, if an improvement in a department's morale had halved its *absenteeism* rate, the cost savings could be estimated and recorded.

**limited company:** a firm that enjoys *limited liability*. In other words the owners (shareholders) are only risking the amount they have invested in the company rather than their personal wealth.

**limited liability** is the idea that the owners (shareholders) are financially only responsible for the amount they have invested in the company rather than their personal wealth. Thus if a firm becomes insolvent, the maximum *creditors* can receive is the shareholders' original investment. In order to protect and inform creditors, the word 'Ltd' (standing for Limited) or 'PLC' (standing for Public Limited Company) appear after the company's name. The importance of limiting the amount of a shareholder's liability is that it encourages people to invest with relatively little risk.

**linearity** is the assumption that variables will behave in a constant manner, e.g. that *variable costs* will always be 50p per unit, no matter what the output level. Graphs drawn on such a basis will consist of straight lines. The most commonly used in business studies is the *break-even chart*.

**linear programming** is a method for optimising the allocation of resources within known constraints. It aims to find the *feasible region* (all possible allocations) and then identify the optimum point by the use of *contribution*.

**line extension:** adding a new flavour or model type to a product line. For example, once Walls had launched 'Magnum' successfully, 'White Magnum' soon followed.

Pros:
- a line extension can offer more variety to regular customers, encouraging higher levels of *repeat purchase*
- it can also be used to segment a market, as, for example, a plain chocolate choc-ice will appeal more to adults than to children
- most importantly, a line extension can protect a successful product from competition; once the success of 'Magnum' had become clear, competitors would look for ways of getting into this market sector; the easiest way would be to offer a 'Magnum' imitation (*me-too*) with a point of differentiation; if Walls had not offered 'Magnum White', a rival would have done so

Cons:
- line extensions can cannibalise your existing products, in other words much of the demand for 'Magnum White' may have come from buyers of 'Magnum'. By spreading sales among more products, each one's chance of gaining high retail distribution is reduced

**line management:** managers who have been delegated specific authority over people, decisions and results within the management hierarchy. Line personnel are distinguished from staff because the latter hold no direct responsibilities for meeting *company objectives*. The term 'line manager' comes from the line of command (also known as *chain of command*) that forms a vertical line of delegated authority within the organisational structure.

**liquid assets** are the assets that are closest to cash, namely bank deposits (cash) and *debtors*.

**liquidation** means turning assets into cash. The term is usually used in the context of a firm ceasing to trade in its current form, probably due to *insolvency*. The closure may be the result of a *creditor* taking the firm to court to seek compulsory liquidation due to non-payment of debts. In this case a *receiver* will be appointed to attempt to raise the cash to satisfy the creditors. If the firm has sufficient assets, or a fundamentally strong trading position, it may well be that the receiver is able to find a buyer for the firm or to keep it going. More common is *voluntary liquidation*, in which the firm's directors decide that they wish to stop the firm continuing to trade as at present. This might be because an elderly proprietor wants to retire and can find no buyer for the firm. The main alternatives to liquidation are *administration* and financial restructuring.

**liquidity:** the ability of a firm to meet its short-term debts. As bills can only be paid with cash, liquidity can also be understood as the availability of cash or near-cash resources. Liquidity can be estimated from a firm's published accounts using the *liquidity ratio* or *acid test ratio.*

**liquidity crisis:** a loss of confidence in a firm's ability to meet its short-term debts. This may encourage bankers or *creditors* to demand payment before others get at the firm's money. Inability to meet those payments might lead to *liquidation.*

**liquidity management:** controlling the *liquid assets* of a business to ensure that the organisation can always pay its bills. This involves monitoring the *liquidity* and acid test ratios and also checking that stock is saleable and debtors are reliable. By ensuring that cash flowing in is always enough to meet cash flowing out, the organisation preserves its *credit rating* and can also place spare cash on deposit to earn interest.

**liquidity ratio:** a measurement of a firm's ability to meet its short-term debts. This is found by the following formula:

$$\text{FORMULA: } \frac{\text{current assets}}{\text{current liabilities}} = \text{liquidity ratio}$$

The organisation must monitor this ratio carefully as it is a main test of *liquidity*, the ability to settle debts as they fall due by having available the necessary cash. There is no particular value of this ratio which can be used as a universally reliable guide to a firm's health as it will depend on the industry and the particular circumstances. Although accountants recommend a figure of around 1.5, the trend is probably more important. A value at or below 1.0 indicates concern and values greater than 2.0 may mean that too much finance is tied up in short-term assets. The way the *current assets* and *liabilities* are valued is crucial, as is the date on which they are valued. If these are untypical, then the ratio may be distorted. (See also *acid test ratio* and *window-dressing.*)

**listed company:** a firm that has its shares listed on the main London Stock Exchange. In order for this to be possible, the firm must be a *public limited company* (PLC). See below for how to obtain a *listing.*

**listing** refers to those public *joint-stock companies* (*PLCs*) which appear on the Stock Exchange list. Among the advantages and disadvantages of a full listing are:

Pros: • gives access to a large potential source of capital
 • shareholders receive some protection from fraud because of the stringent requirements of the Stock Exchange Council
 • raises the profile of the company, giving it publicity and therefore (perhaps) greater credibility

Cons: • the *flotation* process is time consuming and expensive, requiring a lengthy *prospectus* prepared by a *merchant bank*
 • it makes the company more vulnerable to *take-over bids*; this may lead to *short-termism* in managerial decision-making
 • a great deal of information about the firm has to be made public. It is possible to be quoted on the *Alternative Investment Market (AIM)* which has less stringent requirements, and which is intended for small firms.

**Lloyd's** insurance market is one of the world's main centres for obtaining insurance cover on anything from a car to an oil rig. Lloyd's members underwrite risks from throughout the world, earning Britain considerable sums of foreign currency; making insurance one of Britain's main *invisible exports.*

**loan capital:** medium- to long-term finance, either from banks or from *debenture* holders. Loan capital plus *shareholders' funds* represent a firm's *capital employed.* When raising extra loan capital, a firm should consider its *gearing* level, i.e. the extent to which it is reliant on borrowed money. If loans represent more than 50 per cent of capital employed, the firm is considered over-geared.

**Loan Guarantee Scheme (LGS):** a government-backed loan insurance scheme which guarantees bankers that up to 80 per cent of the money they lend to a business will be guaranteed by the *Treasury.* This was introduced in 1980 as a way of encouraging banks to lend to small and medium-sized companies thought too risky to justify a conventional loan. In return for its financial risks, the government charges a fee of around 2.5 per cent of the annual value of the loan. The precise terms of the LGS are often changed in the annual *Budget,* but would easily be available from the *Department of Trade and Industry* or from any high-street bank.

**lobbying:** putting your viewpoint across directly to a person in a position of power and influence. The term comes from the central lobby of the Houses of Parliament, which is where members of the public go to put their case to their Members of Parliament. Although intended as an aid to the democratic process, lobbying has become tainted by the number of MPs who are paid to represent special interests such as the tobacco industry. (See *pressure groups.*)

**local area network:** the linking of personal computers within a network operating system, usually within the same company.

**local content:** the proportion of the value of output that is produced within the country where the product is assembled. This is an important issue within the *European Union,* because products imported directly from the Far East are subject to restrictions and taxes, whereas free trade exists for products made within the EU. Yet that opens the possibility that a Japanese firm might set up in Britain, import all components from Japan, and simply bolt them together in this country. Other European countries are keen to ensure that a product with such a low local content is treated as if it is a direct import from Japan.

**location of industry:** see *industrial location*

**lock-out:** when an employer decides to bring an *industrial dispute* to a head by preventing the workforce from getting in to work. This might happen if a *trade union* has organised a successful *work-to-rule* or series of disruptive, one-day strikes. Management might fear that the workers will be able to continue *industrial action* indefinitely, as they are continuing to receive a high proportion of their regular wages. A lock-out will ensure that the dispute becomes a shorter, harsher affair in which the workforce receives no income, and may therefore feel forced to settle on the employer's terms.

**logistics** is the process of ensuring the right supplies and products are in the right place at the right time, at a competitive cost. The main functions covered are:

- materials ordering and handling
- *stock control*
- *distribution* and delivery

**logo:** a visual symbol of an organisation or brand. It might be the design of the brand name (such as the Coca-Cola signature) or pure creation, such as the 'golden arches' yellow M that symbolises McDonald's.

**London Derivatives Exchange:** the financial exchange formed from the 1990 merger of the Traded Options Market with the *London International Financial Futures Exchange.*

**London International Financial Futures Exchange:** LIFFE (pronounced 'life') is the financial market where companies can obtain forward currency or hedge their future currency commitments. In 1990 LIFFE was merged with the Traded Options Market to form the *London Derivatives Exchange.*

**long-term liabilities:** debts (*creditors*) falling due after more than one year. These include medium- and long-term loans, *debentures* and (possibly) *provisions* for tax payments or other long-term debts.

**loose economic policy** is the relaxation of fiscal and monetary measures to allow greater consumer spending, cheaper loans and lower taxes. The result is an increase in the rate of economic activity, leading to higher levels of employment, output and expenditure. It is a policy likely to be pursued when an economy is emerging from *recession.* It suffers from the potential danger of sucking in more imports if there is no spare productive capacity. This can lead to a *balance of payments* crisis, and/or to rising rates of *inflation,* especially if demand for goods and services increases too fast in certain sectors of the economy for output to rise to match it.

**loss leader:** a product sold at or below cost in the hope of generating other, profitable sales. The method is most commonly used in retailing, where a shop may advertise a loss leader heavily, enticing in customers who will probably buy other, full-priced items as well. The same term can also be used to describe a manufacturer who prices a lead item cheaply, knowing that usage of the item requires further, full-priced purchases. For example, publishers of sticker collections may charge only 50p for a large, glossy album, but 30p per pack for the cheap stickers that go inside.

**lower order needs:** see *hierarchy of needs*

**lower turning point** is the lowest point in the *trade cycle,* where the economy moves out of *recession* or *depression.* During the downswing of a recession, economists and politicians attempt to forecast when the lower turning point is to be reached. In fact it is often only six to nine months afterwards that it becomes clear when it happened.

**LST:** see *latest start time*

**Ltd:** see *limited liability*

# M

**Maastricht** is the name of the Dutch town where the Treaty on European Union was signed by all the member states in December 1991. The Treaty envisaged the introduction of a single currency by 1999 and formulated a number of areas for combined policy action including industrial and social policy, health and education. The UK negotiated a number of 'opt-out' clauses, especially one on the *social chapter*. This exempted UK firms from complying with a number of measures such as minimum pay and maternity benefits. The Maastricht Treaty attempted to push the pace of European unity forward, but perhaps too quickly for countries such as Denmark and Britain. In addition, the events of September 1992, when the pound was forced out of the *ERM*, suggested that monetary union was still a long way off. The Treaty came into force on November 1, 1993.

**McGregor D** (1906–1964): an American psychologist whose book THE HUMAN SIDE OF ENTERPRISE (first pub. 1960; Penguin, 1987) popularised his view that managers can be grouped into two types: *Theory X* and *Theory Y*. McGregor had researched into the attitudes of managers towards their employees. He found that the majority of managers assumed that their workers were work-shy and motivated primarily by money; he termed this type of manager Theory X. The alternative, minority, view was that workers look to gain satisfaction from employment and therefore evidence of low achievement levels should make managers question whether they were providing the right work environment. In other words, the Theory Y manager's first assumption should be that the blame for poor workforce performance lies with management rather than the workers themselves.

The Theory X Manager assumes:

- workers are motivated by money
- unless supervised closely, workers will under-perform
- that workers will only respect a tough, decisive boss
- that workers have no wish or ability to help make decisions

The Theory Y Manager assumes:

- workers seek job satisfaction no less than managers
- that, if trusted, workers will behave responsibly
- that low performance is due to dull work or poor management
- staff have a desire and the right to contribute to decisions

McGregor's use of the easily memorable X and Y has made his work widely used in management training. This is despite the fact that it is largely derived from other theories. Theory X is derived from the work of F W *Taylor* and from Adam *Smith*'s notion of 'economic man'. Theory Y stems clearly from *Mayo*'s human relations approach and *Maslow*'s work on human needs. Nevertheless, just the introduction to THE HUMAN SIDE OF ENTERPRISE will give the reader a clear understanding that McGregor's writing has much more to contribute than just the memorable X and Y.

**machine tools:** the capital equipment needed to make the machines used in manufacturing. In other words, not the robot welder on the car *production line,* but the machinery to make robot welders.

**macroeconomic:** a term indicating the study of the whole economy and the way it interacts (macro means 'large'). The main elements within the macroeconomy are firms, consumers, the government and other countries, which depend on each other in a way described as the *circular flow of national income.* The macroeconomy is the sum or aggregate of all the elements within it. Thus the *sales revenue* of an individual firm is a part of the microeconomy; by adding up the sales revenue of all firms (their aggregate income) the size of the macroeconomy can be measured. The study of the macroeconomy is concerned with making the most efficient use of its resources (*factors of production* such as land, labour and capital).

**magistrates' court:** a local court presided over by a trained volunteer (a magistrate) rather than by a fully qualified judge. This type of court deals only with relatively minor local matters, which might include prosecutions by trading standards officers concerning the hygiene at a local restaurant.

**mainframe computers** are the largest computers in the series beginning with *microcomputers* and going through *minicomputers.* Their size enables many functions to be processed simultaneously with large reserves of memory. They are mainly used by large corporations, research organisations and where defence or space applications are needed.

**maintenance factors:** another term for *hygiene factors.*

**make-or-buy decision**: the management choice between buying in components or making them in-house.

**management accounting:** the production and use of accounting information for internal managerial purposes of analysis, planning, review and control rather than for historical financial record. The diagram below sets out the main types of information considered part of the management accountant's function. In all cases it will be treated as highly confidential, in contrast with the completed company accounts that are published after the *financial year* has been completed.

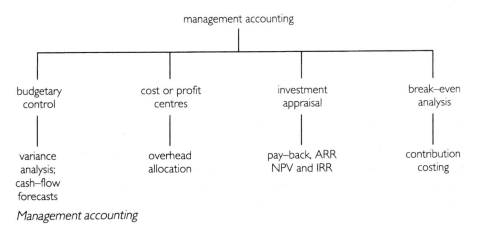

*Management accounting*

**management:** the art of getting things done through people' is the classic definition according to the management theorist Mary Parker Follett. The idea that management is purely about managing people is questioned by others, who believe it over-simplifies. In their book *Effective Management* (Prentice Hall, 1989) Derek Torrington and others put forward the mnemonic GROUP, standing for goals, responsibility, organisations, uncertainty and people:

- managers have conflicting goals
- managers are held responsible for results
- managers work in organisations
- managers must cope with uncertainty
- managers work with and through other people

**management buy-in:** when managers from outside a company buy up the shares in order to take control. The managers do it because they (and their financial backers) believe that they can run the firm more efficiently than the current management. As with a *management buy-out*, a buy-in is likely to be financed largely by borrowed money, causing *gearing* to be uncomfortably high.

Note that a buy-in differs from a buy-out because the latter is when managers buy their **own** firm from the shareholders, whereas a buy-in is when **outside** managers buy in to a firm.

**management buy-out (MBO):** when the managers of a business buy out the shareholders, thereby buying ownership and control of the firm. It is hoped that this will give the management the incentive it needs to maximise the productiveness of the organisation. Many MBOs involve buying a single business unit from a large parent company. This gives the added benefit of separating the firm from its potentially *bureaucratic* (and therefore high overhead) parent.

However, some MBOs have been financed in a risky manner, with high debt levels. If the business is successful, the managers stand to make millions as the value of their shareholding soars. Failure, however, may lose not only the managers' investment but also the workforce's livelihood. So whereas the managers are taking a risk which may pay them handsomely, the workforce stands to gain nothing, but may lose everything.

**management by exception** is the principle that because managers cannot super-vise every activity within the organisation, they should focus their energies on the most important issues. This notion – devised by *Taylor* – sums up the feelings of *authoritarian* managers everywhere; that it is their job to deal with important issues, and that only trivial matters should be delegated.

**management by objectives:** a method of coordinating and motivating a workforce by dividing the company's overall goal into specific targets for each division, depart-ment, manager and possibly employee. Peter Drucker, in his book THE PRACTICE OF MANAGEMENT (Heinemann, 1955) put forward the view that management by objec-tives is the only effective way of delegating authority in a large firm. He urged that targets should be agreed after discussion, not imposed from above. A *Theory Y* man-agement would be expected to take the former approach; *Theory X* managers would impose targets from above.

**management by walking about (MBWA):** an extension of *human relations* theory suggesting that managers can best express their interest in and focus on shop-floor activity by regular, informal visits. By inviting complaints or ideas, senior managers can cut through the *layers of hierarchy* that hinder *vertical communication*. As with many developments in motivation theory, this idea originated in America but was adopted most enthusiastically in Japan.

**Management Charter Initiative (MCI):** an attempt at providing widely accepted qualifications confirming that a manager has reached a recognised competence level. This initiative was a response to the acknowledged weaknesses of managers in Britain compared with overseas competitors. MCI will provide three qualification levels:

- a certificate aimed at supervisors and first-line managers
- a diploma for middle managers
- a Master's degree for aspiring or actual senior managers

A feature of this scheme is that no college attendance or exams are involved. The cer-tification will stem from a *mentor* within the candidate's company, who will be judging whether the manager has displayed the necessary qualities within his or her daily work. It remains to be seen whether this system provides the quality and consistency necessary for a qualification to become recognised and valuable.

**management consultant:** an individual or firm which specialises in giving inde-pendent advice to companies. The advice may relate to internal management issues such as *delayering* or *restructuring*, or on divisional issues such as obtaining better pro-duction technology or tackling a marketing problem. Management consultants are expected to have greater breadth of experience than the company's own manage-ment, since they are likely to have tackled the same problems before at a different firm. No less important is that the consultant has no *vested interest* in ensuring that one department triumphs over another in a reorganisation.

**management succession:** the issue of who will take over the key positions in the company when the current directors retire. This can be a very important issue for family businesses, should there be no obvious successor. It can also worry the share-holders in a large *public limited company* that has been dominated by one or two people. Such worries might lead to a flagging share price that would leave the firm vulnerable to a *take-over bid*.

**management trainee:** an employee selected to participate in a training programme designed to equip the individual for a management post. This is likely to be a process lasting between six and 24 months, including:

- a personal development programme designed to encourage self-confidence, assertiveness and time management
- an academic programme based on finance, marketing, motivation theory and the law
- a work experience programme in which trainees will spend some weeks or months in several different departments in order to gain a full understanding of the workings of the organisation

**manager**: an employee with authority over a number of subordinates and the responsibility to plan and monitor short- and medium-term strategies. See *management*.

**M and A:** see *mergers and acquisitions*

**manpower planning:** deciding on the type and number of staff required in the future, given the firm's sales forecasts, plans and *objectives*. Having decided how many workers are needed and what their skills should be, the *human resource* manager can plan by:

- carrying out a manpower audit, i.e. checking on the skills of all the present workforce
- identifying the known future leavers (those reaching retirement, for example), to exclude them from the calculations
- consulting, then deciding on how many existing staff could and would like to retrain for the job functions of the future
- preparing a recruitment plan stating how many new staff need to be recruited and how the firm will set about the process

**Manpower Services Commission (MSC)** has been replaced by the *Training Agency*.

**manual worker:** an employee who works with his or her hands, usually in a factory context. Manual workers are often subdivided into three categories:

- skilled, e.g. welders and qualified electricians
- semi-skilled, e.g. van drivers and production line workers
- unskilled, e.g. cleaners and road sweepers

**manufacturing resource planning (MRP II)** is a computer-driven, universal planning system for the whole of a company's production processes. It is designed to translate sales forecasts (or actual orders) into purchasing requirements for raw materials and components, factory production schedules, individual work instructions and completion deadlines. Complex as this sounds, it only underestimates the real task. Most firms will have many different product lines and many different orders from a variety of customers. The MRP II system must coordinate and schedule all of these in such a way as to maximise *capacity utilisation*. If it is impossible to produce all the orders within the desired delivery deadlines, the computer will show the overtime requirement, or warn that customers must be alerted to delivery delays.

Once such a system is running effectively, it is easy to see that it not only replaces the planning role of production management, but is likely to lead to huge gains in efficiency. However, the process of setting up MRP II may be chaotic, unless the firm takes time to test every element of the programme before bringing the whole system on stream.

A further, key benefit for MRP II is that because it has a complete computer model of the entire workings of the firm, managers can 'consult' it. *What if? questions* can be asked such as, 'What are the cost, capacity and materials ordering implications of running a 10 per cent extra promotion?' Using this facility makes it easy for managers to experiment in theory, before risking the firm's resources in practice.

**mapping** means selecting the key variables that differentiate the brands within a market and then plotting the position of each one. Usually this is done on a two-dimensional diagram as below. Here, ice-cream brands are plotted against the key criteria of customer age and product price. By contrast, the criteria for cider might be trendy or traditional and strong or standard (alcoholic strength). Brand mapping enables a firm to identify any gaps or niches in the market that are unfilled.

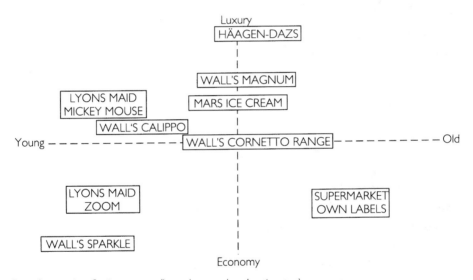

*Brand mapping for ice-cream (based on authors' estimates)*

**margin:** a commonly used shorthand way of referring to a *profit margin*, i.e. the proportionate difference between revenue and cost.

**marginal cost:** the change in the total cost of a product or service which results from changing output by one unit more (or less). In the short run, only *variable costs* can be altered so marginal cost in the short run is entirely variable cost. Marginal costing is an alternative term for *contribution costing*.

**margin of safety:** see *safety margin*

**market**: the term used to describe the meeting place between customers and suppliers.

When considering entering a market for the first time, a company must consider:

- the consumers
- the competitors
- the distribution outlets

The main ways of measuring a market are by volume (the number of units sold) and by value (the money spent on all the goods sold).

**market-based pricing:** a collective term for pricing methods that are based on market rather than cost considerations. (See *pricing methods.*)

**market capitalisation:** the value placed on a company by the *stock market.* It is the number of shares issued multiplied by their market price. It is important to realise that this is only one way of valuing a company and there are others based on asset values. A *take-over bid* is another way.

**market economy** is an economy which allows markets to determine the allocation of resources. Within it there are factor markets where the price of *factors of production* are determined by the *supply* and *demand* for those factors, and product markets, where the price of goods and services are determined in the same way.

Pros:
- automatic: no need for regulation
- offers freedom of choice
- efficiently allocates resources
- leads to greater economic growth

Cons:
- means those with the most money have greatest power
- leads to inequality of income
- the price of a good may not reflect its cost to society; these costs are called *externalities*
- monopolisation within market-places can lead to inefficiency and exploitation

The main advantage of relying on the *market mechanism* is that it is automatic and leads to greater efficiency. However, because markets possess disadvantages, in particular they tend to exploit the weakest members of society, they are always modified or regulated in some way by governments. The extent to which this regulation takes place is a political decision: in the formerly communist countries, free markets were almost completely eliminated and replaced by central planning, but this proved to be a mistake, not only because it was expensive and inefficient to operate, but also because it stifled initiative, and led to lower living standards. A compromise between a wholly planned and a market economy is called a *mixed economy.*

**market failure** occurs when the mechanism of *supply* and *demand* fails to allocate resources in the most efficient way. Alternatively it may fail to produce goods that are wanted. Market failure shows through in a number of ways, including the growth of *monopolistic* firms and other non-competitive organisations, and when *factors of production* stand idle, in particular when large sections of the workforce are unemployed. Markets also fail when *externalities* such as water and air pollution are not costed, so that firms make private profit at the cost of social welfare. In these cases it is argued that governments should intervene.

**marketing:** the all-embracing function that links the company with customer tastes to get the right product to the right place at the right time. Marketing decisions are made through the *marketing model,* based on the findings of *market research,* and carried out through the *marketing mix.* At all stages in the marketing process, the firm needs to work closely with the production department and *research and development,* to ensure that what is promised is delivered.

**marketing activities** are all the actions an organisation can take to achieve its marketing objectives. These would include *market research*, product *mapping*, *market positioning* and carrying out the different elements of the *marketing mix* - product, price, promotions and place. In the past, marketing activities were conducted differently among not-for-profit compared with profit-making organisations. For example, direct sales techniques might be used by double-glazing companies but not by charities. Today charities, *pressure groups* and even political parties use aggressive techniques such as telesales and direct mail because of their proven effectiveness.

**marketing functions:** these are the main areas in which marketing activity helps to achieve the marketing objectives/principles, such as:

- managing changes in technology, competition and consumer taste
- coordinating marketing with production planning and control
- establishing a distinctive identity for a product (partly through *branding*) or company (through the *corporate identity*)
- planning, coordinating and monitoring the *marketing mix*

**marketing mix:** the main variables through which a firm carries out its marketing strategy, often known as the four Ps:

- product (including range of pack sizes and/or flavours or colours)
- price (long-term *pricing strategy* and *pricing method*)
- promotion (*branding*, *advertising*, *packaging* and *sales promotions*)
- place (choosing *distribution channels* and seeking shop distribution)

Textbooks tend to treat each of the elements of the mix as of equal importance. Few marketing companies would agree. The most important element of the mix is the product, which needs to be designed to meet the requirements of those within the *target market*. If this process has been achieved successfully (probably through extensive *market research*) the other three elements of the mix become clear. The price must be suited to the pockets of the *target market* and to the image of the product. The promotion will be through the media that they watch or read, while the place should be the shops visited by those types of people.

The only one of these elements that is outside the company's control is place, for obtaining shop distribution is a very difficult task in crowded modern market-places. No retailers have spare shelving, so in order for your product to gain distribution, another product will probably have to be removed from the shelves. Needless to say, every manufacturer is fighting hard to keep its distribution as high as possible, so it is never easy to gain or to keep hold of high distribution levels.

**marketing model:** a framework for making marketing decisions in a scientific manner. It is derived from F W *Taylor*'s method of basing decisions on scientifically gathered research evidence.

The model has five stages.

1 Set the marketing objective based on the company's *objectives*. For example, if the corporate goal is *diversification*, the specific marketing objective may be to launch a product into a new market that can achieve minimum sales of £5 million within 18 months.

2 Gather data: this will require the collection of *quantitative* and *qualitative* data about the market's size, competitive structure, distribution pattern and consumer attitudes.

3 Form *hypotheses*, theories about how best to achieve the objective. For example a producer of canned food might consider whether to:
- move into the frozen-food market
- move into the chilled-food market
- take the more radical route of moving into petfoods

4 Test the hypotheses: this may be done solely through *market research* or, more thoroughly, by *test marketing* new product ideas. After the results are evaluated, a decision can be reached on how to proceed.

*Marketing model*

5 Control and review: making decisions is only one part of the marketing function; implementing them is no less important. The means of implementation will be via the *marketing mix*. The effectiveness of the distribution, pricing or promotion policies must be controlled, with careful conclusions drawn from the success or failure of the project.

Having completed the task, the managers must look towards new objectives. So the process begins again.

**marketing myopia** means a short-sighted approach to marketing by ignoring the need for customer orientation. The originator of the phrase, Theodore Levitt, suggested that too many firms see marketing as a tool for selling the firm's output. Instead, the seller should, 'take his cues from the buyer in such a way that the product becomes a consequence of the marketing effort, not vice versa.' Within this model of good practice, 'building an effective customer-orientated company involves far more than good intentions or promotional tricks, it involves profound matters of human organisation and leadership.'

**marketing plan:** a report detailing a firm's marketing objectives and strategy, including: costings, forecast results and contingency plans. The stages of constructing a marketing plan are as follows:

1 Conduct a marketing audit to ensure full knowledge of the firm's marketing assets. This could be supplemented by a *SWOT analysis* (identifying the firm's marketing strengths, weaknesses, opportunities and threats).

2 Set clear objectives for the coming year based on goals for three to five years ahead. These might include targets for sales, *market share*, distribution levels and brand image ratings.

3 Devise a strategy for achieving the objectives that operates within a defined budget and covers: new product development, new product launches and going brands, looking at the *above the line* and *below the line* requirements.

**marketing principles:** this term can be used in two ways:

- to mean fundamental truths of marketing, such as its role as the link between the producer and the customer
- to mean the underlying goals of marketing, such as to anticipate market needs and opportunities, satisfy customer expectations, generate income, manage the effects of change and competition and to enhance customer perception of the organisation.

The more common use is the latter.

**marketing research:** see *market research*

**marketing strategy:** a medium- to long-term plan for meeting marketing objectives. The word 'strategy' suggests a carefully thought-out, integrated plan. It should set out the balance of marketing activity between new and existing products – with carefully costed budgets. The strategy is likely to be fully researched and then implemented through the *marketing mix* – the four Ps of product, price, place and promotion. A successful marketing strategy is one that achieves the objectives without going over budget. See also *marketing plan*.

**market-led pricing:** setting a price for your product based upon what the market can bear. This contrasts with producer-led pricing methods such as cost-plus. Market-led pricing will be particularly important in markets where *product differentiation* is low and therefore *price elasticity* is high.

**market manipulation** occurs when companies influence markets to make them less than perfectly competitive. Firms attempt to manipulate markets in a number of ways, for instance by *collusion* with other producers, or by cross-subsidising one market by another in order to force out the competition. Even *advertising* could be said to represent manipulation, if it makes consumers willing to pay a premium price for a good which is not really any different from one produced by other firms.

**market mechanism** is the operation of *demand* and *supply*, which together determine price. If the market mechanism works smoothly it should allocate *factors of production* in the most efficient way to produce those goods which consumers want in the right amount and at the right time. In practice there is bound to be a degree of *market failure*, especially since there is a time lag between changes in demand and changes in supply.

**market niche:** a gap in the range of products or services offered within a market. Having identified that such a gap exists, a business must decide whether the niche is large enough to be profitable and if so, how best to fill it. (See *niche marketing*.)

**market orientation:** the extent to which a firm's strategic thinking stems from looking outwards to consumer tastes and competitive pressures. The main alternative is *production orientation*, where the firm looks inward to its own production needs and limitations. For many years, British firms were criticised for their lack of market orientation, but that changed in the 1980s. However, there is a danger that market orientation results in lost power and status for engineers and production managers, which might affect long-term technological competitiveness. (See also *asset-led marketing*.)

**market penetration:** a pricing strategy for a new product based on a desire to achieve high sales volume and high *market share*, perhaps with the effect of discouraging competitors from entering the market. Penetration pricing would mean setting the price relatively low, thereby accepting low *gross profit* margins with the expectation that the high *turnover* will allow *overheads* to be covered.

Pros:
- very useful if the market is one in which customers build up *brand loyalty* (prices can be pushed up later)
- sensible if you have only a small technological edge, because competitors will be arriving soon

Cons:
- loses the opportunity to charge higher prices to those willing to pay them for being first or innovators
- once a low-price image has been established in the customers' mind, it is hard to shift, and may always be associated with low quality

**market positioning:** where a manufacturer positions a brand within a marketplace, in terms of image, pricing and distribution. *Upmarket* or *downmarket?* Young and trendy or old, established? For specialists or for the general public? Such a decision is fundamental to the long-term marketing strategy of a product. (See *mapping*.)

**market power:** the degree to which a firm has power over its market. A firm like Heinz, for instance, has a more than 50 per cent *market share* in several large food market segments. It therefore has power when negotiating with raw material suppliers, power over the retailers whose customers expect Heinz on the shelves, and influence over consumers through the strength of its brand names and the size of its advertising budget. Market power leads to reduced *price elasticity*, and therefore presents an opportunity for increasing prices and *profit margins*.

**market price** is where the demand for a product exactly matches its 'supply'. It is therefore also known as the 'market clearing' price (labelled MP on the diagram).

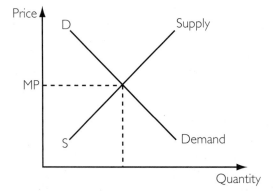

**market research:** the process of gathering *primary* and *secondary data* on the buying habits, lifestyle, usage and attitudes of actual and potential customers. The intention is to gather evidence that can enable marketing and production decisions to be made in a more scientific way than would otherwise be possible. Most large consumer goods firms would agree with Sherlock Holmes (in SCANDAL IN BOHEMIA), 'It is a capital mistake to theorise before one has data.'

Market research can be subdivided as follows:

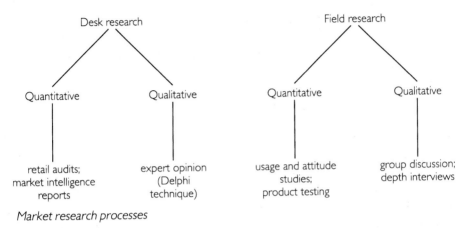

*Market research processes*

**market saturation** occurs when all those who want a product already have one. If the product is a *durable* (such as a freezer), demand will dry up until wear and tear creates a replacement market. With *consumables*, market saturation should not result in falling sales, but will inevitably prevent sales growth.

**market segmentation:** analysing a market to identify the different types of consumer. By matching the consumer categories to the types of product on offer, unfilled *market niches* may emerge. The potential profitability of filling these gaps can then be assessed. The main ways in which a market can be segmented are:

- demographically, e.g. by age, social class or sex
- psychographically (by attitudes and tastes) e.g. trendy versus staid, or home-loving versus adventurous
- geographically, by region

**market share:** the percentage of all the sales within a market that are held by one brand or company. This can be measured by volume (units sold) or by value (the revenue generated). Analysing trends in market share is important for a firm because it shows its position in relation to the market as a whole. It may not be good enough, for example, to have a 5 per cent sales increase if the market is rising at 10 per cent, as market share is being lost. The 5 per cent sales increase may boost profits this year, but if the market becomes highly price competitive as it reaches *maturity*, the firm's products may not be strong enough to survive.

**market-sharing agreement:** a *restrictive practice* in which a number of firms in an industry agree to allow each a profitable part of the total market. Generally this is illegal as it means that price competition is being suspended (forcing consumers to pay excessive prices). A market-sharing agreement is only likely if supply is dominated by a small number of firms (an *oligopoly*), and if it is hard for new competitors to enter the market.

**market size:** the total sales of all the producers within a market-place, measured either by volume (units sold) or by value (the revenue generated). This information is needed to:

- assess whether the market is big enough to be worth entering
- calculate the *market share* held by your own products and brands
- identify whether the market is expanding or contracting

**market standing:** the reputation of a firm amongst its suppliers, distributors and customers. If its market standing is high, a firm can feel confident that its new products will get *distribution* and *product trial*.

**market structure** describes the competitive forces within a market. For example, in the biscuit market, one firm has 50 per cent of all sales, whereas the market for frozen food has many competitors, each with less than 20 per cent of sales.

**market testing** is an investigation by a *public-sector* business of the price that *private-sector* firms would charge to supply a service. As a consequence they might contract private companies to supply services such as accounting (and, by implication, make their own accountants redundant).

**mark-up** is the amount of *gross profit* added on to the direct cost per unit, usually expressed as a percentage.

$$\text{FORMULA:} \quad \frac{\text{gross profit}}{\text{cost of sales}} \times 100 = \text{profit mark-up}$$

---

Worked example: A shirt bought by a shop for £8 and sold for £12 has a mark-up of:

$$\frac{£4}{£8} \times 100 = 50\%$$

---

**market value** is the price determined by *supply* and *demand*. Sellers often say things like, 'My motorbike is worth £1000', but when they come to sell it the bike realises only £400, which is its true 'value'. In the harsh world of economics, goods have no intrinsic value; in other words it makes no difference how much it costs to produce them, their true value has to be related to the amount people are willing to pay for them.

**Maslow A** (1908–1970): an American psychologist whose work on human needs has had great impact upon management theorists. Best known for his work on the *hierarchy of needs*.

**mass production:** the system devised by Henry Ford that turned raw materials into finished product in a continuously moving, highly mechanised process. Mass production's great strength was its high *productivity*, but this relied on manufacturing vast numbers of an identical product. This was epitomised in Henry Ford's famous phrase about his Model T, 'You can have any colour you want … as long as it's black.' As modern markets have become increasingly segmented, mass production has given way to *lean production* or *flexible specialisation*.

**Master of Business Administration (MBA):** a post-graduate degree in management science and methods. Associated mainly with Harvard University (USA) and teaching through case-studies.

**matching principle:** according to this, *expenses* (and *revenues*) are to be allocated in the accounts to the time period in which the cost (or benefit) to the organisation is felt. When the cost or benefit is felt may well differ from when the cash is paid or received. The benefit of a machine may be felt over a number of accounting periods so its cost is allocated to those periods by means of *depreciation*: thus, the cost is allocated against the revenues of those periods.

**materiality** the accounting convention which states that accounts should focus on matters of financial significance to the business, not on precision in trivial matters. For example, pencils in an office are not depreciated but are considered used up when bought.

**materials handling:** the management of the transfer of materials and parts through different stages of production and supply. The intention would be to minimise the distance, time and *wastage* of the materials supply process.

**materials requirement planning (MRP)** is complex computer software that can be programmed to calculate the precise materials requirements for completing a particular order. For example, a builder might use the MRP system to calculate the quantity and type of materials required to produce a two-storey office block. Generally, MRP has been superseded by MRP II (*manufacturing resource planning*).

**matrix management:** the willingness to organise the management of a task along lines that cut across normal departmental boundaries. A new product development team might be formed from an engineer, a research chemist, a marketing manager and a designer. This means that each team member can end up with two bosses: their department boss and the project leader. This has the potential to cause problems, though the Japanese seem to use this system effectively.

Pros:   • ensures that projects are better coordinated than with four departments meeting occasionally
       • if many different project teams are organised, it gives more people an opportunity to use their abilities

Cons:   • individuals may suffer if both bosses make heavy demands on them
       • there is a failure to provide the clear line of accountability present when everyone has just one boss

**maturity** is the peak sales period of a *product's life cycle*. It is likely to be a phase of fierce competition from new producers attracted to the market during the growth stage. This may cause a shake-out in which the less successful withdraw in the face of heavy losses. The survivors could then enjoy a highly profitable decline stage. Alternatively, mature products may be relaunched in *extension strategies* designed to rejuvenate and thereby postpone sales decline.

**Mayo E** (1880–1949): Elton Mayo was a follower of F W *Taylor* whose experiments led him to conclude that scientific management could not explain key aspects of people's behaviour at work. Many of his findings derived from his direction of research studies at a factory at Hawthorne, USA, from which stemmed the phrase the *Hawthorne effect*. He gave rise to what became known as the *Human Relations School* of management thinking.

**MBA:** see *Master in Business Administration*

**MBO**: either *management buy-out* or *management by objectives.*

**MBWA:** see *management by walking about*

**MEAL:** see *Media Expenditure Analysis Ltd*

**mean:** see *arithmetic average*

**measured day-work:** a method of organising work schedules and payment whereby workers have to complete a measured amount of output per day in order to achieve their basic wage.

Pros: • ensures that the company achieves the exact output level wanted on each day (whereas *piece-rate* can lead to over-production)
• a 'transparent' payment system, i.e. workers know exactly what is expected of them and exactly how their pay-packet is calculated

Cons: • could encourage hasty work, if staff decide to complete their tasks as fast as possible in order to finish early
• when used in the motor industry, embarrassing examples were publicised of workers completing their day's work in four hours, then sleeping for the rest of their shift

**measure of central tendency:** an attempt to describe a *frequency distribution* in a single measure. There are three main measures: *mean, median* and *mode.*

**media advertising:** paying for advertising space or time in national, regional or local media. Media advertising aimed at consumers is known as *above the line* marketing.

**Media Expenditure Analysis Ltd (MEAL):** the producers of a widely used, monthly reference book that shows how much every advertiser has spent, and in which type of media. So if a soft drink producer is wondering how much to budget for the launch advertising of a new fizzy orange, MEAL will help by showing how much has been spent by Tango, Fanta and Sunkist.

**median:** a *measure of central tendency* which divides the distribution into two equal parts. If the items in the distribution are ranked in ascending order, the *median* is the middle item. One advantage of the median is that it is not affected by extreme values. A disadvantage is that it gives findings that are biased towards the most numerous and (perhaps) away from the most important.

**media planning:** the process of selecting media to advertise to your target market as cost-effectively as possible. This function is usually carried out by the media department of an advertising agency. It is a four-stage process:

1 Gather the research data to identify your target market.
2 Decide (in discussion with the creative team) the broad media choice: television, newspapers, magazines, cinema, radio or posters.
3 Select exactly which magazines or television regions would be most cost-effective (e.g. VOGUE for reaching wealthy, fashion conscious women).
4 Allocate the media budget as cost-efficiently as possible between the chosen media (e.g. buy more television commercials on the station that reaches your market more economically).

Stages 3 and 4 are undertaken by comparing the cost of an advertising space with the number of readers that publication has in your target market. The following table shows how this might work for a brand of cider targeted at 18–35-year-old women.

| Publication | Cost of colour page | Thousands of 18–35 women readers | Cost per thousand readers |
|---|---|---|---|
| Cosmopolitan | £24 000 | 1 650 | £14.55 |
| Woman | £32 000 | 2 950 | £10.85 |
| Hello | £18 000 | 2 422 | £7.64 |

In this example each thousand women in the target market could be reached at half the cost in HELLO magazine than in COSMOPOLITAN, so HELLO would be the best value medium.

**media selection:** see *media planning*

**mediation:** another term for *conciliation*

**memo:** short for *memorandum*

**memorandum:** a conventional way of conveying written information that is too brief or too urgent to be produced as a report. It is like a letter, but is distributed within the organisation. Usually a memo starts with a format such as:

> Memo to: J Rowlands, Marketing Manager
> From: S Tanna, Marketing Executive
> Date: 25 June
> Subject: The sales decline in May

**memorandum of association** shows the *objectives* of the company, the amount of *authorised share capital* as well as the classes of shares and the voting rights of the shareholders. It is one of the two documents needed for a firm to become incorporated as a *limited liability* company (the other being the *articles of association*).

**mentor:** an experienced and trusted advisor to a new recruit; in effect, an appointed father-figure. This is a modern development of *human relations* theory that ensures that all recruits have a senior figure they can turn to for advice. The mentor will keep any comments or complaints confidential, and could therefore be a more effective advisor than the recruit's boss.

**merchandising:** visiting retail outlets to ensure that a company's products are displayed in as attractive and prominent a way as possible. Merchandisers might offer special display stands or shelves to retailers, hoping that they will use these, in effect, *point-of-sale* advertisements for the company.

**merchant bank** is a form of specialised commercial bank which performs a variety of banking functions, although rarely those directly concerned with the public. Merchant banks developed through the activities of overseas traders who dealt originally with the financing of imports and exports. They still fulfil this role, but their most important functions today are as issuing houses, and as advisers to businesses, particularly on matters concerned with *mergers* and *take-overs*. As issuing houses they advise firms on the right time and how to raise capital on the *Stock Exchange* or the *Alternative Investment Market*. They also act as underwriters to the issue by guaranteeing to buy stock which is not immediately sold at the time of issue. In recent years, many merchant banks have become part of larger banking *conglomerates*, but their names live on. Employees of Hambros, Rothschilds, Lazards and Schroders are often seen on the television offering expert advice on economic and financial matters.

**merger:** an agreement between the managements and shareholders of two companies of approximately equal size to bring both firms together under a common board of directors. (See *take-over*.)

**mergers and acquisitions (M and A)** is a collective term used by American-influenced City institutions to denote the general area of corporate *mergers* and *take-overs*. Many *merchant banks* have M and A departments that can charge substantial fees for advising companies on how to win or to defend against *take-over bids*.

**merit pay:** a form of bonus payment received by employees considered to have performed at a high standard during a year or half-year. To evaluate who deserves a merit pay award, *performance appraisal* is often used.

Pros: • merit pay is a reward system that can apply to all employees (whereas commission, for example, will only be received by those involved in direct selling)

Cons: • often involves tiny sums: a 5 per cent bonus may seem poor reward for outstanding work
• offers scope for mistrust and misunderstanding if some workers suspect there has been favouritism in the allocation of the bonuses

**merit ratings** are a scheme by which employees' performance can be appraised in a semi-quantified way, by giving individuals a mark out of ten for each of a series of job-related criteria. For instance a supermarket worker might be rated on:

|  | Mark awarded | Out of |
|---|---|---|
| Attendance and punctuality | 4 | 5 |
| Checkout-till speed | 9 | 10 |
| Politeness to customers | 2 | 5 |
| Helpfulness to fellow staff | 2 | 5 |
| TOTAL | 17 | 25 |

**methods of transportation** of goods can be via road, rail, water or air. The key factors determining firms' choice include: the importance of speed, freshness, cost, reliability and convenience.

**method study:** analysis of the method by which workers approach a task with the intention of identifying opportunities for improvement. This was F W *Taylor*'s scientific companion to *work study*. First, the consultant would decide how to subdivide the whole production process into small units of work, then method study would decide how each task should be carried out. Method study was carried out by timing each action and recording the motion and effort used. The presence of the so-called time-and-motion men was quickly to become a cause of *industrial relations* disputes.

**me-too product:** a new brand that is largely an imitation of a successful existing one. Usually me-toos struggle to get distribution in shops and are looked down on by customers. So they can only gain sales if they sell at an unprofitably large discount to the price of the original product. Occasionally, though, a firm with an exceptionally wide and powerful distribution network can make me-toos more successful than the original. Walls Cornetto was a me-too of Lyons Maid's King Cone, and Magnum a me-too of the Häagen-Dazs Stick Bar. In both cases, consumers became so familiar with the Walls product that its origin was soon forgotten.

**mezzanine debt** is a source of business finance that is halfway between debt and *equity*. Like a loan, mezzanine finance pays a fixed interest rate. Unlike most loans, however, mezzanine finance is not secured to asset-backed collateral. Therefore it represents a high-risk loan. When sold on to the *Stock Exchange*, such debts are often called *junk bonds*.

**microcomputers** are the smallest computers in the series beginning with *mainframe computers* and going through *minicomputers*. They are generally used by small or medium-sized businesses.

**micro-economics** is the study of how markets work. It provides a theoretical framework for the way firms and *factors of production* operate. Taken together, the workings of small-scale (micro) markets lead to the macroeconomy.

**middleman:** the *agent* or wholesaler who brings together buyers and sellers. It is often assumed that middlemen serve little function, but merely add their *mark-up* to the retail prices of items. Some middlemen could be regarded as parasitic (such as arms dealers), but most are fulfilling the normal *wholesaling* function of breaking bulk.

**milking a product:** maximising the profit from a brand, usually by pushing its price up as far as possible without forcing regular purchasers to switch to another brand. This high price level is likely to discourage new users from starting to buy the product, therefore the brand's *product life cycle* will be shortened. So milking a product implies short-term profit maximisation, even at the cost of the brand's long-term prospects.

The *Boston Matrix* shows the situation in which a firm might milk a product. If the firm has two brands with a high *market share*, one in a growth sector and another in a declining sector, the correct strategy would be to milk the *cash cow* and use the funds to support the 'rising star'. A typical example is the way that cigarette manufacturers have pushed up the prices of long-standing, untipped brands such as Woodbines. Many elderly smokers are still loyal to these brands, and they have been the tobacco industry's cash cows for over 20 years.

**milk round:** the slang term used for the annual practice of some large firms to visit many universities and recruit the best of those interviewed as management trainees.

**minicomputers** are medium-sized computers, lying between *mainframe computers* and *microcomputers*. They are generally used by medium to large organisations.

**minority interest:** this arises where a *subsidiary* of a *holding company* is not wholly owned and a minority of the shares is owned by others. In the holding company accounts, the minority shareholdings of the subsidiaries are *long-term liabilities* and the profits due to the minority shareholders are deducted from profit after tax.

**Mintel,** standing for Marketing Intelligence, is one of the leading sources of secondary marketing information. Every month Mintel analyses the consumers, producers, advertising and distribution within a range of markets. One month they might look at chocolate confectionery, ice-cream and washing-up liquid; the next it might be cosmetics, fruit juice and detergents. A Mintel report is likely to contain most of the *secondary data* a firm needs for its marketing planning (or a student needs for the background to a business project). As Mintel is very expensive to subscribe to, few public libraries have it. It is held at universities or at specialist libraries such as London's *City Business Library* and Birmingham's Central Reference Library.

**Mintzberg H** (b. 1939): an American writer on organisation theory who sought to explain what managers actually do. He rejected the traditional notion that managers plan, organise, coordinate and control. His research showed that most senior and middle managers spend little time thinking ahead. Their days are spent on a series of small tasks related to the problems of the moment and use mainly *oral communication*. Mintzberg recommended that managers should undergo far more training into their role and their use of time.

**minutes** of a meeting are a record of who attended, what the discussions were about and the conclusions that were reached.

**mission statement:** the document detailing the aims that should provide the sense of common purpose to direct and stimulate the organisation. Advocates of mission statements believe that their focus on goals such as high quality and customer service are far easier for employees to relate to than profit. Critics suggest that the statements are little more than *public relations* exercises.

**mixed economy:** one which combines a *market economy* with centrally planned or State-run enterprises. A wholly market-led economy has certain disadvantages, the most important of which is the exploitation of certain members of society, usually those who are economically the weakest. Consequently governments regulate the workings of the market either through laws, or by running parts of the economy through state enterprises. This is known as a mixed economy. In the UK, those industries run indirectly by government have included coal, steel, gas and electricity production, and services such as British Rail and the Post Office. Since 1979, there has been extensive *privatisation*, which has resulted in a greater influence of the market.

| Centrally planned economy | Mixed economy | Market economy |
|---|---|---|
| Production organised and run by the State | Some production State-run, e.g. large-scale 'essential ' services | Production market-driven |
| Labour forced directed and paid in by the State | State and private firms compete for factors of production and customers | Wages determined by the market |
| Prices of goods and services controlled | | Prices determined by supply and demand |

**mobility of labour** is the ability and willingness of workers to move from one job to another. This is an important issue because economic change is so rapid that unless people are able and willing to change jobs they may become permanently unemployed if their type of job becomes obsolete. There are two parts to this mobility: geographical and occupational. In practice, however, they are closely connected, since it is often necessary to change geographical location if a worker's occupation changes. Because of social, cultural and economic ties, efforts to encourage greater mobility in the UK have largely failed.

**mode:** the most frequently occurring result within a set of data. This is a *measure of central tendency*.

**model:** a representation of reality designed to provide insights into how and why an event has occurred or is expected to occur. Usually models are presented in a graphical form (such as a *break-even chart*), though they may be stored as a series of equations within a computer program.

**modem:** a device that allows computers to 'talk' to each other by converting electrical digital signals to signals that can be transmitted along telephone lines. A modem is one of the pieces of equipment that can be used for e-mail or accessing the Internet. The word modem comes from MOdulator/DEModulator.

**Mondex card:** a plastic card that can be used as cash for making small purchases. A bank account holder can use an automatic cash dispenser to transfer any sum from their account to the card. Then, for example, if £100 has been transferred to the card, the user can spend up to that limit. No credit is provided. In 1995 the Natwest and Midland banks trialled the Mondex card in Swindon, where 720 shops were signed up to accept it. If the trial proved successful it would be launched nationally.

**monetarism** is an economic theory associated with the American economist Milton *Friedman*. It states that the supply of money is at the centre of economic activity, and since the government is the only authority which can increase or decrease the supply of money, it is the government's responsibility to control the supply with care. If governments print too much money or allow too much credit, *inflation* will result, since *supply* will outstrip *demand*. If too little money is available, people and firms will have to find a way around the scarcity and so employ less-efficient mechanisms, such as *barter*. As a result, trade will suffer. Monetarists believe that controlling money is the only essential function of governments, who should remove themselves from other areas of economic activity and let markets decide on the efficient allocation of resources.

**monetary policy** is concerned with the *money supply*, rates of interest, exchange rates and the amount of *credit* available, in order to control the level of spending within the economy. There is a great deal of dispute as to the importance of monetary policy, with the monetarists arguing that it is the vital determinant of *aggregate demand*. *Keynesians* believe that the importance of monetary policy is often overstated. They consider *fiscal policy* to be at least as important an influence upon the level of economic activity.

**monetary squeeze** is used to describe a *monetary policy* which attempts to restrict spending in the economy by raising interest rates and limiting the amount of *credit* available. This can be done by restricting *hire-purchase* terms, e.g. raising the required deposit as a percentage of the total price and limiting the repayment period; or by acting on the *commercial banks* either directly or indirectly to limit the amount of lending that they undertake.

**monetary union:** see *European Monetary Union*

**money cycle:** the flow of cash out of and in to a business over the course of fulfilling an order (the *trading cycle*). The table below shows a money cycle for a £240 order costing £200 to make; the firm starts with £150 and ends with £40 extra (the profit).

| | 1 | 2 | 3 | 4 | 5 | 6 |
|---|---|---|---|---|---|---|
| | Initial cash | Purchase materials | Produce goods | Sell on credit | Customer pays | Residual cash |
| Cash in | £150 | - | - | - | £240 | - |
| Cash out | - | £80 | £120 | - | - | - |
| Cash | £150 | £70 | (£50) | (£50) | £190 | £190 balance |

**money income** is the measure of a person's income without taking price levels into account. So, if your money income was £10 000 this year and it rises to £20 000 next, you are twice as well off in money terms. If prices have doubled during the same period (ignoring taxes etc.), your *real income* will not have changed at all.

**money market:** where buyers and sellers of financial securities and loans come together at an agreed price, usually a rate of interest called the discount rate. There is no single physical market-place, since transactions are usually conducted over the phone, through on-line computer links or through faxes.

**money supply** can be measured in a number of ways, from a very narrow definition simply including notes and coins in circulation, to a much wider one which includes *credit*. The reason why broad definitions are used is because goods and services can be bought on credit as well as with cash, and so that will affect overall spending power. In the UK there are a number of ways in which the money supply is measured, the most common being 'M0', 'M1', 'Sterling M3' and 'PSL2'. From the point of view of business, it is important that there is always enough money in circulation, but not too much. Insufficient money leads to inconvenience, and ultimately the necessity to *barter*, whereas too much money leads to *inflation*. The judgement of how much money and credit to allow to circulate is a difficult one, but should mirror the growth of the real economy.

**Monopolies and Mergers Commission:** a government-financed organisation whose function is to oversee proposed *mergers* and to check that where *monopolies* do exist, they are not against the public interest. The Commission was established by the *Fair Trading Act 1973*, although it had existed as the Monopolies Commission since 1948. As a general rule, any merger which is likely to lead to a 25 per cent or greater market dominance will be investigated by the Commission. It will also look into existing cases of the apparent abuse of monopoly power. The Commission itself cannot take legal action; it can only advise the *Office of Fair Trading* that action is necessary. Increasingly, the UK's merger policies have come under the influence of the *EU*, in particular Articles 85 and 86. These, amongst other things, look at Europe-wide market dominance to determine whether to allow a proposed merger to proceed.

**monopolistic competition** occurs when the firms competing within a market-place have sufficient product differentiation to achieve a degree of monopoly power. This usually results from the development of brand names strong enough to prevent competition being purely on the basis of price.

**monopoly** is in theory a single producer within a market. This represents one end of a spectrum of competition, at the other end of which is *perfect competition*.

In practice such dominant producers rarely exist, especially as the definition of the market widens. The potential danger of monopolies is that they will exploit the *consumer*, either by charging excessive prices, or by offering a poor service, or they will simply waste scarce resources by being inefficient. In some cases, monopolies exhibit all these characteristics, and hence governments exercise legal or voluntary restraints on their activities. In the UK monopolies can be investigated by the *Monopolies and Mergers Commission*. The former nationalised utilities such as gas, electricity and water have *regulators* appointed to control them.

MONOPOLY – – – – – OLIGOPOLY – – – – – MONOPOLISTIC – – – – –PERFECT
COMPETITION COMPETITION

INCREASING NUMBER OF FIRMS IN THE MARKET
INCREASING COMPETITION

*Market dominance*

**monopsony** means a single buyer, as opposed to a *monopoly* which is a single seller. A single buyer is in a strong position to exploit the supplier of the good or service required. This can be done by forcing the supplier to lower the price, delay payment, or impose quality standards which he might otherwise not be able to do. It is sometimes said that large Japanese corporations act as monopsonists, pushing stock holding requirements to their suppliers and forcing each to compete very strongly for business.

**Monthly Digest of Statistics:** the publication that provides regular government statistics on output, the *balance of payments* and many other business, economic and social topics. It is an invaluable *secondary data* source and is stocked by many public libraries. It is published by HMSO.

**morale** is a measurement of the confidence and pride of a workforce. High morale should lead to good quality work and a commitment to participate in problem-solving and decision-making. For a manager, few challenges are more daunting than the attempt to transform a group with very low morale into one with far higher self-confidence and pride.

**morality** (in business): the willingness to make decisions on the basis of principle rather than profit, self-interest, or convenience. This may be easier to achieve for the proprietors of a family business than for the directors of a *public limited company*. The former run the business they own, whereas the latter are answerable to shareholders for whom *profit* may be an overriding consideration.

**Morita A** (b. 1921): co-founder of the Sony Corporation, Akio Morita built up his business through innovations such as the transistor radio, the portable television and, most famously, the Walkman. The latter was Morita's conception and he pushed it through to worldwide success even though research suggested that people would have no use for it. From a British viewpoint, Morita's other contribution was to set up one of the first Japanese factories in Britain: the Sony factory in South Wales. This was successful in achieving Japanese standards of productivity and quality, helping to prove that Japanese management methods can work with a British workforce. More inward investment from other Japanese firms followed, as did a substantial shift in attitude by British managers. (See the *Japanese way* and *Japanisation*.)

**mortgage:** a form of commercial loan, secured against a specific property asset. It may or may not be at a fixed rate of interest.

**motivation:** as defined by Professor *Herzberg*, is the will to work due to enjoyment of the work itself. He urges that it should be distinguished from 'movement'. According to the Professor, 'If you do a good job because you want to do a good job, that's motivation. If you do it because you want a house or a Jaguar, that's movement' (JUMPING FOR THE JELLYBEANS BBC Books, 1973). Many other writers and business people use the term motivation differently, to mean anything that causes people to achieve more than they would otherwise do.

**motivation theory:** the writings of industrial psychologists and sociologists which shed light on the factors determining the satisfaction and motivation of employees. The ideas involved can be grouped into two: 'needs' theory and 'expectancy' theory:

- 'needs' theory examines workers' physical, social and psychological requirements from a job; well known theorists include *FW Taylor, Elton Mayo* and *Frederick Herzberg*
- expectancy theory suggests that people are not all driven by the same needs; their motivation is determined by how sure they feel that a desired outcome will be achieved. This approach is associated with Victor *Vroom*.

**motivational research:** see *qualitative research*

**motivators** are the aspects of a job that can (according to Professor *Herzberg*) lead to positive job satisfaction on the part of the employee. They include:

- achievement
- recognition for achievement
- meaningful, interesting work
- psychological growth and advancement at work (such as learning new skills or learning more about yourself)

**moving average:** a calculation of the trend that exists within a series of data over time. It enables erratic and seasonal factors within the data to be smoothed out so that the underlying trend can be identified (see the diagram on page 185).

There are three steps required to calculate a moving average.

1 Decide on an appropriate number of time periods for calculating the average; usually this will be to cover a full year, e.g. four quarters.
2 Add up the values over the first available time period and average them, e.g. year 1 quarters 1, 2, 3 and 4 (divided by 4).
3 Repeat the process for the next time period, e.g. year 1 quarters 2, 3 and 4 plus year 2 quarter 1 (divided by 4). Carry this process through until the last four quarters within the data series.

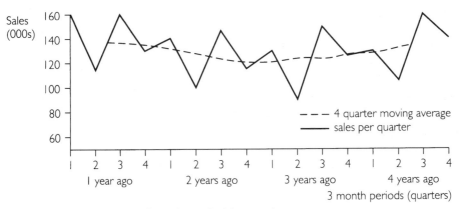

*Using a moving average to show the underlying trend*

**MRP:** see *materials requirement planning*

**MRP II:** see *manufacturing resource planning*

**multilateral** negotiations or agreements are those conducted between many parties (usually countries). The negotiators might be representatives of the major *trading blocs*, such as the *European Union*. The most widely known multilateral trade agreement is GATT, the *General Agreement on Tariffs and Trade.*

**multimedia** involves the use of different media in, for instance, a presentation. Thus the speaker may use television, audio cassette tapes, computer images and so on to make the message carry more impact. The same approach is also widespread within the personal computer (PC) market.

**multinational:** a firm which has its headquarters in one country, but with bases, manufacturing or assembly plants in others. Developing countries are often delighted to welcome multinational companies, but there are two sides to the argument:

Pros:
- they provide employment and income and therefore better living standards
- they may improve the level of expertise of the local workforce and suppliers
- they improve the country's *balance of payments* because imports are reduced

Cons:
- the jobs provided may only require low-level skills
- they may export all the profits back to the 'home' country
- they may cut corners on health and safety or pollution, which they could not do in their 'home' country
- they have been known to exert excessive political muscle

**multiple** (retailer): a store chain which has a number of shops that run on similar, head-office dominated lines. Their size provides the opportunity for tough negotiation over the unit prices of the stocks being purchased.

**multiplier:** the concept that an increase in *injections* to the *circular flow of income* will be multiplied as it goes through the economy, raising incomes as it goes, although by smaller increments. For instance, if the government decides to build a new rail link it will inject say, £100m. into the economy by paying for wages, raw materials and so on. The money will go to the workers and shareholders of the companies concerned, and they will in turn spend more on goods and services, raising wages and profits in consumer-orientated industries. Steadily, then, beneficial knock-on effects are spread through the economy.

**multi-serving** is the ability of a file server to deal with the individual needs of hundreds of computer terminal users simultaneously. It works by interrupting the messages to each terminal to deal with others, but the interruption is so brief that the human operator at the terminal sees no break.

**multi-skilling** means training a workforce to be able to work effectively across a wide range of tasks. This is necessary if *demarcation* barriers are to be broken down and the scope of jobs is to be enlarged. Multi-skilling has many short- and long-term benefits:

Short-term:
- staff can cover for absent colleagues
- trained staff can spot maintenance or other problems before they become serious
- faults can be corrected without the need to wait for a series of different tradesmen

Long-term:
- staff promoted from the shop-floor will have a far wider knowledge and understanding of the process they are now managing
- changes to working practices or to products will be far easier to achieve with a multi-skilled workforce
- wider responsibilities and expertise may help to improve motivation

**municipal services:** council-run facilities such as leisure centres, community centres, refuse collection and street cleaning. Many of these have been contracted out in recent years, meaning that they have been taken out of local authority direct control.

**multi-tasking** is the ability of a file server to download multiple software applications to network users from its hard disk, so that for instance, one person can be word processing whilst another is simultaneously using a spreadsheet package.

# N

**narrow band** is the term used to describe a currency which is allowed to float, but only within certain quite restricted limits before there is *central bank* intervention. Within the European *Exchange Rate Mechanism*, the limits of the narrow band are 2.5 per cent above and below a currency's central rate.

**national bargaining** occurs when *trade unions* negotiate with employers on behalf of members throughout the country. This has become far less common as firms have looked towards plant (local) bargaining or rejected *collective bargaining* totally, in preference for individual contracts.

**National Council for Vocational Qualifications** (NCVQ) is the government body that supervises the certification of vocational qualifications within Britain. It is attempting to provide a series of widely accepted certificates that demonstrate the competences of individuals at levels of achievement between Level 1 and Level 4. By ensuring comparability, a qualification in Level 3 catering should indicate the same ability level as in Level 3 manufacturing. This should make it easier for employees made redundant to switch to alternative jobs. The two main types of qualification offered by NCVQ are the *National Vocational Qualification* (NVQ) and the more academic *General National Vocational Qualification* (GNVQ).

**national income** is the sum of all incomes within an economy after allowing for depreciation. Through the *circular flow of national income* it will necessarily equal the value of annual national output. It includes wages, salaries, profits (whether distributed to shareholders or not), rents, and net income from abroad.

**National Insurance** is the social framework established in the UK after the Second World War whereby all employers, employees and the self-employed make contributions which provide a number of benefits. These include a safety net in the event of illness or unemployment, pensions beyond retirement age, child and maternity benefits, and various other grants. The increasing cost of state benefits, especially as the population ages into the twenty-first century, has become a matter of concern and some debate since a smaller working population will have to support an ever-growing number of dependents.

**nationalisation** describes the transfer of firms and industries from the *private* to the *public sector*. In the UK most nationalised industries were private concerns which had failed e.g. the railways, steelmaking, coalmining, British Leyland (now Rover), and Rolls-Royce, but since 1979 there has been a policy of denationalisation or *privatisation* which has returned most of them to the private sector.

**National Saving** is a form of government borrowing which encourages people to save by offering not only a reasonable interest rate free of tax, but also perhaps more importantly offering absolute security for the money itself.

**National Vocational Qualification (NVQ):** a government initiative to provide young people and employees with a widely accepted, job-focused qualification at a variety of different skill levels.

**natural monopolies** exist where the scale of business operation is so large that it is only economic and practical to have one supplier of the service. For example, to have competing gas mains running side by side to every house would be a waste of resources. It was often argued by those who believed in *nationalisation*, that many industries represent natural monopolies, including power supply, water supply and telecommunications. Admirers of *privatisation* say that this is no reason for the state to have direct control, and many of these industries have now successfully been passed into private hands. The debate continues, however, since many public *monopolies* which have been privatised are now perceived as private monopolies instead, with little or no effective competition.

**natural wastage:** the process of natural labour turnover as employees retire, leave to have children, or leave for other jobs, i.e. for any reason other than *redundancy* or *dismissal*. The rate of natural wastage will differ depending upon demographic factors such as the number of older workers and the proportion of young women. If the rate is relatively high (for instance 12 per cent per annum), then it is possible for the company to reduce its workforce rapidly without needing to resort to redundancies.

**NCVQ:** see *National Council for Vocational Qualifications*

**negative cash flow** occurs when the *cash flow* entering the company is less than that leaving it, i.e. cash outflow is greater than cash inflow. This may be perfectly normal for a firm in its off-season, but if negative cash flow persists it will drain the business of its *liquidity*.

**negative skew** is a *bias* within a distribution towards low values. In other words the majority of the values are below the average. For example, the diagram below shows a research finding into the frequency of school library usage by age of user. It shows that although the average age of a school library user is 15 years, the distribution is skewed towards younger, less-frequent users.

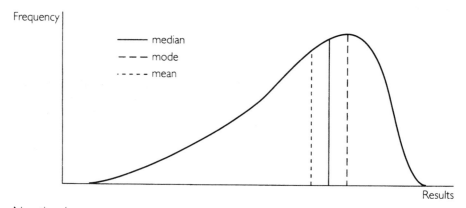

*Negative skew*

**negligence** is a legal term implying that an individual or company has failed in its duty to have regard for the interests of others. It may therefore be possible for the injured party to sue for *damages*.

**negotiation** is a method of joint decision-making involving bargaining between different firms or between workforce and management representatives within a firm. The objective is to arrive at mutually acceptable terms. A distinction can be made between negotiation and *consultation*, as the former term implies competitive rivalry between conflicting interests.

**net**: short for *Internet*.

**net assets** is taken by some exam boards to mean the same as assets employed, i.e. *fixed assets* plus *net current assets* (*working capital*). In published company accounts, however, *long-term liabilities* are deducted, making net assets mean the same as *net worth*. When faced with exam questions about accounting terms such as net assets, candidates can be assured that the examiners will allow any of the different versions in usage:

Examiners' version:  fixed assets + net current assets = net assets

Business practice:    fixed assets + net current assets – long-term liabilities = net assets

**net book value** is the *historic cost* of a *fixed asset* minus its accumulated *depreciation* and is the figure which is written down in the company's *balance sheet*. It is not necessarily a measure of the market value of the asset, which depends ultimately on what someone is prepared to pay. Where an asset is sold for more than its net book value a surplus is recorded under *shareholders' funds*.

**net current assets**, also called *working capital*, comprise *current assets* minus *current liabilities*. It is the finance available for the day-to-day running of the business.

> FORMULA:   current assets – current liabilities = net current assets

**net margin** is the percentage of *sales revenue* which is *net profit*. Unlike the gross margin, fixed *overheads* have been taken into account within this ratio. Therefore it is of far greater business significance.

> FORMULA:   $\dfrac{\text{net (operating) profit}}{\text{sales revenue}} \times 100 = \text{net margin}$

**net present value (NPV)** is the value today of the estimated *cash flows* resulting from an investment. It is found by discounting the future cash flows to make allowance for the *opportunity cost* of tying up *capital* in the investment. Each year's discounted cash total is added together and taken from today's cash outlay on the project. If the resulting figure (the NPV) is positive, then the project is viable. The worked example shows an investment where the *discounted* (future) *cash flows* are not enough to justify the initial outlay.

Worked example: calculating the NPV on the purchase of an industrial robot

Assumptions:
- the robot costs £200 000 and should last four years
- it will cost £20 000 per year to run but save £80 000 of labour costs
- interest rates and therefore the discount factors are at 10 per cent

|        | Cash in | Cash out | Net cash | Discount factor | Present value |
|--------|---------|----------|----------|-----------------|---------------|
| Now    | –       | 200      | (200)    | 1               | (200)         |
| Year 1 | 80      | 20       | 60       | 0.91            | 54.6          |
| Year 2 | 80      | 20       | 60       | 0.83            | 49.8          |
| Year 3 | 80      | 20       | 60       | 0.75            | 45.0          |
| Year 4 | 80      | 20       | 60       | 0.68            | 40.8          |
|        |         |          | Net present value: |       | (9.8)         |

All figures in £000s; negative figures in brackets.

**net profit** is *gross profit* minus expenses such as the *overhead* costs. In other words it is *sales revenue* minus all the operating costs of the business. It can therefore also be termed *operating profit.*

**net realisable value** is the money an *asset* could be sold for, after allowing for any expenses involved. Stock is usually valued on a *balance sheet* at the lower of *historic cost* or net realisable value.

**network:** a diagram used in *network analysis* that shows the activities needed to complete a project, the order in which they should be completed, and the activities that can be completed simultaneously.

**network analysis** is a term describing techniques for planning and controlling projects that consist of a series of interrelated activities. The object is to break a project down into its component activities, placing them in the right sequence, then deciding when to schedule them. Many projects, such as building work or new product development, can be divided into separate activities which can be put into a logical sequence on a network diagram. The duration of each activity can be estimated. There are two alternative methods for completing the network analysis:

- *critical path analysis* focuses upon the longest activity route through to the completion of the project
- programme evaluation review technique (PERT) follows a similar system, but acknowledges that the time allowed to complete activities cannot be predicted exactly, and makes allowance for this

**networking:** the establishment of business contacts and communication links by socialising, attending professional meetings or by belonging to the right clubs. People do this in the belief that 'it's not what you know, it's who you know.'

**networking (IT):** interlinking computer hardware to enable users to have access to information, applications software and computer resources without knowing where any of them are located. As many schools and colleges are aware, computer networks sound excellent in theory, but can be a disappointment due to their unreliability.

**net worth:** the value of a firm's *assets* after all external *liabilities* have been allowed for, i.e. assets employed – *long-term liabilities.* This figure balances with *shareholders' funds,* which gives a good indication of its meaning. A firm's net worth is its net wealth, the real value of the firm according to its *balance sheet.* Therefore if the company is liquidated, by selling off all the assets and paying off all the debts the firm should arrive at a cash sum equal to its net worth. This sum would then be distributed to the shareholders.

FORMULA:   assets employed – long-term liabilities = net worth

**newly industrialised country (NIC):** one which has moved from having a dominant *primary sector* (agriculture and mining) to a fast growing and substantial *secondary sector* (manufacturing). The best known examples are countries around the Pacific Rim such as Singapore and Taiwan. They experience rapid growth, often through attracting *multinationals,* especially while wage rates remain far behind those of developed economies such as Japan and the United States.

**new product development (NPD)** implies all the functions required to identify, develop and market new product opportunities. This requires close cooperation between *research and development, market research* and general marketing functions. A great deal of new product development is based on *qualitative research,* in which psychologists probe for the reasons behind consumer attitudes and actions. This is because radical new products are rarely the result of scientifically conducted research; they stem from insight into the minds of the customer.

**new technology** is used to describe the rapid changes in communications and other processes resulting from the exploitation of the silicon chip. The innovations resulting from the use of new technology can be split into three main types:

- by process, that is advancements in manufacturing technology and automation
- by product, that is new product opportunities using micro-electronic technology such as the fax machine and the electronic games
- by communication links, that is *information technology*

**niche marketing:** a corporate strategy based on identifying and filling relatively small market segments. This can enable small firms to operate profitably in markets dominated by large corporations. It can also be a strategy pursued by a large firm that prefers to have five brands selling 50 000 units in each of five niches, rather than one brand selling 250 000 in the mass market.

Pros: • the first company to identify a niche market can often secure a solid market position as consumers see the original product as superior (e.g. Findus French Bread Pizza)

- consumers are willing to pay a price premium for a more exclusive product

Cons: • lack of *economies of scale* may make costs too high to achieve satisfactory *profit margins*

- the firm's production system must be flexible enough to cope with relatively small quantities of several products (see *flexible specialisation*)

**Nielsen:** a *market research* company best known for their *retail audits.*

**Nikkei Index** is Japan's Stock Exchange Index, equivalent to London's Financial Times Stock Exchange (FT-SE100) index (*Footsie*).

**NIMBY:** see *not in my back yard*

**nineteen ninety two (1992)** became symbolic for the completion of the *single European market*, which was supposed to have happened by the 31st December 1992. In fact many aspects have yet to be resolved, though there has been some progress towards freer trade within the *European Union*.

**node:** the point on a *network* diagram that represents the end of an activity and/or the start of the next. Nodes are drawn as circles within which can be put information such as the *earliest start time* of the activities that follow, or the *latest finish time* of preceding activities. All networks start and end on a single node.

**noise:** factors that can distract from the accurate reception of a piece of communication. These include communication overload, i.e. when too many points are being communicated simultaneously to the same person; and a poor or faulty *transmission mechanism*.

**nominal value** means a face value, not a *market value* or a value based on cost. It most commonly applies in the case of financial securities or shares where the value written on the face of the certificate is not related to its market price. In other words a £1 share may currently have a market price of £3 because the firm is prospering. The term nominal value also applies when something is sold at a trivial or merely nominal price.

**non-discriminatory legislation:** Acts of Parliament that make it illegal to discriminate against an employee on grounds of sex (Sex Discrimination Act) or race (Race Relations Act) when selecting staff for recruitment, training or promotion . The Equal Pay Act also outlaws men and women receiving different pay levels for work of equal value.

**non-executive director:** a part-time director of a company who has no day-to-day involvement or executive powers. The function of a non-executive director is to supply unbiased advice, specialist expertise and act as a control on the executives. Often a non-executive director may represent a large shareholder such as a pension fund. Following the scandal of Robert Maxwell's raid on his employees' pension fund, the *Cadbury Committee* report on *corporate governance* recommended a strengthening of the role of non-executive directors. The Committee's view was that non-executive directors are far more likely than executives to show independence from the senior management. They can therefore act as a brake on the actions of a dominant chief executive.

**non-price competition** is all forms of competitive action other than through the price mechanism. Examples include advertising, sales promotions, packaging, branding, point-of-sale activity and sponsorship.

**non-profit-making organisations** may be run in a businesslike way, but their objective is not the conventional one of the profit motive. Examples include charities, *Training and Enterprise Councils* and schools that have opted out of the local authority funding system.

**non-recourse finance** (or *factoring*) means that the bank (or *factor*) cannot reclaim up-front funding from the client, if the client's customer defaults on the debt. This protects the user of a factoring service from *bad debts*.

**non-tariff barriers** are hidden barriers to trade imposed by governments because they wish to restrict imports without being seen to do so, perhaps because it would be contrary to international regulations under *GATT*. Such barriers may take several forms:

- constantly changing technical regulations which make compliance difficult for importers
- forcing importers to use specified points of entry where documentation is dealt with only slowly
- regulations which favour domestic producers e.g. packaging, and labels which conform to local language requirements

**normal curve:** the bell-shaped curve of the *normal distribution* as shown below.

**normal distribution:** a *frequency distribution* which is bell-shaped so that half of the variables lie to the left of the *mean* and half to the right. Due to the symmetry of the curve, the mean, *median* and *mode* all coincide at the same value. If data is collected on an event that occurs many times over, variations in the result will tend to form a pattern that is known as normal distribution. This means that the results will tend to be clustered around the average, and will be split equally between results above and below the average (see the diagram above). Normal distributions can be standardised so that the width of the distribution is about six *standard deviations*. The areas within each standard deviation can be very useful in statistical analysis, for example in *significance testing*.

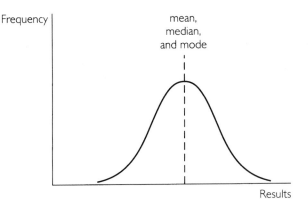

*Normal distribution*

**normal goods** have demand that responds positively to changes in the *real incomes* of customers. In other words if people become better off, they buy more of this type of product. Typical examples include hairdressing, furniture, cars and eating out. All luxury goods fall into the category of normal, as do the majority of everyday items. Those that are not normal are termed *inferior goods* (for which demand rises when consumers are worse off).

**North American Free Trade Area (NAFTA),** whose members consist of the United States of America, Canada and Mexico, is an attempt to create the equivalent of the *single European market* within the North American continent. It may become a *trading bloc* with an even more protectionist outlook than the *European Union*. This would create the risk of a serious *trade war*.

**no-strike agreement:** a contract signed as part of a firm's *negotiation* and *disputes procedure* that bars the *trade union* signatories from calling or encouraging a strike. When signed with Japanese employers, British trade unions have ensured that the disputes procedure provides for binding *arbitration* by an independent person or panel (usually appointed by *ACAS*). Often the binding element has been in the form of *pendulum arbitration*. Although no-strike agreements have been quite common with Japanese firms, by no means all Japanese companies insist on them.

**not in my back yard (NIMBY)** is applied in a number of areas of economic life. It generally applies in situations where everyone agrees that something has to be built for the good of all, but no one wants it near their own home. The most common example is motorways, which everyone agrees are extremely useful and which most people use, but which cause uproar and extreme resistance from those immediately affected by their construction. The same thing happens with potentially dirty or hazardous production processes. This is why both motorways and these factories are often located in areas where residents are poor, lack access to the media and are therefore unable to resist effectively.

**NPD:** see *new product development*

**NVQ:** see *National Vocational Qualifications*

# O

**objective function:** a term used in operations research to denote the criterion by which success is being measured.

**objectives** are the medium- to long-term targets that can give a sense of direction to a manager, department or whole organisation. If a team can be given a sense of common purpose, it becomes much easier to coordinate actions and to create a team spirit. For maximum effect objectives should be measurable and have an explicit timescale, for example to boost *market share* from 8 per cent to 10 per cent within the next three years. They must also be realistic, as an objective that seems unattainable can be demotivating. Consequently it is desirable for objectives to be agreed rather than set.

Objectives form the basis for decisions on strategy, i.e. the plan for the achievement of your goals. Therefore questions about business strategy should not be answered until the individual or company's objectives have been considered fully. (See *aims, corporate objectives,* and *strategy.*)

**objectivity:** the principle that accounts should be drawn up on the basis of objectivity, i.e. without being influenced by personal opinion or bias.

**observation:** a survey technique that requires the researcher only to watch and record behaviour rather than to ask questions. For example, to help decide where to locate a new shop on a high street, it would be helpful to measure the number of passers-by at the sites of the available shop premises. Unless the rental is too high, the retailer should choose the shop where customer traffic flow is highest.

**obsolescence** occurs when a product, service or machine has been overtaken by a new idea that provides the same function in a better or more attractive way. Obsolescence may occur as a result of *new technology*, or due to changing lifestyles or fashions. The threat of obsolescence encourages firms to update their products regularly and to look for new products to replace declining ones. Some firms look to gain financial advantage from two specific types of obsolescence: built-in and planned.

Built-in obsolescence means designing and building failure into a product, in order that the user needs to buy a replacement. This is a way of overcoming the effect of *market saturation* upon the sales of a *durable* item. In other words if everyone who wants a lawnmower has one, sales will fall to zero. This tempts manufacturers to build the products so that they wear out after three or four years. The customer must then go and buy a new one.

Planned obsolescence is the creation of a feeling on the part of customers that they should replace items that are in fact still usable. This is largely done through restyling or adding new features. For example, although your Liverpool shirt may look as good as new, you want to get the new season's styling.

Environmentalists would regard both built-in and planned obsolescence as equally undesirable ways of encouraging wastage of the earth's resources.

**OECD:** see *Organisation for Economic Cooperation and Development*

**off-balance-sheet financing** is 'the creative accounting trick which improves companies' balance sheets' (Roger Cowe, THE GUARDIAN). It is a device by which the business's debts can be removed from the *balance sheet*. This shrinks the firm's stated *gearing* and therefore apparent risk level. The most common method is by the creation of a *subsidiary* company which the firm controls, but does not consolidate into its accounts. This subsidiary may have obtained the loans essential for running the entire business, but these may not need to be listed on the firm's consolidated accounts. The *Accounting Standards Board* is trying to ban off-balance-sheet financing.

**Office of Fair Trading (OFT)** is the government body set up to ensure that firms are complying with the *Fair Trading Act 1973*. The OFT's director-general has four main duties:

- to consider whether *take-over bids* should be investigated by the *Monopolies and Mergers Commission* on the grounds of being against the public interest
- to investigate suspected anti-competitive practices (such as *market-sharing agreements*)
- to investigate existing monopolies
- to consider whether to register or reject *restrictive practices* notified by firms

**off-the-job training** includes all forms of training apart from that at the immediate workplace. It may be conducted internally, for example in a conference room, or externally, at a college. Employees attend college during working hours either through *day release* or *block release*. The training is likely to be focused on skills, attitudes and theories that relate to work.

**OFGAS** is the regulator for the privatised gas industry, which has potentially wide-ranging powers, including the ability to limit price increases when it is felt that excessive profits are being earned. When *privatisation* took place many commentators felt that a private *monopoly* was being substituted for a state one and it would inevitably exploit its *market power* unless it was held in check by some form of outside body.

**OFT:** see *Office of Fair Trading*

**OFTEL** is the regulator for the privatised telephone industry, which has potentially wide-ranging powers, including the ability to limit price increases when it is felt that excessive profits are being earned. When *privatisation* took place many commentators felt that a private *monopoly* was being substituted for a state one and it would inevitably exploit its *market power* unless it was held in check by some form of outside body.

**OFWAT** is the regulator for the privatised water industry, which has potentially wide-ranging powers, including the ability to limit price increases when it is felt that excessive profits are being earned. When *privatisation* took place many commentators felt that a private *monopoly* was being substituted for a state one and it would inevitably exploit its *market power* unless it was held in check by some form of outside body.

**ogive:** another term for a cumulative *frequency distribution* curve.

**oligopoly** exists when a market is dominated by a small number of large firms (see *monopoly*). Such a market can appear highly competitive, because each producer fights hard for particular *market niches*. However this competition is usually in non-price form, such as special offers and *advertising* because there is often a degree of *collusion* which keeps overall prices and therefore profits at an acceptable level. Analysing oligopolists' behaviour is difficult because each producer will be aware that whatever action it takes will inevitably result in a reaction from its competitors. Therefore, it must attempt to take this reaction into account before undertaking anything. The UK markets for soap powder, chocolate, and ice-cream are often quoted as examples of oligopolies.

**on-balance-sheet financing** means generating extra cash using internal or external sources of finance that will show up on the firm's balance sheet. This contrasts with the deceptiveness of *off-balance-sheet financing.*

**one-off profit** is a financial surplus that has resulted from an event that is unlikely to be repeated. For example, if a firm sells a plot of land for £2m. that is on its books at £600 000, it has made a £1 400 000 one-off profit. When company accounts include one-off items, it is wise to try to extract them from the figures. Then a judgement can be made about the underlying position of the business.

**one-way communication** is the passage of a message without gaining *feedback* on whether it has been received or understood by the right person or people. It is an undesirable form of communication, as it lacks effectiveness and the potential to motivate. Examples of one-way communication include the newsletter, the lecture and the notice-board.

**on-line:** the linking of computer terminals so that information can be passed instantaneously. A common example is the electronic checkout at supermarkets that can provide on-line information to head office or even to suppliers about the numbers of each item being sold.

**on-the-job training** is instruction at the place of work on how the job should be carried out. It may be a matter of observing how an experienced employee carries out the task, or being talked through the job by a supervisor.

**OPEC:** see *Organisation of Petroleum Exporting Countries*

**open communication channels** provide information freely to all staff. Methods include notice boards, company newspapers and multi-user networked information on computer.

**open questions** are those that invite a wide-ranging, reflective or imaginative response. On a questionnaire, they are questions that do not have specific answers to be ticked. In an interview, they are the (harder) questions that demand more than just a factual answer. An example of an open question would be, 'Tell me a bit more about yourself.'

**operating profit:** the measure of profit which an organisation earns on its normal operations and excluding any *extraordinary* or *exceptional items*, which might distort a true appreciation of its usual business. Therefore, clear comparisons with previous years or with similar firms may be made.

**operational gearing** measures the extent to which a firm's costs are fixed in relation to output. If *fixed costs* form a high proportion of total costs, the firm has high operational gearing. This is risky because a fall in demand and therefore revenue will have little impact on costs. Therefore, as shown in the left-hand diagram overleaf, profit can turn to loss very quickly (in this case if demand falls by 20 per cent). A good example of this is the airline business, in which very few costs are variable. Therefore a bad trading year can cause huge operating losses. Note that the firm with low operational gearing (on the right) suffers far less, as the 20 per cent fall in demand cuts total costs sharply, as well as total revenues.

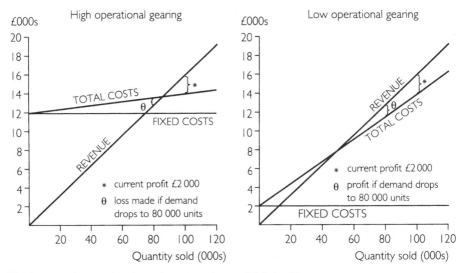

The impact of operational gearing when demand falls by 20 per cent

Individual managers can usually do nothing about their operational gearing, as it depends on the type of industry they work in. They should take it into account, however. If they work in a business such as airlines, they should ensure that *capital gearing* is low in order to provide the financial security to cope with their operational risks.

**operational objectives** are targets that must be achieved by particular departments or divisions in order that the strategic objectives are achieved. For example the marketing department might be set the objective of developing new products with overseas sales of £10 million a year, in order to help a firm meet a *strategic objective* of reducing its dependence on its home market.

**operational research (OR):** a set of multi-disciplinary techniques which are an aid to organising and planning operations such as production, scheduling and resource allocation. An *optimum* is usually sought, subject to a set of *constraints*. The distinctive approach is to develop a mathematical model of the system under investigation, including measurement of factors such as chance and risk. This model can then be used to predict and compare the outcomes of alternative decisions, strategies or controls. Devised at the time of the Second World War, OR techniques predated modern computers, yet are ideally suited to them.

**operations management:** the modern term for production management. It suggests a wider brief than just factory management. For example, it allows for service industries to be seen as requiring management of their operations, as has always been acknowledged in manufacturing.

**opportunity cost** measures cost in terms of the next best or highest-valued alternative foregone. It may be measured in money terms or not. The cost of an evening of studying might be the missed opportunity of seeing a film. One important use of this concept is in *investment appraisal*. The cost of a project is the rate of interest paid on the funds invested. Even if an organisation uses its own funds, it foregoes the interest on its money, so the real cost is the same.

**optimise:** to aim for the most favourable point or circumstances. For example the optimum strategy might be one that is profitable, but not so much so as to attract *me-too products*.

**optimum** means the best possible outcome e.g. maximising *capacity utilisation* or minimising cost.

**option:** the right to buy or sell an item at a price agreed in advance.

**OR:** see *operational research*

**oral communication** means conveying information by the spoken word. This carries certain advantages and disadvantages compared with written communication.

Pros: • enables feeling and emphasis to be conveyed more clearly
  • has the potential to generate far more powerful *feedback* (especially if one-to-one or small-group communication)
  • creates no specific costs, such as paper and filing cabinets

Cons: • lacks the legal status (evidence) provided by written communication
  • ineffective for conveying detailed information such as regional sales figures
  • prone to get distorted if used for a message that must pass through many *intermediaries*

Large firms can suffer from the difficulty of communicating orally through many intermediaries. They become overly dependent on written communication, which can slow down decision-making and cause heavy *overhead* costs.

**order book:** the total number of orders taken from customers, usually expressed in terms of time. Thus an order book of three months means that the factory has that amount of work on order.

**ordinary share** or equity represents part ownership in a *joint-stock company*. Ordinary shareholders receive a *dividend* on the *capital* they invest, but only after *debenture* holders, *preference* shareholders, long-term debt holders and the government (through taxes) have been paid. If the company goes into *liquidation*, ordinary shareholders are the last group of people to receive any return, after all other *creditors*. In return for these potentially high risks, ordinary shareholders enjoy the chance to benefit fully from their company's successes. Rising profits will lead to higher annual dividend payments and an increase in the market value of the shares they hold.

**organic growth** means expansion from within the firm, i.e. not as a result of acquisitions. It also implies that the finance for the expansion has come from internal sources rather than from shareholders or loans. As a result, organic growth is likely to be steady, even slow, but very secure.

**organisational chart:** a diagram showing the lines of authority and *layers of hierarchy* within an organisation. To be effective, the *chain of command* should be clear, with no one answerable to two people. An organisational chart should show:

- the different business functions and divisions
- who is answerable to whom
- the *span of control* in each division
- the official channels of communication

**organisational structure:** the way in which management is organised, both horizontally (*layers of hierarchy*) and vertically (by function, by operation or by *matrix*). The traditional approach was to divide an organisation into functional areas such as marketing, production and finance. Each had many layers of hierarchy, leading to many rungs on the career ladder. Today, many companies have reduced the number of management layers and have reorganised away from functions towards operations (e.g. Walls Ice Cream structures its organisation towards: impulse purchase products; take home products; and the catering market). Within each operation, marketing, production and other staff would work together on the same projects.

**Organisation for Economic Cooperation and Development (OECD)** was set up in 1961 and aims to coordinate international aid for less-developed countries as well as providing a forum for discussion on economic growth and trade. Its members are mainly drawn from the developed world, but some of its most effective work has been in the collection and publication of worldwide economic and social data, standardised so that inter-country comparisons are possible.

**Organisation of Petroleum Exporting Countries (OPEC)** is the name of the *cartel* which sets output quotas in order to control crude oil prices. The members of OPEC are countries of the Middle East, South America and Africa, but not the United States, Russian or European producers. OPEC wielded great power in the 1970s when it controlled 90 per cent of the world's supply of crude oil exports. However, by forcing up the oil price the exploration of marginal fields such as the North Sea and Alaska became worthwhile, thereby reducing OPEC's influence.

**OTC market:** see *over-the-counter market*

**output** is the finished product coming from a production process. It can be measured by volume or by value (volume times price). The level of output should not be confused with output per worker (*productivity*).

**outward bound training** is the use of rural adventure, endurance or sporting events to promote self-reliance and team spirit. A typical course might include absailing, canoeing and building a raft. A cynic might accuse such courses of being a *paternalistic* way of adding excitement to dull jobs; a supporter would point to the communication benefits that can flow from the team-building.

**overcapacity** exists in a market where the maximum capacity of all the producers is significantly above current and anticipated demand. This threatens each producer with the possibility that demand will fall below the *break-even point*. The likely consequences of overcapacity are:

- that the weakest producers will sell out or go into *liquidation*
- that all producers will try to cut their fixed *overheads* by *rationalisation*

- that prices will fall as producers try to utilise their own capacity by boosting demand

**overdraft:** a facility that enables a firm to borrow up to an agreed maximum for any period of time that it wishes. An overdraft is a very flexible way of raising credit in that it need not even be drawn at all and the amount borrowed may fluctuate daily. Banks may offer overdrafts without security, though for larger sums they will take security by a floating charge on all the assets of the business. The actual sum borrowed through an overdraft facility at the end of the financial year is recorded as a *current liability* on the *balance sheet*.

**overhead allocation:** the *overheads* or *fixed costs* of an organisation are difficult to allocate to *cost centres* as they do not vary with activity in the short run. Most methods of allocation are arbitrary and run the risk of being influenced by those who want their own department to look efficient. The best method in theory is *activity-based costing*, which attempts to measure the overheads attributable to each cost centre.

**overheads** are costs that are not generated directly by the production process. The term is often used interchangeably with *indirect costs* or even *fixed costs*. In fact overheads can be fixed or variable, though the overwhelming proportion are fixed.

Examples of fixed overheads: salaries, rent, heating and lighting. Examples of variable overheads: *salesforce* commission, postage (for a mail-order company), advertising (for a direct marketing company).

**over-the-counter (OTC) market** exists to buy and sell stocks and shares outside the *Stock Exchange*, usually through banks.

**overtime ban:** a form of *industrial action* that attempts to disrupt the employer while keeping employees' basic wages unaffected. It can only be effective if a significant proportion of work in a key section is done on overtime. This is only likely to occur in seasonal production peaks.

**overtrading** occurs when a firm expands without securing the necessary long-term finance, thereby placing too great a strain on *working capital*. Increased demand creates the need for more cash to finance extra raw material stocks and *work in progress*. In the absence of extra long-term funds, the firm is forced to apply pressure to *debtors* and *creditors*. If a creditor demands early payment, there is a severe danger of being forced into *liquidation*.

Overtrading is a particular problem for small firms in high growth sectors, but is also difficult for many firms when the economy moves out of recession. Rising demand during the recovery encourages overtrading which, in turn, can result in company failure.

**overvalued currency** is one which is trading on the foreign exchange markets at a price which makes the country's exports uncompetitive, and imports very desirable. This results in a *balance of payments* deficit. Since the deficit causes a greater supply of the foreign currency than there is a demand for it, the exchange rate will eventually fall back to an equilibrium position.

**own-label** (own-brand) products are branded with the retailer's own name, or with a name invented by the retailer. Such products are made by manufacturers to the

keeping employees' basic wages unaffected. It can only be effective if a significant proportion of work in a key section is done on overtime. This is only likely to occur in seasonal production peaks.

**overtrading** occurs when a firm expands without securing the necessary long-term finance, thereby placing too great a strain on *working capital*. Increased demand creates the need for more cash to finance extra raw material stocks and *work in progress*. In the absence of extra long-term funds, the firm is forced to apply pressure to *debtors* and *creditors*. If a creditor demands early payment, there is a severe danger of being forced into *liquidation*.

Overtrading is a particular problem for small firms in high growth sectors, but is also difficult for many firms when the economy moves out of recession. Rising demand during the recovery encourages overtrading which, in turn, can result in company failure.

**overvalued currency** is one which is trading on the foreign exchange markets at a price which makes the country's exports uncompetitive, and imports very desirable. This results in a *balance of payments* deficit. Since the deficit causes a greater supply of the foreign currency than there is a demand for it, the exchange rate will eventually fall back to an equilibrium position.

**own-label** (own-brand) products are branded with the retailer's own name, or with a name invented by the retailer. Such products are made by manufacturers to the recipe or specification laid down by retailer. The products are usually made with a particular price level in mind, often around 10 per cent below the price of the *brand leader*. From the retailer's point of view, the advantages and disadvantages of own label products are:

Pros: • can build a brand identity for your own shop (for example Marks and Spencer) and thereby add value
 • gives a much stronger bargaining position than when dealing with the owners of powerful brand names, therefore buy supplies more cheaply

Cons: • unless your own brand has a good name, the shop's image will be cheapened
 • requires backroom staff to check quality of own-brand produce, adding to *overheads*

---

If you want to get the best results from your coursework, **The A–Z Business Studies Coursework Handbook** is designed to be the answer. Written by the chief examiner of the main Business Studies syllabus, it explains what to do at every stage in the project process from 'How to get started' through to 'Writing effective conclusions'. It contains an A–Z of research sources, key libraries and key organisations which is guaranteed to prove invaluable, while in addition there are sections throughout to give the student practical advice on the best way to write and present their project. For ordering information, please see page 330.

**packaging:** all the design and cost elements involved in the physical protection and presentation of a product. Packaging has been referred to as the 'silent salesman'. An eye-catching pack design that conveys the right image and information about the product can be a highly effective promotional tool. It is a key element in the *marketing mix* for any consumer good.

**pacman defence:** a defence to a *take-over bid* in which the firm under attack turns round and bids for the *predator* company. In other words if Firm A bids for Firm B, the pacman defence is for Firm B to make a counter-bid for Firm A. The intention is that the combination of threat and confusion will encourage Firm A to give up its bid and perhaps look for an easier target.

*The pacman defence*

**P and L account:** see *profit and loss account*

**panel discussion:** a form of *qualitative research* in which the same 6 – 8 consumers meet regularly for a group discussion led by a psychologist. The respondents are selected on very tightly defined criteria, such as 18–30-year-old men who spend at least £100 per month on clothes. The panel might meet every three months to give a clothing manufacturer a feel for changing attitudes to products, fashions and prices.

**pan-European marketing** means treating Europe as a single market by selling the same products in the same way throughout Europe. This strategy is used by *multinationals* such as Levi's, Kelloggs and Ford. It reduces marketing staff costs in each country and can help ensure a consistent image (especially important for firms such as Levi's). Most commentators believe that pan-European marketing will spread rapidly as the *single European market* develops.

**parallel imports** are goods brought into a country by *entrepreneurs* working outside the official *distribution* network of the manufacturer. If cans of Coca-Cola were being sold for 60p per can in France and 40p in Britain, it would be profitable for a parallel importer to bring container loads of the drink in from Britain to distribute in France. Producers try any legal way they can to stop parallel imports, as they interfere with the pricing differentials that enable profits to be maximised. (See *price discrimination.*)

**Pareto analysis:** see *eighty/twenty rule*

**Parkinson's Law** is that, 'Work expands so as to fill the time available for its completion.' (C. Northcote Parkinson (1965) PARKINSON'S LAW Penguin Books). This golden rule points to the danger of assuming that, because managers look busy, they must necessarily be doing useful work. Parkinson's Law is a warning against bureaucracy.

**participative leadership** involves consulting with subordinates and evaluating their opinions and suggestions before making a decision.

**partnership** is a legal form of business organisation where two or more people trade together under the Partnership Act of 1890. It is usual for partnerships to have *unlimited liability*, which means each partner is liable for the debts of the other partners, including their tax liability. Because this requires a high degree of trust, partnerships are most common in the professions, such as in medicine and the law. Forming a partnership allows more capital to be used in the business than is the case with a *sole trader*, and some of the strain of decision-making is taken off the shoulders of individuals. It also allows partners more personal freedom, for example, they can take holidays when they like, but unlike private or public companies they retain major responsibilities for the success of the organisation, and their ability to raise finance remains somewhat limited.

**par value:** see *nominal value*

**passed dividend** is when a firm decides that it cannot afford to pay any dividend to shareholders this year. It is then said that the dividend has been passed.

**patent:** the right to be the sole user or producer of the *invention* of a new process or product. To register a patent the inventor must:

- provide full drawings of the invention for the *Patent Office*
- demonstrate that the ideas have original features
- promise that the ideas are his or her own

Under the Copyright, Designs and Patents Act 1988, patent holders have the monopoly right to use, make, license or sell the invention for up to 20 years after it has been registered. Although this grants the inventor rights that can be very valuable, there is no agency for enforcing patents. Therefore the holder has to be willing to take to court those that infringe the patent. An individual inventor is very unlikely to be able to afford the legal costs, so new patents are often sold on to larger firms.

**Patent Office** is the only authority with the right to grant *patents* and *trade marks* within the UK.

**paternalistic leadership style** is reminiscent of the way fathers treat their children, i.e. deciding what is best for them. The paternalistic approach is *autocratic*, though decisions are intended to be in the best interests of the workforce. The leader is likely to explain the reasons for his or her decisions and may even have consulted staff before making them, but *delegation* is more unlikely. The paternal company treats its workforce as family, taking care of its social and leisure needs. Its emphasis is on *human relations* (*Mayo*) and social needs (*Maslow*).

**payback period:** a method of *investment appraisal* that estimates the length of time it will take to recoup the cash outlay on an investment. Although regarded by academics as simplistic, this is the most commonly used method of investment decision-making by businesses in Britain. Most set a *criterion level* such as two years. Projects will only be considered by senior management if they have a shorter payback period than that. If forecast cash flows are constant, the following formula applies:

$$\text{FORMULA:} \frac{\text{investment outlay}}{\text{contribution per month}} = \text{payback period}$$

---

Worked example: calculate the payback period from a £450 000 investment given the following forecast cash flows:

|        | Cash in      | Cash out    |
|--------|--------------|-------------|
| Now    |              | + £450 000  |
| Year 1 | + £180 000   |             |
| Year 2 | + £180 000   |             |
| Year 3 | + £180 000   |             |
| Year 4 | + £180 000   |             |

Monthly contribution towards the investment outlay is:
£180 000 ÷ 12 = £15 000

$$\text{Payback} = \frac{\text{initial outlay}}{\text{contribution per month}} = \frac{£450\ 000}{£15\ 000} = 30 \text{ months}$$

---

Payback has several advantages and disadvantages over the other methods.

Pros:
- particularly useful for firms with difficult *cash flow* positions, as it helps them to identify how long it will take for the cash to be restored
- the further ahead a forecast looks, the less likely it is to be accurate, as uncertainty increases over time; since payback only focuses on the short term (the period until the money is recouped) it is less likely to be inaccurate

Cons:
- the method focuses on time but ignores *profit*, making it of limited use unless supplemented by other methods such as *average rate of return*
- may encourage *short-termism*

**PAYE** stands for 'pay-as-you-earn' which is a system of *income tax* payment allowing employees to have their tax assessed for the year and then divided into 12 if they are paid monthly, or 52 if they are paid weekly. It avoids people receiving a large income tax bill at the end of the year, and so discourages *tax avoidance*.

**payment by results (PBR)** wage systems provide financial incentives for achieving a high or a fast rate of output. The best known methods are *piece-rate* and commission.

**pay round:** the annual pay bargaining round in which *trade unions* attempt to gain pay rises for their members that at least match *inflation*. Although there is no precise starting date of the pay round, it was long thought that the Ford Motor Company pay negotiations in the autumn were the effective starting point. The pay rise achieved at Ford often sets the *going rate* for other groups of workers within that pay round.

**PBR:** see *payment by results*

**peer group:** the circle of friends and workmates whose views on workplace behaviour and attitudes may be highly influential. (See *group norms*.)

**pendulum arbitration:** a system of binding *arbitration* in which the independent arbitrator must decide in favour of one side to the dispute or the other. No compromise is allowable. For instance, if a *trade union* claims a 10 per cent pay rise while the management offers 4 per cent, the arbitrator must decide which is closer to the 'correct' outcome. If the arbitrator believes 6 per cent to be appropriate, the management's 4 per cent offer will be imposed on both sides.

Although it sounds extreme, pendulum arbitration encourages compromise, as both sides learn to adopt softer bargaining strategies. For example, a trade union official who expects the arbitrator to judge that 6 per cent is a fair outcome should pitch the wage claim at 6.5–7 per cent. A higher claim will increase the risk that the management side will win. Similarly, the management should push their offer towards the anticipated 6 per cent.

Pendulum arbitration agreements are medium-term contracts entered into by union and management. They have legal force, so if one side refuses to accept the arbitrator's decision, it can be sued. As a consequence of the binding nature of the agreement, some trade unions have also accepted *no-strike agreements* as part of the arrangement. This has been helpful in giving Japanese firms the confidence to set up in Britain.

Underpinning a pendulum arbitration agreement must be trust. The union, in particular, puts itself in a difficult position. It might present its case for a 7 per cent pay rise in good faith, based on available information on *inflation* and the firm's latest accounts. However the management side might present to the arbitrator confidential forecasts of a profit shortfall, and thereby win the award. So a trade union would be foolish to enter a pendulum arbitration arrangement unless it trusted that the management side would not take advantage of its greater access to information.

**pension funds** are investment institutions that gather the pension contributions made monthly by employees and employers and invest them for long-term growth. The money is invested in well spread portfolios of shares, property and *government securities* with the intention that the growth achieved will enable the contributors to receive generous pensions when they retire. Pension funds, together with insurance companies and *unit trust* firms are the main institutional shareholders that own the majority of shares in most of Britain's *public limited companies.*

**pension plans** are the provisions made by individuals to ensure that their retirement income is not limited to the state pension. These plans may be made through personal pensions or via additional voluntary contributions (AVCs) to company pension plans. In either case individuals must show vigilance, because high management charges and commissions can greatly reduce the value of the eventual pension.

**pensions holiday:** when a firm with a company pension fund in surplus decides to stop paying in further employers' contributions for a year or two. This cuts the firm's costs and thereby boosts its *profits* temporarily. It can be used by firms suffering from a poor trading position to *window dress* their accounts. Employees and their trade unions are often outraged when the employer benefits from the pension fund surplus (instead of the pensioners), but this practice is legal.

**PEPs:** see *Personal Equity Plans*

**per capita** means 'per head', and is often used in data where an individual measure is required, such as income per capita as opposed to total income.

**per employee** means the same as per capita, though it is more commonly used in a business context such as sales per employee. That would represent a ratio measuring the effective productivity of staff, especially the *salesforce*.

$$\text{FORMULA:} \quad \text{sales per employee} = \frac{\text{total sales}}{\text{number of employees}}$$

**perfect competition** exists when a market exhibits the following characteristics:

- a large number of small buyers and sellers, none of whom can influence price on their own
- a *homogeneous product* i.e. all the rival products are identical
- perfect knowledge i.e. all consumers know the prevailing price
- perfect freedom of entry into, and exit from, the market
- all the firms in the market are profit maximisers

These unrealistic conditions mean that perfect competition is simply a model which has some use as the starting point to analyse the behaviour of firms in the real world, but which cannot be a true representation. It does show how both short- and long-run efficiency can be achieved, however, if at least some of the conditions prevail.

**performance appraisal** is the process of judging the effectiveness of an employee's contribution over a period of time. It might be conducted every quarter, every six months or, most commonly, every year. The appraisal is carried out by a fellow employee, often the immediate superior, though it is usually based more on discussion than inspection. A performance appraisal might follow these stages:

- at the start of the year, discuss the appraisee's personal objectives, i.e. hoped-for achievements and developments
- towards the end of the period, ask the employee to complete a self-appraisal form
- use the latter as the basis for discussion of the employee's achievements, strengths, weaknesses, training needs, career intentions and future objectives

The process is intended to provide employees with *feedback* on their performance and therefore be motivating. However it can be stressful if the appraisal is used to judge *performance related pay* awards.

**performance evaluation** is the judgement made on an individual's achievements in relation to the targets set at the start of the year. This is usually done through a self-evaluation form, consideration of the employee's *performance indicators*, plus a *performance appraisal* interview.

**performance indicators** are ways of measuring achievement in relation to an objective. The form of measurement is likely to be quantitative, such as sales figures, speed of response, or the quality reject rate. Schemes such as *performance appraisal* need an element of numerate data, so performance indicators are often devised as a way of making appraisal more meaningful.

**performance ratios** are measures of managerial or asset efficiency such as return on *capital, asset turnover, stock turnover*, debtors' and creditors' turnover.

**performance-related pay (PRP)** is a bonus or salary increase awarded in line with an employee's achievements over a range of criteria. For a receptionist the criteria might include helpfulness, efficiency, appearance and attendance. An employee performing well above average might get an 8 per cent pay rise while average achievers get only 3 per cent.

**period costs:** another term for *fixed costs*, since they are allocated to a time period rather than specific output, for example, rent and *straight line depreciation*.

**peripheral** (workforce or business) means business elements or activities that do not form part of the core. As a result they are the most vulnerable to an economic downturn or a change of corporate strategy. Professor Handy has suggested that in the future, organisations will have a core of lifelong, highly rewarded and highly skilled employees supplemented by peripheral workers who are hired and fired as seasonal, cyclical or market changes dictate.

**peripheral workers** are those on the edges of an organisation's labour force. They may be employed part-time, on temporary contracts or on zero hours contracts. Unlike the salaried, core workforce, these people are used flexibly, allowing the firm to avoid fixed costs that prove a burden during periods of low demand. If the firm employs too high a proportion of peripheral workers, there is a risk that communication, teamwork and efficiency may be harmed. Also see *core workers*.

**personal computer (PC):** a computer small enough to be either desktop or laptop, yet with the computing power of the *mainframe computers* of some years ago. PCs can either be stand-alone systems or networked to other PCs and data sources. The main uses of PCs are for word processing, *spreadsheet* recording and analysis and *database* information processing.

**Personal Equity Plans (PEPs):** a government scheme that allows shareholders to protect their dividend income and capital gains from any tax liability. Advocates of the scheme praise the stimulus it has on the purchase of shares (and therefore investment in industry). Critics say that it allows wealthy shareholders to earn tax-free income, whereas working people have to pay 20 per cent or more on income earned from real labour.

**personal plan**: a systematic way of analysing and evaluating personal attributes and targets for employment or self employment. The plan will cover both the short term (up to one year) and the long (one to five years); it should cover:

- relevant legal considerations such as the payment of taex and national insurance contributions
- sources of help and support such as the careers service
- the information needed to help make decisions, such as employment trends in the chosen industry, wage rates, terms of employment and so on
- the actions to be taken to execute the plan

**personnel department:** the section of the organisation that is responsible for the recruitment, training, welfare and discipline of staff. This has often been seen as a passive bureaucratic function, hence the modern shift towards *human resource management*.

**person specification**, another term for *job specification*.

**persuasive advertising** is communication to customers designed to appeal to the emotions. Favourable or distinctive images are used to encourage the target market to identify with the product or service being promoted. A long-running example of persuasive advertising is 'Bounty – a taste of paradise'. The power of the moving image makes television and cinema advertising the favourite media for persuasive advertising campaigns.

Some pressure groups criticise the power of persuasive advertising to press people to buy – or long to buy – products that may have little merit (such as expensive children's toys) or actually be harmful, such as fatty foods or alcohol. *Informative advertising* rarely attracts such criticism.

**PEST analysis** (political, economic, social and technological analysis): a systematic means of analysing the external factors that may present opportunities or threats to a business.

**Peter Principle:** that 'in any hierarchy, an employee tends to rise to his level of incompetence, and that's where he stays.' This idea of Dr Laurence Peter's became one of the best known critiques of the modern corporation. He quoted examples of excellent motor mechanics being promoted to become second-rate foremen and of fine teachers becoming incompetent school heads. Dr Peter pointed out that the main criterion for gaining promotion is success, so competence is rewarded with promotion until the individual rises to a hierarchy level where he or she can no longer cope. On arriving at this level of incompetence, the overpromoted employee would be subject to frustration, stress and be at risk of an identity crisis.

**Phillips Curve** is named after A W H Phillips (1914–1975) who studied the data on increases in money income and levels of unemployment between 1851 and 1957, and showed that as unemployment rose, the rate of increase of wages and hence prices (*inflation*) declined. This conclusion appears obvious, since higher levels of unemployment mean that workers are in a less-powerful position to bargain for wage increases, and so the pressures on inflation are reduced. From a government policy point of view it did have important implications however, because a low-inflation policy became inconsistent with full employment, and vice versa. Indeed, a recent *Chancellor of the Exchequer* was quoted as saying unemployment was a price well worth

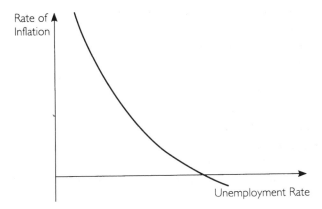

*Phillips curve*

paying to get inflation down, and that in itself justified pursuing a policy of less than full employment.

**physiological needs** are the physical needs of human beings, such as food, warmth and the avoidance of pain. They form the lowest level of *Maslow's hierarchy of needs* and are therefore often referred to as lower order needs.

**picketing** occurs when strikers stand at entrances to the venue of an *industrial dispute* in the attempt to persuade others not to cross the *picket line,* thereby breaking the strike action. Employment legislation limits the number of pickets to six. This makes illegal the use of mass picketing, which can intimidate those thinking of going in to work.

**picket line:** a group of workers on an *industrial dispute* who gather at the factory gate to attempt to dissuade people from strikebreaking. Employment legislation limits the number of pickets to six.

**pictogram:** a *histogram* or *bar chart* in which the bars are presented in pictorial form. An example would be chocolate bars stacked on top of each other, with the number of them denoting the growth in overall sales of chocolate.

**piece-parts:** the components used within a production process. They form part of the raw material stock and *work in progress* of a manufacturing business.

**piece-rate:** the payment of wages solely on the basis of the number of items each worker has produced. This appears an attractive way of providing staff with an incentive to work hard, but piece-rate can cause various problems, including:

- encouraging staff to concentrate on quantity at the expense of quality
- making the firm's output level a function of workforce needs rather than customer demand (piece-rate workers speed up in July and again in December, in order to boost their earnings)

**pilot study:** a preliminary stage in *market research* in which a small number of interviews are conducted to see whether the questionnaire achieves the research objectives. Any unclear questions can be rewritten before the full survey is undertaken.

**place:** the term given to *distribution.* The key marketing questions regarding place are:

- which types of outlet do we want to be distributed in? (Newsagent, supermarket or Harrods?)
- what level of distribution should we seek to achieve?
- how are we to achieve that level?

Of far lesser significance is the choice of *distribution channel* by which the goods change hands between the producer and the customer.

**planned obsolescence:** see *obsolescence*

**planning permission** (or planning consent) is required from a local authority before any new construction can be started. This applies to shop signs, house extensions and change of use as much as to house, factory and office construction. It is designed to protect the environment from haphazard development.

**plant** is the *infrastructure* of a factory, especially the buildings and services (such as ventilation). It would be represented as *fixed assets* on a company *balance sheet.*

**ploughed-back profit** is another term for *retained profit*. It signifies the profit left after all deductions that is reinvested into the business to finance renewal and expansion.

**poaching** employees means attracting workers from a rival firm that have already been trained in the skills you need. This saves you the cost of the training process and means that your competitor has wasted its resources. If done widely within an economy, employers would stop (or cut down on) training new employees since it would become a pointless exercise. This would damage the skill-level and therefore competitiveness of the workforce. It was for this reason that Industrial Training Boards were set up, levying a charge on all firms within a trade and then offering free training to employees. These Boards were scrapped in the 1980s during the period of government hostility to intervention in industry.

**point-of-sale (POS)** materials are used to display and promote products at the retail outlet. A window poster might remind the customer of the brand they saw advertised the night before; a dump-bin may draw the eye to the product and a shelf-sticker may proclaim the price.

**poison pill:** a defence to a *take-over bid* by which the company under threat signs an agreement or buys out another firm that would represent a long-term drain on the resources of the bidder. As a consequence the bidder should decide against swallowing up the poisoned pill (company), and give up their bid. An example of a poison pill is giving staff *employment contracts* with a three-year notice of termination clause. This would add greatly to the cost of taking over and reorganising the firm.

**policy:** another term for *strategy*. In other words, a plan for meeting *objectives*.

**political donations** are gifts made by organisations to political parties in order to get the party concerned elected or re-elected. The donating organisation clearly expects that, having made such a donation, the party will repay the gift in some way once it comes to power. Traditionally, British business has supported the Conservative Party with donations and *trade unions* have given to the Labour Party.

**poll:** a *quantitative research* survey, either into political or consumer opinions.

**pollution** means contamination of some kind. It is usually referred to in the context of the environment, where pollution can take many forms: air, water, noise and many others. Increasingly, firms are being held responsible financially and otherwise for any pollution they produce. (See *environmental audits*.)

**population:** a statistical term meaning all the people within the criteria chosen for a *market research* exercise. For example, it might be all lager drinkers. In which case a sample would be drawn from the lager-drinking population.

**portfolio:** a spread of assets or interests to provide *diversification*. A share portfolio would be spread among large and small, UK and overseas companies. A brand portfolio should have *inferior* and *normal, price elastic* and *price inelastic* products. In this way, it would be extraordinary for circumstances to arise in which the firm cannot succeed.

**portfolio analysis** is the examination of all the brands held by a firm to identify their strength and potential. A useful method is the *Boston Matrix*, which analyses products in terms of their *market share* and market growth. This helps a firm allocate its resources, usually away from brands in declining markets and towards those with growth prospects.

**positive skew** is *bias* within a distribution towards high values. In other words, the majority of the values are above the average. For example, the diagram below shows the frequency with which people take driving tests, analysed by age.

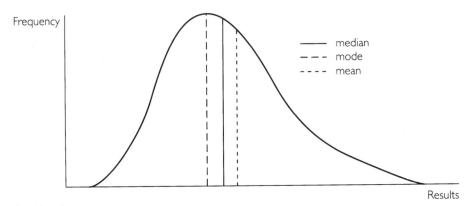

*Positive skew*

**post-tax profit:** profit after the deduction of *corporation tax*. This is the profit that is available for distribution to shareholders. It is also known as 'earnings' which, when divided among the number of shares issued by the firm, provides the ratio *earnings per share*.

**PR:** see *public relations*

**predator:** a company attempting to buy up another firm in a hostile *take-over bid*.

**predatory pricing:** setting a price low enough to drive competitors out of the market, or out of business. This anti-competitive practice is hard to prove, though the pest control firm Rentokil has been warned by the *Office of Fair Trading* to stop doing it. Their tactic had been to target small but successful local competitors; whilst keeping their national prices high (thereby remaining profitable) they cut their local prices in a predatory manner. Once the competitor had withdrawn from the market, Rentokil's prices were pushed back up. Carried out on a rolling basis around the country, this enabled the firm to keep overall prices high, yet maintain their high *market share*.

**preference share:** a share paying a fixed *dividend* that offers greater security than an ordinary share. It is like a compromise between an *ordinary share* and loan capital (*debenture*). If the company goes into *liquidation*, preference shareholders would be repaid in full before ordinary shareholders receive anything. This is also true of dividends, which are paid to them after loan repayments have been made, but before ordinary shareholders receive theirs. From the investors point of view the preference share carries less risk than an ordinary share, but no right to a share of the firm's profitability.

**prepayments** are items paid for in advance, or on which a deposit has been paid. The *balance sheet* item *debtors* is really debtors plus prepayments.

**present value** is the *cash flow* for a future year discounted to become a present-day value. When all the present values are totalled and the initial outlay is deducted, the result is the *net present value* (NPV) of an investment.

**press release:** a *public relations* statement issued to the media in the hope of obtaining favourable editorial publicity. Successful press releases will offer stories that can either be treated as news items or form the humorous items and pictures that press media and television like to use.

**pressure group:** an organisation formed by people with a common interest who get together in order to further that interest. Pressure groups exist in a wide variety of forms, such as the Licensed Victuallers Association, who pressure the government in the interests of the brewing trade; Greenpeace, who fight for environmental issues; and *trade unions*, who look after the interests of their members.

**pre-tax profit:** profit before the deduction of *corporation tax.*

**preventative maintenance** means building into a production schedule the maintenance programme for equipment and machinery. In this way, mechanics can work to prevent faults rather than cure them. This is essential to ensure that a production schedule can be relied upon 100 per cent, without which a *just in time* production system cannot operate efficiently.

**price controls** are government restrictions on the pricing freedom of firms that can be acquired through legislation. In the mid 1970s, firms could only put their prices up by more than 5 per cent if the government's Price Commission approved. This was a way of limiting *inflation* by the use of *direct controls* on the economy.

**price discrimination** means charging different prices to different people for what is essentially the same product. This is done in order to maximise revenue by charging more to those that can afford, and are willing to pay, more. Price discrimination is a response to the recognition by a firm that different types of people may have different *price elasticities* of demand for a product. For example, under 16s get half-price entrance to most cinemas and football grounds because the owners know that higher prices will cut demand substantially. In this case, as in all considerations of price discrimination, it is essential that there should be the minimum of crossover between market segments. In other words, if many adults could get in for half-price, the point of the discrimination would be lost.

**price : earnings ratio (PE ratio):** a measurement of how highly a firm's shares are valued in the *stock market*. The ratio divides the stock market value of the shares by the firm's earnings (profit after tax). The higher the PE figure, the higher the company's share price in relation to its profit.

FORMULA: $\dfrac{\text{market share price}}{\text{earnings per share}} = \text{PE ratio}$

---

Worked example: PE ratio

$\dfrac{£1.50p}{10p} = 15 \text{ times}$

Conclusion: the stock market rates the share at 15 times earnings; this means it would take 15 years of this year's profit level to justify the current share price. Is this realistic? If the firm is Marks and Spencer, one could feel confident of sustained profits. If it is a small computer software firm however, 15 years of profitability cannot be guaranteed. Therefore the share may be overpriced.

---

**price elastic:** is where a proportionate increase or decrease in price leads to a proportionately greater increase or decrease in the quantity sold, i.e. its elasticity is greater than one. (See *price elasticity.*)

**price elasticity** is a measure of the way the *demand* for a good responds to a change in its price. In order to avoid the problems with absolute numbers, it is always measured in proportionate or percentage terms, thus:

FORMULA:  $\dfrac{\text{percentage change in quantity demanded}}{\text{percentage change in price}}$

So if the price of a good rises by 10 per cent, and its demand falls by 20 per cent as a result, the value of price elasticity is:

$$20\% \div 10\% = 2$$

A value greater than one is called *price elastic*, whilst a value of between zero and one is called *price inelastic.* In purely mathematical terms, the value of price elasticity should be negative, since an increase in price will cut demand, and a fall in price will increase demand. Since this is always true it is conventional to ignore the minus sign.

**price inelastic:** where a proportionate change in a product's price leads to a proportionately smaller change in the quantity sold, i.e. elasticity is greater than zero but less than one. Such goods tend to have high *product differentiation*, meaning that consumers perceive them as having no acceptable substitutes. This may primarily be due to the effectiveness of their *branding* and *advertising*, e.g. Levi's. For the manufacturer, the advantage of a price inelastic product is that if its costs rise, it can pass them on to its customers with minimal effect on demand.

**price leader:** a brand that is in such a powerful position within its market-place that it can largely dictate the prevailing price level. The managers of rival brands know that consumers see the price leader as **the** salad cream, baked beans, coconut chocolate bar or whatever. Therefore the price set by the rivals has to be in relation to the leader. For instance, HP baked beans has to be priced at least 2–3p below Heinz, otherwise its market share will dwindle. If HP's costs rise, it may be unable to risk putting its price up until Heinz decides on a price increase. Therefore being second-best in a market with a price leader can be a dangerous position.

**price maker:** another term for *price leader.*

**price mechanism** is the interaction of *demand* and *supply* which determines prices, and hence the allocation of scarce resources.

**prices and incomes policy** is a way of controlling *inflation* by government restrictions on increases in prices, wages and salaries. The difficulties of controlling wages and salaries are bad enough (see *incomes policy*), but they are nothing compared with attempting to control prices. This is because it is almost impossible to police price increases because of their number, and because they respond to market signals. If these signals are ignored, markets become distorted. For example, firms might stop producing items for which the price is being kept too low to be profitable. Governments can try to control prices in the *public sector*, but again this leads to distortions if the *private sector* is not also constrained.

**price sensitive** refers to a good whose demand will react very strongly to a change in its price. For instance, a small increase in price will result in a large reduction in quantity sold. Therefore price sensitive means the same as *price elastic.*

**price taker:** a firm with products that are insufficiently distinctive to stand out amongst the competition. As their *price elasticity* is high, these products must be priced at or below rival brands. This *competitive pricing* is the only way to ensure satisfactory sales levels.

**price variance:** a measurement of how much a price change is responsible for a revenue variance. The only other factor that can be responsible is a change in the sales volume.

---

Worked example: a company's monthly budget is as follows:

|        | Budget   | Actual   | Variance       |
|--------|----------|----------|----------------|
| Price  | £50      | £45      | £5 adverse     |
| Volume | 1 000    | 1 050    | 50 favourable  |
| Revenue| £50 000  | £47 250  | £2 750 adverse |

The company has made £2 750 less revenue than it planned. Both the price and the sales volume have changed. How much of the change in total revenue is due to price variance?

To calculate this, keep the sales volume at its budgeted level. So the price variance is:

$$1\ 000 \times -£5 = -£5\ 000$$

---

**price war:** a clash between rival companies in which prices are being cut in a cycle of thrust and counter-thrust. The situation in which a price war is most likely to start is when there is oversupply, i.e. *capacity utilisation* is low. So firms attempt to keep their *overheads* covered by boosting their *market share.* If only one firm cut price to boost market share, it could benefit. When a price war breaks out, however, no company benefits, only the consumer. Even that is only in the short term, however, because many price wars end when one firm withdraws from the market. In the longer term, that may enable the remaining producers to push up their prices sharply.

**pricing methods** are the different ways in which a firm can decide on the price level to set for its products. The methods can be split into two: cost-based and market-based methods. In either case however, psychological factors can and should be taken into account (see *pricing psychology*).

Cost-based: • *mark-up* pricing, as used by most small firms, means adding a standard profit proportion to the direct costs; clothes shops, for instance, tend to work on a 100 per cent mark-up, so a dress bought for £40 will be priced at £80

• *cost-plus pricing* is similar, except that a profit is added to the full cost of the good or service; in other words an allowance for *overheads* is added to the *direct costs* and then a profit percentage added to the total

Market-based: • *competitive pricing* means taking your price level from the prices set by others within the market-place; a new petrol station, for example, would have to charge prices in line with local competitors; too high a price would mean inadequate sales volume

- *contribution pricing* is more sophisticated, taking advantage of the fact that different prices can be charged in different circumstances for the same product (as long as all prices exceed *variable costs*)
- *profit maximising pricing* is achieved by researching to find the likely level of demand at different prices, then calculating which is the most profitable

In addition to the above, firms may price tactically, in other words to achieve a short-term goal. Examples of pricing tactics include *loss leaders* and *predatory pricing*.

**pricing psychology** is of importance because consumer perceptions and images of products have a major impact on *demand*. In particular, price cutting will boost demand in the short term, but may undermine the long-term image. Consumers do not want 'cheap' Mercedes or Chanel. (See *psychological pricing*.)

**pricing strategy** is the medium- to long-term plan of the price level that a firm wishes to set for a product. For a new product there are two fundamental strategies: *market penetration* (pricing low to maximise sales) or *skimming the market* (pricing high to maximise profit margins). A further possibility for an existing product is *price leadership*. This is only feasible if the product in question has the dominant image within the mass market (examples would include Hellman's Mayonnaise and Benson & Hedges King Size cigarettes). There are many other ways in which a firm might determine the price of product: see *pricing methods*.

**primary data:** first-hand information that is related directly to a firm's needs. *Secondary data* may be useful, but is unlikely to provide the answers to the exact questions you are interested in. For example, secondary data might provide information about total consumer spending on soft drinks. To find out about consumer attitudes to 7Up would require *primary research* to gather primary data.

**primary efficiency ratio:** another term for *return on capital*.

**primary research** is the gathering of first-hand data that is tailor-made to a firm's own products, customers or markets. This is carried out by fieldwork, whereas *secondary* (second hand) *data* is gathered by *desk research*.

**primary sector** is that part of the economy consisting of agriculture, fishing and the extractive industries such as oil exploration and mining.

**Prince's Trust** was set up by the Prince of Wales to provide *grants* for young people wishing to start up their own businesses.

**private label:** a retailer's own brand, which often carries the company name (such as Sainsbury's) but may also be an invented name (such as John Lewis's 'Jonelle' brand). For the retailer, the great advantage of a strong private label is that instead of buying supplies from a powerful branded goods manufacturer (at high prices), it can obtain supplies from whoever is willing to provide the right quality at a low price. Accordingly, private label goods generate far higher profit margins for the retailer than branded goods. (See also *own-label*.)

**private limited company:** a small to medium-sized business that is usually run by the family that owns it. Within such a firm, the family can determine its own *objectives* without the pressures towards short-term profit that are so common among *public limited companies*. The main characteristics of a private limited company include:

- must have 'Ltd' after the company name
- must have less than £50 000 of *share capital*
- is not allowed to gain a listing on the *stock market*

**private sector** is that part of the economy operated by firms that are owned by shareholders or private individuals. In Western economies it is the dominant sector; the remainder is called the *public sector.*

**privatisation** or denationalisation is the process of returning firms or industries to the *private sector* after being run by the state. The policy of privatisation was vigorously pursued by Conservative governments in the 1980s and 1990s. It became a model for many other countries where it was felt that the mix between state and private sector-run organisations had become unbalanced.

Privatisation has a variety of meanings, from the contracting out of refuse services within a local authority, to the *deregulation* of bus routes. It is as much a way of thinking as a closely defined programme. However, the majority of people when they talk of privatisation tend to mean the high profile transfers of nationalised industries into public *joint-stock companies*. The detailed programme of such privatisation in the UK is as follows:

| 1979 | BP |
| | ICL |
| | Ferranti |
| | Fairey |
| 1981 | Cable & Wireless |
| | British Sugar |
| | Amersham International |
| | British Aerospace |
| 1982 | Britoil |
| | National Freight |
| 1983 | Associated British Ports |
| | Forestry Commission |
| | British Rail Hotels |
| 1984 | Sealink Ferries |
| | Enterprise Oil |
| | Jaguar |
| | British Telecom |
| 1986 | British Gas |
| | TSB |
| 1986–8 | National Bus Company |
| 1987 | Unipart |
| | British Airways |
| | Royal Ordnance |
| | Rolls Royce (aerospace) |
| | British Airports Authority |

| 1988 | British Steel |
|------|---------------|
|      | Rover Group |
| 1989 | Water Authorities |
| 1990 | Electricity Supply |
| 1991 | Electricity Generation |
| 1994 | British Coal, plus the splitting up of British Rail with a view to its privatisation. |

Arguments in favour of privatisation and the critics' responses are as follows:

For: As has been proved in the former communist countries, the state is not a good decider of how to distribute *factors of production*. The *bureaucratic* processes involved with decision making prevent efficiency gains which come about through the *market mechanism.*

Against: Many state-run enterprises operate in areas where people have a basic right to enjoy the good or service without effective rationing by price. Examples would include water, gas, and electricity.

For: Many state-owned companies were *monopolies* which exploited the public. Privatisation introduced competition, such as Mercury competing with BT.

Against: Many nationalised industries were *natural monopolies* meaning that there was only room for one producer in the market. The creation of privatised monopolies has allowed the water companies and others to exploit customers more than ever before.

For: The government can reduce its borrowing by selling these companies, and thus follow other policies which it believes increase efficiency, such as lowering *income tax.*

Against: Such privatisation 'bonuses' are one-offs. One Conservative ex-Prime Minister described it as 'selling off the family silver'.

For: *Industrial relations* and *productivity* should improve as workers recognise that there is no state support if the company fails. Managers will also have greater responsibilities for ensuring continuity of production.

Against: Industrial relations have improved in terms of days lost in strikes, but that is true of the whole economy. This may have more to do with legislation or unemployment than anything else. Accusations of greed against some privatised industry bosses may have soured underlying industrial relations in companies such as British Gas.

**proactive:** a decision or action that initiates rather than responds to the initiatives of others. For example, if a *recession* occurred, the proactive company might develop a range of new, lower-priced products. The reactive firm would copy that initiative.

**probability** is the likelihood of an outcome occurring, expressed as a numerical value. Most managers would tend to refer to probabilities in percentage form ('a 50/50 chance') or as a fraction ('the chances are only 1 in 10'). Statisticians use a third method which is based on the fact that all the possible outcomes from an event must add up to 1. Therefore if the chances are 1 in 10, the statisticians describe that as a 0.1 chance.

The most important aspect of probability for business students is to recognise what is known as the gambler's fallacy. If a roulette player sees the ball land on red four times in a row, there is a tendency to think, 'Ah, well next time it's bound to be black.' In fact, every time the ball is put into play the chances of red and black are even. Therefore a firm that has launched two new product flops should not be kidding itself that, 'Our luck should turn.'

**probability tree:** a diagram that sets out all the possible outcomes within a process that has a series of stages.

---

Worked example: what is an interviewer's chance of finding a respondent at home within three calls, assuming that the respondent is out 60 per cent of the time? A probability tree sets out this problem and makes it easy to give an answer.

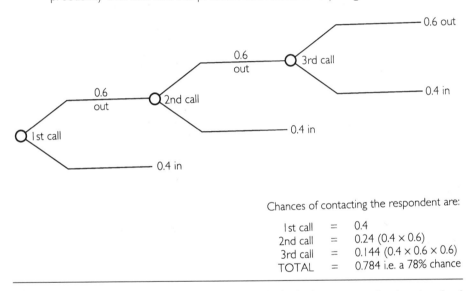

Chances of contacting the respondent are:

|  |  |  |
|---|---|---|
| 1st call | = | 0.4 |
| 2nd call | = | 0.24 (0.4 × 0.6) |
| 3rd call | = | 0.144 (0.4 × 0.6 × 0.6) |
| TOTAL | = | 0.784 i.e. a 78% chance |

---

**process theory** is an examination of the psychological processes that are involved in *motivation*. This contrasts with content theories such as those of *Maslow* and *Herzberg*. The best known element of process theory is *Vroom*'s work on the importance of people's expectations about the chances of an action achieving a desired outcome.

**product:** a term used by manufacturing and service businesses to indicate the goods or services they provide.

**product awareness:** the proportion of all those within a *target market* who are aware of a particular brand/product. *Brand leaders* such as Coca-Cola may have almost 100 per cent awareness, whereas only 60 per cent of soft drink buyers are aware of 7-Up. For companies, product awareness is a crucial first step towards product trial. High product awareness is usually a function of:

- heavy advertising or sales promotion
- gaining favourable public relations (PR) media coverage
- the age and past prominence of the product
- the level of distribution and display
- the distinctiveness/memorability of the product

**product development**: fulfilling marketing objectives by developing new products or upgrading existing ones. This might be in order to boost sales/market share or to add value and therefore price. Successful product development relies upon excellence in research and development and in design, plus the technical ability to turn good designs into well engineered products or services. Product development can be through marginal changes (low risk, small reward) such as 'new, improved Ariel' or major innovations (high risk, high reward) such as Sony's wide-screen TV.

**product differentiation** is the extent to which consumers perceive one product as being different from its rivals. A highly differentiated product is one which people think of as so distinctive that it has no acceptable substitutes. With low differentiation, a product would be one among many, with many direct, acceptable competitors. As a result, products with weak differentiation need to charge relatively low prices in order to hold their *market share.*

There are two main sources of product differentiation:

- actual product advantages, such as better design, better manufacture and higher quality standards
- psychological factors such as *branding* and *advertising*

**production** is the process of organising resources in order to meet a customer requirement. In a manufacturing context, production is the whole process from: obtaining raw materials to goods inward inspection, to production processes, to assembly and finishing, to delivery. The term 'production' can also be applied to the supply of services.

**production chain:** the entire sequence of activities required to turn raw materials into a consumer purchase. The chain will include *primary, secondary* and *tertiary sector* activities, with the latter involved at every stage. A highly simplified example for beer production is shown on the diagram.

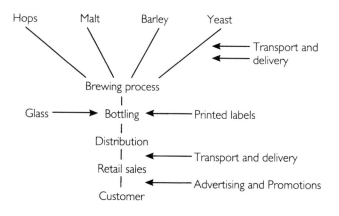

*Production chain for beer production*

**production line:** the arrangement of a flow production system so that parts move systematically from one stage to the next. Within such a process, *division of labour* is likely to be high and production line workers may feel threatened by the prospect of automation.

**production orientation** is a term used by many writers to indicate an old-fashioned business that ignores customer tastes and needs. The management is assumed to be inward-looking, focusing upon the convenience of producing the same old product in the same old way. This is contrasted with more thrusting, market-oriented companies that spot new trends and devise the products to meet them. Although there is truth in this, production orientation does have some important strengths:

- implies a commitment to focus on the firm's strengths rather than diversifying into unknown markets
- will often be associated with high quality, even to the point of producing an item that is stronger or better than the market thinks it needs (but that can boost long-term *corporate image*)
- may lead to longer-term planning for new capital investment than in a market-orientated firm

**production plan**: a detailed account of how a business intends to create the goods and/or services to satisfy forecast demand. This will include:

- the number and type of workers required
- the costs involved
- the time available to achieve the target production level
- the material and capital resources required

**productivity** is a measurement of the efficiency with which a firm turns production inputs into *output*. The most common measure is labour productivity, i.e. output per worker. This is important because output per worker has a direct effect on labour costs per unit. The higher the productivity, the lower the labour cost per unit, as in the following example:

Worked example: productivity and costs for widget manufacture

| | Weekly wage | Productivity (output per worker) | Labour cost per unit |
|---|---|---|---|
| Best UK firm | £250 | 25.0 | £10 |
| Worst UK firm | £250 | 12.5 | £20 |
| Average Japanese firm | £280 | 40.0 | £7 |

Differing levels of productivity (efficiency) are the main single explanation for variations in industrial performance and levels of national wealth. Rising productivity can cause job losses, if demand does not rise as fast as the productivity gains. Yet despite this threat, high productivity remains vital to the competitiveness of every company and country.

**productivity bonus:** a financial *incentive* to encourage a workforce to work hard. Employees receive a basic wage supplemented by a bonus related to their output level. The bonus rate can be calculated on a group or individual basis. *Herzberg* would describe such a system as a way of achieving movement, not *motivation*.

**productivity deal:** an agreement between management and union representatives that the former will provide some financial or other benefits in exchange for higher output per worker. If a 5 per cent pay rise has been granted in exchange for 5 per cent higher *productivity*, this would leave labour costs per unit unchanged and therefore have no harmful effects upon competitiveness or *inflation*.

**product life cycle:** the theory that all products follow a similar life course of conception, birth, growth, maturity and decline, although products pass through these stages at different speeds. The modern cigarette was born in 1873 and sales peaked in 1973 (implying a product life cycle of around 200 years), whereas the entire sales life span of the Power Rangers was three years.

Factors affecting the length of a product's life cycle:

- durability: if the item need be bought only once (such as a sandwich toaster) then *market saturation* can hit demand, as all those who want the item, have it
- fashion: if the item's sales grew because of fashion, it is likely that they will die quite quickly, for the same reason
- technological change can be very significant in turning the customer away from a product that now seems obsolete

An important implication of the theory is that as every product will eventually decline and die, it is necessary for firms to carry out continuous new product development programmes. Ideally, new products should be financed from the *cash flows* generated by mature brands, and should be launched before maturity turns to decline. The product life cycle relates to company cash flow in the following way (see also diagram below):

- during the development phase there is substantial negative cash flow from the money spent on research and development, *market research*, product design, and setting up a *production line*
- if birth turns to growth, more cash must be ploughed into expanding factory capacity

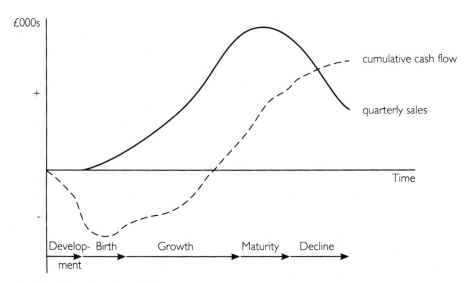

*Product life cycle and cash flow*

- once sales have stabilised, the firm can reap the cash rewards from their success
- in the decline phase, brands with a high *market share* can provide the cash for the development of replacement products (see *cash cow*)

**product mapping:** see *mapping*

**product placement** occurs when a manufacturer gets a brand placed in a scene of a film or television programme. If the hero of a worldwide box-office hit insists on Bacardi and Coke several times in the film, it may be because the producers have paid for the product to be placed there. In effect this is a form of advertising.

**product portfolio:** the range of products or brands held by a company that provide it with diversified sources of income. Ideally this portfolio should range over different markets and different stages in the *product life cycles*. A well-known and very useful way of analysing a firm's product portfolio is through the *Boston Matrix*.

**product proliferation** is the tendency for successful market sectors to become overcrowded by a large number of new product launches. This proliferation makes it hard for shopkeepers to find shelf space for all the products available, and can lead to confusion on the part of the customer.

**product range:** the full listing of the products offered by a firm.

**product recall** is when a manufacturer has to withdraw a brand from sale due to a production fault or to a saboteur tampering with the products. This is expensive in the short term and possibly damaging for the indefinite future, if customers get used to an alternative product.

**product trial** is the rate at which consumers in your *target market* buy or try your brand for the first time. It forms one of the three prime objectives for a firm launching a new product:

1 distribution
2 product trial
3 repeat purchase

Most firms set quantitative targets for each, such as to get a chocolate bar distributed in 80 per cent of sweetshops, tried by 50 per cent of chocolate buyers and repeat purchased by 12 per cent of trialists. In markets such as chocolate, product trial is heavily influenced by *packaging, promotions* and *advertising*. If the market is more fashion orientated, word of mouth is likely to be the main single influence upon the rate of trial.

**profit:** what is left from *revenue* after costs have been deducted. There are many types of profit; each is listed within the *profit and loss account* (see below).

FORMULA:   revenue − costs = profit

**profitability** is the measure of an organisation's ability to earn revenues above its expenditures. Profitability is usually assessed in relation to some yardstick such as *net assets* or *sales revenue*.

**profitability ratios** measure profit in proportion to a yardstick such as *net assets* (*return on capital*) or *sales revenue* (*profit margin* ratio).

**profit and loss account:** a statement recording all a firm's *revenues* and costs within a past trading period. Although firms have a degree of leeway about how they present their 'P & L account', most adopt the format set out in the example below. To show how the calculations work, sample figures are included on the right-hand side.

Worked example: profit and loss account

|  |  | £000 |  |
|---|---|---|---|
|  | Revenue | 940 |  |
| minus | Cost of sales | 610 |  |
| equals | **Gross profit** | 330 |  |
| minus | Overheads | 180 |  |
| equals | **Trading/Operating profit** | 150 |  |
| plus | One-off items | (30) | (a £30 000 loss) |
| equals | **Pre-tax profits** | 120 |  |
| minus | Tax | 30 | (25% of pre-tax) |
| equals | **Profit after tax** | 90 |  |
| minus | Dividends | 40 |  |
| equals | **Retained profit** | 50 |  |

**profit centre:** a division or department of a company that has been given the authority to run itself as a business within a business, with its own *profit and loss account*. Before the start of the year, a senior manager will discuss with the leader of the profit centre the likely *revenues* and costs for the forthcoming year. From this a *budget* will be drawn up from which the profit statement will be derived.

Pros:
- enables power to be delegated to the local level, which should speed up decision-making
- the local profit and loss account can form the basis of financial incentives for all the workforce at the centre

Cons:
- hard to coordinate the activity of several different 'small firms', all wishing to grow rapidly, but with the possibility that they may end up competing with each other
- the performance of a profit centre may bear no relation to the effort and skill of its management; after all, a blazing summer would make high profits in the ice-cream market an inevitability

**profit margin:** *profit* as a proportion of *sales revenue*. It can be expressed as a total (the percentage of sales revenue which is profit), or it can be calculated on a unit basis (profit as a percentage of the selling price). The margin is different from the *mark-up* as the margin is a percentage of price while the mark-up is profit as a percentage of cost.

Worked example: a sofa is bought by a furniture shop for £550 and sold for £625

Profit margin

$$\frac{\text{profit}}{\text{selling price}} \quad \frac{£125}{£625} \times 100 = 20\%$$

Mark-up

$$\frac{\text{Profit}}{\text{cost}} \quad \frac{£125}{£500} \times 100 = 25\%$$

**profit motive:** here the pursuit of profit is the governing force behind a person or organisation's decisions. This is most likely to be influential within the *private sector,* since shareholders require *dividends* large enough to justify the risks taken when investing in a business venture.

**profit maximisation** is often taken to be the reason why firms exist and to be their primary *corporate objective.* In practice, most firms have a hierarchy of objectives. When a firm's survival is threatened, it may profit-maximise in order to restore its financial health. Otherwise it is likely to pursue longer-term *objectives* such as *diversification.*

**profit-maximising pricing** is achieved by researching to find the likely level of *demand* at different prices, then calculating which is the most profitable. If the product has a relatively low *price elasticity,* the price set through this method is likely to be quite high. That is likely to attract new competitors who may make serious inroads into your medium-term *market-share.* Therefore profit-maximising pricing may benefit the firm's short-term performance at serious cost to its longer-term future.

**profit quality** refers to the likelihood of a profit source continuing into the future. If a profit has arisen from a one-off source (such as selling property at above its *book value*), its quality is said to be low. High quality profit is *trading profit* that can be expected to be repeated in future years. These points are illustrated below.

| Worked example: high- versus low-quality profit | | |
| --- | --- | --- |
| | Low quality £000 | High quality £000 |
| Revenue | 840 | 840 |
| Cost of sales | 540 | 460 |
| Overheads | 260 | 190 |
| Trading profit | 40 | 190 |
| One-off profit | 160 | 10 |
| Pre-tax profit | 200 | 200 |

**profit-related pay:** a system of *remuneration* in which a proportion of each employee's salary varies in line with the firm's profit level. So, instead of being paid £20 000 a year, an employee might be paid £15 000 plus 0.01 per cent of the firm's trading profit. If the firm's profit last year was £60m., then the employee can expect a salary of £15 000+(0.01% of £60m. = £6 000), i.e. £21 000. Since 1987 the government has offered *income tax* incentives to encourage the adoption of profit-related pay, but take-up has proved slow.

**profit share:** a bonus paid on top of employees' salaries to ensure that a proportion of the firm's profit is shared out among staff.

Pros: • could help to bridge any '*them and us*' divide between staff and management or shareholders
 • provides staff with a personal *incentive* to keep costs down and *productivity* up (at John Lewis, for example, the profit share has amounted to over 20 per cent of annual salary)

Cons:
- unless it amounts to a substantial sum, the profit share may be disregarded by staff, or even seen as insultingly low
- research evidence has shown that profit sharing, on its own, has little effect on performance, partly because individuals cannot believe that their own efforts will make a significant difference to the whole firm's profit level

**pro forma:** a projected table of data. Hence a business plan for a new firm might include a pro forma *profit and loss account* for the first 12 months.

**programmed trading** is the use of computer programmes that decide when to buy or sell shares or foreign currencies. The computer might be instructed, for example, to automatically sell any share that has fallen by 10 per cent or more (to prevent a client from losing everything).

**progressive tax** takes a higher proportion of an individual's income the more that individual earns. An example is *income tax.*

**project planning:** when undertaking a project such as launching a new product, firms need a planning procedure that ensures that all the project elements are coordinated and scheduled so that the outcome is achieved on time and within the *budget.* This process can be achieved by:
- task analysis, i.e. breaking the project down into its component parts to identify what activities are involved, the order in which they should be completed, and the quality standards necessary
- risk analysis, i.e. estimating the factors causing uncertainty about the achievement of the tasks (such as bad weather delaying factory construction) then making an allowance for them in the project timings
- *network analysis,* i.e. producing a diagram showing the order in which the activities must be carried out and the time by when each one should be completed
- *critical path analysis* then calculates the activities within the network thatmust be completed on time if the project is to be finished as soon as possible

**promotion** has two different meanings:
- being appointed to a more senior or more desirable job (though see *horizontal promotion*)
- the promotion of a product as part of the *marketing mix* by the use of *advertising, branding, sales promotion* and *public relations*

**promotional techniques:** see *sales promotion*

**proprietor** is the person who owns and runs a business, usually a *sole trader.*

**prospectus:** a document which companies have to produce when they go public i.e. become *quoted* on the *Stock Exchange.* It gives details about the company's activities and anticipated future profits. It has to conform to the *Companies Act 1985* and be handed to the *Registrar of Companies.* Any false declarations in the prospectus carry heavy penalties because it is construed as fraud to encourage people to buy shares on the basis of incorrect information.

**protectionism** describes policies of erecting barriers to trade such as *quotas, tariffs* and *non-tariff barriers.* Because of the benefits of trade derived from the law of *comparative advantage,* protectionism is banned under *GATT* agreements. The most notorious period of protectionism was between the wars, during the *Great Depression*, where country after country put up barriers in the hope of maintaining its level of employment.

**prototype:** a sample product manufactured on an experimental basis to see if the engineering and design ideas work in practice. The prototype can be tested both from an engineering and from a *market research* perspective, before the firm decides whether to start full production.

**provisions:** allowances made in accounts for likely, but not definite, future *liabilities*. An example would be if a firm has been sued for damages which it believes it will probably have to pay.

**prudence:** the principle that accounts should be drawn up on cautious assumptions. This would ensure that any errors would tend to be in the company's favour. Examples of prudence include:

- stock being valued at the lower of cost and *net-realisable value*
- profit being recorded when a delivery is made to the customer, rather than when an order arrives

Although theory states that accounts are drawn up prudently, there are many past cases of firms whose financial difficulties could be blamed on imprudent practices.

**psychological price barrier:** the price level that changes consumer perceptions of the product's value for money. £10 000 would represent such a barrier for many car buyers, hence the large number of cars on offer for £9 950. Technically, *price elasticity* increases at the psychological price barrier. Therefore a 1 per cent price increase from £9 950 to £10 049.50 will have a far greater effect upon demand than a 1 per cent change from £9 500 to £9 595.

**psychological pricing** means setting a price based on the expectations of the consumers within your *target market*. If, for example, a perfume producer has identified a *market niche* for a special occasion fragrance for mid-teenage girls, the price may be set above the level of the competition. This will help to reinforce the image set by the perfume's packaging and advertising messages. In this way, the price level becomes an integral part of the product's *marketing mix*.

**psychometric test:** a selection test designed to reveal the personality of a candidate for recruitment or promotion. It is usually done through multiple-choice questions which may use word association to look for candidates' sense of teamwork, their honesty or their sense of commitment. Japanese employers are very keen on this, because it tests whether the individual is likely to fit in.

**public corporation:** the technical name for a nationalised industry, i.e. an enterprise that is owned by the state but offers a product for sale to *public* and *private sector* customers. It should not be confused with a *public limited company*, which is in the *private sector*.

**public enquiry:** a way of judging a *planning permission* case that is thought to be of particular public interest. A typical example might be the building of a motorway through a site of outstanding natural beauty.

The case is usually heard by an inspector appointed by the *Department of Trade and Industry*, and will hear evidence from the proposers and the protesters. The enquiry has the power to turn the planning application down.

**public expenditure** consists of all spending on goods and services by central and local government, and public corporations.

**public limited company (PLC):** a company with *limited liability* that has over £50 000 of *share capital* and a wide spread of shareholders. PLCs are the only type of company allowed to be quoted on the *Stock Exchange*. The drawbacks of being a quoted company are illustrated by Richard Branson of Virgin and Alan Sugar of Amstrad. Both decided that having become public companies they wished to return to the status of *private limited companies* again to avoid the loss of control and the share-price fluctuations which accompany quotations on the Stock Exchange. (See also *divorce of ownership and control.*)

**public relations (PR)** is the process of obtaining favourable publicity via the editorial columns of press media, or in television or radio broadcasts. The PR expert has the contacts within the media to ensure that the client's story or side to a dispute is reported sympathetically. Public relations can be a positive process of organising interviews on Breakfast TV shows or setting up launch parties for new products. However, there have also been many cases where PR personnel have been engaged in spreading negative, even malicious stories about rival firms. This can border on the illegal and is most certainly unethical.

**public sector:** the organisations and activities that are owned and/or funded by national or local government. These include *public corporations* (nationalised industries), public services (such as the National Health Service) and municipal services (such as local council-run leisure centres).

**public sector borrowing requirement (PSBR)** is the gap between government income from taxes and other sources, and its expenditure on such areas as defence, education and social security payments.

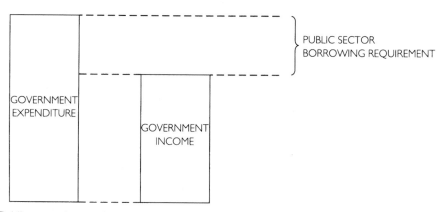

*Public sector borrowing requirement (PSBR)*

**public services** are services within the *tertiary sector* made available to all members of society. They include waste collection, street lighting, education and health services. They are often 'free at the point of delivery', i.e. when you receive the service, but of course they are not 'free' as such. For instance, householders do not have to pay the operator every time their dustbin is emptied, but of course they do pay for this service indirectly through taxation.

**public service motive:** the force that drives people to work for a greater good than simply personal gain or profit. Nurses' pay is often said to reflect their special motivation – it is so low that few would join the profession unless they had a special desire to help people who are ill.

**public spending** is the amount of expenditure which governments undertake with the *revenue* which they obtain from taxes and other sources. (See *fiscal policy*.)

**purchase documents:** the paperwork to initiate or confirm the placing of an order for goods or services. An order form will usually include sections for: the product type, the catalogue number, the price, the number being ordered, the discount level (if any) and the total value of the order.

**purchasing manager:** the individual responsible for obtaining the right supplies at the right price to arrive at the right time. This job function should be conducted in close collaboration with the marketing and production departments.

**put option:** the right to sell shares in the future at today's price. Such a transaction would be entered into by someone who believes that the share price is about to fall. It is the way in which an investor who feels 'bearish' about the *stock market* can make money out of their pessimism.

**pyramid:** this usually refers to the company hierarchy, in other words the formal management structure, including the numbers of management layers and the *span of control*.

**pyramid of ratios:** a popular text book device for showing how accounting ratios interrelate. It also gives an indication of the rank order of importance of the ratios. At the apex of the pyramid is usually the *return on capital* (ROC) ratio. This is then split up into component parts such as *profit margins* and *asset turnover*. These can then be split further into their constituents; profit margins, for example into *sales turnover* and *profit*. This is illustrated in a simplified version.

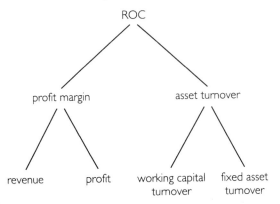

*Pyramid of ratios*

**pyramid selling:** is a clever (though generally illegal) way of encouraging inexperienced people to part with their cash in exchange for the right to sell a questionable product to others at high prices. Those at the top of the pyramid can benefit hugely from the commissions that those lower down pay on anything they sell. The nearer to the bottom you go, the more you encounter disillusioned people who realise that they have spent up to £100 on items that most consumers do not want.

**qualitative research** is in-depth research into the motivations behind consumer behaviour or attitudes. It is usually conducted by psychologists among small groups of people within the *target market* for the product (these are called *group discussions* or *focus groups*). The other main technique used by qualitative researchers is the *depth interview*.

The idea behind qualitative research is that when people are asked direct questions (as in a *questionnaire*) they may give answers that make them sound sensible or rational. Yet many purchasing decisions are based on emotion, not logic. Consumers pay £20 extra for the 'right' pair of jeans. Qualitative researchers aim to find out consumers' real thought processes during a relaxed discussion that has no pre-set questions. It can therefore lead wherever the psychologist feels the truth lies.

Pros:
- can reveal the motivations behind consumer decisions
- as discussion can range freely, it can discover the unexpected (whereas questionnaires can only consist of questions that were known beforehand to be significant)
- group discussion can provide ideas about how to solve a marketing problem from the most important people of all: the customers

Cons:
- each interview or discussion is expensive, therefore few firms can afford to conduct many; this leads to possible concerns about whether the sample is representative
- the unstructured nature of the responses means that the data cannot be quantified

**quality assurance:** the attempt to ensure that quality standards are agreed and met throughout the organisation, to ensure customer satisfaction. Among the key factors that must be considered are:

- the time, effort and technology input into product design
- the quality of supplies of materials and components
- the commitment of the workforce
- the system of quality monitoring and control
- the ability to deliver on time
- the quality of advice and *after-sales service* provided.

**quality circle:** a discussion group that meets regularly to identify quality problems, consider alternative solutions, and recommend a suitable outcome to management. The members are usually drawn from the factory-floor, but may include an engineer, a quality inspector and a member of the sales team (to provide the customer angle). This method was first devised at the Toyota Motor Company in Japan in the 1950s. Its success as a form of *consultation* and *job enrichment* led to its wider adoption in Japan and then, in the 1980s, in the West. The two principles behind the quality circle are that:
- no manager or engineer can understand production problems as fully as the shop-floor workers, therefore their knowledge is a huge untapped asset for the firm

- workers appreciate the opportunity to show their knowledge and talents in a problem-solving environment

**quality control:** the process of checking the accuracy of work bought-in or completed. This is usually carried out by quality inspectors, though some modern factories encourage employees to check their own quality. This conforms to *Herzberg's* view of the importance of personal responsibility and self-checking.

**quality newspapers** are generally accepted as non-tabloid in format, offering both news and comment but requiring a fairly developed vocabulary and command of the language.

**Quality of Work Life (QWL):** a campaign by industrial psychologists to persuade managers to consider more seriously whether their employees benefit from the work they are doing. It is largely based upon the work of *McGregor* and *Herzberg*, especially the latter's advocacy of *job enrichment.*

**quantitative research** means research using pre-set questions among a large enough *sample size* to provide statistically valid data. In practical terms that means using a *questionnaire* to poll at least 200 consumers within each segment of a market. It is a way of discovering data such as:

- a product's *consumer profile*
- the way a market can be segmented
- probable sales at a given price level
- estimated sales of a new product
- the results of a *blind product test*

Large firms tend to use group discussions (see *qualitative research*) to help understand customer views and then write a questionnaire based upon them. Interviewers can then be employed to conduct the survey upon a representative sample of the population. The three main ways of drawing a sample are: *random, quota* and *stratified.*

**quantity surveyor:** the independent construction expert who estimates the amount, type and cost of materials required and used within a building project.

**quartile:** the total accounted for by one quarter of a population. For instance, a computer might rank all of a firm's 1 000 customers in order of sales value. The 250 biggest customers (the top quartile) could then have their sales totalled, which might reveal that they buy 80 per cent of the firm's *output.* The smallest 250 customers (the bottom quartile) might be worth less than 2 per cent of the firm's output. This information would help the company to make decisions on its sales and distribution strategies (see the diagram on page 233).

**Queen's Award for Industry** is given for an outstanding contribution in particular business areas such as exporting or training.

**questionnaire:** a document containing a series of questions designed to discover the information required to meet a firm's research objectives. When writing questionnaires there are four main principles to bear in mind:

- each question should ask only one point
- questions should not contain *bias* (e.g. 'How much do you like cider?')
- the time, cost and ability to quantify the analysis of the answers depends on whether the questions are closed or open. *Closed questions* are far more

common (e.g. 'Have you bought cider within the last week?' Yes [  ] No [ ])

- the questions must be asked in the right sequence, leaving personal details such as age, address and occupation until the end, and making sure that earlier questions do not bias the answers to later ones

**queuing theory** (also known as simulation) is the construction of a model to simulate the effect on queues of randomly occurring events, such as customer arrival times, that take varying lengths of time to process. The technique works when there are just two key variables. It could be used to decide how many service counters a bank should open if its objective is to allow a queue of no more than three people to develop.

Pros:
- takes into account the random factors in human behaviour
- enables a manager to try out new methods on paper before experimenting in practice
- can easily be computerised, thereby allowing experiments to be conducted into how to achieve a particular customer service objective

Cons:
- a complex procedure for non-mathematicians to grasp, therefore of limited value in a general meeting
- can only be accurate if the *sample size* of the observations is large enough (and taken at the right times)

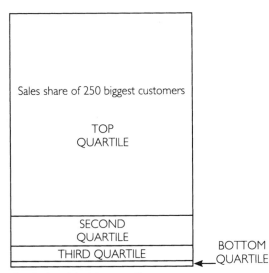

*Analysing data into quartiles*

**quick ratio:** see *acid test ratio*

**quorum:** the minimum number of group members present at a meeting to enable decisions to be valid. For example in a committee of 12 it may be agreed that a minimum of six members must be present for a quorum to exist.

**quotas (import):** a form of import protection that limits the sales of foreign goods to a specified quantity or *market share*. This will reduce the *supply* of the item, so if *demand* stays constant either the price will rise or a rationing system will be needed.

**quota sample:** the recruitment of respondents to a *market research* exercise in proportion to their known *demographic profile*. Therefore if you know that 25 per cent of your buyers are men, you would instruct interviewers to recruit one man for every three women within your sample. This is a far cheaper method of recruitment than *random sampling*.

**quoted company:** a firm that has its shares listed on the *Stock Exchange*.

# R

**Race Relations Acts 1968** and **1976** make it unlawful to discriminate at the workplace against any person on grounds of colour, race, ethnic or national origin. Specifically, the Acts make it unlawful to refuse employment, training or promotion on these grounds, or to select someone for *dismissal* on grounds of race. The 1976 Act set up the Commission for Racial Equality with power to investigate and issue non-discrimination notices against employers or *trade unions* found to be acting in a discriminatory manner. Individual complaints should be taken to an *industrial tribunal*.

**R and D:** see *research and development*

**random numbers** are numbers that have no pattern to them if used systematically. They can be drawn from a hat or, more probably, be generated by computers. Random numbers are useful in certain operations research techniques, such as *simulation*.

**random sample:** contacting survey respondents so that every member of the population has an equal chance of being interviewed. This sounds straightforward but is, in fact, both hard and expensive to achieve. The reason is that random must not be confused with haphazard. If all that an interviewer did was to stand outside Marks and Spencer one Tuesday afternoon and interview as many people as necessary, various distortions would occur in the sample:

- relatively few men would be interviewed
- few working women would be interviewed
- few hardworking students would be interviewed
- in other words, the sample would be biased towards pensioners, parents of preschool children and the unemployed.

In order to avoid these pitfalls, random samples are drawn from local electoral registers, and interviewees are contacted at home. The interviewer must call three times before giving up on an address. This is to overcome the problem that busy people are the least likely to be at home. The need to visit and revisit specific addresses adds considerably to fieldwork costs. So although random sampling is common in social research, businesses tend to use *quota samples*.

**ratio analysis:** an examination of accounting data by relating one result to another. This facilitates more meaningful interpretation of the figures. On its own, the knowledge that a firm's stock total is £5m. provides little insight. However, when related to its £10m. turnover (at cost), the analyst can judge the efficiency implied by holding onto its stock for six months, on average. (See also *inter-firm comparison* and *intra-firm comparison*.)

There are four main users of ratio analysis:

- internal managers, wanting to measure their own performance compared with previous years and with their rivals: the main ratios of interest would be those relating to performance (such as *return on capital, stock turnover, debtor days* and *asset turnover*) plus those relating to profitability, such as *gross* and *net margins*

- *creditors* or potential creditors, for whom the security of their loans or credits would be the prime consideration: *liquidity* measures such as the *current* and *acid test ratios* plus the *creditor days* figure would be of particular interest
- shareholders or potential shareholders should start with key indicators such as return on capital, acid test and *gearing*: this would be followed by investigation of the main shareholders ratios: *earnings per share, dividend yield* and the *PE ratio*
- the staff (perhaps through *trade union* representatives) would be interested in the financial security of the firm (acid test and gearing ratios) and in its profitability: widening *profit margins* would make a substantial pay claim seem far more plausible

**rationalisation** means reorganising to increase efficiency. The term is mainly used when cutbacks in *overhead* costs are needed in order to reduce an organisation's *break-even point*. This may be achieved by:

- closing one of a company's factories and reallocating the production to the remaining sites
- closing an administrative department and delegating its tasks to the firm's operating divisions
- *delayering* (removing a layer of management)

*Public relations* officers often use the term rationalisation as a euphemism for *redundancies*.

**rationing** means imposing a physical limitation on individuals' consumption of a good or service. For instance, in time of war it might be necessary to limit each car driver to one gallon of petrol per week. Rationing is often achieved through the *price mechanism*, in that only those who can afford a good will be able to have it.

**raw data** is unprocessed *primary data*. Usually the term refers to statistical information such as the sales figure for a product. Even after elementary processing such as collection into a time series (month 1, month 2 etc.) it is still considered raw. Among the main forms of analysis of raw data are: *indexing, seasonal adjustment, smoothing* and weighting.

Until it is processed it may be hard to use and interpret raw data, as shown in the following figures for sales of T-shirts.

Worked example: T-shirt company sales

|  | Raw sales figures | Seasonally adjusted sales index (base: Jan–Mar) |
|---|---|---|
| Jan–Mar | 1 647 920 | 100 |
| Apr–Jun | 2 486 729 | 105 |
| Jul-Sept | 3 842 166 | 107 |
| Oct-Dec | 1 946 771 | 112 |

It is only after allowing for the seasonal influences on *demand* that the underlying pattern of sales growth can be identified.

**raw materials** are *commodities* bought by a firm in a virtually unprocessed state. Examples would include sugar for making chocolate and sand for making glass.

**Reaganomics** was the term given to the *monetarist* or *supply side* economic policies which were pursued by President Reagan when he was in office during the 1980s.

**realignment** (of currencies) occurs under a *fixed exchange rate* system when currencies get out of line, perhaps one country has a persistent *balance of payments* deficit for instance. In this case, a realignment occurs so that that country can export more and import less. In other words the currency is devalued.

**real incomes** are money incomes deflated by the level of prices. For instance, if you earned £100 last year and £200 this, but in the meantime prices had doubled, your real income would remain the same. So, to calculate real incomes, divide money incomes by price.

**real interest rates** are the rates above (or below) prevailing rates of *inflation*. For instance, if inflation is 5 per cent per annum, and interest rates are 8 per cent, real rates are 3 per cent. During periods of rapid inflation, a seemingly attractive rate will often be negative. For instance, an attractive interest rate of 20 per cent will actually be minus 5 per cent, if inflation is 25 per cent per year.

**realisation** is the accounting concept that enforces a consistent interpretation about <u>when</u> a profit can be recorded in a firm's books. It states that a profit is realised when a delivery has been made in response to a customer's firm order. Note that this is not the same as when the cash is received, since most businesses give their customers time to pay, i.e. a credit period.

**rebasing an index** means changing the base period, probably in order to update the information and make it easier to interpret.

METHOD:  **1** decide on the new base period
**2** let the figure for that period equal 100
**3** divide the figure for each other period within the sequence by the base period figure, then multiply by 100

Worked example: rebasing an ageing index.

|  | Old index, with March Year 1 = 100 | Index rebased, with March Year 7 = 100 |
|---|---|---|
| Feb Year 7 | 462 | 95.0 |
| Mar Year 7 | 486 | 100.0 |
| Apr Year 7 | 491 | 101.0 |
| May Year 7 | 482 | 99.0 |
| Jun Year 7 | 488 | 100.4 |

**recapitalising:** injecting more *capital* into a business that has insufficient to trade effectively and safely. The alternative to recapitalisation is probably *liquidation*, though in this case existing or new shareholders believe it preferable to keep the business going.

**receiver** is appointed by creditors when a company has insufficient assets to cover its *liabilities*. The receiver's job is to try to sell the company to any other interested parties as a going concern so that those who are owed money can get it back. If he or she fails to find a buyer, then the company will be sold off in parts, and will be liquidated.

**recession** is that part of the *trade cycle* which is characterised by falling levels of demand, very little investment, low business confidence and rising levels of unemployment. It is neither as long lasting nor as severe, however, as a *depression*. The official definition of a recession is two successive declines in quarterly *gross domestic product*.

**recognition:** see *union recognition*

**recommended retail price (RRP):** the price that the manufacturer suggests that the retailer should charge. With most products the manufacturer has no legal right to force retailers to sell at this price, so some charge more and some charge less.

**recovery** is that part of the *trade cycle* which is characterised by slowly rising levels of demand, some investment, patchy business confidence and falling levels of unemployment.

**recruitment** is the process of identifying the need for a new employee, defining the job and the appropriate person for it, attracting a number of suitable candidates, then selecting the one best suited to the job. (See *seven-point plan*.)

**recruitment procedure:** the complete process of turning the need for a new employee into a successful appointment. This would include advertising the vacancy (or *headhunting*), shortlisting, dealing with references, assessing candidates, deciding on the most suitable and then debriefing the unsuccessful candidates. Throughout the process it is necessary to avoid discrimination by sex, race, disability or age. This not only avoids legal challenges to decisions, but also ensures that the best candidate is appointed to the job.

**recycling** means dismantling and/or sorting products so that they can be collected and reused. This reduces the need for more raw materials to be mined or grown. As the cost of *raw materials* increases, technology improves, and the legal, moral and ethical implications of polluting become more critical, firms will move into recycling more of their own and other firms' products.

**redeployment** means moving people to new job functions either because their department has been closed down or because they are not good enough in their current post. It is often used as a polite way of telling staff that they are being moved sideways or even demoted.

**reducing balance method** is another term for *declining balance method* (of *depreciation*).

**redundancy** occurs when a job function is no longer required. Therefore the employee holding the job becomes redundant through no fault of his or her own. If an organisation requires a large number of redundancies in order to reduce its *overheads*, it may ask for volunteers, offering financial inducements to those that accept. If insufficient numbers of the right types of employee apply to leave, compulsory redundancies may have to follow. The staff involved are legally entitled to the following minimum payments:

| Age of employee | Payment per year of service |
| --- | --- |
| 18–21 years | Half a week's pay |
| 22–41 years | One week's pay |
| Over 41 years | One and a half week's pay |

These terms only apply to those employed for more than 16 hours per week and with over two years of continuous employment.

**re-engineering**: the complete reinvention of how work is carried out within an organisation, including fundamentals such as *organisational structure, job design* and production layout. Such a radical approach has rarely been attempted throughout a large firm, but American Express has reported reducing its annual costs by over $1 billion through re-engineering.

In their bestselling book *Reengineering the Corporation* (Harper Collins 1993) Michael Hammer and James Champy suggested that the driving force behind re-engineering were the 3 Cs: customers, competition and change. Critics suggest that re-engineering is little more than a management consultants' gimmick – and merely another term for *rationalisation* and *redundancy*.

**referee:** someone who supplies a *reference* on a job applicant.

**reference:** an account by someone of independent standing of the suitability, capability and character of a job applicant. Employers may worry about possible *bias* within job references, as it is the candidate who chooses the referee, and the author may have an interest in the applicant gaining the job. Despite this, references are one of the most important elements in most firms' *recruitment* selection procedures.

**refinancing** means much the same as *recapitalising*, though the latter carries the implication of being based rather more on equity finance. A refinanced business might, therefore, have received a high proportion of its extra *capital* in the form of loans.

**reflation** is the economic policy of stimulating aggregate demand by using *Keynesian* measures in order to reduce unemployment (such as tax cuts or increases in government spending).

**regional policy** is the government's attempt to correct imbalances of income and employment by stimulating the local economy of less prosperous areas. (See *enterprise zones* and *development area*.)

Pros:
- reduces inequality of incomes and of opportunities
- reduces the hardship associated with structural decline
- reduces congestion in other regions
- by reducing unemployment it reduces the waste and cost of keeping workers on the dole

Cons:
- there is little evidence that it works to change long-term trends
- firms often move a very short distance to take advantage of the incentives, but in so doing create no extra jobs or incomes
- to be effective it requires substantial government spending; successful firms might argue that they are subsidising less successful ones

**regional test:** a form of test marketing in which a real experiment is undertaken within a whole marketing region. An example would be launching a new product within the North-West. This would find out whether the product can achieve a high enough *market share* to be profitable if launched nationally. A regional test is a far more expensive experiment than *market research*, but should yield far more accurate information. (See also *test marketing*.)

**Register of Members' Interests:** a document in which Members of Parliament specify any group with which they are associated which might influence the way they speak or vote in the House of Commons. By declaring such interests it is allowable for MPs to advance the causes of those groups.

**Registrar of Companies** maintains a record of all *joint-stock companies* in the UK, including their *memorandums of association* and for larger companies, their *annual report and accounts*. All the information held by the Registrar is available to the public at *Companies' House*.

**regressive tax:** one which takes a smaller proportion out of someone's income the more they earn. It is important to realise that a tax like *VAT* which is set at a fixed rate, is in fact regressive. If two people buy identical goods on which there is £10 of VAT, the £10 represents only 1 per cent of someone's income if they are earning £1 000, but 10 per cent if they are earning £100.

**regulator:** an independent person appointed by the government to exert control over the activities of privatised *monopoly* companies such as British Gas. (See *OFGAS, OFTEL, OFWAT.*)

**regulation** is one way in which companies are constrained by law, for instance on the maximum permitted level of pollution. Many firms complain that the existence of many consumer protection, employment and pollution regulations imposes excessive overhead costs upon business. For example, many staff are required to ensure that laws are being complied with. Furthermore, dislike of dealing with rules and regulations may put people off starting new businesses.

One of the objectives of privatisation was the removal of excessive restrictions, but it was necessary to introduce regulators such as OFGAS, OFTEL and OFWAT to limit the activities of British Gas, British Telecom and the water companies and so avoid their exploitation of powerful market positions.

**remembered pain:** a grievance so acute as to be an unforgotten scar on an individual or group memory. Professor *Herzberg* used the term as a warning against underestimating the importance of *hygiene factors* (such as pay, status and working conditions). He found that his *two-factor theory* was being misinterpreted to suggest that only *motivators* matter. In fact, the exploitation of a productive individual or group by underpaying could lead 'to a remembered pain that leads to *revenge psychology* on the part of workers. They'll get back at you some day when you need them' (JUMPING FOR THE JELLYBEANS BBC Books, 1973). The Professor pointed out that many *industrial disputes* appeared to be sparked off by a trivial issue, but the origins could be traced back to a remembered pain.

**remuneration:** the entire package of material rewards received by an employee. These may comprise: pay, pension contributions, and *share options* plus *fringe benefits* such as a company car and private health insurance.

**reorder level:** the quantity of stock considered the minimum before more need be ordered from the supplier. To decide on the appropriate reorder level a firm must take into account the following factors:

- how long suppliers take to deliver after an order has been placed (their *lead time*)
- the level of *demand* for the product
- the level of *buffer stock* set by a firm

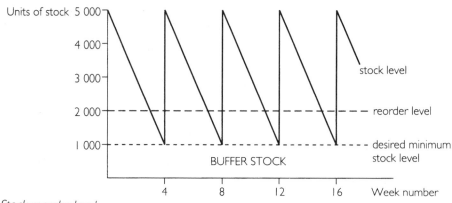

*Stock reorder level*

**repeat purchase** occurs when a first-time buyer purchases the same brand again. If this keeps happening, the process could be described as developing *brand loyalty*.

**repeat sales**: another term for *repeat purchase*.

**repetitive strain injury (RSI)** is an acute muscle pain brought on by overrepetition of a small physical movement. Journalists found themselves hit by RSI when new technology printing led to them doing far more keyboarding within their jobs. Some found that RSI proved permanent, forcing them to leave their profession. RSI has proved to be the modern equivalent to health and safety issues such as excessive factory noise, and is watched carefully by *white collar unions*.

**resale price maintenance** is a regulation forcing retailers to abide by the prices set by producers. This protects small independent shops from price competition, thereby ensuring that more survive to serve their local communities. Only after resale price maintenance was abolished in Britain in 1964 was there a substantial shift towards the concentration of *market share* among multiple retailers such as Sainsbury's and Tesco.

**research and development (R and D)** means scientific research and technical development. This is directed at improving the product, rather than at finding out what the consumer wants and thinks. The latter information is the function of *market research*.

**reserves** are a company's accumulated, retained *profit*. When they were made, these profits represented an important source of long-term finance for the business. There is no reason to assume, however, that they are still held in the form of cash. Therefore it is a mistake to suggest that a firm can 'use its reserves' to finance investment; it can only use cash.

**residual cash**: the cash total a firm is left with at the end of a trading period or at the end of the *trading cycle* for a particular order.

**residual value** is the forecast value left in an *asset* at the end of its useful lifetime. This requires a guess as to the resale value of a second-hand asset in, perhaps, three or four years' time. This may be subject to considerable inaccuracy, yet it is a key element in the calculation of *depreciation*, whether by the *declining balance* or *straight line* methods.

**resistance to change** occurs as a result of: fear of the unknown; mistrust of the motives of those proposing change; and worries about loss of job security, income or status on the part of the staff concerned. Research has shown that in most organisations, middle managers are the staff most resistant to change. This is because middle managers have more to lose in any reorganisation than those below them in the hierarchy.

To reduce resistance to change, senior management needs to:

- have established in advance a sense of common purpose and of trust between the employees and management of the organisation
- explain and discuss the reasons for change in an attempt to achieve a consensus that it is essential
- if possible, guarantee staff that the changes will not result in any compulsory *redundancies* or pay cuts
- consult fully on the options available for implementing the change, ensuring that employee views have a significant impact on the eventual strategy
- set a clear timetable for the entire process of change; this prevents rumours circulating about what may happen next

**resource histograms** measure the use of a resource (such as manpower) over time. They are presented as block diagrams. Managers may combine their use with *critical path analysis* to see where holdups may occur because of limited resources and how to reschedule the work.

**respondent:** an individual who responds to a *market research* exercise and is therefore part of the actual *sample*.

**response rate:** the proportion of those contacted within a *market research* survey who become *respondents*. This is an important element in determining how representative the *sample* is. A low response rate might introduce *bias*, as those who choose to respond may have different views from those that do not. This is a major disadvantage of using *self-completion* or postal questionnaires instead of *face-to-face interviews*.

**responsibility** i.e. for decisions or results can be implied by *delegation*, but should remain with the directors, for they are ultimately responsible for the organisation's strategy and for the appointment of the staff involved. Nevertheless, there have been many occasions in business and in politics when the chief executive or government minister has refused to accept responsibility for actions taken by subordinates. In which case no one appears to be responsible for organisational errors or misdeeds.

**restricted communication channels** are those that deliver information to specified people only. For example management accounts or minutes of board meetings may only be sent to selected senior executives. *Electronic mail* can be channelled in the same restricted way to maintain the control, confidentiality and security of information.

**restrictive practice:** a term used in two separate contexts.

Restrictive trade practices are active interferences by producers into the free working of markets. This reduces competition and is therefore likely to lead to higher consumer prices. Among the main restrictive trade practices are *full line forcing*, *market-sharing agreements* and the sharing of technological or marketing information. Practices such as the latter can be registered with the *Office of Fair Trading* and would therefore be legal. Unregistered restrictive practices can result in prosecution under the *Fair Trading Act 1973*.

Restrictive working practices are past agreements between producers and workers that limit the management's flexibility to decide who should work where and in what way. A common example is tight job *demarcation*, whereby a plumber may refuse to change a fuse because that is the job of an electrician. As the Japanese have demonstrated the benefits of workforce *flexibility*, British managements have tried to negotiate or to force through an end to job demarcation.

**restructuring** means reorganising with a view to improving efficiency. This may involve a restructuring of the management hierarchy (perhaps through the introduction of *profit centres*) or of the production capacity. Often, in fact, the word 'restructuring' is used as a euphemism or excuse for large-scale *redundancies*.

**retail audit:** a form of secondary research that measures the retail sales and *market share* of all major brands within a representative sample of shops. Individual producers may then decide to subscribe to this service on a weekly or monthly basis. Among the benefits of retail audits are:

- provides analysis of the composition and trends of sales within different types of outlet (supermarkets, chemists etc.)
- gives producers an early warning of changes in consumer purchasing patterns that will soon feed through to demand (via changes in wholesale stock levels)
- provides data on shop *distribution* levels

**retail cooperatives** are usually part of the national cooperative movement, which was established to provide consumers with goods at a fair price and with all the profits being paid back to the shoppers themselves.

**retailer:** a shop which sells goods to the general public.

**retail margins:** the percentage *profit* received by a shop on each item (or the average item) it sells. This is the retailer's *gross margin*, i.e. it does not allow for *overhead* costs.

$$\text{FORMULA:} \quad \frac{\text{selling price} - \text{purchase price}}{\text{selling price}} \times 100 = \text{retail margin}$$

---

Worked example: if a furniture shop buys chairs from a manufacturer for £200 and sells them for £500 its retail margin is:

$$\frac{£300}{£500} \times 100 = 60\%$$

---

**retail prices index (RPI):** shows changes in the price of the average person's shopping basket. The RPI is the main measurement of *inflation* in the UK and is calculated through a *weighted average* of each month's price changes.

It starts with a study of people's spending patterns, to try to assess the average household's weekly expenditure. This is in order to provide the base weights. About 16 per cent of household spending is on transport; it therefore carries a weight of 0.16 within the RPI. So if transport prices rise by 10 per cent, this adds 1.6 per cent to the overall RPI (10% × 0.16). The bigger the proportion of household incomes spent on an item, the bigger the effect of any price change upon the overall inflation figure.

A problem with the RPI is that it is weighted towards the average household's spending pattern. Yet many people who rely on the level of the RPI for annual increases in their government benefits or pensions have quite different spending patterns. For instance, pensioners spend twice the proportion of their income on heating as the average household. So if electricity and gas prices rise 10 per cent in a year when most prices have risen by 3 per cent, the RPI figure (of perhaps 4 per cent) will fail to reflect the inflation experienced by pensioners.

**retail selling price (RSP)** is the actual price of an item charged to customers in a shop. This will differ from the wholesale price to a degree that depends on the price *mark-up* decided on by the retailer. In making calculations about manufacturers' revenues or profits, it is important to remember that they will not receive the RSP of the product. They will only receive the *ex-factory price*. This is shown in the table below which assumes a traditional *distribution channel*.

| Event | Term |
| --- | --- |
| Manufacturer charges £4.20 to wholesaler | Ex-factory price |
| Wholesaler charges £5.40 to retailer | Wholesale price |
| Retailer charges £8.99 to customer | Retail selling price |

**retained profit** is the profit left after all additions and deductions from *sales revenue*. These include trading costs, one-off profits or losses, taxation and *dividends*. Retained profit (the so-called 'bottom line') represents an important source of long-term, internal finance for the business. It adds to the *balance sheet* reserves, and therefore to *shareholders' funds*.

**retention** of staff is a measurement of how good a firm is at keeping its employees loyal. An annual retention of 95 per cent would mean just 5 per cent leave. A firm's retention rate is likely to be a function of how well it provides for its employees' *hygiene factors* and *motivators*.

**return on capital (ROC)** is the percentage return the firm is able to generate on the long-term capital employed in the business. Its importance is illustrated by the fact that it is sometimes referred to as the primary efficiency ratio. A firm's ROC enables a judgement to be made on the financial effectiveness of all its policies. If, for example, it is unable to generate a higher ROC than the prevailing rate of interest, it could be argued that the firm should close down, sell off its *assets* and put the money in the bank. Apart from in times of *recession*, the average firm generates a return of around 20 per cent on its capital employed. Within its growth phase, however, the Body Shop generated figures closer to 100 per cent, which meant that the firm was generating enough profit to double the size of the business each year.

FORMULA: $\dfrac{\text{operating profit}}{\text{capital employed}} \times 100 = \text{return on capital}$

Worked example: if a firm has an operating profit of £252 000 and capital employed of £2m., its ROC equals:

$\dfrac{£252\ 000}{£2\ 000\ 000} \times 100 = 12.6\%$

**return on equity** is the percentage return the firm is able to make on its *share-holders' funds* (the capital owed to the holders of *ordinary shares*). This is a similar ratio to *return on capital* and can be evaluated in much the same way. The only difference is that return on equity ignores any loan capital held by the firm.

$$\text{FORMULA:} \quad \frac{\text{pre-tax profit}}{\text{share capitals + reserves}} \times 100 = \text{return on equity}$$
$$\text{(shareholders' funds)}$$

**return on investment (ROI):** an American term that is sometimes used to mean *return on capital* employed (ROC), and sometimes to mean return on capital outlay or average rate of return (ARR).

**revaluation** is an upward valuation of the *assets* of a firm, probably as a consequence of *inflation*. The only asset that is commonly subject to revaluation is *freehold* property. In the interests of objectivity, the new valuation would be carried out by independent surveyors. However, the firm's own directors would still have influence over the new figures.

**revenge psychology** is Professor *Herzberg's* warning about the mental state of those who have suffered a *remembered pain*.

**revenue** is the total value of sales made within a trading period.

FORMULA:  price × quantity sold

**revenue expenditure:** another term for *revenue spending*.

**revenue spending** is expenditure on all costs other than *fixed asset* purchases. It is charged in full against *sales revenue*. Examples include materials, expenses and salaries.

**reverse take-over** takes place when a smaller company takes over a larger one. This could be where the issued *share capital* of the victim is larger than that of the aggressor, in which case financing the reverse take-over involves raising more loan capital or issuing more shares. An alternative is where a *private limited company* takes over a *public limited company*.

**reward for risk:** a way of evaluating profitability through comparison with the presumed risk-free investment of resources in a bank deposit account. The reward for risk is the amount by which the percentage rate of profit exceeds the prevailing interest rate. The higher the reward, the greater the risks it is worth taking.

---

Worked example: a new computer software firm is making a 16 per cent return on capital while interest rates are 10 per cent. Is this satisfactory?

Quantitive analysis: the reward for risk is 16% – 10% = 6%; if research shows that, each year, one in ten software firms goes into liquidation, the 6% reward would not justify the 10% risk.

Qualitative analysis: if the firm has a well-diversified product range, a wide spread of customers and management of proven quality, the level of reward may outweigh the low level of risk.

---

The same method of analysis can be applied to the investment appraisal methods: *average rate of return* and (without subtracting the interest rate) *internal rate of return*.

**rework** is the extra labour and material cost involved in correcting manufacturing faults on a production line. Most modern procedures for improving quality (such as *total quality management, quality circles* and *zero defects*) aim to eliminate rework altogether. This would cut costs and enable customer deliveries to be speeded up.

**rifle marketing** is the attempt to target specific consumers who are the most likely purchasers of a firm's products. Firms selling life assurance, for instance, buy lists of the names and addresses of likely consumers in order to direct their mail shot as accurately as possible. Whereas a soap powder manufacturer is likely to use *shotgun marketing* (such as TV advertising) in the hope that likely consumers will be watching.

**rights issue:** so called because it offers existing shareholders the right to buy more shares before anyone else. It occurs when a company wishes to raise more *capital* relatively cheaply. The company will ask its existing shareholders if they wish to buy more shares at what might seem an advantageous price i.e. lower than the price at which the shares are currently trading. However, because the rights issue has the effect of supplying more shares to the market, the share price will fall after the rights issue has taken place. For the original shareholders who do not wish to take up the rights issue their share value is protected because they are able to sell their rights to make up the difference.

**risk identification** is the attempt to determine and then quantify any threats to the firm's continued operations. Identifiable risks may include:

- financial risks, arising from the firm's *liquidity* position (short-term ability to meet debts), or from its *gearing* level (its dependence on debt): these risks can be quantified using *ratio analysis*
- trading risks, stemming from the price sensitivity of the firm's products, the degree of competition, and whether producers are working at full capacity or far below it: quantification could be achieved if the firm could discover its *price elasticities*, its *market shares* and the degree of *capacity utilisation*
- transactional risks, arising from reliance on large orders for materials that are subject to changes in market prices, or from reliance on foreign currency: substantial shifts in the price of materials or currencies may turn expected profits into heavy losses
- crises, such as when Perrier Water became contaminated

**risk management** is the attempt to identify and plan for threats to the firm's stability or profitability (*see risk identification*). Managers can apply a long-term strategy of risk minimisation by addressing each of the main areas of business risk:

- financial risks: avoid low *liquidity* and high *gearing*; ensure careful *cash-flow forecasting* and control
- trading risks: avoid over-reliance on one product or market; work at strengthening the *product differentiation* of your brands
- transactional risks: hedge your forward risks if they are substantial; consider buying on the forward market (giving a guaranteed price today for your needs in three, six or 12 months' time)
- crises: prepare *contingency plans*

**risk : reward ratio** is an assessment of the risks of making an investment compared with the anticipated rewards. This ratio is rarely quantified because of the difficulty of determining precise data. A typical example of its use is by investors in West End musicals. The failure rate is known to be very high, but the rewards from investing in a successful production can be so huge as to make some people consider that the risk:reward ratio is favourable.

**robotics** is the science of using robots in production processes to replace people, especially where such processes are monotonous or hazardous. Increasingly, however, scientists are investigating wider ranges of activities for robots involving primitive 'thought' processes.

**ROI:** see *return on investment*

**role-play exercises:** a standard element in management training courses in which individuals adopt roles assigned to them in a problem-solving or decision-making context.

**rolling over** (of debts) is an agreement between a company and its bankers that loans due to be repaid at a certain date will instead be 'rolled over' into the future. In other words, the company is being given longer to repay the debt. This is not necessarily a charitable act by the banks as they will not only receive extra interest on the debt, but are also likely to charge a substantial arrangement fee to the company concerned.

**royalty:** an agreed percentage of sales revenue paid to the owner of a *patent* or *copyright* for the use of the idea, process, name or work.

**RSI:** see *repetitive strain injury*

**RSP:** see *retail selling price*

**safety margin:** the amount by which *demand* can fall before a firm incurs losses, i.e. how close the firm is to the *break-even* level of output.

     FORMULA:   demand – break-even output = safety margin

**safety policy:** the term for the legal requirement that firms should display a written statement of their policy towards the health and safety of the workforce. This is laid down in the *Health and Safety at Work Act 1974.*

**sale and leaseback** is a contract to raise cash by selling the *freehold* to a piece of property and simultaneously buying it back on a long-term lease. This ensures that the firm can stay in its factory, shop or office premises and therefore can carry on trading as if nothing has happened. Yet the capital released through this process can enable the firm to expand or to survive a difficult trading year. On the face of it, carrying out a sale and leaseback deal is a short-termist act, enjoying extra cash today at the cost of future annual rental payments plus the threat of becoming 'homeless' at the end of the lease period. As the diagram below shows, however, as long as the profits generated by the cash raised are greater than the annual rental payments, the firm's long-term future should be sound.

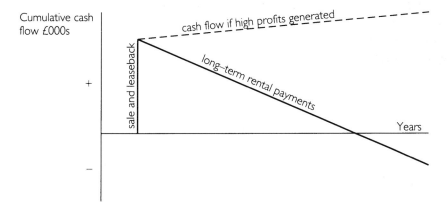

*Impact on cash flow of sale and leaseback*

**Sale of Goods Act 1979** lays down the contractual arrangements implied by the purchase of an item. It specifies that goods must be of 'merchantable quality', i.e. fit for the purpose for which they were purchased.

**sales administration** is the process of controlling paperwork and electronic systems to ensure efficient delivery to, and payment from, customers. The most important aspects of sales administration are order processing, *credit clearance, credit control,* security checks and delivery schedules.

**sales budget:** the target level of sales revenue for a period of time, usually twelve months. Budgets are set after adjusting the forecast sales figures in line with the firm's overall strategy. For example a Sales Director might agree a budget that is 12 per cent higher than the previous year, even though trends indicate a 5 per cent rise in sales. This might be to provide an incentive for every member of the firm's sales-force to work harder. If the 12 per cent rise is achieved, substantial bonuses might be available for all sales staff.

**sales campaign:** the package of measures used to communicate to, and motivate, a firm's distributors or salesforce. For example, if McVities have a new biscuit brand they are about to launch, the sales representatives will need to learn about its con-sumer benefits so that they can persuade retailers to stock the product. The sales campaign could include:

- a sales conference
- sales brochures and information packs
- sales letters and memos
- regular sales meetings to keep morale high

**sales conference:** a meeting where a company's salesforce is brought together to be given a presentation on new products and promotions. The sales conference should motivate the salesforce to sell the firm's products with renewed enthusiasm. To help achieve this, major new products may be launched to the sales staff in expensive locations.

**sales documents:** the paperwork used to ensure that a customer's order is supplied efficiently and accurately. The documents include:

- a delivery note – showing what products have been supplied
- an invoice – showing the products supplied and their prices, plus a request for payment and the payment terms (such as 'payment should be made within 30 days')
- a statement – a monthly confirmation of the sums of money due for payment

**salesforce:** the team of sales representatives employed to achieve high *distribution* in wholesale and retail outlets, or to sell direct to consumers. A national sales force rep-resents a major *overhead* cost to firms, as representatives will be required for every region. As a result, building up an effective salesforce is a major financial strain for new, small firms. Yet without a strong salesforce, a firm may find too few outlets to achieve a *demand* level above the *break-even point*.

**sales promotion** is the use of short-term incentives to purchase, such as free offers, *sampling and selling*, competitions and *self-liquidators*. The strategy behind the use of sales promotions may be aggressive or defensive. An example of the latter would be to defend the brand against a competitive attack by a new or existing product. An aggressive promotion would be attempting to gain sales and *market share*, and would therefore be targeted at purchasers of rival brands.

The main purposes of sales promotion are:

- to create the initial surge of demand to persuade shops to stock a newly launched product
- to attract new buyers who the firm hopes will become regular customers
- to lock customers in to buying your product when under threat from a new competitor

**sales revenue** is the value of sales made within a trading period. For ordinary calculations, it is enough to realise that:

FORMULA:   quantity sold × price = revenue

This does require some explanation however, in order to distinguish revenue from cash received. This is because a firm includes within revenue any sales made on credit. Therefore revenue comprises cash sales plus credit sales. This may sound a trivial matter, but because profit calculations are based on sales revenue, it follows that company accounts can present a healthy-looking profit position even though the firm is desperately short of cash.

**sales turnover:** another term for *sales revenue*.

**sales value** means total sales measured at selling price, i.e. quantity times price. It is usually used as a way of measuring *market size*. For an individual firm, sales value is the same as *sales revenue*.

**sales volume** is the quantity of goods sold, either by an individual firm or throughout a market-place.

**salinating** is the process of hiding company *assets* overseas, usually illegally. The term is derived from 'salting away' one's savings.

**sample:** a group of respondents to a *market research* exercise selected to be representative of the views of the *target market* as a whole. There are four main methods of sampling: *random, quota, stratified* and *cluster*. In consumer research, the quota sample is the one used most commonly.

**sample size:** the number of *respondents* to a research survey or to a specific question within the survey. The sample size is important as it needs to be large enough to make the data statistically valid. A sample of 20 people, for example, is so small that a different 20 could easily have quite separate views. When deciding on an appropriate sample size for a survey, a firm should bear in mind the following:

- the higher the sample size, the more expensive the research and the longer the fieldwork will take
- the lower the sample size, the greater the chance that random factors will make the results inaccurate
- if the research is to assist in a decision of great importance to the firm, it should invest the time and money into a large sample size (if affordable)

**sampling and selling** is a way of promoting product trial by using demonstrators to offer potential customers a free sample. While the customer is testing the product the demonstrator explains the product's key features and benefits. This is a useful way of tackling *consumer resistance* to, for example, an unusual foreign food. (See *sales promotion*.)

**sandwich courses** are academic (often degree) courses that have an extended work placement sandwiched between periods of study. A 'thick' sandwich consists of a year at work within three years of academic study. A 'thin' sandwich has between two and four shorter spells of work experience.

**satisficing:** a term used to describe the acceptance of what is satisfactory instead of pursuing the best or maximum result. There are two main circumstances in which this applies:

1 Setting a strategy based on a satisfactory compromise between objectives. For example, if two divisional directors are each attempting to persuade the firm to pursue a different strategy, the managing director might satisfice by deciding on a mixture of both.

2 Aiming for an achievement that is less than the maximum, perhaps because the firm does not want to draw attention to its powerful *market position*. For example, instead of aiming for *profit maximisation* a firm might pursue a profit level just high enough to finance its expansion plans.

**savings ratio:** that proportion of household income which is saved. The proportion can have a considerable impact on the development of an economy. Savings provide funds which can be used to invest in new *plant* and equipment, which clearly helps growth. On the other hand, if consumers save rather than spend then *demand* will be insufficient to sustain business confidence, and therefore growth. So in the long term, the growth of an economy depends upon a high rate of saving, but in the short term a rise in the savings ratio would cut consumer spending and might lead to *recession*.

**scab:** a term of abuse by strikers or *pickets* to describe strikebreakers. Hence 'scab labour' means workers who cross picket lines and take the jobs of those on strike.

**scale of production**: a measure of a company's output level, usually in relation to competitors or to trends over time. So 'large-scale production' implies that the firm is one of the major producers in its market place; 'increased scale of production' may be from very small to quite small. As their scale of production increases, firms are likely to enjoy *economies of scale*. To a certain extent these will be counterbalanced by *diseconomies of scale*.

**scenario planning** is the process of anticipating possible changes in a firm's situation and then devising ways of dealing with them. For example a chocolate producer could ask itself: 'What if next summer brings a three month heat-wave? How will we cope with the collapse in demand for our products?' Having conceived the scenario, the management could consider options such as providing special display cartons suitable for retailers' chilled cabinets, or even supplying their own chocolate chillers.

**Schonberger, R** (b. 1937): an author whose books JAPANESE MANUFACTURING TECHNIQUES (Collier Mac., 1983), WORLD CLASS MANUFACTURING (Collier Mac., 1987), and BUILDING A CHAIN OF CUSTOMERS (Hutchinson Business Books, 1990) made him one of the world's most sought-after business consultants and speakers. He has done much to popularise Japanese management methods in America and Britain.

**Schumacher, F** (1911–1977): a writer whose book SMALL IS BEAUTIFUL (Vintage, 1993) began a serious rethink of the effectiveness of large business corporations, and of the environmental damage caused by modern business practices.

**science park:** an industrial estate placed next to a university or research centre with the intention that the businessmen and the academics can get together to discuss practical applications of new developments or theories.

**scientific decision-making** is the use of a formal procedure to ensure that decisions are arrived at in an objective manner. It attempts to eliminate *hunch* or *bias* by ensuring that decisions are based on factual, numerical evidence. The following decision-making model is widely used:

*Scientific decision-making model*

**scientific management** is the attempt to make business decisions on the basis of data that is researched and tested quantitatively. The principles were laid down by F W *Taylor* in his book THE PRINCIPLES OF SCIENTIFIC MANAGEMENT (Harper Collins, 1947). He considered it to be management's duty to identify ways in which costs could be accounted for precisely, so that efficiency could be improved. Although F W Taylor is remembered mainly for his advocacy of financial incentives and high *division of labour*, his most influential legacy has been his advocacy and part-invention of such tools of scientific management as cost accounting, *work study* and *method study*. (See *scientific decision-making*.)

**scrip issue:** issuing extra, free shares to existing shareholders in proportion to their holdings; for instance one new for every one held. Although there are technical reasons for doing this, the main motive is to reduce the market share price. The problem here is that if a company is very successful and its share price shoots up to reflect this (perhaps to 380p each), sharebuyers are put off by a price that looks expensive. A one-for-one scrip issue would double the number of shares in circulation and therefore should halve the value of each share. At 190p each the shares appear to be priced more reasonably, which may make them more attractive.

**SD:** see *standard deviation*

**seasonal adjustment** is a method for identifying and eliminating regular seasonal variations from a data series in order to identify the underlying trend. This statistical procedure is especially important for data that has a direct impact on decision-making. The monthly unemployment figures might affect government economic policy, and a poor month's sales might lead a firm to halt a 'failed' advertising campaign. Yet unless seasonal influences have been taken out of the figures, the data might look gloomy when the underlying trend is quite positive.

**seasonal adjustment factor:** the average variation from trend within a season, measured over a number of years. This can then be applied to forecasts of future trends in order to predict actual sales in seasons to come.

Step 1 Average the variations from trend within a season

|  | Actual | Trend | Variation |
|---|---|---|---|
| January Year 1 | 80 | 100 | 0.80 |
| January Year 2 | 86 | 100 | 0.86 |
| January Year 3 | 96 | 120 | 0.80 |

Average variation = 0.82

Step 2 Apply the adjustment factor to future trend estimates

January Year 4:  if the trend is estimated to be 125, the January Year 4 actual figure can be forecast at: $125 \times 0.82 = 102.5$

**seasonal variation** is the degree to which actual figures vary from the trend within a given month or quarter. Although some text books measure the variation as a number (actual minus trend), it seems more logical to take it as a proportion (actual over trend).

**secondary action** is *industrial action* at a place other than where the dispute originated. All such forms of action were made illegal through a series of *Employment Acts* during the 1980s, culminating in the 1990 Employment Act.

**secondary data** is information collected from second-hand sources such as reference books, government statistics or market intelligence reports. Such data can provide information on *market size* and market trends for most product categories. It may be accessible publicly and therefore free, but is in any case not as expensive to gather as *primary data*. See the entries for: *Annual Abstract of Statistics, Business Monitors, Economic Trends, Economist Intelligence Unit, employers' association, Mintel.*

**secondary picketing** means setting up a *picket line* at a place other than where an *industrial dispute* originated. As with all other forms of *secondary action*, this is illegal.

**secondary sector:** the part of the economy concerned with the manufacture of products. *Primary sector* industry extracts materials from land or sea, while the *tertiary sector* provides business and consumer services. Although the secondary sector is Britain's most important supplier of exports, less than a quarter of the workforce is employed in manufacturing. It is a feature of developing economies that the secondary sector grows faster than primary industry. In developed economies such as Britain, however, the secondary (manufacturing) sector tends to grow less fast than service businesses.

**secondment:** a posting to another division of a firm or even to a different firm altogether, partly with a view to learning new methods and partly perhaps, because there is not enough for the employee to do currently.

**secured loan:** A loan made secure by the *collateral* put up by the borrower. This collateral (security) is usually land or property. A lender will be more willing to provide a loan if certain of repayment. Therefore secured loans are less expensive (carry a lower interest rate) than unsecured ones.

**seedcorn capital** is the initial *share capital* that enables a new business to be born. It might be invested by family or friends, or by a *venture capital* firm. It should provide sufficient funds for an *entrepreneur* to test out a business idea fully. Many business start-ups fail, therefore providing seedcorn capital is very risky. However, the occasional great success may make sufficient profit to more than cover the losses made on the failures.

**segmentation:** see *market segmentation*

**segregation of duties:** separating employee job functions to make it clear where one job ends and another begins. This should ensure that there is no duplication of effort by staff (which would waste time). Segregation of duties is a similar concept to that of *demarcation*.

**self-actualisation** is psychological self-fulfilment, i.e. feeling enriched or developed by what one has learned or achieved. *Maslow* considered this the highest need of human beings (see *hierarchy of needs*).

**self-completion questionnaires** are questionnaires that respondents must fill in themselves (unlike a *face-to-face interview*). They may be sent by post or left for people to pick up and complete. This represents a much cheaper form of *market research* than the face-to-face interview, but is likely to suffer from low *response rates* (which can *bias* the results).

**self-employed** workers operate as their own bosses, either working *freelance* or with the permanent task of running their own business. Self-employment has various tax advantages over regular employment, especially in claiming expenses that can be offset against *income tax* bills. In 1990, it was estimated that 12 per cent (3.4m.) of the labour force was self-employed.

**self-investment:** the questionable business practice of persuading (or instructing) your company *pension fund* to buy shares in your own company. This may be done for good motives, but there have been several cases in which a company in deep financial trouble has used this method to prop the company up for some months. Then, if the firm collapses, workers may find that not only have they lost their jobs, but also their pensions may be at risk.

**self-liquidators** are *sales promotions* designed to generate enough income to pay for themselves. An example would be a Smartie eggcup promoted at a price of 99p plus two Smartie tube lids. Consumers buy the product to collect the pack qualification, but in any case the promotion self-liquidates because the 99p covers the cost of the eggcup.

**self-regulation** occurs when an employers' organisation decides to issue codes of behaviour to encourage the firms in an industry to act more responsibly. Traditionally such organisations have been founded when pressure for regulation from the public or parliament has become too great to ignore. The employers hope that the agreement to regulate themselves will pre-empt the need for government intervention.

**selling off-the-page** occurs when a purchase is made as a direct response to a press advertisement. The customer may have placed a credit card order by telephone, or cut out a coupon and sent it off together with a cheque. Selling off-the-page is common in the mail order business and in the financial services industry. It is a major form of *direct response* marketing.

**semi-variable costs** are costs that vary with *output*, but not in direct proportion. Therefore, in order to calculate total costs at a specific level of output, a manager would have to work out the semi-variables especially. This makes them hard to deal with, notably in break-even analysis. Examples of semi-variables include maintenance expenditure and telephone bills. In the latter case, it is clear that although a doubling of customer demand would not necessarily double a firm's telephone calls or bills, it is reasonable to expect that they would increase. Therefore the telephone is neither a fixed nor a variable cost. (Note that if a cost such as a telephone bill comprises a fixed rental element plus a variable usage charge, a firm would split the cost up into its fixed and variable elements.)

**sensitivity analysis** means building variations into a forecast, to enable a manager to see what happens if the outcome proves better or worse than expected. For example, when forecasting cash inflows for an investment appraisal, a firm could measure the effect (the sensitivity) of demand being 10 per cent above or 10 per cent below the expected level. It is a form of *contingency planning*.

**separate legal entity** occurs when a firm becomes incorporated as a limited company, in which the business becomes legally separated from the owners or shareholders. After that, if the company runs into debt or is sued for negligence, it is not the owner who is liable, but the company.

**separate status** occurs when the employment terms and conditions for managers are quite different from those for the workforce. Although this is considered a very old-fashioned, '*them and us*' approach, it remains quite common. Typical examples of separate status include:

|  | Factory workers | Clerical and managerial |
|---|---|---|
| Working hours: | 08.00–16.30 | 09.30–17.30 |
| Remuneration | Hourly wage or piece-rate | Monthly salary |
| Pension: | State only | Company pension scheme |
| Notice: | One week | Three months |

**sequestration order:** a court order placing the *assets* of an organisation into the hands of an independent sequestrator, who will then pass the funds on to the court. This technique has been used to force *trade unions* to accept *industrial relations* laws, since the rejection of court rulings has led to their funds being confiscated. This has threatened the union with *insolvency* and closure.

**service contract:** an *employment contract* covering the length of notice and compensation arrangements (in case of dismissal) for company directors or senior managers. Such contracts often specify lengthy notice periods, and therefore form the basis of high compensation payments.

**seven-point plan:** a procedure for carrying out *recruitment* interviews in a methodical manner, devised by A Rodger. Job candidates are judged on the following criteria: physical make-up, achievements, intelligence, aptitudes, interests, personal manner and personal circumstances.

**Sex Discrimination Act 1975:** a law forbidding discrimination against either sex in relation to *recruitment*, terms and conditions, and access to training or promotion. Despite the existence of this Act, the difficulty of obtaining legal proof has meant that much discrimination has persisted. As with other issues of *social responsibility*, the passing of laws has not proved a substitute for ethical behaviour.

**Sex Discrimination Act 1986:** an Act enabling a common retirement date to be imposed on men and women. In 1993, the government stated its preference for a retirement age of 65.

**sexual harassment** is distress caused by unwelcome verbal or physical advances of a sexual nature. Although the term usually refers to men harassing women, it may be vice versa. Sexual harassment can be a reason to claim *constructive dismissal* from an *industrial tribunal.*

**shadow costs:** a method of obtaining an optimum solution to a transportation problem by calculating the *opportunity cost* of each unused route. Costs are proven to be at their minimum when there are no remaining routes with negative opportunity costs.

**shamrock organisation:** a term invented by Professor *Handy* to describe the modern business with three types of workforce:

- a permanent, highly valued and skilled core, assured of lifetime employment
- the contractual fringe (suppliers of services that can be contracted out, such as cleaning)
- a flexible labour force, hired and fired to cope with seasonal and cyclical changes in demand

Handy suggests that such an organisation will be slimmed down, with core staff taking on highly responsible tasks including the coordination of the fringe and flexible workforce. The shamrock organisation can be contrasted with the traditional *paternalistic* but *bureaucratic* corporation.

**share:** a certificate entitling the holder to *dividends* and *shareholders' rights* in proportion to the number of shares owned.

**share capital:** the value of the sum invested into the company by ordinary and preference shareholders. As these investors cannot get their money back from the firm, the managers know that they can rely on these funds permanently into the future. Investors can, of course, sell their holdings to other investors through the *Stock Exchange.*

**shareholder value:** the 1990s term that has become the stated primary objective of most public limited companies in Britain. The only problem is that no-one is quite sure what it means. The book IN SEARCH OF SHAREHOLDER VALUE by A. Black (Pitman, 1997) does little more than equate it to the share price. Others see it as a compromise between today's share price and the price (plus dividends) in the medium term future. Either way, it means focusing upon the needs of shareholders over the needs of the other stakeholders.

**shareholders' funds** are that part of a firm's long-term finance owed by the company to its shareholders. It comprises the *share capital* invested by the shareholders plus the accumulated profits made by the firm over its years of trading (the *reserves*).

FORMULA:   share capital + reserves = shareholders' funds

**shareholders' rights** are the legal entitlements of owners of ordinary shares. These include:

- the right to attend the *annual general meeting*

- the right to vote on new directors
- the right to take part in a *vote of confidence* in the *chairman*
- the right to receive an *annual report* into the financial state of the business

In practice, small shareholders have rights, but usually very little power. On occasions, however, they can exert considerable influence, as when Alan Sugar, founder of Amstrad, wished to end his company's Stock Exchange *listing* and return the company to the status of a *private limited company*. Mr Sugar offered to buy Amstrad shares at a price which his shareholders considered derisory; they gathered together and turned the offer down.

**share options:** a financial incentive that offers managers the right to buy shares in the company they work for at a future date, at a price set today. For example, a director might be given an option to buy 250 000 shares at a price of 50p at any time between three and five years hence. If the share price rises to 90p, they can take up the option and sell the shares on the *stock market*. By buying at 50p and selling at 90p, a profit of 40p × 250 000 = £100 000 will have been made. Supporters of this kind of scheme believe that share options will provide key employees with the incentive to perform at their best. Critics suggest that it might lead to *short-termism* (when the options are due), and can lead to excessive financial rewards in the boardroom, when the workforce may deserve just as much credit as the directors.

**share premium** is that part of the *share capital* received in excess of the face value of the shares issued. For example:

- a firm is started up with 1 000 £1 shares
- later, after a successful spell, it decides to issues a further 1 000 £1 shares at the prevailing market price of £1.50 per share
- therefore it has a share premium of 50p × 1 000 = £500
  plus share capital of £1 × 2 000 = £2 000
  giving a total share capital of £2 500

**share register:** the list of all the shareholders in a company together with the size of their holding. Firms regularly check their share registers to see if a particular person or company is building up a large enough share stake to launch a *take-over bid*.

**shifts in demand curves** occur when something has an impact on the market which causes people to demand more (or less) of the product at its old price (see diagram). This commonly occurs when:

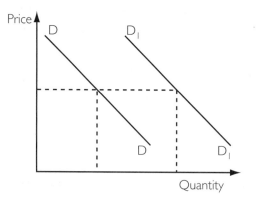

- there is a change in taste or fashion
- there is a change in the price of substitutes or complements
- people expect prices to rise (or fall) some time in the future
- there is a change in people's incomes

**shifts in supply curves** occur when something has an impact on the market which causes people to supply more (or less) of the product at its old price (see diagram). This commonly occurs when:

- there is a change in the price of one of the inputs with which the good is made, e.g. when the price of a raw material rises, the supply curve shifts to the left
- there is a technological change which enable producers to supply more at the same price
- taxes and subsidies are put on a good, e.g. the European Union subsidises farmers to make their beef competitive on world markets. Without the subsidy the supply curve would shift to the left

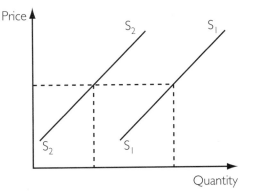

**shift work** is regular work that takes place during non-standard working hours. It may be a morning shift (e.g. 2 a.m–8 a.m.) or a night shift (8 p.m–2 a.m.). Shift work is essential in services such as the fire brigade and is often used in manufacturing, especially if there is an expensive, *flow production* process requiring high *capacity utilisation*. Some organisations recruit workers for a specific shift; others have a rotation of two weeks of days, two of evenings etc. There may be shift payments that offer a higher rate of pay to compensate for the unsociable hours worked.

**shop-floor:** the place where direct labour is carried out, either by shop assistants or by factory workers.

**shop steward:** an elected representative of the *trade union* members at a workplace. The post is voluntary, so the shop steward is an ordinary employee paid by the employer and allowed to conduct union activities within ordinary business hours. As the shop steward is not employed or paid by the national union, he or she need not feel bound by union policy unless the local membership supports it. Functions of a shop steward include:

- acting as a communication link between management and the shop-floor, and also between the local members and the national union

- negotiating on local issues such as local wage rates or *working conditions* (especially if *negotiations* are on the basis of plant bargaining)
- taking up local cases of health and safety, discrimination or *unfair dismissal* with management, bringing in legal advisors when necessary

A common mistake is to confuse a shop steward with a *foreman*. The latter is a supervisor with no connection to trade union organisation.

**short-termism** is a phrase describing the state of mind of managers for whom rapid results are the top priority. Examples of short-termism include:

- setting a short *payback period* as an investment criterion
- increasing prices up to their most profitable level (thereby attracting competition)
- cutting back on spending on research and development or training

Such an approach can be contrasted with the Japanese pursuit of long-term goals such as total quality and technological superiority. It seems likely that the main causes of British short-termism are:

- the absence of a tradition of loyalty to one company, which may make our executives too keen to make their mark quickly
- the greater number and influence of accountants in British boardrooms (compared with engineers in Germany and Japan)
- the threat of a *take-over* may encourage firms to keep short-term profit high in order to bolster up the share price: British firms are much more likely to have a majority shareholding available on the *stock market*, so this is a more important issue in Britain than in Germany or Japan

**shotgun marketing** is fired at all possible consumers in the hope that some will be hit. Television advertising tends to be of this type, whereas advertising in trade magazines is *rifle marketing* since it is aimed at a particular, specialised readership.

**significance testing:** checking the statistical validity of a sample result, usually in relation to an objective of 95 per cent certainty. An example would be checking whether a 54 per cent preference for product A is statistically significant compared with the 46 per cent choice for product B. If the *sample size* is very small, this difference is of no significance since it can be explained by purely random factors.

**silent salesman:** see *packaging*

**simulation** (also known as *queuing theory*) is the construction of a model to simulate the effect on queues of randomly occurring events such as customer arrival times that take varying lengths of time to process.

**simultaneous engineering** means organising product development so that the different stages are carried out in conjunction with each other instead of in sequence. This reduces the time taken to get an idea to the marketplace, which cuts costs and provides a competitive advantage over slower rivals. Key elements include:

- project teams comprising specialists from the different business and engineering functions (such as *research and development*, design, machine tools, *materials handling, market research, cost accounting* and so on)
- improved communications between functions

- simultaneous development of the product, the production and the marketing processes.

Simultaneous engineering is a crucial element in the *time based management* approach to *lean production*.

**single currency** would mean that a single *central bank* would issue bank notes and coins that would be usable anywhere within the EU. That would eliminate the costs and risks involved in exchanging foreign currencies when trading with (or holidaying in) European Union countries. A single currency is the objective of the *European Monetary System*, to be achieved under the *Maastricht* Treaty by 1999. It is most unlikely, however, that a single currency will be established for all the member states by that date.

**single European market:** the agreement between the EU countries that from January 1 1993, the trading differences between member countries were to be eliminated so that businesses could treat the whole of the Community as their home market. This was intended to be achieved by the abolition of three trading restrictions: *non-tariff barriers*, physical customs controls, and different technical standards and taxation levels. Despite the early 1990s optimism about the '*1992*' (single market) changes, its completion remains a long way off.

**single sourcing** means purchasing from only one supplier. This was thought foolish until the 1980s, when Japanese firms such as Nissan adopted it successfully in their British factories. Advantages and disadvantages of single sourcing include:

Pros:
- allows a strong, long-term bond to be built between the firm and its supplier
- bulk purchasing keeps fixed costs per unit down
- dependence upon a single source forces both sides to be 100 per cent efficient, as any supply shortfall will halt production

Cons:
- no day-to-day competitive pressure to force the supplier to stay efficient and good value
- no back-up just in case of a completely unexpected problem, such as the severe earthquake in Kobe in 1995, which forced many Japanese firms to rethink their single-source approach.

**single status** occurs when a firm has eliminated all the physical and contractual barriers between grades of staff. These forms of class discrimination might include: separate canteens, different working hours, different pay terms and conditions (management on salaries, workers on *piece-rate*), or *clocking in* for shop-floor workers only. Once a firm has removed such divisive features, it can hope to eliminate the feeling of '*them and us*' that pervades many organisations. Japanese firms go so far as to insist on the same overalls for all managers and workers, or even morning exercises. Both are to establish single status by demonstrating that all employees wear the same work clothes and participate in the same morning activity.

**single union agreement** means the recognition by a firm of only one workforce representative body for *collective bargaining* purposes. This removes the potential disruption caused by *inter-union disputes* and reduces the time spent on negotiations. Toshiba's agreement with the electricians' union (the EEPTU) in 1981 is believed to have been the first of its kind in Britain. Such agreements have often included *pendulum arbitration* clauses, with some adding *no-strike* agreements.

**situational audit**: a check upon a firm's financial, marketing and strategic position at a point in time. It is an attempt to answer the question:'Where do we stand?' Once this has been answered, the business can decide where to aim in future. The situational audit will usually include:

- analysis of the market growth and market shares within the product categories the firm operates in
- analysis of the firm's financial position compared with rivals
- assessment of the strengths and weaknesses of the staff
- consideration of the degree of success at achieving current objectives.

**skewed result:** a *frequency distribution* in which the number of findings is not balanced around the *mean* figure. The findings may be skewed towards values below the mean (a *negative skew*) or above the mean (a *positive skew*).

**skimming the market** means pricing a new product at such a high level that it is only purchased by trend-setters, enthusiasts or the very rich. The firm may choose to hold this high price in the long term, or cut prices when competition arrives. Skimming the market is a viable option only for an innovative product. (See *market penetration*.)

Pros:
- the price tag placed on a product affects consumer perceptions of its quality and desirability; pricing high can be an important element in establishing an up-market image
- skimming can be used as a form of *price discrimination*, ensuring that trend-setters pay the high price they are willing to pay, then lowering the price to attract the mass market later on

Cons:
- a high price may make it easy for a competitor to launch a successful, lower-priced imitation
- by failing to maximise sales at the start, the firm may not be able to hold on to a viable *market share* when competitors arrive

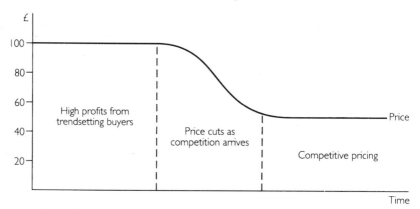

*Skimming the market*

**sleeping partner:** a contributor of finance to a business partnership who takes no active role within the firm, and therefore can arrange to hold *limited liability* status.

**slogan:** a catch-phrase used regularly by an advertiser to communicate a sales message in a highly memorable way.

**slump** is a period of low demand and investment, and high unemployment. It is a rather vague term used interchangeably with *depression* to mean a severe *recession* within the *trade cycle*. It is often seen in the context of 'booms and slumps' to indicate the way the economy tends to fluctuate between these two extremes.

**small claims court:** a local court that will hear cases of dispute concerning sums of up to £3000. A typical problem might concern a householder claiming against an electrician over a £250 job that proved to be faulty. At the small claims court individuals speak for themselves without the use of expensive legal advice.

**small firm:** a phrase that is taken to mean a firm with limited financial resources which has little or no power over its market-place. The government uses the more precise definition of a firm with fewer than 200 employees. This, however, would allow firms with substantial earnings and high *market shares* to be termed small. As with every type of business, the attempt to define or generalise about them usually falls foul of their wide diversity. It is safer to consider the financial position and market strength of each firm individually than to overgeneralise.

**Smith, Adam** was the eighteenth-century author of much of the classical economic theory which still forms the basis of free-market economics. His best known book THE WEALTH OF NATIONS (Penguin, 1982) set out, in 1776, his faith in market mechanisms as a means of promoting efficiency and customer satisfaction. The book's key phrase referred to the *invisible hand* that ensures that customer *demand* can be matched by *supply* without needing a planning authority. The invisible hand is the *price mechanism.*

**smoothing** is the statistical process of ironing out the erratic or short-term elements within data in order to identify the longer-term trends. See *seasonal adjustment* and *moving averages.*

**social audit:** an independent quantification of the elements of a firm's activities that affect society, such as pollution, waste and workforce health and safety. A social audit can be used internally, by managers wanting to measure their degree of success at environmental improvement; or externally, by pressure groups or shareholders concerned about the firm's long-term health and reputation. The potential value of this technique can be seen in the example below. It shows how a social audit of two firms might lead to different conclusions about their real efficiency than a calculation of financial ratios might.

Worked example: bicycle manufacturing firms

|  | Firm A | Firm B |
| --- | --- | --- |
| *Financial ratios* | | |
| Trading profit margin | 6.8% | 8.8% |
| Return on capital | 18.5% | 19.8% |
| *Social ratios* | | |
| Average lifetime of bike | 5.5 yrs | 3.0 yrs |
| % made from recycled material | 60% | 20% |
| Industrial accidents per 100 workers per year | 1.5 | 8.0 |

**social benefit** measures the benefit to the whole of society of a production process or business decision. So when an individual purchases a good or service not only does he/she receive an internal benefit through its consumption, but there may also be an external benefit to society as a whole.

FORMULA:  internal benefits + external benefits = social benefits

**social chapter** is that part of the *social charter* which was agreed by all twelve member states of the *EU*, apart from the UK, under the *Maastricht* Treaty.

**social charter** is a set of statutory and non-statutory measures designed to harmonise social legislation within the *EU*, alongside economic measures. It covers twelve areas: freedom of movement, social protection, vocational training, health and safety, elderly persons, protection of children and adolescents, disabled persons, sexual equality, living and working conditions, employment and remuneration, *collective bargaining* and the right to strike, information, consultation and participation.

**social cost** measures the cost to the whole of society of a production process or business decision. This means that not only are the firm's *internal costs* accounted for, but also the costs imposed on society as a consequence of the action (such as pollution or unemployment). These latter costs are external to the company.

FORMULA:      internal costs + external costs = social costs

**social grade** is the occupational category that shows the social class to which each household belongs. Interviewers ask respondents for the occupation of the head of the household and the answer is placed into one of the groupings listed below. This categorisation is used in *market research* as evidence has shown that social class has a large effect on people's lifestyle and purchasing habits. The social grade bands are:

GRADE A:  top professional (e.g. lawyers) or directors of large companies
GRADE B:  senior managerial
GRADE C1:  clerical, e.g. secretary
GRADE C2:  skilled working class, e.g. welder
GRADE D:  semi- or unskilled working class
GRADE E:  state dependent, e.g. long-term unemployed

**social responsibilities** are the duties towards employees, customers, society and the environment that a firm may accept willingly, or may treat as a nuisance. The historical record of firms' acceptance of their responsibilities is patchy. Some religiously motivated firms such as Cadbury's and Rowntree treated their workforce and customers with respect as far back as the nineteenth century. Yet at the same time, a brand of cigarettes called 'Heartsease' was promoted as an aid to recovery from illness. Such deceptions led to the passing of laws to protect consumers, workers and residents from socially irresponsible companies. Today, many firms believe it is in their best interests to behave correctly, since customer image and workforce contentment are important elements in business success. The key to a firm's attitude to its responsibilities is probably the timespan of its company objectives. A get-rich-quick building firm will have a very different approach to an established family business that thinks in terms of generations rather than months.

**sole trader:** an individual who may or may not employ other people, but who owns and operates the business. Sole traders generally have little capital for expansion, and are heavily reliant on their own personal commitment to make the business a success. Should the business be unsuccessful, there is no cushion from *limited liability* as a sole trader is unincorporated; in other words, the firm's finances are inseparable from the proprietor's.

**solvency** is when a firm or individual's assets exceed its external debts. Therefore it has the financial stability that comes from positive asset backing. If external debts are greater than the asset values, a state of *insolvency* exists.

**solvency ratios** measure the ability of an organisation to cover its external liabilities with its assets. Two main ratios are *gearing* and *liquidity* (or acid test).

**sources of finance** indicate where an organisation might obtain funds for expansion or the replacement of plant and equipment. It is important to establish the size, type and historical development of the firm in question before deciding which of the following is appropriate. Clearly a multinational will not be using family and friends as a source, whereas a newly established firm may do so.

| Type | Pros | Cons |
|---|---|---|
| Family/friends | • Usually inexpensive<br>• Little collateral required | • Usually limited in size<br>• May provoke unwanted interference |
| Bank loans and overdrafts | • The bank may be a source of advice<br>• Overdrafts are quite flexible and interest only charged when overdrawn | • Bank may 'pull the plug' if things go wrong<br>• Overdraft repayable on demand<br>• Usually requires collateral |
| Trade credit | • Offers an easy way to improve cash flow | • Loss of early payment discount<br>• May affect business relationship if payment delayed too much |
| Shares | • May be an easy and relatively painless form of finance<br>• Firm must be a plc to issue shares on the Stock Exchange<br>• Issues can be expensive | • Control is diluted |
| Debentures , | • No dilution of control<br>• Very long-term finance (usually 20+ years) | • Only very large companies are able to generate funds in this way<br>• Raises gearing |
| Hire purchase | • Low initial outlay<br>• Avoids straining cash flow | • Asset not owned until finally paid for<br>• Expensive |

| Leasing | • Low initial outlay | • Asset never owned |
| | • Good for cash flow | • More expensive than |
| | • May be able to update equipment at low cast | buying outright |
| | • May be able to purchase the asset at the end of the term at low cost | |
| Factoring | • Low administration costs | • Fee may take a high proportion of profits |
| | • Improves cash flow and makes it more predictable | • Factor may refuse to let you deal with a company thought untrustworthy |
| | • Reduces danger of bad debts | • Credit procedures may upset some customers |
| Internal/ploughed-back profits | • Firm has control | • Only effective when profits are good |
| | • Reduces gearing | |
| | • This is the most important source of business capital | • Refusal to use loans in addition to profits can result in *over-trading* |
| Government/EU grants | • Inexpensive | • Hard to obtain |
| | | • May depend on location |
| | | • Nationally, grants represent a trivial proortion of business finance |

**span of control:** the number of subordinates answerable directly to a manager. It can be described as 'wide' if the manager has many direct subordinates or 'narrow' if there are few. Within an organisation, the span of control bears an inverse relationship to the number of layers of management hierarchy. In other words, if the span is wide, fewer layers would be needed to manage a given workforce. This is illustrated below, where a span of control of three results in five *layers of hierarchy*, while a span of nine requires only three layers (assuming a shop-floor workforce of 81).

Advantages of a wide span of control include:

- the boss has less time for each subordinate, therefore must delegate effectively
- fewer layers of hierarchy are needed, therefore improving vertical communications (reducing the number of *intermediaries*)
- allows subordinates 'the opportunity to use their ability' which is Professor *Herzberg*'s definition of *job enrichment*

Advantages of a narrow span of control include:

- tighter management supervision may be necessary in a business where mistakes cannot be allowed (such as the production of components for passenger aircraft)
- less stress involved for each employee, as the scope of each job is limited
- more layers of hierarchy mean more frequent promotion opportunities, i.e. the career ladder has more rungs

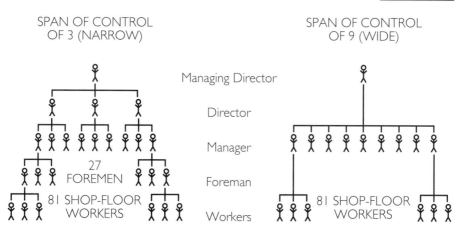

SPAN OF CONTROL OF 3 (NARROW)

SPAN OF CONTROL OF 9 (WIDE)

Managing Director

Director

Manager

27 FOREMEN

Foreman

81 SHOP-FLOOR WORKERS

Workers

81 SHOP-FLOOR WORKERS

**specialisation:** the division of a work process into separate job functions so that individuals can develop expertise by specialising. This was a vital element in Adam *Smith* and F W *Taylor*'s perception of the benefits of *division of labour*. This has been called into question by the effects of specialisation on motivation and the success of the Japanese approach to multi-skilling.

**sponsorship** is a form of promotion in which funds are provided for a sporting, cultural or social event in return for prominent display of the sponsor's company or brand name.

**spreadsheet** is a set of numerical data inputted and displayed on a computer which is connected in such a way, via a number of formulae, that changing one figure will automatically update all the others. In business, spreadsheets are often used to predict events, because it is simple to ask *what if...? questions* and immediately see a result. For instance, if it was suggested that sales might rise by 10 per cent next year, the company could see at a glance what the implications for sales revenue, costs and profits would be.

**staff associations** represent the employees of an organisation in discussion or negotiation with the employer. They usually operate with the approval of – and with financial support from – employers. Where they exist alongside *trade unions*, the staff associations are usually forums for *consultation*, not negotiation. Where there is no trade union representation, the associations may be allowed a more active role by the employer. In either case, however, trade unionists would criticise staff associations for their lack of independence from management.

**staff functions** are those of employees who provide advice or assistance to the line managers, who hold responsibility for achieving specific business objectives.

**staff status** means that office staff have privileges that are not available to production workers. These might include a separate canteen, longer holidays and no requirement to clock in and out of the premises.

**staff turnover**: see *labour turnover.*

**stagflation** is the economic phenomenon of stagnation and *inflation* happening simultaneously. This had been thought to be impossible, since the effect of stagnation would be to depress wages and hence prices. In practice it was found during the mid-1970s that levels of inflation could rise to the point where people expected it to continue, and acted accordingly. Thus, although unemployment was rising, *trade unions* still negotiated for high pay rises because of the expected levels of prices next year.

**stagging** is the purchase of shares in a company *flotation* with the sole purpose of selling them quickly on the *Stock Exchange* for a profit. New issues are very often offered at an attractive price in order to ensure that all the shares are sold, thus offering stags a chance to make a quick profit. This was the case with many *privatisation* flotations.

**stakeholder:** an individual or group with a direct interest in an organisation's performance. The main stakeholders are: employees, shareholders, customers, suppliers, financiers and the local community. Stakeholders may not hold any formal authority over the organisation, but theorists such as Professor *Handy* believe that a firm's best long-term interests are served by paying close attention to the needs of each of these groups.

**standard cost:** the desired average cost for producing an item. This can be compared with the actual achievement to discover whether the firm is working effectively.

**standard deviation (SD):** a standardised measure of the distribution of data around a *mean* value. Statisticians use the term 'standard deviation' in this precise way, whereas most managers treat it more loosely. In particular, managers often refer to the term standard deviation when they mean the *standard error* from a sample result.

**standard error** estimates the *standard deviation* of sample means around the true population *mean*.

**standardisation** is the production or use of products or components that are so identical as to allow them to be fully interchangeable. The achievement of standardised parts is a necessary condition for efficient *mass production* to take place. Without it, skilled workers would have to spend time filing down parts to fit them into the right slots. Standardisation is also a key element in *economies of scale*, as modern firms use the same components in different products to enable longer production runs to take place and to save on design costs.

**standard of living** is a rather imprecise term which refers to the ability of people to buy the goods and services they desire. It could be measured as people's real incomes, i.e. wage levels in relation to price levels. Increasingly it also takes into account non-quantifiable factors such as levels of crime, the time and ease of travelling to work and so on. This is sometimes referred to as the 'quality of life'.

**standards certification:** the paperwork that confirms that a particular consignment or product has conformed to the standards laid down by an agency such as the *British Standards Institute*.

**standard time:** the estimated, desired time for an employee to complete his or her task, or for all staff to complete the job. When multiplied by the hourly labour rate, this will give a figure for the average labour cost (a key element in the *standard cost*).

**statement of account**: an up-to-date statement of an individual's trading or financial position with a company or a bank.

**statistical process control** is the use of statistical monitoring systems to ensure that production is proceeding efficiently and at high-quality standards. Modern laser scanning-based systems can check production rates and accuracies at various stages in the production process at very low cost. If performance falls outside pre-set standards, an alarm will be sounded or displayed.

**statistical quality control** uses the same approach as above, but focused solely upon product quality.

**statistics:** in a business context, this means the statistical data that firms gather and may try to present in a light that favours themselves. When seeing numerate 'facts' presented, Benjamin Disraeli's famous statement should be borne in mind, that, 'There are lies, damned lies and statistics.'

**status:** how highly a person is rated by other members of a group or workforce. This might derive from the individual's own abilities and achievements or from institutional factors such as job title or remuneration. *Maslow* regarded status as an important social need, while *Herzberg* considered it a *hygiene factor*, i.e. a potential source of dissatisfaction.

**statutory requirements** are those that are laid down by law and which every firm has to conform to. Laws are said to be 'in the statutes' or 'on the statute books'.

**sterling** is the name given to the UK's internationally traded currency, the pound sterling, to distinguish it from other countries which also use the word 'pound' for their currencies.

**stick to the knitting** is a curious phrase that urges firms to concentrate on what they know best, rather than take the risks involved in diversifying into numerous other sectors.

**stock:** materials and goods required in order to produce for, and supply to, the customer. There are three main categories of stock: *raw materials* or components, *work in progress* and finished goods.

**stock appreciation:** an increase in the value of a company's stocks, generally due to *inflation*. As company profits are boosted by increases in stock values, stock appreciation gives a rather artificial boost to profits (causing higher tax and perhaps *dividend* payments). The standard accounting procedure for preventing this distortion of real profitability is the adoption of *last in, first out* (LIFO) stock identification.

**stockbroker:** a person who trades in, and can give advice on the buying and selling of, shares.

**stock control** covers the procedures needed to ensure that stock is ordered, delivered and handled with efficiency, so that customer demand can be met cost effectively. This is achieved through careful *stock rotation* and may also involve a stock reordering system based upon predetermined minimum and maximum stock levels. (See *reorder level.*)

**Stock Exchange** is a market for securities (the collective name for stocks and shares). The London Stock Exchange is one of the biggest in the world after Tokyo and New York, with an annual turnover of over one million million pounds. Its main functions are to enable firms or governments to raise capital and to provide a market in second-hand shares and government stocks.

Advantages of the Stock Exchange:

- offers firms a reliable source of investment funds, especially equity capital
- by offering a second-hand market in shares it encourages people to channel their savings into industry
- the Stock Exchange insists on stringent rules for admittance by firms and these, along with other legal requirements, offer a degree of protection to savers.

Disadvantages of the Stock Exchange:

- the share price does not necessarily reflect the true value of a company. It may be the result of rumours, or the overall state of the market
- being quoted on the Exchange removes some control from the management and may encourage *short-termism*, as directors focus upon *dividends* and the share price
- recent scandals suggest that the degree of investor protection is in fact quite small, and call into question the ability of the Exchange to regulate itself

**stockholding costs** are the *overheads* resulting from the stock levels held by a firm. These include:

- warehouse rental and insurance costs
- energy costs (refrigeration, for example)
- manpower costs, including security guards
- interest charges on the money tied up in the stock

By moving to a *just in time* system of minimal stock levels, all these costs could be cut dramatically.

**stock market:** see *Stock Exchange*

**stock options:** see *share options*

**stockpiling:** building up stock levels, perhaps in preparation for a seasonal sales peak or before the advertising launch of a new product.

**stock rotation** is the administrative and physical process of ensuring that older stock is used first. This is necessary to prevent wastage due to the stock rusting, becoming obsolete, or going past its sell-by date. The procedure recommended in all stock rotation systems is FIFO: *first in, first out.* This is why fresh and chilled food shelves should always be filled from the back, thus encouraging customers to buy older stock first.

**stocks and shares** is a general term for investments that are traded on the *stock market*. In this case, stocks means fixed interest securities such as *debentures* (*loan capital*), while shares give a part-ownership of a company (*equity capital*).

**stocktaking:** a periodical physical count of the items held in stock, usually carried out on the *balance sheet* date at the end of the financial year. This is to ensure accurate stock records and thereby determine the levels of *wastage* and pilfering that are occurring.

**stock turnover** is a measurement of the speed with which a firm sells out its stock. A fruit stall which, every day, buys stock in the morning and sells it all by the evening is turning its stock over 365 times per year. A car dealer might find that he takes an average of three months to sell a car (his stock). Therefore his stock turnover is four times per year.

The formula for calculating stock turnover is set out below. Note that the relevant sales figure is *cost of sales*: this is to make the figure comparable with stock, which is always valued at cost.

FORMULA: $\dfrac{\text{sales (at cost)}}{\text{stock}} = \text{stock turnover}$

Advantages of a high stock turnover figure:

- spreads stockholding costs over many units of stock
- minimises the amount of *working capital* tied up in stock and therefore frees capital for other uses
- ensures that stock does not become out of date

Disadvantages of a high stock turnover figure:

- unless the firm can reorder quickly and efficiently enough, the stock may turn over so fast as to lead to empty shelves and disappointed customers may never come back
- high stock turnover means keeping stocks low; this may mean that the firm is not able to buy in bulk, which will increase *variable costs*

**stock valuation:** the method used by a firm to place a value on the stocks it holds. Published accounts state the method as 'the lower of cost and net realisable value'. In other words stock is valued at cost, unless its resale value has fallen below cost, in which case it should be valued at the lower figure. Although *LIFO, FIFO* and *AVCO* are, strictly speaking, methods of stock identification, many examiners treat them as if they are ways of determining a stock valuation.

**stop-go** was a term used to describe policy measures taken by governments in the 1960s and 1970s. When unemployment became unacceptably high in political terms the government stimulated demand through lower taxes (*fiscal policy*) and interest rates (*monetary policy*). This created the 'go' phase of the cycle. Unfortunately, the stimulus eventually resulted in skill shortages, rapid increases in imports and caused *balance of payments* crises which forced the 'stop' phase through higher taxes and interest rates. 1980s governments boasted that they had abolished stop-go, but in fact stoked up one of the biggest ever 'go' phases in the mid-to-late 1980s. This was followed by the longest post-war 'stop' (*recession*) from 1990 onwards.

**straight line depreciation** means spreading the cost of a *fixed asset* equally over its expected useful lifetime. For the purpose of straight line depreciation, 'cost' is the difference between the purchase price of the asset (its *historic cost*) and the second-hand scrap value expected at the end of its life (its *residual value*).

FORMULA: $\dfrac{\text{historic cost} - \text{residual value}}{\text{years of useful life}} = \text{straight line depreciation}$

Worked example: a machine with an expected six years' life is bought for £23 000. If its expected scrap value in six years' time is £2 000, annual straight line depreciation will be:

$\dfrac{£23\ 000 - £2\ 000}{6} = £3\ 500 \text{ per year}$

Pros: • if an asset is to be used equally over a period, it is logical that its cost should be spread equally (and it conforms to the *matching principle*)
  • it is the only method accepted by Inland Revenue for the calculation of profit (and therefore *corporation tax*)

Cons: • does not reflect the reality that assets depreciate much more heavily in the first year than in subsequent years; this causes fixed assets to be over-valued on the *balance sheet*
  • the method requires two key assumptions in order to get the figures right: the asset's length of life and its residual value

**strategic alliance:** see *joint venture*

**strategic decision:** a decision that will have considerable long-term effects on the organisation and therefore requires discussion and approval at a senior managerial level. An example might be whether to sell off a poorly performing division, or to invest sufficient extra capital to restore its competitiveness.

**strategic objectives** are wide-ranging, long term goals of significance to the operations of a whole organisation. For example, a firm that has 70 per cent of its sales in Britain might set itself the strategic objective to reduce its dependence upon the home market to below 40 per cent within 5 years.

This might force a rethink about the location of its factories, the type of products it sells, the background or nationality of the staff it employs and so on. Among the most common strategic objectives are:

  • to diversify
  • to focus (un-diversify or *stick to the knitting*)
  • to achieve a dominant market position
  • to develop a technological advantage over rivals.

**strategy:** a medium- to long-term plan for how to achieve an *objective*. The plan itself would include not only what is to be done, but also the financial, production and personnel resources required.

**stratified sample:** a research sampling method that draws respondents from a specified subgroup of the population. An example would be a lager producer deciding to research solely among 18–30-year-old men, since they represent the heart of that market-place. Within the chosen group, individuals might be chosen on a random basis, hence the term 'stratified random sample'. (See also *random* and *quota samples*.)

**stress** is often assumed to be a symptom of an over-pressurised working life. Research evidence shows that managers are rather less prone to stress than shop-floor workers with repetitive jobs. This suggests that stress is mainly a function of feeling out of control of one's life. Stress can lead to migraines, high blood pressure and excessive drinking.

**strike pay** is a payment by a *trade union* to members who are on an official strike. This is usually of a sum that is far below the striker's regular wage.

**structural change** means a fundamental change in the way a business, a market or a whole economy operates.

  • economic change such as a switch from traditional, heavy industry to the 'sunrise' industries such as electronics can lead to *structural unemployment*

- structural change within a market might be caused by *privatisation*, two large companies merging or by the *liquidation* of a once-powerful firm
- for an individual business, structural change might take the form of a shift to decentralisation or the decision to handle products on a global basis rather than country-by-country.

**structural unemployment** occurs when there is a change in demand or technology which causes long-term unemployment. Very often this occurs in particular regions which have been heavily dependent on certain industries, such as coal in Wales, and shipbuilding in the North East. There is little any government can do to alleviate such unemployment other than offering retraining for those made redundant.

**sub-assembly** means putting together a component that will later be part of the final assembly of the finished product. Therefore, on a car *production line*, the assembly of a gearbox would be termed a sub-assembly.

**subcontracting:** finding a supplier to manufacture part or all of your product. The main circumstances in which subcontracting is used are:

- when a firm is already operating at maximum capacity and therefore cannot meet further demand in any other way
- when there are elements of a product that you are ill-equipped to manufacture efficiently
- to cope with seasonal peaks in demand

**subjective decision:** a decision that has been made either without, or in spite of, the evidence of researched data. Such decisions might be made by a lazy or prejudiced manager, or might be the result of an inspired *hunch*. A good example of the latter was the Sony Chairman's support for the 'Walkman', despite research evidence that consumers saw no need for it.

**subjective factors** are those for which personal judgement is necessary since they cannot be quantified effectively. They may be very important in business decisions such as capital investment, though there is a tendency to treat figures as facts and therefore downgrade non-quantifiable issues. Subjective factors include: effect upon morale, expectations of competitors' actions, and the effect on, and importance of, the *corporate image*.

**subliminal advertising** is the unethical practice of flashing hidden messages into TV commercials for such a short time that only the subconscious mind can take them in. This is against the *Code of Advertising Practice*.

**subordinate:** an employee who is answerable to a specified manager.

**subsidiarity** is the idea that decisions which affect certain people should be made as locally as possible. The word has been much used within the context of the *European Union*. UK governments have used it as an argument to prevent what they see as the over-centralisation of power in the hands of the EU, and in particular the *European Commission*. Local authorities in England and Wales have also used it as an argument against the same UK governments for removing their traditional roles within local communities of looking after such things as health and education.

**subsidiary:** a business that is owned by another business (the *holding company*). The subsidiary is likely to be trading under its own name, but as the holding company owns more than 51 per cent of its shares, it is the latter that will have effective control. The subsidiary's financial figures will form part of the parent company's *consolidated accounts.*

**subsidy** is paid by governments to lower costs of production, either for social reasons, or for strategic military reasons, or to raise incomes (e.g. hill sheep farmers), or to keep down prices of essential goods.

**substitute**: a brand or product that fulfils the same function as another and can therefore be used in its place. For example Persil is a substitute for Ariel and vice versa. Products that have several direct substitutes are likely to be highly *price elastic,* as consumers will switch to whichever of the competitors is the cheapest.

**suggestion schemes** are formal procedures for collecting ideas from the shop-floor. The suggestions might relate to new products, improved working methods or cost-cutting measures. Often, such schemes offer financial or promotional bonuses to suggestions that are adopted by the company. Many firms have suggestion boxes for workers to place their ideas, but not many are successful. They lack the personal involvement and group spirit of *quality circles* or *kaizen* (improvement) groups.

**summary dismissal** is the on-the-spot sacking of an individual due to behaviour believed to make his or her *employment contract* invalid. Examples include theft, violence or being offensive to customers. In such circumstances, instant dismissal is not wrongful or *unfair.*

**sunrise industry:** one positioned in a rapidly growing market, usually based on new technology and innovation.

**sunset industry:** one believed to be in terminal decline, with obsolete technology and an obsolete product.

**superordinate goals** are the aims that can provide the sense of mission that is so beneficial to *motivation.* The superordinate goal of many Japanese firms has been the achievement of worldwide acclaim for quality and technology. For others it may be to save the Brazilian rainforests, or to preserve craft skills.

**superstore:** a large retail outlet with substantial car parking that offers a very wide range of goods within a self-service shop.

**supervisor:** a shop-floor manager, in daily contact with those on the lowest grade within an organisation. In F W *Taylor*'s time, the norm was for 'driving supervision' whereby a supervisor achieved satisfactory output levels through threats or violence. The modern era tends to look for self-discipline from the workforce, allowing supervisors to take a more positive role in recruitment, training and the leadership of *quality circles* or *kaizen* groups.

**supply** is a term used in economics to denote a firm's willingness to produce and deliver goods or services demanded by customers. Supply is a key part of the *market mechanism* by which supply and *demand* are kept in balance through the price level. In other words if supply is short (e.g. few tomatoes due to bad weather), the price will rise in order to reduce the level of demand to match the available supply.

**supply curve:** a graphical representation of the likely level of supply of a product at a range of different prices, i.e. the relationship between price and supply. As one might expect, the curve indicates that as price rises, firms will be keen to supply more. In the short term, however, they may be unable to do so because of capacity constraints.

**supply side measures** are those designed to encourage the free working of markets, including that for labour (by restricting *trade union* activities and reducing unemployment benefit), *capital* (by ending *monopoly* controls and *restrictive practices*) and land (by dismantling such things as rent control). The notion of supply side economics was derived from *monetarism*, which argues that government's only two legitimate functions are to ensure that markets are free to operate efficiently and to control the amount of money or *credit* in circulation. Any other government activity, particularly that concerned with manipulating *aggregate demand* (see *Keynesian*), is a waste of time since any increase in demand only bids up prices (see *demand-pull inflation*), and therefore is soon cancelled out.

**supportive leadership** implies a friendly and approachable manner, displaying concern for the needs and welfare of subordinates. Such a focus upon good *human relations* is in keeping with the theories of *Elton Mayo*.

**survey:** another term for *quantitative* market research; in other words, research among a large enough sample of consumers to provide valid data.

**sweat shop:** a workplace where exploitation is common, with low wages in return for high effort levels. Such a situation is most likely to occur if local unemployment is high and unionisation is low.

**sweating your assets** is a commonly used phrase indicating the importance of achieving a high *asset turnover*; in other words, generating a high sales level from the firm's asset base. The higher the asset turnover, the harder the assets are working, therefore the more they are 'sweating'.

**Switch card**: a payment card that debits a person's bank account automatically, within a few days of use. It is a plastic version of writing out a cheque.

**SWOT analysis** is the assessment of a product, division or organisation in terms of its strengths, weaknesses, opportunities and threats. Its simple, four-box format makes it easy to use as a visual aid in a management meeting or conference. The strengths and weaknesses are the actual position of the product or company, while opportunities and threats represent future potential.

| **Strengths** | **Weaknesses** |
|---|---|
| • expertise at financial services | • short-termist approach partly due to take-over threat |
| • low-cost production due to deregulated labour markets | • poor education and training within workforce |
| • influence of Japanese firms on British management | • capacity cutbacks during the 1980 and 1990 recessions |

| **Opportunities** | **Threats** |
|---|---|
| • to gain market share or develop new markets within Continental Europe | • that foreign firms may prove more competitive, thereby taking a rising share of UK markets |
| • to build Europe-wide brands (such as Kit Kat) thereby enjoying large economies of scale | • that future European laws may restrict business decisions by British firms |

*SWOT analysis of British firms in the single European market*

**synergy** occurs when the whole is greater than the sum of the parts, i.e. when $2 + 2 = 5$. This is often anticipated in *take-over bids,* when directors assert that the purchase of a rival will provide such *economies of scale* as to make the combined firm a world-beater. Research evidence suggest that synergy is achieved far less often than it is forecast.

**systems analysis** is the detailed examination of how procedures such as stock control actually work, in order to identify the features required of computer software in order for efficiency to be maximised. (See *systems approach.*)

**systems approach** to management regards organisations as groups of inter-relating elements that require coordination and information to turn a wide range of inputs into a variety of outputs. Systems theorists believe that managerial success depends on a careful analysis of how the organisational system does and should work.

---

### Doing a Business Research Assignment?

**The A–Z Business Studies Coursework Handbook** provides a full, clear account of how to set up, research and write up a business project. See page 330 for details.

**tacit agreement** between firms means *collusion*, perhaps over-pricing or market sharing.

**tactical decisions** are those based on short-term considerations such as meeting this year's budgets or plans. For instance if a product's sales are 4 per cent below the annual forecast with one month until the year end, the sales manager might decide to run a *sales promotion* or cut the price. Usually, tactical decisions are made by middle management, though a decision to start the winter sale before Christmas would be a senior managerial decision for a clothes or jewellery retail chain.

**tactics** are the measures adopted to deal with a short-term opportunity or threat. Although managers would want to adopt tactics that fit in with the long-term strategy, there may be occasions when this is not possible.

**take-over:** obtaining full management control of another firm as a result of purchasing over 50 per cent of its *share capital*. This process is also known as acquisition. Usually, the bidder (*predator*) is sufficiently bigger than the target company to make the acquisition relatively easy to finance. However it is possible for a small firm to raise the finance to buy a larger firm; this is known as a *reverse take-over.*

**take-over bid:** the attempt by a *predator* company to buy a controlling interest in another firm. This is done by offering the target firm's shareholders a significantly higher price for their shares than the prevailing market price. The offer can be made in any of the following ways:

- a cash bid e.g. 150p per share
- a paper bid or share swop e.g. three Firm A shares for every two of Firm B's
- a combination of cash and paper e.g. 50p cash plus two Firm A shares for every two of Firm B's

**tall hierarchy:** an organisation with many *layers of hierarchy* and a narrow *span of control.*

*Tall hierarchy*

**tangibles:** a term used to distinguish physical *fixed assets* such as land and machinery from *intangible assets* such as patents and *goodwill*.

**target audience** is another term for *target market*.

**target market:** the precise profile of the customers a firm wishes to sell to. For a new cider, the target market may be working women aged 18–30; for an iced lolly it might be children aged 8–12. A firm will decide on its target market after conducting extensive *market research* including, perhaps, a *market segmentation* analysis. The choice of the target market will then affect every section of the *marketing mix*, including:

- distribution outlets: supermarkets or sweetshops?
- pricing
- style of *advertising* and choice of advertising media
- product characteristics such as sweetness or colour

**target setting:** the process by which an employee agrees performance targets with his or her boss. This gives the individual a clear idea of what to aim for during the year and can form part of an annual *appraisal* interview.

**tariff:** a tax imposed on an imported good. This is likely to reduce demand, and makes any domestic competitor more attractive to consumers. The importer may seek to redress the imbalance by cutting *profit margins*, or by becoming more efficient, or in extreme cases by setting up a production plant inside the country itself. Import tariffs are banned between members of the European Union. Tariffs can be levied in one of two ways:

- an 'ad valorem' tax, i.e. a percentage added to the price of the imported good
- a 'specific duty', such as £1 per item, regardless of whether the good is valued at £10 or £100

**task analysis:** see *project planning*

**tax avoidance** is the use of legal measures to minimise personal or corporate tax bills. Typical business examples include the use of *tax havens* and of *transfer pricing*.

**tax haven:** a country that levies low or no direct taxation, such as the Cayman Islands. British firms may set up *holding companies* based in the tax haven, enabling company profits to attract much lower tax levels.

**tax relief** is a means by which the government encourages individuals or firms to act in ways thought to be beneficial to the economy. It works by enabling taxpayers to set certain types of expenditure against tax, thereby providing an effective subsidy. For instance, firms may be able to claim tax relief for *capital expenditure* on high technology machinery.

**Taylor F W** (1856–1915): an American engineer who invented *work study* and founded the scientific approach to management. He emphasised the duty of management to organise the working methods of shop-floor labour, so as to maximise efficiency. Then, by setting financial incentives that would provide high rewards for hard work, both the worker and the business should benefit. Taylor used work study and *cost accounting* to analyse business efficiency, and advocated high *division of labour*, specialised tools, *piece-rate* payments and tighter management control as the main methods for productivity improvement. Taylor's most important work with companies was between 1895 and 1905, though his widest contribution to management was through his 1911 book PRINCIPLES OF SCIENTIFIC MANAGEMENT (W W NORTON, 1980).

His methods had considerable impact in America and then in Britain, notably through *mass production* at the Ford Motor Company. Taylor's impact on shop-floor labour was equally substantial but far less happy. The alienation caused by *deskilling* and loss of power led to the drive for unionisation that characterised the industrial scene between 1925 and 1975.

**team briefings:** a form of *oral communication* in which supervisors inform the members of their team about production requirements, quality problems or company successes. Such sessions are often held at the start of a working day or week.

**teamworking** occurs when production is organised into large units of work, instead of by a high division of labour. The team of people working on the large task (such as making complete shoes, instead of just making the soles) will need to be:

- multi-skilled and therefore well-trained
- motivated by something more than the piece-rate rewards they received while working on the single, repetitive task

**TEC:** see *Training and Enterprise Council*

**technical insolvency** occurs when a firm has negative net assets, i.e. its *share capital* has been outweighed by losses. This might be due to an accounting technicality, such as a large write-off of *goodwill* following a *take-over bid*. If so, financial markets may support the firm's continued trading.

**telemarketing**: contacting customers by telephone in order to persuade them to buy from you.

**teletext:** an information service provided through ordinary TV sets in which advertising space can be purchased relatively cheaply.

**teleworking** means working at home, though linked to the office by instant communications such as telephone, *fax* and computer *modem*. This can benefit the employer by reducing the *overhead* costs per worker, and provides a route back into work for employees who have been looking after dependent relatives.

**tender** has two meanings within business and economics. The first is the closed bidding for a contract such as the construction of a building, where firms are asked to submit their price for a job and the lowest is accepted. The second is where offers are made to buy *Treasury bills* at a fixed price on the *Stock Exchange*.

**tertiary sector** is that part of the economy concerned with service businesses. It is the largest sector in terms of employment in the UK, accounting for over two-thirds of the workforce.

**test market:** the launch of a new or improved product within a tightly defined area, in order to measure actual sales potential. Launching a product nationally is so expensive in production costs, advertising expenditure and *opportunity cost* that many firms will not take the risk of assuming that successful *market research* findings will mean successful sales. They first want to test a promising idea out in an area that may be as small as a town, or as large as the Midlands.

Pros: • provides more accurate sales forecasts, therefore the right-sized factory can be set up
• enables lessons to be learnt before the national launch

Cons: • gives competitors a chance to evaluate your product and decide how to respond
• management and *salesforce* focus on a small area, which may cause higher sales than are realistic nationally

**Thatcherism:** the term given to the range of policies and attitudes developed during Mrs. Thatcher's period as Prime Minister (1979–90). The underlying attitudes were based upon her dislike of *public sector* activities, extreme faith in the effectiveness of the free market and an *authoritarian* approach to leadership in general and unionised labour in particular. The main policies implied by the term Thatcherism include:

• *deregulation* of *private sector* businesses
• *privatisation* of state- and local-authority-controlled trading organisations
• *centralisation* of control of the remaining *public sector* activities
• *monetarism*
• switching from *direct* to *indirect taxation*, due to concerns about the effect of direct taxes on work incentives
• income redistribution towards the 'wealth creators' (the better off) as part of her desire to promote an *enterprise culture*

**them and us** is a traditional statement of the divide between managers and workers. Managers see the workers as 'them'; workers see the managers as 'them'. This situation is fostered by *separate status*, by the recruitment of graduate trainees who do not start at the factory floor, and perhaps by the very existence of *trade unions*. Many feel it originates in a class-obsessed society or in the school divide between grammar and comprehensive and state versus private education. Whatever its origins, most commentators would agree that its elimination is an important management task.

**Theory X** is *McGregor's* term for the common management attitude that most workers have an inherent tendency to dislike work. In his own words:

Behind every managerial decision or action are assumptions about human nature and human behavious. A few of these are remarkably pervasive:

1 The average human being has an inherent dislike of work and will avoid it if he can.
2 Because of this human characteristic, most people must be coerced to get them to put forth adequate effort toward the achievement of organisational objectives.
3 The average human being prefers to be directed, wishes to avoid responsibility, has relatively little ambition, wants security above all. (D McGregor THE HUMAN SIDE OF ENTERPRISE Penguin, 1987; first published 1960)

(See also *Theory Y*.)

**Theory Y** is a managerial approach based on the belief that human beings can be stimulated by and energetic towards work, providing it has the potential to engage their interest. A common mistake is to believe that *McGregor's* theory is about differ-

their effects. The main assumptions identified by McGregor as Theory Y were:

> The expenditure of physical and mental effort in work is as natural as play or rest …
>
> The average human being learns, under proper conditions, not only to accept but to seek responsibility …
>
> The capacity to exercise a relatively high degree of imagination, ingenuity, and creativity in the solution of organisational problems is widely, not narrowly, distributed in the population. (D McGregor, THE HUMAN SIDE OF ENTERPRISE (Penguin, 1987; first published 1960))

It has often been remarked that McGregor's theory Y anticipated by more than 10 years almost all of the management approach known as the *Japanese way*. (See also *Theory X* and *Theory Z*.)

**Theory Z:** the writer Ouchi's term for the Japanese approach to management, which he distinguished from McGregor's *Theory Y* in the following ways:

- the Japanese focus on lifetime employment
- the intense attempt to make the employee conform to company practices and attitudes
- a strong emphasis on *human relations*

**tight (fiscal) policy** is a government economic strategy which raises taxes and/or reduces public expenditure. Its purpose is to restrict demand, usually to keep *inflation* in check. It is usually combined with a tight *monetary policy*.

**time-and-motion study** is the investigation of the efficiency with which a task is carried out. It is a popular term for *method study*.

**time rate** is payment for the length of time spent working, rather than the quantity of output achieved.

**time-based management:** focusing on time as a key business resource. In the 1970s price was the key competitive tool. In the 1980s it was quality. Now, speed of delivery, speed of response and speed of development are all-important. Speed adds value, as you can see in the price list of every photo-processing outlet.

**time-series analysis** is the processing of data into sequences of figures over time. Such data can consist of four main elements:

1. the longer-term trend, perhaps growth or decline
2. seasonal or cyclical factors, i.e. ups and downs that occur in a regular pattern
3. erratics: unpredictable fluctuations in the figures, caused by known elements (such as the weather) or by unknown ones (e.g. variations in the trendiness of a particular product)
4. responses: results of specific measures you have taken to affect the series (e.g. advertising spending causing a temporary sales increase)

To analyse this data effectively it is necessary to process it by:

- smoothing out the erratics (by the use of *moving averages*)
- smoothing out the seasonal variations (by *seasonal adjustment*)
- identifying and measuring the responses

This would make it possible to identify the underlying trend and then extrapolate it forwards in order to forecast the future position.

**time sheet:** a form on which staff can record how long they have spent working on different projects. This enables salary overheads to be allocated more accurately.

**top-down management** is a leadership style based on decisions and orders being issued from the top, without *consultation* or *delegation.*

**tort:** a legal wrong against an individual which gives that person the right to take civil action for the payment of damages. The law of tort is intended to defend the rights and interests of individuals against wrongful conduct such as:

- trespass
- nuisance (such as pollution of a river)
- defamation
- negligence

**total float:** see *float time*

**total quality management (TQM):** the attempt to establish a culture of quality affecting the attitudes and actions of every employee. This is usually attempted by trying to get every work group (or department) to think of those they work for as customers, even if they are fellow employees. An example would be for the maintenance engineer to treat a shop-floor worker with a defective machine as a valued customer, rather than as a nuisance. Other main features of TQM include:

- the use of *quality circles*
- emphasis upon service and *after-sales service* quality as well as quality manufacture
- the idea that high quality (and low cost) stem from getting things right first time

American firms with a long experience of TQM have reported that change occurs far more slowly than managers expect, leading to a phase of disenchantment with the whole process. This should not be a surprise because TQM relies on a workforce that wants to improve quality and has the power to achieve it. Providing that *motivation* is no easy task, especially if the managers' views are rooted in those of F W *Taylor.*

**Townsend R** (b. 1920): the highly successful Chairman of Avis Car Rental, who set out his management philosophy in UP THE ORGANIZATION (Michael Joseph 1970). It was the first ever business best seller, and many feel it has never been surpassed. His key themes were distaste for bureaucracy, advocacy of an extreme version of a *Theory Y* management, and a strong plea for truth and honesty in business.

**TQM:** see *total quality management*

**tracking:** see *continuous research*

**trade advertising:** messages to retail, wholesale or industrial customers that are placed in trade media such as THE GROCER magazine. Usually, consumer firms place advertisements in trade media in the week or two prior to the start of consumer advertising. This is to achieve retail distribution before consumers come in to search for the product.

**trade association**: an organisation set up to represent the interests of all the firms within an industry, notably for *lobbying* government and sharing information.

**trade barriers:** see *barriers to trade*.

**trade credit:** providing business customers with time to arrange for the payment of goods they have already received. This period is one of interest free credit, which helps the customer's *cash flow* at the cost of the supplier's. Although the typical credit period offered to customers is 30 days, the average time the customers take to pay is nearer 80 days.

**trade cycle** is the way the economy moves from boom to slump in a regular fashion over a period. It can also be called the business or the economic cycle. The time taken from boom to boom is controversial; the economist who identified the cycle in the 1860s, Juglar, thought it was 8 to 11 years, whilst others thought it was as little as three and a half years, and *Kondratieff* thought there was a very long cycle of 50 years. Certainly it is possible to identify periods of booms and slumps since the industrial revolution, although they have all been superimposed on an upward trend line.

Because of the general trend upwards, each successive boom has tended to be higher than the previous one.

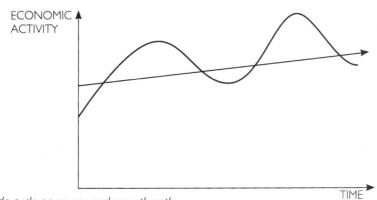

*The trade cycle on an upward growth path*

**Trade Descriptions Act 1968** prohibits false or misleading descriptions of a product's contents, effects or price. This affects packaging, advertising and promotional material. It is one of the key pieces of *consumer protection* legislation.

**trade discount:** the percentage of the consumer selling price being provided as the *gross profit* margin for the retail trade.

**trade exhibition:** an industry market-place, where suppliers in a sector such as fast food can display their products to an audience of fast food restaurateurs or *franchisees*.

**trade fair:** see *trade exhibition*

**trade mark:** a *logo* or symbol displayed on a company's products and advertising to distinguish the firm's brands from those of the competition. For exclusive use, a trade mark must be registered at the *Patent Office*.

**Trades Union Congress (TUC):** the organisation that represents British *trade unions* at a national or international level. The TUC was formed in 1868 and has had periods of considerable influence on government decision-making, notably the 1970s. Its functions are to:

- be the voice of the union movement as a whole
- prevent or solve inter-union disputes
- promote international labour solidarity, especially within Europe

**trade union:** an organisation representing the interests and goals of working people. Membership involves the payment of subscriptions, usually of about £10–£15 per month.

Advantages of trade unions, to union members

- collective bargaining on their behalf
- local *shop stewards* can help in case of unsafe or unfair practices
- access to free legal advice and support

Advantages of trade unions to businesses

- communication link between management and workforce
- avoids the time-consuming need for individual bargaining
- a strong union may encourage managers to take worker needs seriously

**Trade Union Act 1984:** legislation designed to ensure that *trades unions*:

- become liable to be sued by employers if a strike is authorised without a secret ballot of the membership
- elect or re-elect voting members of the union's national executive at least every five years

**Trade Union Reform and Employment Rights Act 1993:** a further piece of legislation that critics say was designed to weaken trade unions, though the government declared its aims as to increase the rights of individual employees and trade union members, and to improve competitiveness. It extended the changes brought about by previous *Employment Acts*. Among its main provisions are:

- requiring unions to provide employers with at least seven days' notice of official industrial action
- requiring union members to give periodic written agreement to the deduction of union subscriptions from their pay (making it more likely that people will let their union membership lapse)
- creating a new 'citizen's right' to restrain unlawfully organised *industrial action* (making it easier to stop unofficial strikes)
- abolish the remaining *wages councils* and their statutory minimum pay rates

**trade war:** a protectionist battle between governments in which *tariff* barriers against a country's imports leads to retaliation. If a trade war becomes serious enough it can cause a widespread downturn in world trade.

**trading bloc:** a group of countries that share *free trade* agreements between each other, but with *tariff* walls that discourage imports from countries outside the block. The *European Union* is a good example.

**trading cycle:** the entire business process from receiving an order through to calculating the profit. It can be seen as having three elements: (see page 283)

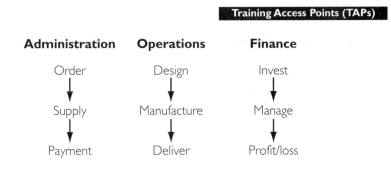

| Administration | Operations | Finance |
|:---:|:---:|:---:|
| Order | Design | Invest |
| ↓ | ↓ | ↓ |
| Supply | Manufacture | Manage |
| ↓ | ↓ | ↓ |
| Payment | Deliver | Profit/loss |

These elements must be managed so that the administration and operations work in conjunction with each other, and are well enough controlled to ensure that the profit or loss can be identified. The trading cycle will determine the *money cycle* (*cash flow*) for a particular order.

**trading forecast:** a prediction of a firm's sales revenue and profit levels over the coming trading period (usually a year).

**trading profit** is the difference between the *revenues* and *costs* generated by a firm's ongoing business. As it is not a consequence of one-off items, it can be assumed that current trading profit is likely to recur in the future. Therefore it is regarded as high-quality profit. Another term for trading profit is 'operating profit'. As shown in the calculation below, trading profit can be calculated by deducting *overheads* from the company's *gross profit*.

Worked example:

|  | £000 |
|---|---|
| Revenue | 920 |
| Cost of sales | 420 |
| Gross profit | 500 |
| − Overheads | 280 |
| = Trading profit | 220 |

**Trading Standards Authority:** the organisation responsible for enforcing consumer protection legislation. It employs trading standards officers who protect consumers in two main areas. First they protect consumers where there is potential exploitation. For example, they check petrol pumps to ensure that they deliver exactly the amount indicated on the pump. Secondly they protect consumers where safety is at risk, such as toys which are potentially dangerous.

**trading standards officer:** an employee of a local council whose responsibility is to ensure that *consumer protection* laws such as the *Weights and Measures Act* are stuck to by businesses locally.

**trainee:** an employee who is being trained to undertake a particular role, such as a *management trainee*.

**training** is the provision of work-related education, either *on-the-job* or *off-the-job*.

**Training Access Points (TAPs)** are the national provision of access points to information about training schemes and their availability. They are based at job centres and major libraries, though there are also mobile centres that visit employers' premises.

**Training Agency:** the government body responsible for the coordination of national training schemes. Its main tasks are to encourage training schemes for the unemployed, to encourage an entrepreneurial spirit, and to assist small businesses. It is the successor to the Manpower Services Commission. Perhaps its best known activities are:

- *Employment Training (ET)*, which trains the long-term unemployed
- *Youth Training (YT)* schemes, which train young people between the ages of 16 and 17 who are not in education or employment
- *Training and Enterprise Councils (TECS)* which are supported by the Agency

A criticism of the Training Agency is that its main function is to 'massage' the unemployment figures by keeping people in sometimes fruitless training schemes rather than having them claim benefit.

**Training and Enterprise Councils (TECs)** were formed in 1990 to organise locally based training, plus business start-up support. The TECs decide what the local skills needs are, then commission local colleges or firms to provide appropriate courses. There are about 80 TECs in England and Wales, each financed by government but run by local business representatives.

**training credit:** an attempt at creating a market in training for young people, by giving school leavers a voucher worth £1 500 which they can use to 'buy' the training they want from a local employer or college. This was hoped to provide more choice for the young person and therefore encourage the providers of training to improve the quality of their service. Critics suggested that £1 500 was insufficient to provide a serious training programme.

**training mentorship:** see *mentor*

**transfer payment** is where government income from one part of society is paid to another part. The best known are pensions and social security payments such as unemployment benefit.

**transfer pricing** is employed where no external market exists which would set a price. It is often used by large companies for internal purposes to control costs, or, in the case of *multinationals* to reduce taxation. This is achieved by one *cost centre* in a low tax country charging another in a high tax country a high transfer price. The first one will make a large profit on which little tax is paid, whilst the other will make low or no profits and so will also have a low tax liability.

**transformational leader:** one who has the vision, the power, and the personality to cause radical change within an organisation.

**transmission mechanism:** the process by which a message or event is transferred from one person or place to another. In business this term has two main applications:

- in communications, the transmission mechanism is the medium by which a message is conveyed, e.g. telephone or memo
- in economics, the transmission mechanism is the way in which economic change in one region affects other regions, e.g. via trade and investment flows

**transnational corporation:** another name for a *multinational*

**transparency** occurs when a deal or decision is made in an open manner, so that all those affected understand the reasons. Lack of transparency can lead to rumours or ill feeling, often directed at particular individuals.

**transportation technique:** the *linear programming* method that tests whether resources have been allocated optimally between two variables. The name stems from the technique's origins in decisions about how best to decide which depot should supply which customer in order that transport costs be minimised. As with any form of *operational research* the method lends itself to computerisation, but is reliant on assumptions that may prove over-simplistic, and vulnerable to *bias* in gathering the data.

**Treasury**: the UK government department responsible for executing the government's taxation and spending policies. It comes under the direct responsibility of the *Chancellor of the Exchequer,* although the Prime Minister, as First Lord of the Treasury has ultimate control. Because it has the power to withhold or spend money it is the most influential of all departments. The Treasury operates a complex *macroeconomic* forecasting model which is designed to help decision making, especially when devising the *Budget.* Unfortunately the Treasury model has proved poor at spotting turning points in the business cycle.

**Treasury bills** are short-term (three months) government securities. They are sold on the *Stock Exchange* in order to make up for any shortfall in government spending in excess of tax revenue. Because they are so short term, they provide a very flexible way for governments to borrow. They are issued in units exceeding £5 000 and since 1988 have also been issued and redeemed in ECUs (*European Currency Units*).

**treasury function:** active management of a firm's financial resources, so that cash is earning the highest returns possible, while financial risks such as foreign exchange losses are minimised. Corporate treasurers can generate high profits for a firm, though there have been several cases of major firms losing hundreds of millions of pounds due to treasury errors. In some firms, corporate treasurer has become a new title for the same old financial director.

**Treasury model:** a computerised economic forecasting model used by the government to estimate future economic trends.

**trend:** the underlying pattern of growth or decline within a series of data. This pattern can be projected forward as a prediction of the future in the process known as *extrapolation* of the trend.

**trend analysis** means examining changes in a data series over time. For example, an examination of ice cream sales would reveal a steady increase in the proportion of sales occurring in the winter months. Fuller detail on trend analysis is in the entry on *time series analysis.*

**trial balance:** a check on the accuracy of the firm's *double-entry bookkeeping* by adding the credits from all the ledgers and comparing them with all the *liabilities*. This is an interim stage between the recording of day-to-day transactions in the firm's ledgers (books) and the presentation of finished accounts.

**troubleshooter:** originating in the oil industry, this term is used to describe an individual who is asked to sort out a business problem of someone else's making.

*Management consultants* may be used in this role, though large firms may have their own head office staff who can troubleshoot.

**true and fair view:** the phrase used by auditors to confirm that a firm's accounts are accurate within the terms of the accounting practices used to draw them up. Occasionally, auditors qualify a set of accounts by stating that they are not happy with one element of the data provided. This occurs if they believe that an aspect of the accounts does not provide a true and fair view of the company's finances.

**TUC:** see *Trades Union Congress*

**turnkey project:** a contract for something as substantial as a whole factory, in which the supplier supplies, installs and tests every aspect of the specification, so that the customer can make it operational at a mere turn of the key.

**turnover** is an abbreviation for sales turnover, which means the same as *sales revenue*.

**two-factor theory:** the view that the factors related to *job satisfaction* can be divided into two: those that only have the potential to provide positive job satisfaction and those that can only cause dissatisfaction. Professor *Herzberg* came to this conclusion in the late 1950s, after conducting research among accountants and engineers in America. The findings of his research are presented below. Many have criticised his research method, but many managers have attempted to put his theory into practice and have enjoyed considerable success.

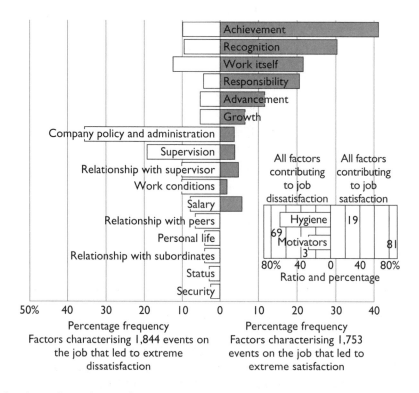

*Herzberg's two-factor theory of motivation*

**two-way communication** occurs when instant *feedback* is possible, thereby enabling a proper conversation to take place. This should be far more effective and motivating than *one-way communication*.

**types of employment:** the categories into which all types of job can be fitted, consisting of:

- full and part-time employment
- self-employment
- permanent and temporary work
- contract and non-contract labour
- skilled and unskilled labour
- homeworking

REVISION: There are two sets of revision lists and a glossary of examiners' terms at the back of this book to help you prepare for exams or unit tests. See pages 307–312 for unit tests in GNVQ Business Advanced and pages 313–325 for examinations in A level Business Studies. See pages 326–329 for explanations of examiners' terms such as 'analyse' and 'discuss'.

**unbundling** means unravelling an organisation in order to identify and then concentrate on its core strengths. This will simplify the management structure and help to ensure that the profits from a company's stronger divisions are not simply being used to subsidise the poor performers. Pressure to unbundle usually comes as a reaction against the excesses of a *take-over* boom. During the latter, growth-orientated firms often buy up unrelated businesses, thereby turning themselves into *conglomerates*. Unbundling will return them to their former position as specialists in one or two *core activities*.

**uncertainty** is the situation that underlies every business decision. This is because decision-making concerns changes that will have an effect in the future, and the future can never be predicted with certainty. An important issue that stems from this is that uncertainty increases over time. In other words, a forecast of next year's sales or costs has a lower chance of accuracy than an estimate of the figures for next week. Therefore decisions that rely upon circumstances in the distant future are subject to very great uncertainty. Examples of this include commercial failures such as Concorde and De Lorean cars.

**underemployment** occurs where people nominally have jobs, but jobs that do not keep them fully occupied. This often results in very low wages, and is particularly prevalent in the agricultural sectors of underdeveloped countries.

**underground economy**: business and work activity conducted outside the official world of banking, auditing and government. The underground economy works for cash, thereby avoiding taxation and regulation. Another term for this is the black economy.

**under-used capacity** occurs when an organisation is producing below its maximum possible level. For instance, if a hotel has an average occupancy rate of 75 per cent, its level of under-used capacity is 25 per cent. This figure is important because it is only by making full use of capacity that *fixed costs* (and therefore total costs) per unit can be minimised.

**underwriting** is the acceptance of a business risk in return for a fee. Lloyd's of London has a worldwide reputation for its willingness to underwrite any type of insurance wanted by a client. For a *stock market* new issue, a *merchant bank* will underwrite it by guaranteeing to buy any shares which are not sold in the company *flotation*.

**unemployment** exists when someone seeking work is unable to find any.

The main types of unemployment are:

- structural, i.e. when the economy changes in a fundamental way people are made unamployed. The coal and shipbuilding industries of the UK are examples
- cyclical, i.e. when demand is low at the bottom of the trade cycle

- seasonal, e.g. people in the building trade are often laid off during the winter when the weather is too bad to work.
- frictional, which is when people are temporarily unemployed between jobs

**unfair dismissal:** terminating the employment contract of a member of staff for a reason that the law regards as unfair. This would include anything other than *gross misconduct,* incapability and genuine *redundancy.* Workers who believe they have been dismissed unfairly must appeal to an *industrial tribunal* within three months.

**Uniform Business Rate** is a tax paid by businesses to cover the use of local goods and services. It was introduced with the poll tax (community charge) and was the successor to the local rating system. It is set nationally but reflects local property values.

**unincorporated** means a firm which operates as a *sole trader* or partnership which has not applied to the *Registrar of Companies* for incorporation as a *joint-stock company.* Those running an unincorporated business have *unlimited liability* for the firm's debts.

**union:** see *trade union*

**union density** measures the proportion of a workforce that belongs to a *trade union.* This is a major influence upon the effectiveness of union activity.

**union recognition** is the acceptance by an employer that bargaining on wages and conditions will be negotiated with the union representing the workforce. Since the *Employment Act 1980* there has been no obligation under UK law to recognise a union, no matter what proportion of staff support it. Therefore employers have found it easy to prevent unions from establishing a meaningful presence in new companies. For unless the firm grants union recognition, the union has no power whatever.

**unique selling point (USP):** the feature of a product that can be focused on in order to differentiate it from all competition. The USP should be based on a real product characteristic, such as the advertising slogan used by Mars for one of their chocolate bars: 'Topic – a hazelnut in every bite'. Stronger still are USPs based on a patented technical advantage. Many firms, however, attempt to create USPs that are based purely on advertising imagery. This can be effective (better to be the sexiest chocolate bar than the hazelnuttiest) but usually at the cost of extensive TV advertising support. (See *product differentiation.*)

**unitary taxation:** an attempt to defeat tax avoidance measures such as *transfer pricing,* by imposing company profit taxes based on a firm's *turnover* within a particular state or country. When introduced in California, unitary taxation caused a storm of protest by *multinational* firms, but it increased sharply that State's revenues from *corporation tax.*

**unit cost** is the average cost of making one item, found by dividing total cost by the number of units produced. This sounds straightforward, but unit (or average) costs are among the trickiest concepts in business. This is because it seems as if you can use unit costs to work out the total cost of producing any specified number of units. In fact, however, unit costs comprise two elements: *variable costs* (which are a true cost per unit) and *fixed costs per unit* (which are only correct at one level of output). Therefore before 'using' unit costs it is necessary to strip out the fixed element.

---

Worked example: unit costs

> At 400 units of demand, unit costs are £2, half of which are fixed. What are total costs if demand doubles?
>
> Fixed costs stay at £1 × 400 = £400
>
> Variable costs are £1 × 800 = £800
>
> Therefore total costs at 800 units = £1 200 (**not** 800 × £2 = £1 600)

---

**unit trust:** a fund that spreads small savers' investments over a wide portfolio of different *stocks and shares*. This is a popular and relatively inexpensive way of investing on the *Stock Exchange*.

**unity of command:** the standard management practice that every employee should be answerable to only one boss. This could be said to conflict with *matrix management*.

**unlimited liability** means that because a business is trading without having become incorporated, its owners are liable for all the debts it may incur. If these debts are greater than the personal assets of the proprietors, they may be forced into *bankruptcy*. The main types of unlimited liability business are *sole traders* and *partnerships*.

**Unlisted Securities Market** (USM): a stock exchange set up during the 1980s for small firms too new to obtain a listing on the full London Stock Exchange. This was part of the 1980s financial boom, offering early access to equity capital for dynamic firms such as Body Shop. Unfortunately, many USM firms were far less successful, leading to a crisis of confidence in the Exchange during the early 1990s. It was replaced in 1995 by AIM – the *Alternative Investment Market*.

**unofficial strike:** a refusal to work that has been agreed locally by union members, but has not been approved by the national union. As a result, strikers will not receive any *strike pay* and will have their legal case weakened should the firm dismiss them. Unofficial strikes are sometimes called *wildcats* or walk-outs. Both terms give the correct impression of a dispute that has arisen so suddenly that workers act before getting official union approval.

**unsecured loan:** borrowing that is not backed by any form of security or *collateral*. This would be hard to obtain and would carry relatively high interest charges.

**Unsolicited Goods and Services Act 1971** was intended to protect customers from the practice of inertia selling. It would no longer be possible to insist that customers pay for goods that they had not ordered, but had not bothered to return. This Act was one of many pieces of *consumer protection* legislation passed in the period 1968–74.

**upgrade** means replacing an existing computer system with superior hardware or software. The main benefits are likely to be larger memory and speedier operation.

**up-market:** a word used commonly in marketing to denote a product that is aimed at wealthier consumers. Its opposite is a *down-market* product.

**upper turning point** is the highest point in the *trade cycle*. It is usually reached where there are shortages of skilled labour and capital goods, and when expectations that the boom will continue begin to fade. The loss of confidence and rising costs reduce levels of investment, and through the *multiplier*, result in a downturn.

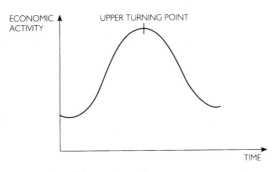

*The upper turning point of the trade cycle*

**upstream activities** are those that focus on earlier stages in the *production chain.* Therefore upstream integration is another term for backward *vertical integration.*

**upturn** is that point in the business or *trade cycle* where business confidence returns, investment restarts, unemployment falls and incomes begin to rise.

**usage depreciation:** spreading the cost of a *fixed asset* over its useful lifetime in proportion to its level of usage within each trading period. This is a rarely used alternative to the standard methods: *straight line* and *declining balance method.*

**USP:** see *unique selling point*

**usury** means lending money at exorbitant rates of interest.

**utilities** are industries which provide the most basic services such as water and power. Before *privatisation* it was generally accepted that utilities were State run, not only because of their importance to the overall economy, but also because they operated on such a large scale, they were *natural monopolies.* For example, it was evident that there was no economic logic in having rival gas pipelines going to every house just to provide some competition to British Gas.

**validity**: measuring or judging the reliability of data such as the findings of *market research*. To assess the validity of research findings, the following should be considered:

- whether the questionnaire was biased
- whether the sampling method was appropriate
- whether the sample size was large enough to provide statistically valid data
- whether the interviewing was carried out consistently and without bias (overenthusiastic, for example)
- whether the research results can be related directly to customer actions (people may say they will try a product , but not bother in real life).

**value added** is the difference between the cost of inputs and the price customers are prepared to pay for the finished product. It is value added that creates the surplus to pay the wages, *overheads* and *dividends*. A product with high value added is likely to have been produced and/or designed with great skill, though it may also be the result of creating a very desirable brand image.

FORMULA:    selling price  –  bought-in goods and services    = value added
$$£4 \quad - \quad £0.80 \quad\quad = £3.20$$

The diagram below shows how the £3.20 value added is distributed. It also indicates that value added can be expressed as a percentage:

% value added    $= \dfrac{\text{value added}}{\text{materials}} \times 100$

$= \dfrac{£4 - 80p}{80p} \times 100$

$= 400\%$

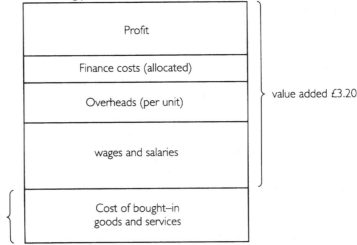

£4.00 selling price

Profit

Finance costs (allocated)

Overheads (per unit) — value added £3.20

wages and salaries

£0.80 — Cost of bought–in goods and services

*Value added*

**Value Added Tax (VAT)** is a percentage tax added on to the price of a good or service. It was introduced in 1973 to replace purchase tax and to harmonise with the rest of the *European Union*. Since each stage of production adds value (the difference between the cost of its inputs and the revenue gained from its output), the tax is added at each stage, and can be claimed back, until it reaches the final consumer, who cannot reclaim it. The tax is *regressive* in that it takes a higher proportion of a poor person's income than someone who is rich. In recent years the British Government has broadened the VAT net, for example by taxing fuel.

**value analysis:** the study of each aspect of a product to see if it adds sufficient value to justify its cost. Companies conduct value analysis to look at both new and existing products to see whether they are designed in a way that satisfies the consumer in terms of what the product looks like, what it costs and how well it performs its job. Achieving this goal requires a combination of *market research*, cost information and engineering skills.

Generally, the term 'value analysis' is used to mean the identification of costs that could be cut, either by using cheaper materials or by redesigning a product to use fewer components. It is this negative approach that has led to value analysis being blamed for reductions in quality and workmanship, for example, cars being made with thinner body steel and window frames becoming much less ornate than in the earlier part of the century.

**value discipline:** a strategic focus upon a single way to provide value to customers. M. Treacy and F. Wiersema, in their book *The Discipline of Market Leaders* (Harper Collins 1995) suggested that there are three categories of value discipline:

- operational excellence, for example British Airways or Marks & Spencer
- product leadership, for example Nike, Sony or Intel
- customer intimacy – products tailored to individual customers, such as Rolls Royce cars.

Identifying and focusing on a value discipline can help concentrate the whole organisation on a known goal.

**value engineering:** another term for *value analysis*, used in connection with manufacturing industry.

**value judgement:** an opinion based on beliefs rather than facts. Although the term could be used to describe *entrepreneurs* who make decisions in an unscientific manner, it is more commonly used as a criticism of student essays. Students often make the error of stating value judgements as if they are facts (for example, 'All firms profit-maximise').

**values:** ethical principles that guide one's actions, enabling one to identify decisions or actions that are morally unacceptable. (See *ethics*.)

**variable:** a variable is a factor that can cause changes to occur in a firm's plans or outcomes. Some variables are within the firm's influence, such as pricing levels, employee *motivation* and *advertising* effectiveness. An efficient firm will measure and evaluate these variables in order to decide what policies to adopt towards them. Others are wholly outside the firm's control, such as the weather, competitors' actions and consumer confidence. These variables should be measured and anticipated so as to aid the firm's planning process. If a weather forecast predicts a heatwave, for example, a soft drink producer should know whether to expect sales to rise 20 per cent or 200 per cent.

**variable cost:** one that varies in direct proportion to changes in output, such as raw materials, components, *piece-rate* labour and energy used in production. In other words, these are costs that should double if output doubles. Although *break-even charts* require the assumption that some costs vary in direct proportion to changes in *output*, in practice it is unlikely that any costs will be totally variable. For instance, raw materials are likely to cost less per unit when buying in bulk. Therefore the materials cost might not quite double when output doubles.

**variable cost per unit:** total variable costs divided by the number of units produced. As the worked example shows, it is assumed that variable costs per unit will not change as output changes.

Worked example:

|  | Yesterday | Today |
|---|---|---|
| Variable costs | £360 | £720 |
| Output (units) | 240 | 480 |
| Variable cost p.u. | £1.50 | £1.50 |

**variable overheads** are costs that vary in proportion to changes in demand or output, but are not related directly to the production process. Examples include any commission paid to sales representatives, and any variable costs associated with delivery, such as the cost of postage for a mail-order company. When making profit or break-even calculations, variable overheads should be added to variable costs, **not** to fixed overheads.

**variance:** the amount by which an actual figure differs from a budgeted one. (See *variance analysis.*)

**variance analysis:** the process by which a firm identifies then analyses any differences between budgeted and actual *revenues* and costs. This is the main single use of computer *spreadsheets* in business. At the start of its financial year, a firm will agree monthly *budgets* with its staff. At the end of each month, actual figures will be recorded alongside the budgeted ones, together with any variations. For example:

January revenues (£000s)

| Budget | Actual | Variance |
|---|---|---|
| 240 | 275 | + 35 |

An unusual feature of the maths of variance analysis is that, instead of the variance being measured as a plus or a minus, it is 'favourable' or 'adverse'. The reason is to avoid confusion over positive or negative variances. For whereas an unexpectedly high *revenue* is good, unexpectedly high costs are not. So if actual costs are £40 000 above the budgeted figure, instead of recording the variance as +£40 000, it would be an adverse (unfavourable) variance of £40 000. An adverse variance is one that reduces *profit*; it is shown on a spreadsheet by putting the figure in brackets.

The other point to note in the example that follows is the bottom line: *year to date.*
This means the cumulative position, i.e. the result from each month is added to the
ones before. This line helps the user to see at a glance whether a single month's variances are a freak, or whether a clear trend is being established.

---

Worked example: variance analysis at the end of February

All figures in £000s

|  | January | | | February | | | March | | |
|---|---|---|---|---|---|---|---|---|---|
|  | Budg | Act | Var | Budg | Act | Var | Budg | Act | Var |
| Revenue | 85 | 80 | (5) | 95 | 86 | (9) | 110 | | |
| Materials | 36 | 34 | 2 | 42 | 39 | 3 | 46 | | |
| Fixed costs | 42 | 44 | (2) | 45 | 45 | – | 45 | | |
| Profit | 7 | 2 | (5) | 8 | 2 | (6) | 19 | | |
| Year to date (Profit) | 7 | 2 | (5) | 15 | 4 | (11) | 34 | | |

Note: to calculate year to date you add up all the corresponding figures, e.g. the
£15 000 budgeted profit for year to February came by adding January's £7 000
to February's £8 000. This makes the data cumulative.

---

**VAT:** see *value added tax*

**VAT registered:** A trader has to register with HM Customs and Excise when its sales
revenue reaches a certain level. Below that level of sales revenue, registration is
optional.

Once a trader is registered the difference between VAT received on sales or supplies
(output VAT) and VAT paid on purchases (input VAT) must be paid over to Customs
and Excise, usually quarterly. A trader who is not registered for VAT is VAT-exempt.
Exemption means that VAT is not added to sales but cannot be recovered from the
cost of purchases.

Zero-rating means thast the trader is registered, charges zero VAT on sales and can
claim back from Customs and Excise the VAT paid on purchases.

**vendor appraisal** means assessing the qualities of potential suppliers in order to
decide which ones to approve. For example, a firm such as Walls might appraise
packaging suppliers on criteria such as reliability, speed of response (for when hot
weather causes a sales boom) and hygienic factory conditions. Walls' staff will only be
allowed to buy from approved suppliers (vendors).

**venture capital** is risk capital, usually in the form of a package of loan and *share capital,* to provide a significant investment in a small or medium-sized business. The
need for it arises when a rapidly growing firm requires more capital, but the firm is
not yet ready for the *stock market.* In these circumstances, *merchant banks* might provide the funds themselves, or arrange for others to do so. A typical venture capital
investment might provide £500 000: half in loans and half in shares.

**verbal warning:** the first stage in the process by which an employee can legally be
dismissed for reasons which do not justify *summary* (instant) *dismissal.*

**vertical communication** is the passage of information up and down the management hierarchy. It may be upward, as in a shop-floor complaint to managers about

safety conditions, or downward, as in a manager-run team briefing session. Successful vertical communication can overcome *them and us* barriers and can enhance the speed and quality of *consultation*. To achieve this, however, requires a clear sense of common purpose and a flat enough hierarchy to minimise the layers through which the communication must pass.

**vertical integration**: occurs when two firms join together that operate in the same industry, but at different stages in the production/supply chain. The integration might come about through *merger* or *take-over*.

Backward (or upstream) vertical integration means buying out a supplier, e.g. a chocolate manufacturer buying a sugar producer. See the entry on *backward integration*.

Forward (or downstream) vertical integration means buying out a customer, e.g. the chocolate firm buying up a chain of newsagents. See the entry on *forward integration*.

**vested interest:** a participant in a decision, action or statement who has a direct interest in the outcome and therefore may prove biased. For example, estate agents have a vested interest in suggesting that the housing market is strong enough for prices to rise.

**vicarious liability:** the legal responsibility of a superior/employer for the actions taken by subordinates/employees in the course of their work.

**video conferencing** is the establishment of a TV and video network that can enable staff working at a distance from each other to 'meet' without travelling.

**video display unit (VDU)** enables computer-generated data or information to be shown on a screen.

**virus** (computer): a software programme that latches on to other programs with the purpose of disrupting them. This might cause the loss of valuable or even vital data.

**visible trade** is concerned with the export and import of goods. The difference between visible exports and visible imports is called the *balance of trade*. (See *balance of payments*.)

**voice** (advertising)**:** a common expression in marketing is 'share of advertising voice'. 'Voice' is the total spent on advertising within a market-place. So a firm's share of advertising voice is how much they have spent as a proportion of the expenditure total. Many firms believe that this is a key factor within their *marketing mix*. It is an important consideration in the setting of advertising budgets. For example, Coca-Cola may want to have a more than 50 per cent share of voice in the cola market. Therefore if Pepsi double their advertising spending, Coke will have to do the same to maintain their share of voice. See diagram overleaf.

**voluntary code of practice:** a formal statement by a committee or organisation of the methods of working recommended as good practice for the firms and individuals within the industry. Such codes are often devised by the *employers' association*, which provides a symbol that participants in the scheme can display to potential customers. The code is voluntary if it has no statutory or legal backing. This is usually what employers say they want, though financial scandals within the City of London have led many within the financial sector to call for statutory and therefore legally enforceable codes of behaviour.

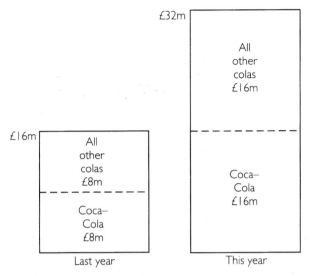

*Maintaining your share of advertising voice*

**voluntary liquidation:** a decision by the company directors or shareholders to ask *receivers* to liquidate the business in the best interests of the shareholders. *Liquidation* meaning turning *assets* into *cash*. This process of winding up the company's affairs may be due to a financial crisis or simply because a firm's directors wish to retire and have no successors.

**voluntary organisation:** a non-profit-making enterprise such as a charity or a youth group. The special difficulties of managing such organisations have been analysed by Professor *Handy*. Key amongst them is the need for a management style that makes staff feel valued, since there is no financial reason for volunteer staff to work effectively.

**vote of (no) confidence:** this is the way in which shareholders who believe that their company has been mismanaged can demand that the current chairman resigns. A vote can be called at the *annual general meeting* between the directors and the share-holders. Although this procedure is an important aspect of the theoretical *accountability* of company managements to their shareholders, in practice it is extremely rare for a vote of no confidence to succeed.

A vote of no confidence may also be carried out when a government policy has been so seriously called into question that the Speaker of the House of Commons accepts an Opposition call for a no-confidence debate. Should the government lose such a debate, it is accepted parliamentary practice that it resigns from office and a general election is held.

**Vroom V:** a highly influential author on *motivation* and leadership, whose most sig-nificant work focused on *expectancy theory*.

**wage-price spiral:** a phrase describing a situation in which wages chase prices, in turn causing prices to rise further, and so on. When *inflation* rises to such a level that workers see their *real incomes* falling, they respond by demanding wage increases to compensate. This is also known as *cost-push inflation*. Whether wages follow prices at the start of the cycle, or prices follow wages is subject to a great deal of political debate.

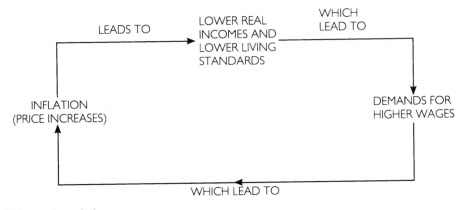

*Wage-price spiral*

**wages councils** were formal wage negotiating forums in industries which traditionally had very low pay rates. The rates set by the councils were legally binding on all employers in the particular industry. Their supporters argued that they protected workers from low-wage exploitation in industries traditionally dominated by employees with few bargaining strengths, such as part-time women workers. Their opponents said that they enforced a wage rate higher than the market equilibrium, and this resulted in a loss of jobs. The government abolished them in 1993 as part of a campaign to deregulate the labour market.

**walk the talk** means that managers need to see and be seen at every level of the organisation, so that their ideas remain practical and their communication stays personal. It is a modern version of the 1960s expression *management by walking about*.

**Wall Street Crash:** the collapse in American share prices that began in 1929 and continued until 1932. It was the result of the American *stock market* rising so far during the 1920s that share prices no longer reflected reality. Investors took risks in highly speculative shares, such as land deals in the Florida Everglades and in Europe. Once rumours of the risks of these shares became common knowledge, the bubble burst and share prices plummeted, helping to bring about the *Great Depression* which continued until the Second World War. The same pattern of share price boom and bust has happened several times since 1929, notably in the 1980s.

**warehouse club:** a form of *cash and carry* for the ordinary consumer. Anyone can pay the fee to join the club, and is then able to buy large quantities of groceries and household goods at sharply discounted prices. Once warehouse clubs are established, conventional supermarket chains may suffer falling *revenues* and *profit margins*.

**wastage** is the rate of loss of resources within a production or service process, either necessarily (such as the weight loss when filleting a fish) or unnecessarily (such as sloppy work). Staff effort should be devoted to minimising the wastage that is within their control or influence.

In manufacturing, the main problems are:

- materials wastage
- reworking (due to poor quality first time)
- defective production (with products sold off as 'seconds')

In retailing, the main problems are:

- customer or staff theft and pilfering
- products passing their sell-by date (due to over-ordering or poor *stock rotation*)
- poor handling, leading to products becoming damaged

**wealth distribution:** a measurement of the proportion of the nation's total assets held by different sectors of society. For instance it may be that the richest tenth of the population own 40 per cent of the country's wealth, while the poorest tenth own just 1 per cent.

**web:** short for *World Wide Web*.

**weighted average:** an average that is weighted in line with the relative importance of its different components. This is necessary to make the final figure a true reflection of the information.

For example, if there are three size categories for British companies: small, medium and large, with *sales turnovers* of £100 000, £5m., and £1bn respectively. What is the average turnover of a British company?

The worked example below shows an unweighted average of this information on the left. It gives a highly misleading answer of £335m. The right-hand column weights the average by the proportion of firms there are in each size category. It takes into account that there are many more small firms than large and therefore results in a more accurate, much lower figure (£40.88m).

| | Simple average | Weighted average | | | |
|---|---|---|---|---|---|
| | | figure | times | weight | = weighted total |
| Small | £100 000 | £100 000 | × | 80% | £80 000 |
| Medium | £5 000 000 | £5 000 000 | × | 16% | £800 000 |
| Large | £1 000 000 000 | £1 000 000 000 | × | 4% | £40 000 000 |
| Total | £1 005 100 000 | | | | |
| | 3 | | | Addition of weighted totals = | |
| | = £335 033 333 | | | weighted average = £40 880 000 | |

**weighted index:** the calculation of a data series with a base figure equalling 100 within which the principles of *weighted averages* are applied. Among the most widely used weighted indexes in Business and Economics are the *retail prices index (RPI)* and the Financial Times Stock Exchange 100 Index (FT-SE 100, popularly known as *Footsie*).

A problem with weighted indexes is that the weights applied can become out of date as market or consumer habits change. This is why some statisticians prefer current year weighting to the more common base year weighting.

**Weights and Measures Acts 1963 and 1985:** legislation making it illegal to sell goods below their stated weight or volume, together with an enforcement procedure through trading standards officers and the *Office of Fair Trading*. The 1985 Act allows metric measures to be used.

**what if . . . ? questions** are hypothetical considerations of:

- what might happen in the future
- what might result if things are done differently today

What if ...? questions are the essential preliminary stage to *contingency planning*, i.e. to the process of preparing responses to possible opportunities or threats. These questions are made far easier to think through if a firm's sales, production, distribution and financial data is kept on a single computer model. This is the attraction of resource planning systems such as *MRPII*.

**whistle blower:** an individual whose sense of moral outrage leads him or her to expose wrongdoing within an organisation, either to the authorities or to the press.

**white collar union:** a *trade union* representing clerical, professional or managerial staff.

**white goods** is a collective term for household kitchen appliances such as fridges, freezers and washing machines, all of which were traditionally produced with white metal casings.

**white knight:** a company that comes to the rescue of a firm that is facing a *take-over bid* from an unwelcome *predator*. The white knight steps in with a counter-offer for the firm, thereby saving it from the predator. A classic example of this was Waterford's rescue of Wedgwood from the clutches of the London Rubber Company (Durex).

**White Paper:** a document setting out proposals for government legislation.

**wholesaling:** the process of buying large quantities of product from suppliers and selling on in smaller volumes to retailers or business users. This is known as 'breaking bulk'. This traditional role as the middleman is often looked down on because the wholesaler's profit margin appears to make goods more expensive for the consumer. As shown by the diagram on the facing page, however, without a wholesaler the number of journeys required for each manufacturer to service each retailer would become prohibitively expensive. Furthermore, there would be serious effects on traffic and the environment from the number of extra journeys necessary.

**Deliveries required without a wholesaler**

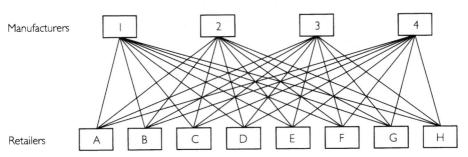

**Deliveries required with a wholesaler**

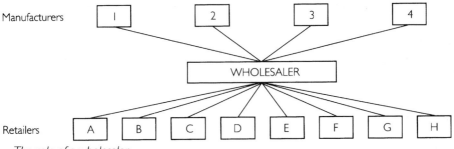

*The role of a wholesaler*

**wide band:** the option within the *European Monetary System* which allows a currency to vary 6 per cent above or below its central rate. This is a flexible version of what is supposed to be a *fixed exchange rate* system. The *narrow band* allows only a 2.5 per cent variance.

**wildcat strike:** spontaneous unofficial industrial action brought on by the sudden emergence of a major grievance. A typical catalyst might be the sacking of a respected *shop steward*.

**windfall gain:** a one-off gain that can aid this year's profit or cash position, but cannot be expected to recur in future.

**winding up** is the process of completing the *liquidation* of a business in order for it to cease trading in an orderly manner.

**window-dressing:** presenting the company accounts in such a manner as to flatter the financial position of the firm. This is a form of *creative accounting* in which there is a fine dividing line between flattery and fraud. In the overwhelming number of cases, window-dressing is no more misleading than tidying up before visitors arrive. Among the different ways of window-dressing accounts are:

- Masking a deteriorating *liquidity* position. This is in order to present a *balance sheet* that looks financially sound. This can be done via the following, three-step process.

  Step   **I** A firm's liquidity ratio has worsened during the past year from 1.5 to 0.9. The latest balance sheet is to be drawn up tomorrow.

Step    **2** So it executes a *sale and leaseback* deal today, bringing in an instant injection of cash.

Step    **3** Tomorrow's balance sheet therefore presents a liquidity figure of 1.5, leaving outsiders unaware that the underlying liquidity position has been bad and is deteriorating.

- Massaging the profit figure: Although firms' revenue totals and cost totals sound like facts, there is a great deal of scope for changing the figures. At the end of a poor year's trading, managers may be asked to bring forward as many invoices and deliveries as possible, to, in effect, push two months' revenue into the last month before the year-end.

**withdrawals** are leakages from the *circular flow of national income*. They consist of taxation, imports and savings.

**word of mouth:** the spread of information or publicity through individuals' decisions to talk about a product or event. This is an especially important form of free *advertising* for fashion-based and/or children's products. Favourable word of mouth will spread if a product has been particularly well designed and made.

**workers' cooperative** is a business owned and controlled by those who work in it. Large scale cooperatives of this kind were attempted in the 1970s, but they failed because, despite the additional commitment of the workforce, the businesses were simply not viable. They also faced another problem, which was one of management. The necessity to bring in outsiders to perform vital management functions, such as accountants and marketing experts runs counter to the cooperative ideal, and this tension can lead to considerable inefficiency. This is less apparent in small-scale cooperatives, and during the 1980s these became far more numerous and successful. Many of these smaller versions were started with the *redundancy* money of workers made structurally unemployed. They have been far more successful, and local Cooperative Development Agencies have grown up to foster their growth.

**worker-directors** are representatives from the workforce who sit on the boards of companies. Although common in Continental Europe, and in particular in Germany, this is rare in the UK. It is seen by some as a way of encouraging participation in decision-making, and was proposed as a way of reducing industrial relations problems by the Bullock Report in 1977. Understandably perhaps, management is generally not keen on the idea because they fear it may slow decision-making, reduce their power and possibly enable confidential financial information about the company to reach the hands of the workers. *Trade unions* are also lukewarm, on the grounds that it emasculates them by making the worker-directors equally responsible for decisions made at board level, and also it reduces their powers of *negotiation*. Greater *industrial democracy* is now seen as coming more from grass roots decision-making via Japanese-style techniques.

**worker participation** is the active involvement of the workforce in the ideas, decisions and actions of the organisation. It can be encouraged by structures such as *quality circles, kaizen* groups and *works councils*. Such structures are only successful, however, if senior management give full support to the suggestions that come up from the factory floor.

**work-in:** an unusual form of *industrial action* in which staff continue working even though the business has collapsed and/or the workforce has been made redundant. A work-in tends to generate favourable publicity and may attract a buyer interested in taking over an enterprise with such enthusiastic employees.

**working capital** is the day-to-day finance for running a business. In exam questions, the term means the day-to-day finance available for running a business.

FORMULA:   current assets − current liabilities = working capital

Working capital is used to pay for raw materials and running costs, and also funds the credit offered to customers (*debtors*) when making a sale. If a firm has too little working capital available, it may struggle to finance increased production without straining its *liquidity* position. Yet if a firm has too much capital tied up in the short term, it may not be able to afford the new machinery that could boost efficiency.

**working capital ratio:** see *liquidity ratio*

**working conditions:** the physical surroundings and atmosphere of a workplace, e.g. state of decoration and amount of pollution. Professor *Herzberg* regards them as *hygiene factors*, for whereas poor working conditions may be demotivating, good conditions become accepted as the norm and therefore give no positive satisfaction.

**work in progress (WIP):** semi-completed components within the production process, either stockpiled or on the production line itself. This is one of the three types of stock: the others are raw materials and finished goods. Although in many factory contexts WIP is a minor element of stock, in others such as shipbuilding and construction, the long production time makes work in progress a heavy user of the firm's *working capital.*

**works measurement** has been defined by the *British Standards Institute* as 'The application of techniques designed to establish the time for a qualified worker to carry out a specified job at a defined level of performance.' These timings combine with a study of the way in which the process is carried out (*method study*) to provide a full *work study*. This is an important element in the *scientific management* approach to production.

**works council:** a regular forum for discussion between management and workforce representatives. Excluded from the agenda would be bargaining over wages, terms and productivity levels, as these matters would be left to *trade union* negotiations. The role of the works council is to look ahead at the company's plans and to draw ideas for improvements from the factory floor. A weakness of works councils has always been that because they include representatives from the whole firm, they lack the focus of a localised *quality circle* or improvement group.

At Maastricht, Britain negotiated an opt-out from the European Union's drive to impose works councils on all large companies in Europe. Despite this, United Biscuits Plc (McVities and KP) has introduced works councils throughout its European bases, <u>including</u> Britain. Many other multinationals are expected to follow this lead towards more consultation.

**work shadowing:** a form of vocational training in which a student or new recruit follows a member of staff around for a day or longer, observing what the job consists of.

**work study** is the systematic measurement of working processes and timings with the intention of identifying the best available method and realistic *output* targets. Also known as *time and motion study*, it was one of the key management tools devised by F W *Taylor* at the end of the nineteenth century.

**work-to-rule:** a form of industrial action in which employees refuse to undertake any work that is outside the precise terms of their *employment contract*. This stops overtime and many forms of participation and communication that are accepted practice. Staff may prefer a work-to-rule to a strike, since they are able to draw their basic pay.

**World Bank** or the International Bank for Reconstruction and Development was established in 1947 to provide aid to developing countries in the form of loans and technical assistance. Originally the Bank supplied loans for capital projects, such as those concerned with improving a country's *infrastructure*, but from 1980 onwards it was allowed to offer help in the case of *balance of payments* difficulties, subject to conditions.

**world-class manufacturing** is a term coined by R *Schonberger* to denote the characteristics of the world's top-performing companies. *Benchmarking* is the technique used most commonly to identify how well a firm's performance stands up against the world's best performing manufacturers.

**World Trade Organisation** *(WTO):* the grouping of over a hundred countries into an international free trade club. The member countries commit themselves to work towards the elimination of barriers to imports and thereby encourage free and fair trade. The WTO is a successor to *GATT* (the *General Agreement on Tariffs and Trade*). Whereas GATT covered only trade in goods the WTO also includes services and the protection of intellectual property (such as patents and copyright).

**World Wide Web:** a menu-based system of software that provides links to other information sources throughout the Internet. It is where most of the information on the Internet is posted for other users.

**write down:** the decision to cut the *book value* of an asset down to a level that is now thought more appropriate. In a sense that is what *depreciation* does each year, but the term 'write down' is usually used to denote any reduction in an asset's book value other than through normal depreciation.

**write off:** the decision to cut the *book value* of an asset down to zero (or to a nominal sum such as £1). This would be done if it became clear that a physical asset had become worthless or a *debtor*'s item had become unrecoverable.

**written warning:** the second stage in the formal procedure by which an employee can legally be dismissed for inadequate performance.

# Y Z

**year to date:** accumulated figures for the months of the year so far. The term is used commonly on *spreadsheets* of monthly budgets.

**yield:** another term for *dividend yield*

**Youth Training (YT)** is the name given to a training programme for unemployed school-leavers that is devised and administered locally by *Training and Enterprise Councils (TECs)*. It aims to provide those on the course with sufficient skills to achieve a Level II *National Vocational Qualification* (NVQ).

**yuppie:** a 1980s label describing a supposedly new class of young upwardly mobile professionals devoted to smart but faddish lifestyles.

**zero budgeting:** the attempt to prevent *budgets* creeping upwards each year by setting the coming year's budget at zero and demanding that managers should give a full justification for every pound of budget they request.

Pros: • should identify departments that no longer need high budgets, thereby releasing funds for growth areas
• a way of reducing the cost base of the whole organisation, especially important when facing a period of weak demand

Cons: • effective zero budgeting requires considerable management time spent in identifying and justifying the appropriate budget level
• no budgeting system is free from the problem that some managers are more cunning about justifying high budgets than others, so the system may not ensure extra funds for those in the most need

**zero defects:** the goal of achieving perfect product quality, time after time. Many believe that this could only be feasible at an excessively high design and production cost.

**zero hours contract:** an employment contract stating that the employee's regular working week amounts to zero hours. This provides the employer with total flexibility, allowing the employer to tell staff the start of each week the hours they are required to work. Such a contract might be given to a hotel receptionist, who might then have to work from 6.00 am to 2.00 pm Monday to Thursday and from 5.00 pm to 3.00 am on Friday and Saturday.

**zero rated:** products for which *VAT* declarations must be made, though the rate of tax is 0 per cent.

**z score** (accounting): a single measurement of a company's financial health based upon a weighted average of several *accounting ratios*. If a company's z score is below one, it is believed to be in danger of complete or partial financial failure. The ratios used include: *acid test*, trends in profitability, *gearing* and *working capital* control.

**z score** (statistics): the proportion of outcomes within a specified part of a normal distribution, measured in terms of *standard deviations*. The z score enables statistical significance to be measured with more precision than just in terms of one, two or three standard deviations.

# BUSINESS STUDIES REVISION LISTS

The following pages provide revision lists for tests or exams. This is to help readers use their A-Z as effectively as possible. The revision lists are split into 3 main sections: GNVQ Advanced Business, AEB A level and Cambridge Modular A level. Students of the Cambridge Linear A level should use the Cambridge Modular lists plus a special Examiners' Terms section on page 326.

# ADVANCED GNVQ BUSINESS REVISION LISTS FOR UNIT TESTS

The authors have been through the NCVQ documents on the content and focus of the Mandatory Units, to identify the key terms for revision. For example, they have identified 40 top revision terms for the Unit 1 test on Business In The Economy.

For the end of unit tests, look up the following terms, making sure that you understand the text and can memorise the definition.

**Unit 1:** Business in the economy

**Unit 2:** Business organisations and systems

**Unit 3:** Marketing

**Unit 4:** Human resources

**Unit 5:** Production and employment in the economy

**Unit 6:** Financial transactions, costing and pricing

**Unit 7:** Financial forecasting and monitoring

## Unit 1: business in the economy – top 50 revision terms

Break-even position (see break-even point)
Competitive pricing
Consumer protection
Corporation tax
Demand
Demand curve
Deregulation
Destruction pricing (see predatory pricing)
Disposable income
Economies of scale

Effective demand
Elasticity of supply
Equilibrium
European Union (EU)
Expansion pricing
Fiscal policy
Government economic objectives
Government intervention (see interventionist policies)
Growth (see economic growth)
Income elasticity

Income tax
Inflation
Interest rate
Interventionist policies

Investment
Monetary policy
Monopoly
Monopolies and Mergers Commission
Office of Fair Trading
Oligopoly

Opportunity cost
Penetration pricing
Planning permission
Price elasticity
Price maker (see price leader)
Price taker
Price war
Pricing strategy (see also pricing methods)
Private sector
Privatisation

Profit motive
Public sector
Public spending
Regional assistance (see regional policy)
Single European market
Skimming
Social benefits
Social costs
Supply
Value Added Tax (VAT)

## Unit 2: business organisations and systems – top 50 revision terms

Budgetary control
Business objectives
Centralised organisation
Communication
Communication channels
Communication net
Company formation
Cooperative
Data Protection Act 1984
Database

Decentralised organisation
Electronic communications technology
Electronic data interchange (EDI)

E-mail (see electronic mail)
Feedback
Fitness for purpose
Flat organisation
Franchise
Function
Incompatible equipment

Information technology
Internet
Limited liability
Market share
Matrix management
Networking (IT)

On-line
One-way communication
Open communication channels
Organisation chart

Organisational structure
Partnership
Personal computer (PC)
Private limited company (Ltd)
Private sector
Public company
Public corporation
Public limited company (PLC)

Public sector
Quality control

Restricted communications channels
Shareholders
Sole trader
Sources of finance
Span of control
Spreadsheet
Stock market
Two-way communication
Unlimited liability
Virus

## Unit 3: marketing – top 60 revision terms

Advertising
Advertising ethics
Advertising Standards Authority (ASA)
After-sales service
Branding
Brand loyalty
Closed question
Cluster sample
Code of Advertising Practice
Consumer profile

Customer loyalty
Customer satisfaction
Customer service
Direct mail
Direct marketing
Direct sales
Distribution channels
Face-to-face interviews
Fast moving consumer goods (FMCG)
Field trials

Fitness for purpose
Focus groups
Indirect sales
Interviewing (and see face-to-face interview)
Market orientation
Market research
Market share
Marketing activities
Marketing functions
Marketing mix

Marketing plan
Marketing principles
Marketing strategy
New product development (NPD)
Observation
Open questions
Panel discussion
Piloting (see pilot study)
Primary data
Product development

Product life cycle
Product orientated (see production orientated)
Public relations (PR)
Qualitative research
Quantitative research
Questionnaire
Quota sample
Random sample
Repeat purchase
Sale of Goods Act 1979

Sales administration
Sales campaign
Sales conference
Sales promotion
Secondary data
Selling off the page
Target audience
Telemarketing
Trades Descriptions Act 1968
Validity

# Unit 4: human resources – top 50 revision terms

Accreditation of Prior Learning
Advisory Conciliation and Arbitration Service (ACAS)
Annual pay round
Aptitude test
Arbitration
Body language
Business objectives
Collective bargaining
Consultation
Curriculum vitae

Director
Disciplinary procedure
Dismissal
Employee share ownership schemes (ESOPs)
Employment contract
Equal opportunities
Equal Pay Act
Ethical code
Feedback
Flexible working

Grievance procedure
Health and Safety at Work Act 1974
Human relations
Human resources management

Individual bargaining
Induction
Industrial action
Industrial tribunal
Interviewee techniques
Interviewer techniques

Job description
Job roles
Job rotation
Job (person) specification
Labour mobility

Manager
Manpower planning
Multi-skilling
Non-discriminatory legislation
Performance appraisal

Productivity
Quality circles
Race Relations Acts 1968 and 1976
Recruitment
Reference
Sex Discrimination Act 1986
Staff associations
Teamworking
Trade union
Working conditions

# Unit 5: production and employment in the economy – top 50 revision terms

Added value (see value added)
Aggregate demand
Automation
Benchmarking
BS 5750 (see British Standard 5750)
Business cycle
Change
Computer aided design (CAD)
Computer aided manufacture (CAM)
Contracting out

Deregulation
Deskilling
Economic growth
Employers' associations

Exchange rate
Flexible working
Freelance
Inflation
International competitiveness
Investment

Investors In People
Japanese Way
Job security
Just in time
Labour flexibility
Labour market
Labour mobility
Motivation

Multi-skilling
New technology

Off-the-job training
On-the-job training
Privatisation
Productivity
Quality assurance
Redundancy
Remuneration
Research and development
Robotics
Scale of production

Self-employed
Single European market
Single sourcing
Structural change
Structural unemployment
Teleworking
Total quality management
Training and Enterprise Councils
(TECs)
Underground economy
World Trade Organisation

## Unit 6: financial transactions, costing and pricing – top 50 revision terms

Absorption costing
Added value (see value added)
Assessing suppliers (see vendor appraisal)
Authorised cheque signatories
Bad debt
Breakeven chart
Breakeven point
Cash flow
Contribution
Contribution pricing

Cost accounting
Cost-plus pricing
Credit clearance
Credit control
Credit insurance
Credit note
Credit terms
Creditors
Debit cards
Debtors

Depreciation
Direct costs
Dividends
Electronic data interchange (EDI)
Electronic Funds Transfer at the Point of Sale (EFTPOS)

Fixed costs
Invoice
Marginal cost
Margin of safety (see safety margin)
Market-led pricing

Money cycle
Overheads
Pricing strategies
Profit
Purchase documents
Purchasing (see purchasing manager)
Residual cash
Retained profit
Sales documents
Sales revenue

Scenario planning
Segregation of duties
Total costs
Trading cycle
Trading profit
Under-used capacity
Unit cost
Variable cost
What if? questions
Work in progress

*GNVQ revision lists*

# Unit 7: Financial forecasting and monitoring – top 50 revision terms

Acid test
Aged creditors analysis
Aged debtors analysis
Asset turnover ratio
Balance sheet
Budget
Cash flow
Cash flow forecast
Creditors
Current assets

Current liabilities
Current ratio (see liquidity ratio)
Debtor collection period (see debtor days)
Debtors
Equity
Factoring
Forecasting
Grant
Gross profit/sales ratio (see gross margin)
Hire purchase

Indirect costs
Insolvency
Inter-firm comparison
Leasing
Liquidity

Mortgage
Net profit
Overdraft
Overheads
Partnership

Private limited company (Ltd)
Public limited company (PLC)
Profitability
Profit and loss account
Profit margin
Ratio analysis
Retained profit
Return on net assets (see return on capital)
Security (see collateral)
Share capital

Sole trader
Solvency
Sources of finance
Stock turnover
Trade credit
Trial balance
Value Added Tax (VAT)
Variance analysis
Venture capital
Working capital

# MAIN CONCEPTS REQUIRED FOR SUCCESS IN AEB A LEVEL BUSINESS STUDIES EXAMS

The following pages set out lists of terms to revise for examinations. When approaching exams, look up each word in the main text, making sure that you understand it and can memorise the definition.

1    Marketing – top 40 revision terms
2    Accounting and finance
2.1  Published company accounts – top 30 revision terms
2.2  Management accounts – top 30 revision terms
2.3  Top 20 financial formulae
3    Operations management – top 40 revision terms
4    People in organisations – top 50 revision terms
5    External influences on business
5.1  Economic environment of business – top 35 revision terms
5.2  Legal and social environment of business – 30 top concepts
6    Business objectives and strategy
6.1  Background to business – top 40 revision terms
6.2  Business statistics – top 20 concepts and terms

AEB revision lists

# 1 Marketing – top 40 revision terms

Asset-led marketing
Brand loyalty
Confidence levels
Consumer durable
Consumer profile
Contribution (marginal cost) pricing
Correlation
Cost-plus pricing
Distribution channels
Distribution targets

Extension strategy
Innovation
Market orientation
Market penetration
Market segmentation
Market share
Market size
Marketing mix
Marketing model
Marketing plan

Marketing strategy
Mass marketing
Niche marketing
Price discrimination
Price elasticity
Primary research
Product differentiation
Product life cycle
Product portfolio analysis (Boston matrix)
Qualitative research

Quantitative research
Quota sample
Random sample
Sales forecasting
Sales promotion
Secondary research
Skimming the market
Stratified sample
Test marketing
Value added

# 2 Accounting and finance

## 2.1 Published company accounts – top 30 revision terms

Assets employed
Audit
Balance sheet
Capital employed
Corporation tax
Cost of sales
Creditors
Current assets
Current liabilities
Debtors

Depreciation
External finance
Fixed assets
Goodwill
Gross profit
Historic cost
Intangible assets
Internal finance

Liquidity
Net current assets

Overheads
Profitability
Profit and loss account
Profit quality
Reserves
Share capital
Shareholders' funds
Venture capital
Window dressing
Working capital

## 2.2 Management accounts – top 30 revision terms

Average rate of return
Break-even analysis
Budgetary control
Cash-flow forecast
Contribution

Contribution per unit
Cost centres
Credit control
Direct costs
Discounted cash flow (DCF)

External finance
Factoring
Fixed costs
Indirect costs
Internal finance
Leasing
Net present value (NPV)
Overhead allocation
Payback period
Profit centres

Reward for risk
Sale and leaseback
Stock control
Stockholding costs
Stock valuation
Straight-line depreciation
Variable costs
Variance
Working capital
Zero budgeting

## 2.3 Key financial formulae – top 20 revision terms

Acid test ratio
Asset turnover ratio
Average rate of return (ARR)
Break-even output
Cash flow
Contribution per unit
Debtor days
Dividend cover
Dividend yield
Gearing (capital)

Gross (profit) margin
Net (profit) margin
Pay-back period
Price-earnings ratio (PE ratio)
Profit
Return on capital (ROC)
Safety margin
Stock turnover
Straight-line depreciation
Total contribution

# 3 Production and operations management – top 40 revision terms

Automation
Batch production
Benchmarking
BS 5750
Buffer stock
Capacity utilisation
Capital intensive
Cell production
Computer aided design (CAD)
Computer aided manufacture (CAM)

Critical path analysis
Diseconomies of scale
Division of labour
Economies of scale
Electronic data interchange (EDI)
Flow production
Information Technology

Innovation
Just-in-time
Job production

Kaizen
Lead time
Lean production
Mass production
New technology
Productivity
Quality circles
Quality control
Reorder levels
Research and development

Specialisation
Standard costs
Standard times
Stock control

*AEB revision lists*

Stock rotation
Teleworking
Time-based management

Total float
Total quality management (TQM)
Zero defects

## 4 People in organisations – top 50 revision terms

Absenteeism
Accountability
Appraisal
Arbitration
Arbitration Advisory and Conciliation
Service (ACAS)
Authoritarian leadership
Autonomous work groups
Chain of command
Communication channels
Conciliation
Consultation
Culture
Decentralisation
Delayering
Delegation
Democratic leadership
Empowerment
Hawthorne effect
Human needs
Human relations
Human resources management
Individual bargaining
Induction
Industrial action
Industrial democracy

Industrial relations
Job enrichment
Job rotation
Kaizen groups
Labour flexibility
Labour productivity
Labour turnover
Layers of hierarchy
Management by objectives
Matrix management
Participation
Paternalistic leadership
Pendulum arbitration
Performance related pay
Piecework
Quality circles
Organisational hierarchy
Resistance to change
Responsibility
Single status
Span of control
Teamworking
Theory X and Y
Trade union
Works councils

## 5 External influences

### 5.1 Economic environment of business – top 35 revision terms

Balance of payments
Consumer durable
Deregulation
Devaluation
Direct controls
Direct taxation
Economic growth
European Union

Exchange rates
Fiscal policy
Fixed exchange rates
Government economic objectives
Government intervention
Gross domestic product
Import protection
Income elasticity
Incomes policy
Indirect taxation

Inflation

Interest rates

International competitiveness

Laissez-faire policies

Monetary policy

Nationalisation

Pan-European business strategy

Privatisation

Regional policy

Quotas

Recession

Reflation

Retail prices index (RPI)

Single currency

Single market

Tariffs

Trade cycle

### 5.2 Legal and social environment of business – 30 top concepts

Advisory Conciliation and Arbitration Service (ACAS)

Bankruptcy

Business culture

Business ethics

Cartel

Contingency planning

Demographic change

Employment Acts (various, 1980–1990)

Equal opportunities

Equal Pay Act 1970

Environmental audit

External costs

Health and Safety at Work Act 1974

Industrial tribunals

Insolvency

Liquidation

Lobbying

Market failure

Market sharing agreements

Monopolies Commission

Office of Fair Trading

Pressure groups

Race Relations Acts 1968 and 1976

Receiver

Regulator

Sale of Goods Act 1979

Sex Discrimination Act 1975

Social costs

Social responsibilities

Trade Descriptions Act 1968

# 6 Objectives and strategy

### 6.1 Background to business – top 40 revision terms

Aims

Business plan

Contingency planning

Corporate objectives

Corporate plan

Crisis management

Decision trees

Ethics

External constraints

Flotation

Franchising

Horizontal and vertical integration

Internal constraints

Limited liability

Management buy-out

Merger

Mission statement

Multinational company

Objectives

Ordinary shares

Overtrading

Partnership

Preference shares

Primary sector

Private limited company

Private v public sector

Prospectus

Public limited company

Secondary sector

Shareholders' rights

Sole trader
Stakeholders
Stock exchange
Strategy
SWOT analysis
Tactics
Takeover
Tertiary sector
Unlimited liability
What if? questions

## 6.2 Business statistics – top 20 concepts and terms

Base year
Bias
Confidence levels
Correlation

Decision trees
Expected value
Extrapolation
Index numbers
Mean
Median

Mode
Moving average
Probability
Raw data
Retail prices index
Sample
Sample size
Seasonal adjustment
Significance testing
Weighted average

# CAMBRIDGE MODULAR BUSINESS STUDIES – KEY REVISION TERMS

The following pages set out lists of terms to revise for examinations. When approaching exams, look up each word in the main text, making sure that you understand it and can memorise the definition.

### Business organisation 4371 (double module) – compulsory
The nature of business – top 15 concepts
The internal organisation of business – top 10 terms
Information and business decision making – top 10 terms
Accounting and finance – top 15 terms
Human resource management – top 15 terms
Operations management – top 15 terms
Marketing – top 15 terms

### Business context 4372 – (compulsory)
The nature of the business environment, and changes within it – top 25 terms
Objectives of the state and their impact on business – top 25 terms
Financial control of business –top 5 concepts
Employer/employee relations – top 5 concepts

### Human resource management 4373
The 30 terms here are in addition to those in the compulsory modules 4371 and 4372.

General terms – top15
Human resources planning – top15 terms

### Marketing 4374
The 30 terms here are in addition to those in the compulsory modules 4371 and 4372.

### Operations management 4375
The 40 terms are in addition to those in the compulsory modules 4371 and 4372.

The production process – top 20 terms
Production management – top 20 terms

### Accounting and finance in business 4376
The 40 terms here are in addition to those in the compulsory modules 4371 and 4372.

Financial accounting – top 20 terms
Management accounting – top 20 terms

### Cambridge Linear A level business studies (9370)
Use the Cambridge Modular lists for modules 4371, 4372 and 4376. In addition, revise the following terms for business statistics and operational research.

Business statistics – top 25 terms
Operations research – top 20 terms

# Business organisation 4371 (double module) compulsory

## The nature of business – top 15 concepts

Aims
Corporate culture
Corporate objectives
Hierarchy of objectives
Mission

Objectives
Primary sector
Private sector
Public sector
Secondary sector

Stakeholders
Strategy
SWOT analysis
Tactics
Tertiary sector

## The internal organisation of business – top 10 terms

Accountability
Centralisation
Chain of command
Decentralisation
Delegation

Informal groups
Managers
Organisational structure
Responsibility
Span of control

## Information and business decision making – top 10 terms

Information technology
Market research
Primary data
Qualitative data
Quantitative data

Sales forecasting
Sample
Sample size

Scientific decision making
Secondary data

## Accounting and finance – top 15 terms

Accounting rate of return (see average rate of return)
Balance sheet
Break-even chart and break-even point
Budget
Cash flow

Direct costs
Fixed costs
Marginal costs
Overheads
Payback period

Profit
Profit and loss account
Ratio analysis
Sources of finance
Variable costs

## Human resource management – top 15 terms

Appraisal
Autocratic leadership
Collective bargaining
Consultation
Contract of employment (see employment contract)

Democratic leadership
Hierarchy of needs (Maslow)
Human resource management
Individual bargaining
Leadership style

Manpower planning
Motivation theory
Theory X and Y (McGregor)
Two-factor theory (Herzberg)
Worker participation

### Operations management – top 15 terms

Capacity utilisation
Cell production
Continuous improvement
Critical path analysis
Diseconomies of scale

Economies of scale
Float time
Just in time
Industrial location
Lean production

Productivity
Quality assurance
Research and development
Stock control
Time-based management

### Marketing – top 15 terms

Boston Matrix
Distribution and distribution channels
Extension strategy
Market growth
Marketing mix

Marketing model
Marketing planning
Market research
Market segmentation
Market share

Pricing and price elasticity
Product life cycle
Product portfolio
Sales forecasting
Sample and sample size

# Business context 4372 – compulsory

### The nature of the business environment, and changes within it – top 25 terms

Business cycle
Cartel
Change and change management
Constraints
Contract of employment (see employment contract)

Culture
Demand
Disposable income
Ethics
Health And Safety at Work Act 1974

Labour flexibility
Labour market
Market economy
Market failure
Market mechanism

Market power
Macroeconomic
Monopoly
Oligopoly
Population (see demographic profile)

Real incomes
Restrictive practices
Sale of Goods Act 1979
Stakeholders
Supply

### Objectives of the state and their impact on business – top 25 terms

Balance of payments
Devaluation
Direct taxation
Economic growth
Employment

European Union
Exchange rates
Export marketing
Fiscal policy
Free trade

Government economic objectives
Gross domestic product
Indirect taxation
Inflation
Infrastructure
Interest rates

Interventionist policies
Monetary policy
Protectionism
Public spending

Reflation
Retail Prices Index
Single currency
Single market
Unemployment

**Financial control of business –top 5 concepts**

Commercial banks
Financial accounting

Financial reporting
Merchant banks
Stock Exchange

**Employer/employee relations – top 5 concepts**

ACAS
Collective bargaining
Employers association
Grievance procedure
Trade union

# Human resource management 4373

(NB the following 30 terms are in addition to those within the compulsory modules 4371 and 4372)

**General terms – top15**

Arbitration
Barriers to communication
Conciliation
Formal and informal communication
Hawthorne effect (Mayo)

Hygiene factors
Industrial democracy
Job enlargement
Job enrichment
Motivators

Paternalistic leadership
Quality circle
Scientific management (FW Taylor)
Single status
Works council

**Human resources planning – top15 terms**

Dismissal
Equal opportunities
Induction
Industrial tribunal
Labour flexibility

Labour turnover
Off-the-job training
On-the-job training
Performance appraisal
Performance related pay

Recruitment
Redundancy
Social charter
Unfair dismissal
Union recognition

# Marketing 4374

(NB the following 30 terms are in addition to those within the compulsory modules 4371 and 4372)

Advertising
Agent
AIDA
Confidence level
Consumer panels

Consumer (demographic) profile
Contribution pricing
Cost-based pricing
Direct response marketing
Face-to-face interviews

Fitness for function/purpose
Income elasticity
International marketing (see export marketing)
Marketing strategy
Market penetration

Market skimming
Mark-up pricing
Pricing policies (see pricing methods)
Product differentiation
Psychological pricing

Public relations
Questionnaire
Quota sample
Random sample
Sales promotion

Self-completion questionnaires
Stratified sample
Surveys
SWOT
Wholesaler

# Operations management 4375

(NB the following 40 terms are in addition to those within the compulsory modules 4371 and 4372)

## The production process – top 20 terms

Batch production
Capacity
Contribution costing
Contribution per unit
Design mix

Diseconomies of scale
Division of labour
External economies
Flow production
Industrial inertia

Internal economies
Job production
Opportunity cost
Pollution and recycling
Primary production

Secondary production
Service and after-sales service

Specialisation
Standard costing
Tertiary production

## Production management – top 20 terms

Buffer stock
Capital intensity
Computer aided design (CAD)
Computer aided manufacture (CAM)
Efficiency

Industrial relations
Lead time
Make-or-buy decisions
Payment systems
Production control

Quality circles
Re-order level
Robotics

Safety at work
Stock-out

Training
Value analysis

Working conditions
Work in progress
Work study

## Accounting and finance in business 4376

(NB the following 40 terms are in addition to those within the compulsory modules 4371 and 4372)

### Financial accounting – top 20 terms

Acid test ratio
Assets
Business entity
Cash flow statement
Creditors

Current assets/liabilities
Debtors
Depreciation
Dividend yield
Earnings per share

Fixed Assets
Gearing
Liabilities
Liquidity
Matching convention

Profitability
Prudence
Return on capital
Stock valuation
Working capital

### Management accounting – top 20 terms

Absorption costing
Average rate of return
Budgetary control
Cost centre
Credit control

Debtors control
Discounted cash flow
Equity capital
Full costing
Investment appraisal

Internal rate of return
Loan capital
Long run
Margin of safety
Net present value

Profit centre
Semi-variable cost
Short run
Standard cost
Variance analysis

## Cambridge linear A level business studies (9370)

Use the Cambridge Modular lists for modules 4371, 4372 and 4376. In addition, revise the following terms for business statistics and operational research.

### Business statistics – top 25 terms

Base year
Bias
Confidence level
Correlation
Cyclical variation
Decision trees

Expected value
Extrapolation
Index numbers
Mean

Median
Mode
Moving average

Normal distribution
Probability
Raw data
Retail prices index
Sample
Sample size
Seasonal adjustment

Significance testing
Skewed result
Time-series analysis
Weighted average
Weighted index

## Operations research – top 20 terms

Blending
Constraints
Critical path

Critical path analysis
Dummy line

Earliest start time
Feasible region
Free float
Latest finish time
Linear programming

Linearity
Model
Network analysis
Node
Operational research

Optimum
Queuing theory
Random numbers
Simulation
Total float

# EXAMINERS' TERMS

## INTRODUCTION

The following entries should help explain what examiners mean by the words they use in exam questions. It is important to remember, though, that the words are only half the story. The other key factor is the mark allocation. This not only gives an indication of the length of answer required, but also the depth. The higher the *mark allocation*, the more likely it is that the examiner is looking for the skills of analysis and, especially, evaluation – and the more likely that the exam question will be marked on the basis of levels of response.

**Analyse:** to break a topic down into its component parts. This should help to identify the causes and effects of the issue and to explain the process whereby the causes bring about the effects. This encourages more depth of study. It implies a writing style that uses continuous prose in fully developed paragraphs. Bear in mind the word 'why?' when analysing.

**Assess:** weigh up and thereby *evaluate* two or more options or arguments.

**Assumptions:** (see *state your assumptions*)

**Comment:** draw conclusions from the evidence, possibly in the form of a stated opinion. For example, in the first part of a question you might be required to analyse a company's financial position using ratios; part b) might ask you to comment on your findings. You might reach a conclusion about the firm's profitability and liquidity, then state your opinion about the firm's overall financial health. Also, it is often helpful to comment upon any further information needed.

**Consider:** another term inviting you to weigh up options or arguments in the form of continuous paragraphs of writing.

**Critically analyse** means to look in depth at an issue (analyse) from the perspective of a critic. In other words the examiner is encouraging you not to take the issue at face value; instead you should be questioning the assumptions or evidence involved. However, it is important to remember that film 'critics' may write a favourable review. You, too, should look at the strengths as well as the weaknesses involved.

**Debate:** put both sides of the case as forcefully as you can, then criticise each side from the perspective of the other. Take, for example, the essay title 'Debate the issue of whether cigarette advertising should be banned completely'. You should put forward the views both for and against, then tackle the arguments of those in favour from the point of view of opponents (and vice versa). You may decide, in the end, to 'vote' or abstain, as in a real debate.

**Decide which:** make a choice between the options, supported by your reasoning.

**Define:** explain the meaning of the term as precisely as you can; giving an example can help, but is not a substitute for explanation.

**Discuss:** put forward both sides of a case before coming to a conclusion. Discussion would require continuous writing and would be likely to be marked on a levels of response basis, with a high proportion of marks awarded for *evaluation*.

**Discuss critically:** a little different from 'discuss', though the examiner appears to be hinting that there may be a reason to be sceptical of the theory or question under discussion. Therefore you should look carefully for weaknesses in the logic.

**Distinguish between:** (as in 'distinguish between revenue and profit'). Here, you should explain each of the two terms and then look for the point of difference between them: 'the difference is that costs have been deducted from revenue to find profit'.

**Draw a graph:** it may sound absurd, but many Examiners' Reports state that students drew bar charts or even pie charts when asked to draw a graph. By graph the examiner means line graph.

**Evaluate:** this vital term means to weigh up evidence in order to reach a judgement. In the context of an essay, you will have to present that evidence (pros and cons, perhaps) before reaching a conclusion. As the term invites your judgement, do be willing to state your opinion within the conclusion, e.g. 'In my view ...'. It can be helpful to keep in mind the phrase 'to what extent ...?'

**Examine** means to look in detail at the argument, evidence or theory presented. It requires continuous writing and should be rounded off with a conclusion.

**Explain:** expand upon in order to show your understanding of the term or theory being tested. The depth of explanation required will be indicated by the *mark allocation*. Giving a well-chosen example will often gain a mark.

**Give:** this means list, as in 'Give three current assets'. All you would need to provide in answer is 'stock, debtors, cash'. There is no requirement to explain the points you make. Point-form answers are acceptable.

**How might:** this phrase suggests a need to explain a process, as in 'How might a firm choose between two investment options?' You must explain the process with care, then consider the *mark allocation* before deciding whether a conclusion is required. If 5 marks are available, no conclusion would be necessary; with 25 marks, however, you would be wise to *evaluate* your answer.

**Identify:** to name one or more examples of the topic being examined. Usually this would require no more than a list, with one mark awarded per point made.

**Justify your answer:** present an argument in favour of the views you are expressing, for example: 'Should the Post Office be privatised? Justify your answer.' Although the question appears to be expecting a yes or no at the outset, it is better to wait until the end to state your opinion, because you will have given the matter enough thought to be able to justify your decision.

**Levels of response:** a way of marking answers based upon different academic skills rather than the quantity of knowledge shown. This is the way in which most high-mark questions are examined. If ten marks are available for 'Explain the impact of higher interest rates upon firms', a levels of response marking scheme would put a ceiling on the number of marks available for listing points (see diagram). Therefore you are better off writing a full explanation of two or three points.

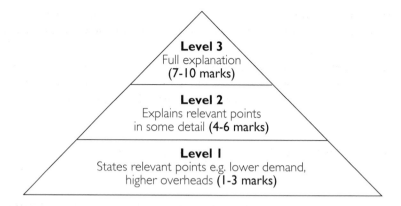

**List:** briefly state, not necessarily in a full sentence (same as give).

**Mark allocation:** the number of marks on offer for each part of a question.

**Name:** same as list or give.

**Outline:** provide a description of an event, theory or method. The length and the level of detail will be governed by the *mark allocation*.

**Report format:** see *Write a report*.

**Show your workings:** this phrase is used often with numerical questions, but should never be ignored. In the pressure of the exam room, almost every candidate will slip up somewhere in a complex calculation. If there are 10 marks on offer for the answer '£24,800', the candidate who gives the answer '£248,000' with no workings will get 0, while a candidate with the same answer will get 9 marks if the workings show where the single slip was made. The secret with numerical questions is not to get 10 out of 10 one time and 0 the next. It is to get 8 or 9 marks every time.

**Sketch a diagram:** this suggests a quick drawing on the ordinary exam writing paper, paying little attention to precision in the lines being drawn. However, to convey any meaning, the sketch will need properly labelled axes and/or lines and a clear title. With sketches, the labelling may carry more marks than the diagram itself.

**State:** means the same as give.

**State and explain:** this should be tackled exactly in this way, i.e. give a reason (in perhaps 4–8 words) then explain it (in perhaps 4–8 lines).

**State your assumptions:** in a numerical question, tell the examiner the decisions you have made when there has been some uncertainty about the correct figures. To gain a mark, your assumption must be based on uncertainty and must be logical. For example, in a recent exam, many students calculating profit assumed that corporation tax would stay unchanged at £40,000 from one year to the next. As corporation tax is charged as a percentage of pre-tax profit, this was not acceptable. Do not confuse an assumption with a conclusion.

**Suggest** means to put forward an idea. If few marks are allocated, this might require no more than a list of points. The word is used more commonly, though, in the context of higher-mark case study or essay questions. In this case it would require a full explanation and justification for the suggestions made.

**SWOT analysis:** an investigation into an organisation's current strengths and weaknesses and potential opportunities and threats. It is usually presented in report format.

**To what extent:** this commonly used examining phrase requires you to reach a judgement about the degree to which a statement, theory or evidence is true. It is likely that the levels of response marking scheme will reward evaluation especially heavily. So focus on relatively few themes, deal with each in depth and then make a judgement about 'to what extent...'.

**What do you understand by?** (or **What is meant by?**): explain the meaning of the term or phrase given. An example may be helpful, but is not a substitute for explanation.

**Why might:** this phrase invites you to suggest possible explanations for why a firm or individual may have chosen a course of action. The use of the word might gives you scope to stray outside the confines of, perhaps, a case study text. Any answer will be accepted as long as it is not too far-fetched; but remember that examiners want to reward your business understanding, so try to draw from relevant theories.

**Write a memo:** present your answer to a question in the form of a business memo (memorandum). This requires headings (To, From, Title, Date) and is likely to be a relatively brief statement of (or request for) factual information. The contents can be written in continuous prose or in point form.

**Write a report:** present your answer to a question in the form of a business report. A report is a document that is likely to provide a great deal of information (written and numerical) and is therefore broken down into sections, each of which is split into sub-sections. The users of the report expect to be able to refer to any part of it at any time and in any order. Therefore it has a contents page and frequent cross-referencing. A busy manager, for example, may just want to see what budget is being requested. When looking that up, a cross-reference to the financial returns expected would be helpful. The managing director may want to do no more than read a summary of the report's findings and recommendations, so most reports start with an 'executive summary'.

In the context of an exam, where only 30 or 45 minutes may be available, little of the above is possible. So the report need only have title headings (To, From, Title, Date) and a structure of numbered sections with numbered sub-sections. If time permits, it is valuable to start with a section on the background to the report and to end with recommendations/points for action.

Further *Complete A–Z Handbooks* are available from Hodder & Stoughton. Why not use them to support your other A levels and Advanced GNVQs? All the *A–Zs* are written by experienced authors and Chief Examiners.

0 340 65467 8   *The Complete A–Z Business Studies* Second Edition  £9.99
0 340 65489 9   *The Complete A–Z Geography Handbook*  £9.99
0 340 64789 2   *The Complete A–Z Leisure, Travel and Tourism Handbook*  £9.99
0 340 65832 0   *The Complete A–Z Sociology Handbook*  £9.99
0 340 65490 2   *The Complete A–Z Psychology Handbook*  £9.99
0 340 66985 3   *The Complete A–Z Economics and Business Studies Handbook*  £9.99
0 340 66373 1   *The Complete A–Z Biology Handbook*  £9.99
0 340 68804 1   *The Complete A–Z Physics Handbook*  £9.99
0 340 68803 3   *The Complete A–Z Mathematics Handbook*  £9.99
0 340 67996 4   *The Complete A–Z 20th Century European History Handbook*  £9.99
0 340 69131 X   *The Complete A–Z Media and Communication Studies Handbook*  £9.99
0 340 68847 5   *The Complete A–Z Business Studies CD-ROM*  £55.00 + VAT
0 340 69124 7   *The Complete A–Z Accounting Handbook*  £9.99
0 340 67378 8   *The Complete A–Z 19th and 20th Century British History Handbook*  £9.99
0 340 72051 4   *The A–Z Business Studies Coursework Handbook*  £6.99
0 340 72513 3   *The Complete A–Z Chemistry Handbook*  £9.99

All Hodder & Stoughton *Educational* books are available at your local bookshop, or can be ordered direct from the publisher. Just tick the titles you would like and complete the details below. Prices and availability are subject to change without prior notice.

Buy four books from the selection above and get free postage and packaging. Just send a cheque or postal order made payable to *Bookpoint Limited* to the value of the total cover price of four books. This should be sent to: Hodder & Stoughton *Educational*, 39 Milton Park, Abingdon, Oxon OX14 4TD, UK. EMail address: orders@bookpoint.co.uk. Alternatively, if you wish to buy fewer than four books, the following postage and packaging costs apply:

UK & BFPO: £4.30 for one book; £6.30 for two books; £8.30 for three books.
Overseas and Eire: £4.80 for one book; £7.10 for 2 or 3 books (surface mail).

If you would like to pay by credit card, our centre team would be delighted to take your order by telephone. Our direct line (44) 01235 400414 (lines open 9.00am - 6.00pm, Monday to Saturday, with a 24 hour answering service). Alternatively you can send a fax to (44) 01235 400454.

Title _____ First name _____ Surname _____

Address _____

Postcode _____ Daytime telephone no. _____

If you would prefer to pay by credit card, please complete:

Please debit my Master Card / Access / Diner's Card / American Express (delete as applicable)

Card number _____ Expiry date _____ Signature _____

If you would not like to receive further information on our products, please tick the box ☐